For Teddy and Hope

FOREWORD

In the following pages I have tried to let the Victorians speak for themselves with as little assistance—or intrusion—from myself as possible. The contemporary sources, therefore, have been faithfully reproduced, with certain minor exceptions: in the first chapter I took the liberty of translating the third-person accounts of the Parliamentary reporter into the probable first-person language of the debaters; and throughout the book I sometimes abridged my sources without always employing ellipses. Wherever in my own commentary my spelling of proper nouns differs from that in the sources, I have followed the preferred modern usage.

R.A.R.

EARNEST VICTORIANS

*Six great Victorians as portrayed
in their own words and those
of their contemporaries*

By ROBERT A. ROSENBAUM

HAWTHORN BOOKS, INC. • *PUBLISHERS*
NEW YORK

FIRST EDITION
March, 1961.

ACKNOWLEDGMENTS

The author and his publisher wish to thank the following for material used in this book:

Appleton-Century-Crofts, Inc., for material in Chapter 4 from *My Story* by Hall Caine. Copyright 1908, 1909, D. Appleton & Company, New York. Reprinted by permission of the publishers Appleton-Century-Crofts, Inc. Also, for material in Chapter 5 from *Life and Letters of Sir Joseph Dalton Hooker* by Leonard Huxley.

G. Bell & Sons, Ltd., for material in Chapter 4 from *Memoirs and Correspondence of Coventry Patmore* by Basil Champneys.

Ernest Benn, Ltd., for material in Chapter 4 from *Letters of Dante Gabriel Rossetti to William Allingham* by George Birkbeck Hill.

Cassell & Company, Ltd., for material in Chapter 4 from *My Story* by Hall Caine.

Chapman & Hall, Ltd., for material in Chapter 5 from *My Life* by Alfred Russel Wallace.

Dodd, Mead & Company for material in Chapter 5 reprinted by permission of Dodd, Mead & Company from *My Life* by Alfred Russel Wallace.

Hurst & Blackett, Ltd., for material in Chapter 4 from *Pre-Raphaelite Diaries and Letters* by William Michael Rossetti (1900) by permission of Hurst & Blackett, Ltd.

Longmans, Green & Co., Ltd., for material in Chapter 4 from *Ford Madox Brown* by Ford Madox Hueffer, reprinted by permission of the publisher.

Macmillan & Co., Ltd., for material in Chapter 5 from *Life and Letters of Thomas Henry Huxley* by Leonard Huxley; for material in Chapter 6 from *Gordon and the Sudan* by Bernard M. Allen.

Methuen & Co., Ltd., for material in Chapter 4 from *The Life and Letters of Sir John Everett Millais* by John Guille Millais.

John Murray, Ltd., for material in Chapter 3 from *The Letters of Robert Browning and Elizabeth Barrett Browning;* for material in Chapter 5 from *The Life and Letters of Charles Darwin* by Francis Darwin and from *Life and Letters of Sir Joseph Dalton Hooker* by Leonard Huxley.

Harold Ford Rossetti for material in Chapter 4 from *Dante Gabriel Rossetti, His Family Letters,* edited by William Michael Rossetti.

Sampson Low, Marston & Co., Ltd., for material in Chapter 6 from *Ten Years' Captivity in the Mahdi's Camp* by Joseph Ohrwalder.

Sheed & Ward, Inc., for material in Chapter 2 from *Autobiographical Writings* by John Henry Newman, Copyright 1957 Sheed & Ward, Inc., New York, N.Y., and from *Young Mr. Newman,* by Maisie Ward, Copyright 1948 Sheed & Ward, Inc., New York, N.Y.

Sheed & Ward, Ltd., for material in Chapter 2 from *Autobiographical Writings* by John Henry Newman and from *Young Mr. Newman* by Maisie Ward.

A. P. Watt & Son, London, for material in Chapter 6 from *Fire and Sword in the Sudan* by Rudolf C. Slatin, published by Edward Arnold, Ltd., and for excerpts from *Mahdiism and the Egyptian Sudan* by F. R. Wingate, published by Macmillan & Co., Ltd.

CONTENTS

LIST OF ILLUSTRATIONS

CHAPTER 1

Lord Ashley

———— ❧ ————

*"The more I labour, the more I see of labour
to be performed."*

I

From the sprawling, blackening industrial cities of the north of England, from the steaming, fetid cotton mills of Lancashire and the woolen mills of Yorkshire, from the wretched cottages and festering slums of Manchester, Preston, Bolton, and Oldham, of Leeds, Bradford, Halifax, and Huddersfield, the factory children came to London, in the summer of 1832, with their brothers and sisters, their parents and friends, their overseers and employers, their doctors and clergymen, to tell their stories to a Select Committee of the House of Commons. The Committee listened for forty-three days, its secretaries transcribing the pathetic testimony elicited by the careful, persistent questioning of its chairman, Michael Thomas Sadler. For the first time Englishmen were to discover, in the dense pages of an official Parliamentary Report, a world of oppression and suffering that most of them had not dreamed existed.

13

What were the hours of labour at the giggs?

The witness was James Kirk, aged seventeen, who had gone to work in the woolen mills at Leeds when he was nine. He had been tending the gigging machines for the past year.

—We began at five o'clock on Monday morning, and went on to Tuesday night at nine.

You began on Monday morning?—At five o'clock.

When did you rest?—At eight o'clock.

For how long?—For half an hour.

From half-past eight to when did you work?—Till twelve.

How long did you rest then?—For an hour.

Was that for dinner?—That was for dinner.

Go on?—We then went on from one till five, and stopped half an hour; from half-past five to nine, and stopped half an hour; from half-past nine to twelve, and stopped an hour; from one to half-past four, and stopped half an hour; from five to eight, and stopped half an hour; from half-past eight to twelve, and stopped an hour; from one to five, and stopped half an hour; and from half-past five to nine, and then we went off.

Then you worked for 40 successive hours, including the intervals you have stated?—Yes.

Of course you had no time to go to bed?—We laid down at 12 o'clock at night.

For how long?—For an hour.

Was that the only rest you could take?—Yes.

What was your daily work on the Wednesday?—From five o'clock in the morning to nine o'clock at night.

With two hours rest?—Yes.

And what was it on Thursday?—The same.

Then on Friday, will you state what your usual labour was?—We began at five o'clock on Friday, and went on till eight, stopped half an hour; from half-past eight to twelve, stopped an hour; from one to half-past four, stopped half an hour; from five till eight, stopped half an hour; from half-past eight till twelve, stopped an hour; from one till five, and then came home.

What were your wages at this time?—Eight shillings per week.[1]

Abraham Whitehead, a clothier of Scholes, lived in the midst of thirty or forty woolen mills. The factory children and their parents were his neighbors. For more than twenty years his business had

brought him regularly into the mills where he had observed the chil-
dren, often as young as seven years, at their work&.

You say you have observed these children constantly for many years going there early in the morning to their work, and continuing at it till so late at night?—Yes; I have seen children during this last winter coming from work on cold dark nights between 10 and 11 o'clock, although trade has been so bad with some of the mills that they have had nothing to do; others have been working seventeen or seventeen and a half hours per day.

How early do you think they leave their homes?—I can tell you what a neighbour told me six weeks ago; she is the wife of Jonas Barrowcliffe, near Scholes; her child works at a mill nearly two miles from home, and I have seen that child coming from its work this winter between 10 and 11 in the evening; and the mother told me that one morning this winter the child had been up by two o'clock in the morning, when it had only arrived home from work at eleven; it then had to go nearly two miles to the mill, where it had to stay at the door till the overlooker came to open it.

This family had no clock, I suppose?—They had no clock; and she believed, from what she afterwards learnt from the neighbours, that it was only two o'clock when the child was called up and went to work; but this has only generally happened when it has been moonlight, thinking the morning was approaching.

Is this practice general in the entire neighbourhood?—It is the general practice of the neighbourhood; and any fact that I state here can be borne out by particular evidences, that, if required, I can point out.

What has been the treatment which you have observed that these children have received at the mills, to keep them attentive for so many hours at such early ages?—They are generally cruelly treated; so cruelly treated, that they dare not hardly for their lives be too late at their work in a morning. When I have been at the mills in the winter season, when the children are at work in the evening, the very first thing they inquire is, "What o'clock is it?" if I should answer "Seven," they say, "Only seven! it is a great while to 10, but we must not give up till 10 o'clock or past." They look so anxious to know what o'clock it is, that I am convinced the children are fatigued, and think that even at seven they have worked too long. My heart has been ready to bleed for them when I have seen them so fatigued, for they appear in such a state of apathy and insensibility as really not to know whether they are doing their work or not; they usually throw a bunch of 10 or 12 cordings across the hand, and take one off at a time; but I have seen the bunch entirely finished, and they have attempted to take off another when they have not had a cording at all; they have been so fatigued as not to know whether they were at work or not.

Do they frequently fall into errors and mistakes in piecing when thus fatigued?—Yes; the errors they make when thus fatigued are, that instead of placing the cording in this way [*describing it*], they are apt to place them obliquely, and that causes a flying, which makes bad yarn; and when the billy-spinner sees that, he takes his strap or the billy-roller, and says, "Damn thee, close it—little devil, close it," and they smite the child with the strap or the billy-roller.

You have noticed this in the after part of the day more particularly?—It is a very difficult thing to go into a mill in the latter part of the day, particularly in winter, and not to hear some of the children crying for being beaten for this very fault.[2]

Matthew Crabtree, aged twenty-two, entered the woolen mills when he was eight. His normal working day extended from six o'clock in the morning to eight at night, but when trade was brisk he started at five and worked until nine.

Will you state the effect that those long hours had upon the state of your health and feelings?—I was, when working those long hours, commonly very much fatigued at night, when I left my work; so much so that I sometimes should have slept as I walked if I had not stumbled and started awake again; and so sick often that I could not eat, and what I did eat I vomited.

In what situation were you in that mill?—I was a piecener.

Will you state to this Committee whether pieceening is a very laborious employment for children, or not?—It is very laborious employment. Pieceners are continually running to and fro, and on their feet the whole day.

The duty of the piecener is to take the cardings from one part of the machinery, and to place them on another?—Yes.

So that the labour is not only continual, but it is unabated to the last?—It is unabated to the last.

Do you not think, from your own experience, that the speed of the machinery is so calculated as to demand the utmost exertions of a child, supposing the hours were moderate?—It is as much as they could do at the best; they are always upon the stretch, and it is commonly very difficult to keep up with their work.

State the condition of the children towards the latter part of the day, who have thus to keep up with the machinery?—It is as much as they can do when they are not very much fatigued to keep up with their work, and towards the close of the day, when they come to be more fatigued, they cannot keep up with it very well, and the consequence is that they are beaten to spur them on.

Were you beaten under those circumstances?—Yes.

Frequently?—Very frequently.

And is it your belief that if you had not been so beaten, you should not have got through the work?—I should not if I had not been kept up to it by some means.

What were you beaten with principally?—A strap.

Anything else?—Yes, a stick sometimes; and there is a kind of roller which runs on the top of the machine called a billy, perhaps two or three yards in length, and perhaps an inch and a half, or more, in diameter; the circumference would be four or five inches; I cannot speak exactly.

Were you beaten with that instrument?—Yes.

Have you yourself been beaten, and have you seen other children struck severely with that roller?—I have been struck very severely with it myself, so much so as to knock me down, and I have seen other children have their heads broken with it.[3]

A tailor from Stanningly, near Leeds, Samuel Coulson had three daughters who had gone to work in the mills when they were twelve, eleven, and eight years old respectively.

At what time in the morning, in the brisk time, did those girls go to the mills?—In the brisk time, for about six weeks, they have gone at 3 o'clock in the morning, and ended at 10, or nearly half-past, at night.

What sort of mills were those?—The worsted mills.

What intervals were allowed for rest or refreshment during those nineteen hours of labour?—Breakfast a quarter of an hour, and dinner half an hour, and drinking a quarter of an hour.

Is that all?—Yes.

Was any of that time taken up in cleaning the machinery?—They generally had to do what they call dry down; sometimes this took the whole of the time at breakfast or drinking, and they were to get their dinner or breakfast as they could; if not, it was brought home.

Had you not great difficulty in awakening your children to this excessive labour?—Yes, in the early time we had to take them up asleep and shake them, when we got them on the floor to dress them, before we could get them off to their work; but not so in the common hours.

What was the length of time they could be in bed during those long hours?—It was near 11 o'clock before we could get them into bed after getting a little victuals, and then at morning my mistress used to stop up all night, for fear that we could not get them ready for the time; sometimes we have gone to bed, and one of us generally awoke.

What time did you get them up in the morning?—In general me or my mistress got up at 2 o'clock to dress them.

So that they had not above four hours sleep at this time?—No, they had not.

For how long together was it?—About six weeks it held; it was only done when the throng was very much on; it was not often that.

The common hours of labour were from 6 in the morning till half-past 8 at night?—Yes.

With the same intervals for food?—Yes, just the same.

Were the children excessively fatigued by this labour?—Many times; we have cried often when we have given them the little victualling we had to give them; we had to shake them, and they have fallen asleep with the victuals in their mouths many a time.[4]

Elizabeth Bentley, aged twenty-three, was six when she went to work in Mr. Busk's flax mill in Leeds.

What was your business in that mill?—I was a little doffer.

What were your hours of labour in that mill?—From 5 in the morning till 9 at night, when they were thronged.

For how long a time together have you worked that excessive length of time?—For about half a year.

What were your usual hours of labour when you were not so thronged?—From 6 in the morning till 7 at night.

Explain what it is you had to do?—When the frames are full, they have to stop the frames, and take the flyers off, and take the full bobbins off, and carry them to the roller; and then put empty ones on, and set the frame going again.

Does that keep you constantly on your feet?—Yes, there are so many frames, and they run so quick.

Your labour is very excessive?—Yes; you have not time for any thing.

Suppose you flagged a little, or were too late, what would they do?—Strap us.

How long did you work at Mr. Busk's?—Three or four years.

Where did you go then?—Benyon's factory.

That was when you were about 10 years?—Yes.

What were you then?—A weigher in the card-room.

How long did you work there?—From half-past 5 till 8 at night.

Was that the ordinary time?—Till 9 when we were thronged.

It was exceedingly dusty?—Yes.

Did it affect your health?—Yes; it was so dusty, the dust got upon my lungs, and the work was so hard; I was middling strong when I went there, but the work was so bad; I got so bad in health, that when I pulled the baskets down, I pulled my bones out of their places.

You dragged the baskets?—Yes; down the rooms to where they are worked.

And as you had been weakened by excessive labour, you could not stand that labour?—No.

It has had the effect of pulling your shoulders out?—Yes; it was a great basket that stood higher than this table a good deal.

How heavy was it?—I cannot say; it was a very large one, that was full of weights up-heaped, and pulling the basket pulled my shoulders out of its place, and my ribs have grown over it.

Did you perceive that many other girls were made ill by that long labour?—Yes, a good many of them.

So that you were constantly receiving fresh hands to supply the places of those that could no longer bear their work?—Yes, there were fresh hands every week; they could not keep their hands.

Did [the dust] make you very thirsty?—Yes, we drank a deal of water in the room.

Could you eat your food well in that factory?—No, indeed I had not much to eat, and the little I had I could not eat it, my appetite was so poor, and being covered with dust; and it was no use to take it home, I could not eat it, and the overlooker took it, and gave it to the pigs.

Did you live far from the mill?—Yes, two miles.

Had you a clock?—No, we had not.

Supposing you had not been in time enough in the morning at these mills, what would have been the consequence?—We should have been quartered.

What do you mean by that?—If we were a quarter of an hour too late, they would take off half an hour; we only got a penny an hour, and they would take a halfpenny more.

Were you also beaten for being too late?—No, I was never beaten myself, I have seen the boys beaten for being too late.

Were you generally there in time?—Yes; my mother has been up at 4 o'clock in the morning, and at 2 o'clock in the morning; the colliers used to go to their work about 3 or 4 o'clock, and when she heard them stirring she has got up out of her warm bed, and gone out and asked them the time; and I have sometimes been at Hunslet Car at 2 o'clock in the morning, when it was streaming down with rain, and we have had to stay till the mill was opened.

You are considerably deformed in your person in consequence of this labour?—Yes, I am.

At what time did it come on?—I was about 13 years old when it began coming, and it has got worse since; it is five years since my mother died, and my mother was never able to get me a pair of good stays to hold me up, and when my mother died I had to do for myself, and got me a pair.

Were you perfectly straight and healthy before you worked at a mill?—Yes, I was as straight a little girl as ever went up and down town.

Have you been attended to by any medical gentleman at Leeds or the neighbourhood?—Yes, I have been under Mr. Hares.

To what did he attribute it?—He said it was owing to hard labour, and working in the factories.

Did he tell your mother so also?—No, she was not alive; I was coming from Leeds, and he asked a good many questions; he asked me if I had a father and mother; I said "No;" he said if I had no objection he would take me in hand; I said I was much obliged to him; he told me to come to his house that night, and I went to the mill and told them I was going to stop away; I stopped at home ten weeks, and my cousins, that I was living with, had to maintain me, and they told me they were sure he would not do me any good, and they could not find me with support, and Mr. Hares told me it would be a year before I should be straight again.

You were obliged to return to your work?—Yes.

Where did you go then?—I went to Mr. Walker's.

Where are you now?—In the poorhouse.

Where?—At Hunslet.

Do any of your former employers come to see you?—No.

Did you ever receive any thing from them when you became afflicted?—When I was at home Mr. Walker made me a present of 1*s.* or 2*s.*, but since I have left my work and gone to the poorhouse, they have not come nigh me.

You are supported by the parish?—Yes.

You are actually incapable now of any exertion of that sort?—Yes.

You were very willing to have worked as long as you were able, from your earliest age?—Yes.

And to have supported your widowed mother as long as you could?—Yes.

State what you think as to the circumstances in which you have been placed during all this time of labour, and what you have considered about it as to the hardship and cruelty of it.

[*The Witness was too much affected to answer the question.*][5]

II

The Select Committee was all that Sadler could salvage of a first attempt to legislate a ten-hour day for the children of the textile mills. Already a sick man, he spent himself without stint in the enormous labors of his chairmanship—the heavy correspondence with the workingmen's committees, the selection and preparation of witnesses, the exhaustive hearings, the careful correction of the shorthand transcripts. A few months later he failed of re-election to the first reformed Parliament; in two years he was dead.

Sadler's removal from the House of Commons compelled the workingmen to seek a new advocate in Parliament. They found him finally in a somber, handsome young aristocrat, member for the agricultural county of Dorset, who for six years had conscientiously supported the Tory leadership. Anthony Ashley Cooper, the future seventh earl of Shaftesbury but then known as Lord Ashley, was thirty-one.

In the autumn and winter of 1832, *Ashley recalled*, I read incidentally in the *Times* some extracts from the evidence taken before Mr. Sadler's committee. I had heard nothing of the question previously, nor was I even aware that an inquiry had been instituted by the House of Commons. Either the question had made very little stir, or I had been unusually negligent in Parliamentary business. I suspect the first to be the true cause, for it had been an active Session, and I had taken my share in the activity of it. I was astonished and disgusted; and, knowing Sadler to be out of Parliament (for he had been defeated at Leeds), I wrote to him to offer my services in presenting petitions, or doing any other small work that the cause might require. I received no answer, and forgot the subject. The House met in the month of February; on the second or third day I was addressed by the Rev. G. S. Bull, whom till then I had never seen or heard of. He was brought to me by Sir Andrew Agnew, and they both proposed to me to take up the question that Sadler had necessarily dropped. I can perfectly recollect my astonishment, and doubt, and terror, at the proposition. I forget the arguments for and against my intermeddling in the affair; so far, I recollect, that in vain I demanded time for consideration; it was necessary, Bull replied, to make an instant resolution, as Morpeth would otherwise give notice of a Bill which would defraud the operatives of their ten hours measure, by proposing one which should inflict eleven.

I obtained, however, a respite till the next morning, and I set myself to reflection and inquiry. Nevertheless the only persons I consulted were Peach and Scarlett, the present Lord Abinger. They strongly urged me to adopt the question, and I returned home armed with their opinions, to decide for myself, after meditation and prayer, and 'divination' (as it were) by the word of God.[6]

In 1833, rural England—the England of Chaucer, Shakespeare, and Wordsworth—was fast passing away. In burgeoning mills and factories, on railroads, highways, and canals, in banks, courts, and Parliament itself, the Industrial Revolution rushed ahead. Old cities spilled out beyond their ancient limits; new cities chewed up the once green landscape. In the countryside, the expansion of large-scale capitalist agriculture had destroyed the traditional pattern of village life. The independent farmer and secure tenant of former years were now often reduced to the status of wage laborers, hopelessly poor and frequently charges upon their parishes. Increasingly, their only prospect of earning a livelihood lay in tending the new machinery. Into the roaring textile mills of the northern counties, into the pestilential slums of new and unplanned cities, poured the dispossessed of the countryside, to work and suffer and sicken and die.

Englishmen discovered the factory problem with astonishment and despair. Philosophical men reflected, with the melancholy Malthus, that the improvident multiplication of the lower classes necessarily doomed them to destitution. Any legislative remedy was precluded by the triumphant laissez-faire doctrines of the political economists, those partial students of Adam Smith. Only increased prosperity, the economists insisted, could in any way mitigate the general misery at the base of society, and this could best be obtained by granting to everyone engaged in economic activity, to buyer and seller, employer and employee, absolute freedom to pursue his individual interests. It was natural and desirable for the mill-owner to hire his labor (including women and children) as cheaply as possible, use it however he chose, and dispense with it without further obligation when it suited him. It was, of course, incumbent upon the operatives (including women and children) to bargain prudently with their employers and sell their labor on the most advantageous terms. Only slowly did Englishmen come to realize that the operatives—propertiless, uneducated, unskilled workers, demoralized by the brutal conditions of their lives, and with no experience of collective action—were unable to bargain on equal terms, that they were in fact entirely at the mercy of their employers and of the violent fluctuations in business activity.

Unpersuaded of the dangers of governmental intervention in the relations of the market place, the operatives looked to Parliament for help. There were precedents for Parliamentary action in factory acts of 1802 and 1819, timid and largely ineffectual attempts to protect children in the cotton mills. Without the ballot, however, the operatives had no direct political influence. They had plunged enthusiastically into the national agitation for reform of the old, grossly unrepresentative Parliament, only to discover that the Reform Bill of 1832, which enfranchised their employers, excluded them altogether from its benefits. Later attempts to obtain universal male suffrage collapsed with the Chartist movement. The operatives could only petition, demonstrate—and wait. Their prospects were not encouraging. Tories and Whigs alike were prisoners of the fashionable economics and devoid of any idea of constructive social legislation. There were, however, men in both parties who rebelled against the new orthodoxy. A group of young Tories condemned the rapacious individualism of the industrial plutocracy and romanticized an English past when the poorest Englishman could claim his share of the national patrimony, when wealth and privilege carried acknowledged obligations of service and protection. There were Whigs who questioned the wisdom of trusting so completely to economic theories that inverted Christian values and produced the monstrous inhumanities that Sadler's investigations brought to light in 1832. Among such men as these the operatives hoped to find advocates who would awaken Parliament to an awareness of their increasingly desperate condition.

The remedy proposed by the operatives was a shorter working day. To this end, a network of Short Time Committees grew up in 1831 in Yorkshire and Lancashire. Their goal was a ten-hour workday, ostensibly for the factory children but, as the operatives and mill-owners immediately perceived, for the adult operatives as well, since the mills could not be kept open without the children, who constituted more than half of the working force. The creation of the operatives themselves, the Short Time Committees wisely enlisted the support of able men outside the operatives' ranks—of mill-owners like John Wood and John Fielden, of newspaper proprietors like John Walter of the London Times *and George Condy of the Manchester* Advertiser, *of powerful agitators like Richard Oastler, George Stringer Bull, and Joseph Rayner Stephens, and of Parliamentary managers like Michael Sadler and Lord Ashley.*

The selection of Ashley as Sadler's successor was a fortunate one for both Ashley and the operatives. Ashley's social position and Parliamentary experience would assure his being heard with respect. His philosophy of Tory paternalism was the same as Sadler's; however far removed it was from the egalitarian radicalism of many of the operatives, its expression in practical humanitarianism was entirely to their satisfaction. By his role in the reform of the lunacy laws, Ashley had already embarked upon what was to prove the most distinguished philanthropic career of the Victorian age. His leadership of the Ten Hours Movement confirmed him in that career. Though he early served briefly in two Tory governments, Ashley never thereafter held political power. By necessity and choice, he remained an independent in politics, coming in time to wield a moral force incalculably greater than any political power he might have achieved. Until his death in 1885 he devoted himself to relieving the hardships and correcting the injustices of the new industrial age that bore so

*heavily on the poor and defenseless—on the factory children, the
colliery children, the chimney sweeps, on the ill-housed, unschooled,
and destitute. Without party or influence, Ashley awoke the national
conscience; he became, in the words of one historian, a guiding force
in the reconstruction of English life.*

*The choice of career was not easy. Ashley was born into the top
rank of the English ruling class. He was ambitious, and his connec-
tions and talents brought the highest offices within his reach. But the
flexible conscience, the spirit of amiable accommodation, so necessary for a political career were not his. In Ashley, a stern evangelical conscience demanded a life of rigorous and active piety. For many
years, duty and ambition struggled in that restless, melancholy, introspective man.*

My birthday, *Ashley noted in his diary on April 28, 1826*,
and now I am twenty-five years old—a great age for one who is
neither wise, nor good, nor useful, nor endowed with capability of
becoming so. People would answer me, 'Why you have not lost your
time, you have always been engaged;' quite true, but always upon
trifles; indeed, since my quitting Oxford, a space now of three years,
I have absolutely done harm to my intellects, by false reasoning
which, however rare it may have been, is the only exercise which has
disturbed my mental indolence. What might have been performed in
three years? but not a study commenced, not an object pursued; not
a good deed done, not a good thought generated: for my thoughts
are too unsteady for the honour of that title. Visions without end,
but, God be praised, all of a noble character. I fancy myself in
wealth and power, exerting my influence for the ends that I sought
it for, for the increase of religion and true happiness. No man had
ever more ambition, and probably my seeming earnestness for great
and good purposes was merely a proof of hotter ambition and deeper
self-deception than exists in others. That I am not completely in
despair must come from God who knows, '*quae sint, quae fuerint,
quae mox ventura trahantur,*' and who, if He wanted me, or knew
that I could be useful, would doubtless call me forward.

A year later, 1827. April 22nd, Sunday.—Time was when
I could not sleep for ambition. I thought of nothing but fame and
immortality. I could not bear the idea of dying and being forgotten.
But now I am much changed. Immortality has ceased to be a longing
with me. I desire to be useful in my generation, and die in the knowl-

edge of having advanced happiness by having advanced true religion.

April 28th [1828].—My 27th birthday. Now let me consider awhile my future career. The first principle, God's honour; the second, man's happiness; the means, prayer and unremitting diligence; all petty love of excellence must be put aside, the matter must be studied, the motives refined, and one's best done for the remainder. No fretting of the mind. No conceited nervousness for fear some sentence should fail in arrangement, some point in fitness, some attempt at display be found presumption. I must not dread coming down to the level of others. If I am already there the descent is nothing, and why be desirous of appearing greater when that illusion can be maintained by silence alone—and that silence I must break? This is the hardest scheme I ever devised, to come forward at once and show myself no cleverer than others; yet it is the wisest if I could but follow it. I must think of my duties and the subject I have to uphold. If I stop to compare myself with others, either vanity overweening will rush in, or else a cruel despondency, arising equally from conceit, but differing in its mode of influence. Oh! what wisdom and power in this saying, 'Do what is right, and trust to Providence for the rest.'[7]

In February, 1833, Ashley reintroduced Sadler's ten-hours bill in the newly reformed Parliament.

I greatly fear my ability to carry on this measure, *he wrote to Richard Oastler*. I wish, most ardently I wish, that some other had been found to undertake the cause; nothing but the apprehension of its being lost induced me to acquiesce in Mr. Bull's request. I entertain such strong opinions on the matter that I did not *dare*, as a Christian, to let my diffidence, or love of ease, prevail over the demands of morality and religion.[8]

The Whig government of Lord Melbourne saw in the proposed measure less an act of Christian charity than a reckless defiance of economic laws that, for their self-evident truth and universality, approached to laws of nature. There was a new factory investigation, conducted this time by zealous adherents of the orthodox political economy, and a new report that justified fundamental amendments to Ashley's bill. Ashley surrendered the transformed bill to the gov-

ernment, and as a government measure it became the Factory Act of 1833. Though not a ten-hours act, it was a significant advance over earlier measures. For the first time, all textile mills, not the cotton mills only, were brought under government regulation. The Act prohibited the employment of all children under nine years; it limited the employment of children under thirteen to eight hours a day and of young persons under eighteen to twelve hours. Most important, the Act established an effective system of factory inspection.

The Act was better than the operatives at first realized. Nevertheless, the Ten Hours Movement had suffered a major defeat, and for the remainder of the long Whig administration it was impossible to get another ten-hours measure before Parliament. Indeed, it was all Ashley and his supporters could do to hold on to the gains of 1833. Frustrated and embittered, the operatives turned to a futile agitation against the harsh poor law of 1834 and to the mass working-class movement known as Chartism that brought them perilously close to revolution. After the Chartist fiasco in 1839, the operatives returned, almost in despair, to the Ten Hours Movement. Their hopes now were fixed on that day when a Tory ministry would eventually succeed the divided and indolent Whigs.

III

The Whig Parliament was dissolved in June, 1841, and in July British electors returned a substantial Tory majority. Ashley, who had campaigned energetically in the Tory cause, saw the hand of God in the result. His partisan elation was dampened, however, by forebodings that factory reform would find less support in his own party than it had among the Whigs. All would depend on the new Prime Minister, Sir Robert Peel.

Shortly will begin a new Administration, and God grant it may open new hopes and new principles, *Ashley confided to his diary on July 24, 1841*. The country has no real confidence in Peel; they have attempted this great experiment under a sense of duty, and many in a spirit of prayer; but they do not disguise from themselves the awful probability that it may not please God to render Peel an instrument of good to this nation. They fear his love of expediency, his perpetual egoistry, his dread of an immovable principle, his delight in the praise of men. I confess they have much and sad truth on their side. I cannot see in him those great qualities which the present times peculiarly require—we need mighty virtues far more than mighty talents. He has abundance of human honesty, and not much of Divine faith; he will never do a dishonourable thing, he will be ashamed of doing a religious one; he will tolerate no jobs to win votes, he will submit to no obloquy to please God; a well-turned phrase of compliment, and eulogy from John Russell or Macaulay, will attract him more than 'Hast thou considered my servant Job?'[9]

What was the temper of the operatives? With renewed interest in a ten-hours bill running high, Ashley traveled north to the mill towns to prepare the operatives for the coming campaign.

August 2nd.—Manchester. Came here on a factory tour to see the latest improvements (!) in machinery. Went to a meeting of operatives and talked to them; poor fellows, the times are heavy, and their position is most distressing, nor can I foresee any possibility of amendment for them; the Ten Hours Bill would come too late for all the practical purposes we once predicted; the evil unchecked has attained so fearful a height that human legislation is mere verbiage. The meeting went off very well. I expressed sympathy and friendship —it soothed their spirits, and somewhat lightened the burthen by an apparent sharing of it. The clergy here, as usual, are cowed by capital and power. I find none who 'cry aloud and spare not;' but so it is everywhere.

August 6th.—Leeds. Convened meetings at Bolton, Ashton, Huddersfield, and Leeds; success went on increasing, and each reception was more hearty and affectionate than the last. What a sin it is to be ignorant of the sterling value and merit of these poor men! A few words of kindness are as effectual with them as a force of fifty thousand soldiers on a French population. Never have I met with such respect and affection as on this journey. I see and feel the truth of Oastler's observation, 'they are neither infidels nor Jacobins; they love the monarchy and they love religion.' It is most correct, though they have been denied the blessings of the one, and excluded from the benefits of the other. O God, the God of all righteousness, mercy, and love, give us all grace and strength to conceive and execute whatever may be for Thine honour and their welfare, that we may become at the last, through the merits and intercession of our common Redeemer, a great and a happy, because a wise and understanding, people.[10]

Ashley had every reason to expect that Peel would offer him an important place in the new government. He was resolved, however, to accept no appointment that would limit his activities on behalf of the operatives. When Peel finally summoned Ashley to a meeting late in August, 1841, it was to offer him a minor and merely decorative position in the royal household, one that would have removed him altogether from the political scene. Mortified, Ashley nevertheless declined only when Peel, after several interviews, still refused to commit his government to the support of a ten-hours bill. In January, 1842, just before the assembling of the new Parliament, Ashley wrote again to Peel to ask if, after five months of deliberation, the government had decided to bring in a ten-hours bill. Peel declared finally that it would not, though the Home Secretary, Sir James Graham, was considering a bill dealing with the education of the factory children. To a second inquiry from Ashley—would the government then oppose a ten-hours bill brought in from another quarter?—Peel had nothing further to add. The mind of the new government was now clear. Ashley, cut off from all power and influence, would have to conduct his campaign from the floor of the Commons against the active hostility of a government of his own party. It was bitter news he had to communicate to the Short Time Committees.

It is with the deepest regret, *Ashley wrote on February 2*, that I am obliged to announce to you that Sir Robert Peel has signified his opposition to the Ten Hours Bill; and I conclude, therefore, as you will conclude, that his reply must be taken as the reply of the whole Government on this important question.

Though painfully disappointed, I am not disheartened, nor am I at a loss either what course to take, or what advice to give. I shall persevere unto my last hour, and so must you; we must exhaust every legitimate means that the Constitution affords, in petitions to Parliament, in public meetings, and in friendly conferences with your employers; but you must infringe no law, and offend no proprieties; we must all work together as responsible men, who will one day give an account of their motives and actions; if this course be approved, no consideration shall detach me from your cause; if not, you must elect another advocate.

I know that, in resolving on this step, I exclude myself altogether

from the tenure of office: I rejoice in the sacrifice, happy to devote
the remainder of my days, be they many or be they few, as God in His
wisdom shall determine, to an effort, however laborious, to ameliorate
your moral and social condition.[11]

&§*The next days were days of "trouble and rebuke"*§&.

Politicians are chameleons, &§*Ashley recorded on February 3,
1842*§&, and take the colour of the passing cloud. My letter ap-
proves itself to their consciences, but obstructs their wishes; they
feel that *I* am right and *Peel* in the Treasury; so the House of Commons will think with *me* and act with *him*. I have had some cold
praise, but no promises of support. I am complimented with some
formal regrets; but they all show me that the right hand of the chair
presents objects in a different point of view from the left hand—
some have suddenly found out that 'I may be going too far;' all seem
secretly to wish that I would go no further. 'Peel has made a pro-
pitiatory sacrifice to Cobden and Co., and why should not *you* to the
whole party?' These are their thoughts, though not, as yet, their
language.

I confess I feel sadly alone; I am like a pelican in the wilderness,
or a sparrow on the house-tops. I have no one with whom I can take
counsel, no one to aid me, no one to cheer me.

Feb. 4th.—By chance I lighted on the *Morning Post*, and found
there the most violent and venomous article I ever read against any
public man, directed against myself. This is only a sample of the
things I shall have to endure. Were I just coming into public life,
fresh from school, and lessons of morality, I should die outright of
astonishment and disgust; but though affected, I am acclimated, and,
having endured an attack, shall recover a part of my health, but no
more.

Those who do not openly desert, discountenance my progress;
some look black, all look cold; the very men who patted me on the
back, praised my exertions, rebuked the apathy of the Government
(while *we* were in Opposition) now reverse all three. Sandon talks of
it as very natural, if not very justifiable—'*to be sure*,' he says, '*when
in Opposition your friends wished to annoy the existing Government,
now, of course, they look more carefully into the thing.*' This he did
not condemn, but called it 'human infirmity!' This was his tone
throughout a long conversation, in which he endeavoured to show

that, as much evil would be left after all that I could do, I might as well leave the whole.[12]

Ashley's disappointment with Peel was inevitable. In many ways the Prime Minister was the antithesis of Ashley. This son of a successful cotton-spinner, who still spoke with a slight Lancashire accent, was a hard-headed man of business, indifferent to general ideas and suspicious of enthusiastic natures. He was wholly a politician, a master of the art of the possible. Single-handed, Peel had revived the once moribund Tory party, persuading it to abandon its posture of blind resistance to change and embarking it upon a course of conservative reform. Now firmly in power, with a brilliant ministry and a secure majority in the Commons, he proposed to deal with the widespread economic distress by legislating important financial, banking, and tariff reforms. The presence in the government of a man of Ashley's severe conscience and religious preoccupations could only have obstructed that program. Peel's opposition to a ten-hours bill did not spring from dishonorable motives. He was not inhumane; his father, the first Sir Robert Peel, had been a prominent supporter in Parliament of the factory acts of 1802 and 1819. His point of view was simply that of the business community. He believed that the welfare of all classes depended on an increased national prosperity, which was to be achieved not by further regulating enterprise but by emancipating it from the trammels of the unenlightened past. In this belief Peel's career as Prime Minister was to prove him partially correct.

All Peel's affinities are towards wealth and capital, *Ashley complained in his diary on February 24.* His heart is manifestly towards the mill-owners; his lips occasionally for the operatives. *What* has he ever done or proposed for the working classes? His speech of last night [on the current distress] was a signal instance of his tendencies. He suppressed all the delinquencies of the manufacturers, bepraised machinery, and treated the distress as severe but temporary. Now, he might have said that no small portion of the suffering was caused by the forced immigration of families in 1836, reducing the already low wages, and aggravating the misery, in the stagnation which followed. He might have said, too, that, while we cannot interdict machinery, we ought not to be blind to its effects: it may cheapen goods for the consumer, but it pauperizes irrevocably thousands of workpeople, who can never resume their position, whatever be the activity of trade. In short, his speech was a transcript of his mind: cotton is everything, man nothing!

Feb. 25th.—Time creeps on, years fly past, and the city of oppression and vice has not capitulated; the factory system stands erect; millions of infants are consumed.

March 3rd.—Matters do not brighten; I see hardly a speck of day. There may be a ray of light to break forth in God's mercy, but it is not yet above the horizon. It is manifest that this Government is ten times more hostile to my views than the last, and they carry it out in a manner far more severe and embarrassing. I find that the [factory] inspectors are terrified by Sir J. Graham. Horner and Saunders are now warmly with me, but they do not dare to say so. Now I fear delay, the Minister knows my position, and can defy me, because he has both power and speciousness on his side. Matters may be postponed to a late period of the Session, when I shall be more than usually helpless through the absence of many supporters. I am particularly dejected. I feel an unusual conviction of incompetency; every one seems more equal to the task, be it what it may, than myself. I am become quite timid. I have undertaken things that are too hard for me, and yet I have asked—at least I thought so—counsel of God in everything; but man oftentimes asks amiss.

March 11th.—Peel has been eminently successful in his plans; his Corn Bill has been sharply debated, but, on the whole, favourably received. His new taxes and new tariffs (to-night) almost gave satisfaction, a thing unheard of in the history of the Exchequer! To be sure, he had an astounding case of necessity, but that plea, even, has oftentimes failed. His success puzzles me; I cannot regard him in any light but as a mere seeker of human praise; his moral phræseology seems the result of calculation. His speech this evening was a *chef-d'œuvre* of self-confidence. This is unquestionably the next best thing to a vigorous faith; it leads to victory. I begin to fear that I have as little of the one as of the other. I am quite down again; easily raised, easily depressed. I catch at a straw, and writhe under disappointment. The fact is, I am almost tired. I have laboured now for nearly ten years, and the haven recedes as I approach. Not a cheer is given to Peel in the House of Commons that does not retard my success, multiply my toil, and add to my anxiety. This is a jovial prospect!

March 18th.—Spoke again last night on the Lunacy Bill. I seemed to myself to do it without force or point, and with difficulty; half left unsaid and the other half said ill. This is humbling and despairing, because I plough not in hope. How can I look to success in the great measures I propose, if I am so weak in the smaller? The house will despise schemes so brought forward. Am I working *in* the truth and *for* the truth? This doubt often arises now, and yet, what is my guide if I am not?[13]

IV

❧*In the midst of his despair over the prospects of a ten-hours bill, there came into Ashley's hands the unpublished first report of the Commission on the Employment of Children in Mines and Factories. Two years before, when the ten-hours cause had seemed hopeless, Ashley had succeeded in obtaining the appointment of a royal commission to investigate the employment of children outside the textile mills. The Commissioners' first report dealt with mines and collieries. Once again, through the sober pages of an official document, passed the wretched, haunting procession of England's working children and those who knew them. The accounts of misery and oppression, more horrible than those of the factory children in 1832, were made especially vivid by the introduction of illustrations calculated to arrest the attention of the hurriedly perusing statesman. Not even Ashley had foreseen the terrifying revelations, or the wave of revulsion and indignation that passed over England when the report was published*☙.

April 9th [1842].—This day is, perhaps, the last of leisure I shall have for a long time. Gave it to the reading of the Colliery Report, that I may be thoroughly furnished to the good work. I can never produce, in a speech, one-tenth part of the truth, and yet, unless that be fully told, I shall not accomplish my purpose. Great labour, great difficulty, first to read, and then to select and arrange the matter.

May 7th.—The report of the Commission is out—a noble document. The Home Office in vain endeavoured to hold it back: it came by a most providential mistake into the hands of members; and, though the Secretary of State [Sir James Graham] for a long while prevented the sale of it, he could not prevent publicity, or any notice of motion.

Perhaps even 'Civilisation' itself never exhibited such a mass of sin and cruelty. The disgust felt is very great, thank God; but will it be reduced to action when I call for a remedy?[14]

⮜§Ashley at once announced his intention to bring in a bill to exclude women and children from the mines and to regulate the labor of young people. The government was cold. The report was indeed damning, and the growing public outcry seemed likely to drive them to some sort of remedial action. But Graham, the Home Secretary, like his colleagues, believed that any such action would be unwise and futile. To attempt to regulate industry would merely drive capital out of the country and leave the working classes in more desperate straits than ever. It was to be regretted that the Commissioners had brought so effectively to public attention an evil that was beyond remedy§⮞.

May 14th.—The Government cannot, if they would, refuse the Bill of which I have given notice, to exclude females and children from coal-pits—the feeling in my favour has become quite enthusiastic; the Press on all sides is working most vigorously. Wrote pointedly to thank the editor of the *Morning Chronicle* for his support, *which is most effective.*

May 21st.—The Government had well-nigh given away Thursday (my day) for the Colliery Bill, to C. Buller. It is clear that they desire to get rid of the motion. This day I received a formal proposition from Freemantle to give precedence to the Bridport case. No reason assigned why the Minister demanded precedence; there is quite as good reason why I should precede Buller, as he precede me. I told him that such a request came with a very bad grace from a Government which was hostile, not only to past measures of the kind, but, I really believed, to this one in particular! I, of course, refused; postponement would be total surrender.

May 23rd.—Peel, knowing my determination not to give way, advised Wynne this evening (Wynne told me so himself) to take Thursday for a *question of privilege,* thereby destroying me altogether. Never was there such treatment, such abominable trickery.

May 24th.—One would have thought that a 'paternal' Government would have hastened to originate, certainly to aid, any measure for the removal of this foul and cruel stain? No such thing, no assistance, no sympathy—every obstacle in my way, though I doubt whether they will dare *openly to oppose* me on the Bill itself. Have

no time for reflection, no time for an entry. I hear that no such sensation has been caused since the first disclosures of the horrors of the
slave trade! God, go before us, as in Thy pillar of a cloud!

May 30th.—26th, day fixed; persisted, having received an assurance from Peel and Freemantle that the privilege question would
not occupy two hours, Peel having engaged to give me a day if I
were disappointed. So it turned out; Wynne was absent; I was
called; the first sentence was all but begun, when cries arose that
Wynne was coming; I gave way, and this famous 'two hours' debate
occupied from five till twelve o'clock! Never did I pass such an evening; expecting, for six hours, without food or drink, to be called
on at any moment—very unwell in consequence, and have been, in
fact, ever since. Peel then gave me Tuesday (to-morrow), and just
now—such is the apparent fate of the question—a horrid attempt
to assassinate the Queen has caused an adjournment of the House.

May 31st.—This is the day; but I fear that all will be so engrossed by this terrible affair [the assassination attempt], that there
will be no hearing for us! Wrote to Peel, and offered to release him
from his engagement (which he was quite ready to hold to), seeing
his great anxiety to finish the Income Tax Bill. He had lost his day
by so terrible an event, that it would be kind and becoming on my
part to anticipate his wishes and postpone my own. He wrote a grateful acceptance of my offer, and now I stand for Tuesday next, like
the god Terminus on the Capitol, resolved not to budge.

June 1st.—I am glad I have done so. Peel has carried his Bill,
and I am not the worse for the delay, at least, I hope so. I foresee a
covert and spiteful opposition; the Great Northern coal-owners
have produced a document of defence of themselves, which throws
the mantle of their comparative merit over the enormities of the general practice. Here is party! It is a vain, insolent, and feeble paper,
quite in the style of the old apologies of the Factory masters. These
repeated delays have tried my patience, and stumbled my faith—
God forgive me. I shall yet see that the harvest is retarded, not
denied.[15]

*Ashley introduced his bill on June 7, 1842, in a long address
summarizing the findings of the Commission and explaining his proposed remedies. His manner was sober. There were no recriminations,
no searing indictments. The facts, selected, organized, and dispassionately presented, spoke for themselves. The enormous effect of the
speech derived from the cumulative power of revelation after revela-*

tion exposing a subterranean world of unimagined cruelty and degra-
dation§❧.

Sir, it is not possible for any man, whatever be his station, if he have but a heart within his bosom, to read the details of this awful document without a combined feeling of shame, terror, and indignation. It has shown you the ignorance and neglect of many of those who have property, and the consequent vice and suffering of those who have none; it has shown you many sad causes of pauperism; it has shown you the physical disorders which our system has engendered, and the inevitable deterioration of the British race; it has shown you in part our condition, moral, social, and religious. We know not what a day may bring forth. I know it will be said, "Vice is not new—danger is not new; this has occurred before, and will occur again." That is true; but I maintain that our danger is absolute, not comparative—our forefathers had to deal with thousands, we with millions. We must address ourselves to the evil boldly and faithfully, or it will soon acquire so enormous a magnitude as to be insuperable by any effort either of genius or principle.

❧§Grimly he recited the facts documented by the Commission: of the employment underground alongside adult men and women of children of both sexes, usually seven or eight years of age but sometimes five or six; of their confinement for sixteen hours a day in barely lit, poorly ventilated, inadequately drained mine shafts; of the crushing labor, brutal discipline, and calloused exploitation to which they were subjected; of the peculiar diseases to which they were heir and the moral ruin that reduced them to a condition scarcely human§❧.

Now, it appears that the practice prevails to a lamentable extent of making young persons and children of a tender age draw loads by means of the girdle and chain. The child, it appears, has a girdle bound round its waist, to which is attached a chain, which passes under the legs, and is attached to the cart. The child is obliged to pass on all fours, and the chain passes under what, therefore, in that posture, might be called the hind legs; and thus they have to pass through avenues not so good as a common sewer, quite as wet, and oftentimes more contracted. This kind of labour they have to continue during several hours, in a temperature described as perfectly intolerable. By the testimony of the people themselves, it appears that the labour is exceedingly severe; that the girdle blisters their sides and causes great pain. "Sir," says an old miner, "I can only say what the mothers say, it is barbarity—absolute barbarity." Robert North says, "I went into the pit at seven years of age. When I drew by the girdle and chain, the skin was broken, and the blood ran down. If we said anything, they would beat us. I have seen many draw at six. They must do it or be beat. They cannot straighten their backs during the day. I have sometimes pulled till my hips have hurt me so that I have not known what to do with myself." In the West Riding, it appears, girls are almost universally employed as trappers and hurriers, in common with boys. The girls are of all ages, from seven to twenty-one. They commonly work quite naked down to the waist, and are dressed—as far as they are dressed at all—in a loose pair of trousers. These are seldom whole on either sex. In many of the collieries the adult colliers, whom these girls serve, work perfectly naked. Near Huddersfield the sub-commissioner examined a female child. He says, "I could not have believed that I should have found human nature so degraded. Mr. Holroyd, and Mr. Brook, a surgeon, confessed, that although living within a few miles, they could not have believed that such a system of unchristian cruelty could have existed."

Now, Sir, it appears that they drag these heavy weights some 12,000 yards, some 14,000, and some 16,000 yards daily. "In the east of Scotland," says the commissioner, "the persons employed in coal-bearing are almost always girls and women. They carry coal on their backs on unrailed roads, with burdens varying from 3/4 cwt. to 3 cwt.,—a cruel slaving," says the sub-commissioner, "revolting to humanity. I found a little girl," says he, "only six years old, carrying 1/2 a cwt., and making regularly fourteen long journeys a-day. With a burden varying from 1 cwt. to 1 1/2 cwt., the height ascended and the distance along the roads, added together, exceeded in each journey, the height of St. Paul's Cathedral." Thus we find a child of six years old, with a burden of at least 1/2 cwt., making fourteen times a-day a journey equal in distance to the height of St. Paul's Cathedral. The commissioner goes on: "And it not unfrequently happens that the tugs break, and the load falls upon those females who are following," who are, of course, struck off the ladders into the depths below. "However incredible it may be, yet I have taken," he adds, "the evidence of fathers who have ruptured themselves by straining to lift coal on their children's backs."

But, Sir, if this is bad for the children and young persons, the case is far worse for pregnant women. For them it is horrible. "I have

a belt round my waist," says Betty Harris, "and a chain passing between my legs, and I go on my hands and feet. The road is very steep,
and we have to hold by a rope, and where there is no rope, by anything that we can catch hold of. It is very hard work for a woman.
The pit is very wet. I have seen water up to my thighs. My clothes
are wet through almost all day long. I have drawn till I have had the
skin off me. The belt and chain is worse when we are in the family
way." "I have had," says a witness, "three or four children born the
same day that I have been at work, and have gone back to my work
nine or ten days after: four out of eight were still-born."

Now, Sir, the physical effects of this system of labour may be
classed under these heads: stunted growth, crippled gait, irritation
of head, back, and feet, a variety of disease, premature old age, and
death. "Several," says Dr. Scott Allison, "become crooked. Diseases
of the spine are very common and very serious. Several of the girls
and women so employed are distorted in the spine and pelvis, and
suffer considerable difficulty at the period of the parturition." Diseases of the heart are very frequent, say all the medical witnesses.
"Many are ruptured, even lads, from over exertion; some are ruptured on both sides." But the most destructive and frequent disease
is asthma. "Some are affected at seven or eight years of age. Most
colliers at the age of thirty become asthmatic." Dr. Scott Allison
adds: "Between the twentieth and thirtieth year many colliers decline
in bodily vigour, and become more and more spare. At first, and,
indeed, for several years, the patient, for the most part, does not
suffer in his general health; but the disease is rarely, if ever, cured.
It ultimately deprives him of life by a slow and lingering process."
"The want of proper ventilation," says an old miner, "is the chief
cause; the men die off like rotten sheep." There is another most
curious disease, of which the House now hears perhaps for the first
time. It is the melanosis, or black spittle. From the state of the
atmosphere in which the people work, there is oftentimes not sufficient
oxygen to decarbonize the blood, and Dr. Thompson, of Edinburgh,
says: "Workmen in coal-mines occasionally die of an affection of the
lungs, accompanied with the expectoration of a large quantity of
matter of a deep black colour." Dr. Makellar calls it "the most
serious and fatal disease which he had had to treat among colliers—
a carbonaceous infiltration in the substance of the lungs." Dr. Scott
Allison says: "The symptoms are emaciation of the whole body, constant shortness and quickness of breath, occasional stitches in the
sides, quick pulse, usually upwards of 100 in the minute, hacking

cough day and night, attended by a copious expectoration, for the
most part perfectly black. The disease is never cured. It invariably
ends in the death of the sufferer." Who, then, can be surprised that
the consequences are premature old age and death? Not only, however, is the death of the collier premature, but so is the exhaustion
of his strength: he is early deprived of the power of earning a livelihood. Mr. Massey, clerk to the Wellington Union, says "that when
about forty years of age, the greater part of the colliers may be
considered as disabled and regular old men."

*The bill Ashley proposed would have excluded all females and
boys under thirteen years of age from the mines; ended the system of
assigning parish apprentices to the colliers, for whom they were
forced to work without pay until they were twenty-one; and prohibited the employment of anyone under twenty-one in charge of an
engine, thus checking the many fatalities attributable to the operation of mechanical lifts and other machinery by careless, meagerly
paid children. Ashley concluded with a final appeal to the humanity
and patriotism of his hearers.*

Sir, we can estimate our loss of acquisition of territory by geographical measurement; and so we can calculate in finance by increase or deficiency of revenue; but it is not so easy to arrive at the
moral statistics of a country. Many persons love to estimate the condition of a kingdom by its criminal tables; but surely these figures
exhibit very scantily the moral state of a people. A people may be in
a frightful condition as citizens, and yet but few appear before the
magistrate or infringe the laws. Criminal statistics are only a symp-
tom, and not the extent of the internal disorder. I hope, Sir, that the
House will not consider that I am speaking dogmatically on these
subjects: my intercourse with the working classes, both by correspondence and personal interview, has for many years been so extensive, that I think I may venture to say, that I am conversant with
their feelings and habits, and can state their probable movements. I
do not fear any violent or general outbreaks on the part of the
population; there may be a few, but not more than will be easily re-
pressed by the ordinary force of the country. But I do fear the
progress of a cancer, a perilous, and, if we much longer delay, an
incurable cancer, which has seized upon the body, social, moral, and
political; and then in some day, when there shall be required on the
part of our people an unusual energy, an unprecedented effort of

virtue and patriotism, the strength of the empire will be found prostrate, for the fatal disorder will have reached its vitals.

There are, I well know, many other things to be done; but this, I must maintain, is an indispensable preliminary; for it is a mockery to talk of education to people who are engaged, as it were, in unceasing toil from their cradle to their grave. I have endeavoured for many years to attain this end by limiting the hours of labour, and so bringing the children and young persons within the reach of a moral and religious education. I have hitherto been disappointed, and I deeply regret it, because we are daily throwing away a noble material!—for, depend upon it, the British people are the noblest and the most easily governed of any on the face of the earth. Their fortitude and obedience under the severest privations sufficiently prove it. Sure I am, that the Minister of this country, whoever he be, if he will but win their confidence by appealing to their hearts, may bear upon his little finger the whole weight of the reins of the British empire. And, Sir, the sufferings of these people, so destructive to themselves, are altogether needless to the prosperity of the empire. Could it even be proved that they were necessary, this House, I know, would pause before it undertook to affirm the continuance of them. What would induce you to tolerate further the existence of such abominations?

Is it not enough to announce these things to an assembly of Christian men and British Gentlemen? For twenty millions of money you purchased the liberation of the negro; and it was a blessed deed. You may, this night, by a cheap and harmless vote, invigorate the hearts of thousands of your countrypeople, enable them to walk erect in newness of life, to enter on the enjoyment of their inherited freedom, and avail themselves (if they will accept them) of the opportunities of virtue, of morality, and religion. These, Sir, are the ends that I venture to propose. The House will, I am sure, forgive me for having detained them so long; and still more will they forgive me for venturing to conclude, by imploring them, in the words of Holy Writ, "To break off our sins by righteousness, and our iniquities by showing mercy to the poor, if it may be a lengthening of our tranquility."[16]

June 9th.—Oh that I had the tongue of an angel to express what I ought to feel! God grant that I may never forget it, for I cannot record it. On the 7th, brought forward my motion—the success has been *wonderful,* yes really wonderful—for two hours the House listened so attentively that you might have heard a pin drop, broken only by loud and repeated marks of approbation—at the close a dozen members at least followed in succession to give me praise, and express their sense of the holy cause.

As I stood at the table, and just before I opened my mouth, the words of God came forcibly to my mind, 'Only be strong and of a good courage'—praised be His Holy Name, I was as easy from that moment as though I had been sitting in an armchair. Many men, I hear, shed tears—Beckett Denison confessed to me that he did, and that he left the House lest he should be seen. Sir G. Grey told William Cowper that he 'would rather have made that speech than any he ever heard.' Even Joseph Hume was touched. Members took me aside, and spoke in a *very serious* tone of thanks and admiration. I must and will sing an everlasting 'non nobis.'—Grant, oh blessed God, that I may not be exalted above measure, but that I may ever creep close by the ground, knowing, and joyfully confessing, that I am Thy servant, that without Thee I am nothing worth, and that from Thee alone cometh all counsel, wisdom, and understanding for the sake of our most dear and only Saviour, God manifest in the flesh, our Lord Jesus Christ! It has given me hopes for the Empire, hopes for its permanence, hopes for its service in the purposes of the Messiah. God prosper the issue!

June 11th.—Has not this carried, in fact, the Ten Hours Bill?[17]

Ashley's speech was greeted by a chorus of praise from both sides of the House. Successive speakers expressed their shock at the state of affairs in the mines, pledged Ashley their support—but assured him that the conditions he described were not to be found in their districts.

A few notes of qualification hinted at the opposition to come. Graham promised the government's cordial support of Ashley's bill, but questioned the wisdom of postponing to the age of thirteen the initiation of boys into the collieries. Lord Egerton earnestly shared Graham's concern. I cannot help stating to the House some information which I have received on this subject, and which was communicated to me by a most respectable gentleman, a clergyman, who has been long conversant with such subjects. This gentleman states, unwillingly, but conscientiously, that he fears that the peculiar bend of the back, and other physical peculiarities requisite to the employment, cannot be obtained if children are initiated at a later age than twelve.[18]

Hedworth Lambton, member for North Durham and himself a

mineowner, cautioned the House that great interests were involved here, not least the miner's right to dispose freely of his own labor❧. A law is necessary to protect the child, ❧*he agreed*❧, but to protect the child, not against the coal-owner and his agent, but against the cupidity of his own parent. There is the great difficulty to contend with. It matters little to the coal-owner, as far as his self-interest is concerned, whether the boy goes down to work in the mine at the age of nine or ten, or eleven and twelve. It matters little whether that boy works three days, or five or six days in the week; but it does matter to the cupidity of the parent.[19]

❧*Two weeks later, at the bill's second reading, the opposition was more outspoken. All conceded the desirability of barring women from the mines but condemned the Commission's report as highly exaggerated and offered evidence of their own to contradict its findings. Throughout South Staffordshire, the member for that district informed the House*❧, mining is generally looked upon as a healthy, cheerful, and pleasant occupation. The "jolly collier" is a proverbial expression all over the county. It is generally considered a remarkably pleasant and cheerful employment. It has been observed that, when any accident happens to a collier, or he is attacked by any disease, he is cured in an incredibly short time. Their general health is much better than that of the rest of the labouring population.[20]

❧*Another mineowner, Peter Ainsworth, member for Bolton, offered further evidence of the health and well-being of the colliery children, but warned that their condition would be harmed rather than improved by Ashley's bill*❧. The state of these children is much better than that of the factory children; but the effect of the noble Lord's bill will be to deteriorate their condition, and to aggravate the distress which already exists amongst the working classes. In the borough with which I am connected there is what is called a relief fund, from which, during the last year, the following persons derived assistance:—373 cotton-spinners; 370 weavers; 134 out-workers or working labourers; but only nine of the colliery population. The noble Lord has already interfered with the cotton-spinners, and gone such great lengths as to cause great privations amongst them, and the result of this measure will be the same with regard to the mining population.[21]

June 23rd.—Last night pushed the Bill through Committee; a feeble and discreditable opposition! 'Sinners' were with me, 'saints' against me—strange the contradiction in human nature! Had I trusted in man, I should have been lamentably forlorn: not a member of the Government, except Manners Sutton, who was necessarily present. Graham, it is true, apologised, as summoned to the Queen; but where were the rest? It is very curious (but so I have invariably found it) that those who promised support, failed, and those who made no promises, were present. I must except a few. Bell and his Northern gentry behaved admirably. Some who came down to support me spoke against me!

June 24th.—A notice given last night, by Mr. Ainsworth, to refer the Bill to a Select Committee, to see whether it would not abate the wages of the working classes! This involves delay—long and serious delay. I suffer much from anxiety. George Anson gave me a kind message from Prince Albert, expressive of his sympathy and the Queen's, adding that he had read every syllable of it [the speech] to the Queen.

June 25.—Late last night, or rather at two o'clock in the morning, forced my Bill through the Report, despite the resistance of Mr. Ainsworth. Thank God! but the day is not yet won. There may be difficulty on the third reading.

June 28.—Deputation from South Staffordshire; very positive, very unreasonable. But they have secured Hatherton's co-operation in the Lords; and I, meanwhile, have not found any one to take charge of the Bill. Buccleuch, even, requires longer time for the exclusion of females. Locke, I hear (the agent of Francis Egerton), is secretly setting men's minds against the 'female clause.' The whole struggle is reserved for the Upper House. God be with us!

June 29.—A day of expectation and hope. Disappointed at the last. The House was counted out, and my Bill again delayed. The mercy of God is ever qualifying evil. I have lost the day, but I have gained the Duke of Buccleuch. He will undertake the charge of the Bill; for him I will extend the time of operation to 1st of March.

July 2.—Resisted again last night. Two divisions on the adjournment of the debate late at night. Peel and Graham voted with me on the first, but went away on the second. *Neither of them said a word in my favour.* Gladstone voted against me, and Sir Edward Knatchbull; Graham, the evening before, had changed his tone, and began to express his doubts to Jocelyn. Here again is 'cordial support!' The Government will *openly* desert me in the House of Lords. Wharncliffe attempted to break his engagement, by desiring me to postpone all parts of the Bill *except that which related to females.* I positively refused.

The opposition in the House of Commons delayed Ashley's bill but could not prevent its passage. The bill was amended, however, in two particulars: a clause was introduced providing for inspection of the mines; and Ashley consented to reduce the age when boys might enter the mines from thirteen to ten, with the stipulation that boys under thirteen should work only alternate days.

July 6.—Ainsworth again resisted it as a 'dropped order;' fixed it, however, *by right,* for the later part of the evening. It came on about nine, and, God be everlastingly praised, received, amid cheers, the fiat that 'Lord Ashley do carry the Bill to the Lords.'

Palmerston told the Ministers that, *'if they* were sincere (and they would soon be tested), the Bill must pass the House of Lords.'[22]

The Lords were altogether hostile, their inherent resistance to legislative innovation stiffened by the presence among them of many great coal-owners. Ashley found it almost impossible to get anyone to sponsor the bill in the Lords after the Duke of Buccleuch, the Lord Privy Seal, who had consented to do so reluctantly and with serious reservations, withdrew.

July 1.—Last night the Duke of Buccleuch informed me that his colleagues [in the government] objected; they refused him permission to undertake the Bill; they would not make it a Government measure. Surely, after such promises of support from Graham, such unanimity in the House, and such feeling in the country, they should have done so; but they are hostile in their hearts. Hatherton has notified his opposition in the Lords. I have no one to take charge of the Bill.

July 8.—Much, very much trouble to find a peer who would take charge of the Bill. It is 'the admiration of everybody, but the choice of none.' So often refused, that I felt quite humbled; I was a wearisome suitor for a moment's countenance. All had some excuse or other; praised it, but avoided it. Have since tried Lord Abercorn, the Duke of Cleveland, Lord Dalhousie, Lord Lansdowne, Lord Carnarvon, who has given me no answer, and Lord Stanhope, who dissuaded me from urging my request by showing how *his* advocacy of the Bill might ruin it in the estimation of their Lordships. He was truly zealous and kind; but his plea was a just one for 'non-interference.'

At last, this very evening, a debate still raging in the House of

Lords, I obtained Lord Devon, who spoke, with shame, of the indifference of the Peers to such a measure.

Never did one body present such a contrast to another as the House of Lords to the House of Commons—the question seemed to have no friends; even those who said a sentence or two in its favour, spoke coldly and with measure. Hatherton gave notice of a Committee, and the Duke of Wellington approved it, and spoke, with contempt and suspicion, of the Commissioners. I could not guess at his motive, unless it were an attack on the late Government. And this, after he had told me two days ago at Buckingham Palace that he entirely approved my speech, and that 'the House of Lords would give us no trouble!' nay, more, in a letter I received from him still later, he assured me that 'he should take the same line in the Lords as the Ministers had taken in the Commons!'

This is the accomplishment of 'cordial and earnest support!' But God will overrule, and turn all things to His glory at last. There is, I doubt not, and will be, more success than I now see, for disappointment and apprehension lie heavy on me. I sent the Bill to the Lords with deep and fervent prayer, consecrating, and committing it to God, as Hannah consigned her son Samuel, to His blessed service. May He, in His mercy, have 'respect unto me and my offering!'[23]

The opposition to the bill in the House of Lords was led by the Marquess of Londonderry, owner of coal mines in Durham and an unreconstructed Tory. His attacks began while the bill was still in the Commons and continued with greater force when it was put on the calendar of the upper house. No aspect of the bill was spared. The commissioners and subcommissioners, Londonderry accused, were untrustworthy. I have statements by me that some of the sub-commissioners are wholly unfit for the duty cast upon them. I am informed that one of the sub-commissioners, named Franks, kept two hat-shops, one in Regent-street, and the other in the city, and failed, and that he afterwards was imprisoned for a libel on the clerk of the Fishmongers' Company.[24]

Nor did he approve of their methods. These gentlemen came to this inquiry fresh from the factory commission, with all the prejudices which that commission is likely to excite, and with an expectation and desire of finding similar oppressions amongst the miners to those which they have found amongst the manufacturing population. Their instructions were to examine the children them-

selves, and the mode in which they have collected their evidence—
communicating with artful boys and ignorant young girls, and putting questions in a manner which in many cases seemed to suggest the
answer—is anything but a fair and impartial mode calculated to
elicit evidence on which the House can rely, and on the basis of which
it should proceed to legislate.[25]

*The report itself he wholly condemned as exaggerated and
highly colored*. Again, I think the manner in which the report has
been accompanied by pictures of an extravagant and disgusting, and
in some cases of a scandalous and obscene character, is not such as
should have been adopted in a grave publication, and is more calculated to excite the feelings than to enlighten the judgment.[26]

*Lord Londonderry believed that the problem of the colliery
children was surrounded by a mass of misconceptions*. With regard to the age at which boys should be employed in these collieries,
I think they are as fit for the work at the age of eight as when they
are ten. If we refuse to permit boys to be employed in this work before they arrive at the age of ten years, how are the colliers to bring
up and educate their children? In most cases the parents are too
poor to maintain them, and utterly unable to procure for them any
education.[27]

*Furthermore, what was the value of a bookish education to
these children*? Much has been said about education, but we must
remember the necessity which exists for employing the children, and
the difficulty in those districts of the country of youths getting any employment, however educated, except in the collieries. On this subject
I invite your Lordships' attention to the following communication
from another of my correspondents. [The noble Marquess read a
communication describing the superior advantages of a practical education in collieries to a reading education, and stating, that at Shina
Row a library had been established for the colliers, but not one ever
came to it.][28]

*Certainly he was opposed to the employment of women in mines,
but other women performed harder labor than those in the collieries,
and excluding the women from the pits would work severe hardships
on both themselves and the mine-owners*. I have received a letter
from a person at Edinburgh, in which the writer states that in the
collieries in Mid-Lothian it is impossible to employ horses for bringing up the coals from the pits; that women are generally employed in
this work, that they bring up the coal on their backs, ascending by
ladders, and that they prefer this mode of gaining a livelihood, be-

cause by this work they can earn higher wages than by other employ-ment. The writer also states, that if the women are debarred from gaining a livelihood by this means they will, in a majority of in-stances, be unable to obtain other employment; and he adds, that the collieries at present yield little profit, and if the owners have to em-ploy men to do the work which is now performed by women, they must require higher prices for the coals, and he believes that eventu-ally many of the collieries will be given up.[29]

The self-styled humanitarians had completely overlooked the problem of what was to become of the women who would be thrown out of work, without compensation, by the bill. I must say, that practical benevolence is more praiseworthy than mistaken humanity. It has been stated, that the result of the bill will be favourable to the morality of the persons affected by it. It may be so; or it may not; and I am an advocate of morality in all its forms. But I would ask your Lordships whether such an uncertainty as contingent morality ought to be purchased at the fearful price of beggary and starva-tion.[30]

July 13th.—Last night fixed for debate in the House of Lords, postponed to Thursday. Lord Londonderry attacked me, Clan-ricarde defended me. Misery makes one acquainted with strange bed-fellows! He did it kindly and well. Government at last declared, by the voice of Lord Wharncliffe, that it would 'be quite passive, it would give no support to the Bill.' This, too, after having promised great things in the House of Commons; and moreover, after having done the Bill a disservice by recommending that it should be referred to a Select Committee.

Now then I am impotent—nothing remains (humanly speaking) but public opinion—were it not for this I should not be able to carry one article of the Bill; but something, please God, I shall at-tain through that His instrument; yet a very small portion of what I desired. It is impossible to keep terms with this Ministry, their promises are worth nothing.

July 26th.—Bill passed through Committee last night. In this work, which should have occupied one hour, they spent nearly six, and left it far worse than they found it; never have I seen such a dis-play of selfishness, frigidity to every human sentiment, such ready and happy self-delusion. Three bishops only present, Chichester (Gilbert), Norwich (Stanley), Gloucester (Monk), who came late, but he intended well. The Bishop of London and the Archbishop of

Canterbury went away! It is my lot, should I, by God's grace, live
so long, to be hereafter among them [in the House of Lords]; but
may He avert the day on which my means of utility in public life
would be for ever concluded![31]

*In the face of public opinion, the Lords could not drop the
bill, though they only narrowly avoided sending it to a Select Committee where it would have been delayed indefinitely. They did, however, seriously cripple it with amendments. In the bill as finally
passed, the employment of women and girls underground was prohibited. The age at which boys might enter the mines was fixed at
ten, without the qualification that those under thirteen should work
only alternate days. The practice of assigning parish apprentices to
the colliers was approved, though restricted to boys between ten and
eighteen. The duties of the mine inspectors were limited to reporting
on the condition of the workers only, not of the mines. The bill did
not at all limit the hours of work in the mines despite the fact that
the colliery children worked longer hours than those in the mills*.

Aug. 1. Said Peel to me the other evening, 'I shall be as great a
sufferer as most people by the Bill, but it was perfectly right; the
evidence could not be resisted—though I shall be so great a sufferer,
I assure you *I have not offered the slightest impediment*.' I told him
'I believed his statement.' I could not, however, pay compliments, for
he ought to have done far more than give this negative aid; *he
ought to have co-operated vigorously*.

12 o'clock, night.—Redesdale moved the third reading. I was much
buoyed up with the notion (which papers, bills, peers, and clerks
confirmed) that the amendments (!) admitting the women into pits
'only not to work,' had been omitted; full of excitement and thankfulness; then I suddenly discovered that the words were added on a
slip of paper. God forgive me for my bitter disappointment; God
strengthen my faith and patience! I am in a fix, shall I accept the
words, or endeavour to strike them out? If they remain, the Bill is
neutralized; if they be objected to, the Bill is lost.

On August 7, 1842, the bill passed. August 8th.—Took the
Sacrament on Sunday in joyful and humble thankfulness to Almighty
God for the undeserved measure of success with which He has blessed
my effort for the glory of His name, and the welfare of His creatures.
Oh that it may be the beginning of good to all mankind! *Novus
saeculorum nascitur ordo?* Whatever had been done, is but the mil-

lionth part of what there is to do; and *even then*, should such an end be accomplished, which man never yet saw, we should still be 'unprofitable servants.' The more I labour, the more I see of labour to be performed, and vain at the last will be the labour of us all. Our prayer must be for the Second Advent, our toil 'that we be found watching.'[32]

V

The government's factory bill, prepared by Sir James Graham, was presented in May, 1843. Graham's chief concern was for the education of the factory children; his bill reduced their workday from eight hours to six and a half and provided for their compulsory education in schools directed by the Church of England. From outraged Nonconformity there immediately descended such a storm of protest upon the astonished ministers that the bill had to be withdrawn. The next February Graham introduced a new bill that avoided altogether the explosive educational issue. This bill limited the hours of children under thirteen to six and a half (the children could be employed in two shifts so as not to affect the hours of the adult operatives), but it lowered the age at which they could enter the factories from nine years to eight. The workday of young persons was limited to twelve hours; in this category Graham included boys from thirteen to eighteen and—an important innovation—all females over thirteen. A number of administrative improvements over the Factory Act of 1833 were also introduced, providing for the safeguarding of machinery and making inspection more effective.

Despite these cautious but significant advances, Graham's bill was still a twelve-hours bill for all the operatives over thirteen years. Ashley's strategy was, therefore, to transform it into a ten-hours bill by moving amendments to the second clause, which specified the hours at night when the protected categories could not work, and to the eighth clause, which fixed the number of hours during the day when they could work. In the north of England the Short Time Committees roused the operatives for their fourth and greatest effort in support of their Parliamentary champion.

On March 15 the government's bill received its second reading, whereupon the House of Commons voted itself a committee of the whole to consider the bill clause by clause. At the second clause Ashley moved "that, the word 'night' shall be taken to mean from six o'clock in the evening [Graham had specified 'eight'] to six o'clock

*in the following morning; and the word 'mealtime' shall be taken to
mean an interval of cessation from work for the purpose of rest and
refreshment, at the rate of two hours a day, with a view to effect a
limitation of the hours of labour to ten in the day." Graham replied
that the government would stand firm for twelve hours; a ten-hour
day for the protected categories would of course impose a ten-hour
limit on the operation of the mill, thereby reducing by one-sixth the
time in which the mill-owner could earn back his investment and
make his profit—and this at a time when the race with foreign manufacturers was perilous in the extreme. "I have been informed," Graham warned, "that such a step would be fatal to many of our manufacturers. A feather could turn the scale; an extra pound weight
would lose the race." The ensuing debate was sharp. This was the
first time that the ten-hours issue had come before the Parliament
elected in 1841, and it was immediately apparent that Ashley enjoyed considerable support§.*

March 16th.—Factory bill last night in Committee; moved, by
arrangement with Sir J. Graham, amendment on word 'Eight' in
second clause. Spoke two and a quarter hours. Never had a greater
weight on my spirits, and yet—God's everlasting goodness be praised
—obtained astounding personal success. Francis Egerton made an
excellent speech; and Sandon, for a wonder, came out manfully.
Bright made a violent assault upon me, with insinuations, because he
could not make charges; brought him to account and to apologies.
What will be the issue? Had we divided last night, we should, I am
told, have beaten the Government! The interval will be favourable to
them; official whips will produce official votes.[33]

*§Peel and Graham were sufficiently concerned about the strength
of ten-hour sentiment in the House of Commons to venture a discreet
appeal to Ashley through Lord Stanley, the Secretary for War and
the Colonies§.*

March 18th.—Jocelyn [Ashley's brother-in-law] came to me yesterday, after morning service, and said that 'he had something important to communicate.' Stanley had taken him aside on Saturday
evening, and had urged upon him the mischiefs arising from the
amendment for 'ten hours' that I had proposed. 'Ashley,' he added,
'does not know the condition in which he places the Government. If
he carries his point, as it seems probable he will, two courses remain:

we must either throw up the Bill, for Graham is pledged to carry it as it is, or throw it into his hands.' He then said a great deal more about the effect such success would have in aiding the repeal of the Corn Laws, and remarked: 'If Ashley is strong enough to beat the Government, he must take all responsibility; if he thinks himself strong enough to defeat them here, perhaps he thinks himself strong enough to take the Government.' Jocelyn said: 'What would you have Ashley do? He has given his life, you may say, to the question; what would you have him do? He could not surrender it.' Stanley replied in a drawling, uncertain tone: 'I don't know; I don't say what he could do.' The upshot was that Jocelyn, without delivering a direct message, was to inform me of the Ministerial mind. He did so. I replied that 'if my perseverance involved the repeal of ten thousand Corn Laws, and the dissolution of as many Governments, I would go on with all the vigour I could command; that, were I disposed to hold back, I could not do so in the smallest degree; that even in a mere question of politics, a man would be regarded as a sad specimen of faithlessness who retired simply to gratify the convenience of his Parliamentary friends, but that in this case, when I had toiled for so many years, and placed the whole matter on the basis of duty and religion, I should be considered, *and most justly, too,* a hypocrite almost without parallel.' We rang the changes on all this, and Jocelyn went away. I saw him again in the street, just before I entered the Chapel Royal. 'I have seen Stanley again,' he said; 'he never thought you could resign the question; you were too deeply pledged.' 'It would be a sad thing,' continued Stanley, 'for the Government to appear as alone resisting the wishes and feelings of the people; it would look very ill to the country if the question had a majority in the House, but was rejected solely by the Government.' Then Lord Stanley added (*O tempora, O mores!*), 'What I meant was that you (Jocelyn) and your friends should not bestir yourselves so much to obtain votes, and Ashley might save his character by maintaining his point, and *yet allow himself to be beaten!*' If ever insult was put on an individual, here it was with a vengeance! I told Jocelyn that 'the only difference was whether I should be an open or a secret scoundrel.' I added that 'I would exhaust all legitimate means to obtain my end, and that if defeated, I would never cease to work on the sympathies of the country.'[34]

The debate on the second clause of Graham's bill, which had begun on March 15, resumed on March 18, 1844. Peel placed himself firmly in opposition to Ashley's amendment. There were many areas of the economy, he argued, where the condition of the workers was as bad as, or worse than, that of the textile operatives. Would Parliament legislate for one group and not for the others? Or would it attempt the impossible task of legislating for all? The cheers of Ashley's supporters astounded the Prime Minister. He would not, he warned in conclusion, accept a ten-hours act. Late that night the House divided. By a vote of 179 to 170, it rejected Graham's definition of night as commencing at eight o'clock, and by a second vote of 161 to 153 accepted Ashley's amendment. For the first time, the House had declared for ten hours. Graham, however, was unyielding. He immediately announced that he would not drop the bill but would proceed to the eighth clause, when the House would have to reconsider its action by voting on the substitution of "ten hours" for "twelve hours" in the definition of the workday for the protected categories.

March 19th.—Last night 'adjourned debate' on Factory Bill and division. Can I believe the result? 'It is a night much to be observed of the Lord.' Oh, gracious God, keep me from unseemly exultation, that I may yet creep alow by the ground to Thine honour, and to the recovery of the people from Egyptian bondage! The Red Sea is yet before me, the enemy are in pursuit, and the wilderness has shut us in; but we will, by His grace, 'stand still and see the salvation of the Lord.' He will cleave a path for us through the mighty waters, and ordain in our mouths a song of praise in the land of promise and hope. My supporters wonderfully firm; had no whipper-in, yet they stuck to me admirably. The Government—that is, Peel and Graham —evidently out of temper. This seems as much the cause of their opposition as anything else. Their speeches, ingenious in argument, but wretched in principle and feeling, purely commercial: Peel urging a decay of trade; Graham, an abatement of wages. Neither touched my facts or arguments; but most unfairly Graham spoke a second time, and at great length, before others had spoken once. Peel argued, in fact, against all interference, and then appealed to the House on the merits of his Bill! denounced our legislation with factories as unjust, quoted the condition of thousands of children who are as yet unprotected (passing, in truth, on me the old sneer of the Millowners & Co., that I was one-sided), and speaking as Prime Minister, in detail, of all these horrors, declared that he had no thought of assuaging them. In the sight of God and man he abdicated the functions of

Government. A curious division. My members included very many who represented the mightiest trading constituencies, and this on a *commercial* question!

The Ministers have signified their intention to try over again the whole question by a division on Friday next. The interval will be employed in every Government method of influence and coercion. What engine can I employ to counteract and extinguish their fire? They are unjust, bitter, headstrong, but powerful. I am alone, but I commit all to God, who will maintain His own work.

It is a wonderful event, an especial Providence; is there a precedent like it? A single individual, unaided by a party, with scarcely a man whom he could trust to second him, has been enabled to defeat the most powerful array of capitalists, overcome the strongest domestic apprehensions, and the most powerful Ministry of the last fifteen years! Struggle as they will, the question is passed; it may be delayed in its final accomplishment, but surely it cannot be reversed. God give us faith, faith, faith!

March 21st.—An oppressive weight appears to have been removed from my shoulders, and yet I cannot recover my elasticity. I feel like a man that has been stunned or bled. I am conscious of a change, but hardly of relief: partly the effect of long habit, partly the effect of the foreseen Government hostility (and their power is great!). I find no real comfort but in beholding God as the *author*, and, I pray, as the *finisher*, of this work in His blessed Son Jesus Christ. Ministers quite mad, using every exertion, no reasoning, no misstatement, no falsehood almost, spared! Expresses sent off the whole of Sunday. I offered to delay 'Ten Hours' for two years and a half. Every one satisfied except Peel and Graham, who are furious in temper.[35]

On March 22 the House of Commons, as a committee of the whole, took up the eighth clause. Ashley's motion that the word "ten" be inserted in place of "twelve" set off a long and intense debate. The opposition, as usual, denied the accuracy of the facts Ashley alleged in support of his proposition and repeated arguments that had become familiar during the twelve years the ten-hours question had been before the country.

Edward Cardwell, member for the cotton town of Clitheroe in Lancashire, denied that the proposal could be treated strictly as a humanitarian measure, as Ashley urged, in disregard of its commercial effects. Now this question has been divided, with reference to its popularity, into two sides, in a very remarkable way; and it has been stated that one side takes a purely commercial view, while the other rests entirely upon a basis of morality and humanity. One hon. Member, who stated this distinction in strong terms, borrowed, perhaps unconsciously, the language of the classical historian of Lancashire, who spoke of "passing children through fire to Moloch, and through filth to Mammon;" and such is the tone in which it is thought right to speak of those who venture to differ from the noble Lord. Now, I altogether deny the soundness of this distinction. I do not deny that it is possible to take a purely and strictly commercial view of this question. I do not deny that it is possible for a sordid man to think of nothing but how he might extract from the toil and sufferings of others the largest fortune for himself. But I do deny that they can altogether discard the commercial view of the subject, and rest solely upon considerations of morality and humanity. Do they know what they are talking of? Is it possible for any man who has the least experience on these subjects—or, if he has no experience, who, in the absence of it, applies to the matter a common capacity—not to know how much both the physical and moral comfort of the manufacturing classes depend upon the commercial view of the question? It is scarcely possible for any of them not to know that the success of the manufacturer of this country can do a great deal more for the poorer classes than the widest efforts of the most diffusive charity, or the happiest results of the best-contrived Legislation.[36]

Sir William Clay, a merchant and shipowner, prophesied that Ashley's proposal would actually harm the factory children and, indeed, depress the wages of the entire working class. What are the temptations to prefer the labour of women to men, and of very young persons to that of persons of middle age, it may be said almost of adults? Why they are twofold, first, because it is cheaper; but secondly, and mainly, perhaps, because as the machinery is improved, becomes more delicate and moves faster, and requires less human labour,—it becomes more essential that that labour should be, that of persons at the precise period of life when there is the utmost amount of quickness and activity, when the nerves of sight and touch are in the utmost perfection. The noble Lord's own statistics show that such is the tendency now. Will that tendency be decreased by the proposed measure? Is it not certain that it will be increased? We are about to take off one entire sixth-part of the time within which the master manufacturer is to obtain a return on his fixed capital.

How must he meet this new condition of things? Why, by greater
economy in his labour in the first place, and by working his machinery faster in the second. He will seek with tenfold avidity to
make his engine, with its Briarean power, do more, and human hands
less. He will make his giant of iron and brass work faster too—so
fast that it can only have for fellow labourers human beings when
the young powers of life are in their utmost intensity and those
powers taxed to their very utmost stretch.[37]

*Henry George Ward, member for Sheffield, voiced the despair
of the political economists who saw no ray of hope in the spectacle
of an ever more numerous people struggling ever more desperately
for shares of an insufficient national subsistence*. We are all
agreed that there is a great pressure upon the labouring population,
not confined to one class of manufactures—I can show its existence
to a great extent in the town which I represent; that all are overworked; and that the stern necessity of living induces this condition
of the people, compelling the children almost universally to be called
to labour too early, and forced to labour too long a time, so that
there is not time for education, for wholesome recreation, or for religious and moral instruction. We do not want Dr. Bissett Hawkins to
tell us that it would be better for children, or that it would be better
for all classes, to work ten hours instead of twelve. We do not want
Mr. Horner to tell us that all classes of the population are over-
wrought. There is no doubt of this. We do not want to be told that
they are not free agents—who is a free agent?—or that their social
and moral condition would be better if they laboured only ten hours;
or that excessive labour tends to debase human nature and to prevent acquirements. I admit the evil as fully as any advocate of a ten
hours Bill; and sitting here as the Representative of one of the
largest working men's communities, I will not consent to be twitted
with any heartlessness, or indifference, to their sufferings because I
do not concur in the remedy proposed. I, and those who think with
me, are called Doctrinaires, Utilitarians, and Theorists, but I hold
on the contrary that they are the Theorists who think they can alter
by Act of Parliament the conditions of life which press hardly, and
harshly, on the population of this country.[38]

*On arguments such as these Ashley's supporters heaped their
scorn*. Let the question, then, be divested of all extraneous matter,
and what does it come to? *demanded the young Tory idealist,*

*Lord John Manners*ᏹᏺ. Are the Representatives of the people of England of opinion that twelve hours, instead of ten, are a fitting duration for the day's labour of English matrons and young children? That is the question, and the solution of it seems to me easy; but then come the hon. Members for Manchester, Stockport, and the rest, and plead two propositions in bar; first, that the commerce and manufactures of this great Empire will be destroyed, unless these mothers and children are allowed to work twelve hours a day; and, in the next place, that the wages of the work-people will be reduced. But with something like indignation, and with something like contempt, I beg to ask, is this possible? That the commerce of this great Kingdom is dependent on longer toil by two hours than it is fitting for man to endure? Yes! that will be the confession made by the rejection of the noble Lord's proposal! It is saying to this country —it is affirming in the face of all Europe—that the whole secret of our vast manufacturing power lies in the one hour before sunrise, and in the one hour after sunset, which we snatch from the poor people of England. And this too, after all we have heard of the iniquity of protection! This, then, is the protection they declare to be necessary for their manufacturing interests? I should rather have imagined that the protection of their manufactures exists in the exemption of machinery from taxation. I should have rather imagined that it exists in the power of a manufacturer to assemble round his dwelling any number of people he pleases, to make addition to his wealth by means of that machinery, if trade is brisk; and who, if trade is dull, would have no claim upon that wealth which they contributed to swell. I should have imagined it to consist in the fact of the very rooms in which that machinery worked, and of that machinery itself, paying nothing to the relief of the poor, or towards the burthens of the State—but now it seems that the only species of protection which is looked upon as essential, consists in the over-working of mothers and infant children. I do not believe—I cannot believe it.[39]

ᏹᏺ*Sir Charles Buller explained his reasons for abandoning the strict laissez-faire doctrines he once held to come to Ashley's support*ᏹᏺ. When I voted with the noble Lord, I deliberately adopted a new and bold principle of legislation. I exposed myself to the charge which is thrown out against all who voted with the majority, that they were voting against all principle; for I voted, I am quite aware, against the principle on which legislation on these matters has hitherto been conducted; a legislation which, while it contented it-

self with protecting the property of the rich, shrunk from giving its
protection to the poor, left the helpless to take care of themselves,
and paid no attention to the revolutions which the progress of time
brings about in the social condition of nations.

New evils require new remedies. A new social state, such as that of
England has become in the present century, requires new principles
of legislation. Can it be said that this is a view of the matter in
which no thinking man concurs with me? I venture to say that no unprejudiced man who looks at the alteration which has been operated,
in the course of the last century, in the social condition of the people
of this country, can contemplate that alteration without feelings of
apprehension. A hundred years ago the great mass of the working
people of this country were agricultural, with little community of interest, scattered over the country, without any means of intercom-
munication, without intelligence, without any idea or capacity of
acting in concert, without any power of combination, and entirely influenced by institutions, feelings, and habits which taught them implicitly to act under the guidance of those to whom they had been
accustomed to look up with hereditary awe, and, I may add, with
hereditary attachment. At that period the population of the towns
was limited, and the manufacturing portion were principally skilled
artizans, who got high wages, were possessed of great intelligence,
and were well able to protect themselves. What is the case now? Millions, I may say, of men have collected together for the first time, in
certain limited spaces; millions, not skilled artizans, but men carrying on, in their several classes, some one particular branch of industry, which they practise from the first moment at which they can
work, till they can work no longer,—the great mass of them, in fact,
just as unskilled as the rudest agricultural labourer. Thus large
masses of unskilled, impoverished labourers are collected together,
subjected to terrible privations and discomforts from their very
agglomeration;—from the same cause almost at the mercy of their
employers;—and from the same cause ready and apt to combine for
mischief.

Is this a state of things which Parliament can regard with satisfaction? Is it a good state of things? Is it better for the working
people? Is it better for the rest of the community? What is the physical condition of these unfortunate people thus collected together? Is
it a satisfactory one? I will not go into any lengthened details, but
let me simply ask the House to remember what has been shown to be
the comparative duration of life in Manchester, for instance, and in

the county of Wilts, an agricultural district. In Wiltshire the average duration of life is thirty-three years: in Manchester, it is only seventeen. I do not mean to say that this difference in the duration of human life springs solely or mainly from the nature of factory labour: but it clearly must arise from the circumstances taken all together, under which that labour is carried on in the great towns. Now, it cannot be doubted that the evils of this physical condition are calculated to grow worse in every succeeding generation. A people whose life is reduced to one-half of the usual average of the working class by no accident, no sudden disaster, no chance epidemic, but by the constant action of circumstances unfavourable to health and longevity, are not likely to propagate a vigorous and healthy race. No legislature can view with indifference a state of things that thus shortens human life, and tends to deteriorate the species.

Nor is their social and moral condition at all satisfactory. No man can venture to say that they are properly educated. No man can say that their religious wants are properly attended to. No man can say that their moral condition is wholesome or natural. The mode of employment is such as to subvert all the ordinary relations of the sexes as to labour; the women and children do the hard work, the men occupy themselves with the household duties. The women and children support the men by their hard labour; though every one must admit that nothing can be of greater importance than that women should be limited to the discharge of their own proper functions.

The political bearings of this state of things call for earnest consideration; for it cannot but be acknowledged that the number of people thus collected together, with manifold subjects of complaint, with great facilities for combination, with no attachment, as a rule, to their employers, in a condition eminently open to the machinations of agitators—are circumstances fraught with much danger to the country, unless a speedy and efficient remedy is applied. Those who may shrink from the taunt of being actuated by mere humanity will find plenty of justification for legislating on this subject on grounds of mere interest. It is the interest of every friend of order and property to provide the remedy for a social state that cannot continue without danger to both.[40]

Graham closed the long debate with a restatement of the position from which he would not be budged: passage of a ten-hours act must either depress the wages of the operatives or cause the ruin of domestic manufactures and the flight of capital abroad. Now, I have been asked by the Hon. and learned Member for Liskeard (Mr. C. Buller), to give the Committee some new arguments, and some fresh reasoning to induce it to reconsider its decision of the other night. I am bound, in answer to that appeal, to state, that whether it be from the weakness of my reasoning powers or possibly from the exhaustion of this subject, I have no fresh arguments—no additional reasons to offer—having stated already most fully all the arguments and all the reasoning which occurred to my mind as conclusive on the subject. I have dispassionately and carefully considered those reasons and those arguments, and the conclusion to which they lead irresistibly, before I stated them to the House; and subsequent consideration and subsequent inquiry have only contributed to strengthen my conviction that the course proposed by my noble Friend (Lord Ashley) is, beyond all doubt, that course and that measure which is most fatal to the interests of those whose cause he espouses, and whose welfare he, in common with us all, is most anxious to promote. My belief is that if our manufacturers, with expensive machinery, are compelled to work only ten hours a day, while their foreign rivals work fourteen—if our operatives are limited to sixty hours a week, while their competitors, whether in America, in France, in Switzerland, on the borders of Austria, or in Germany, and in Belgium, work eighty-four hours in the week—I say competition under such circumstances can only end in defeat; it may be sooner or later; but I am certain defeat must, under such circumstances, inevitably attend the British manufacturer, unless, indeed, the wages of labour be reduced in this country below the level of the Continent. I am satisfied that now, with the power unlimited of transferring our machinery to foreign countries, where there is no limit of hours (for though there is an apparent restriction in France, in the absence of any system of inspection it is not operative, and cannot be carried into effect) and we know of large establishments on the confines of Austria where they work for fourteen hours every day for six days in the week—in Austria, which, next to Belgium and Switzerland, is our greatest manufacturing rival—if you limit us here to ten hours a day we shall find that our manufacturing capital will soon follow our machinery to foreign countries. I am as satisfied as I can be of any mathematical proposition, that the first effect will be, if wages do not greatly fall, to transfer our manufacturing capital to those foreign countries which are already our rivals, and that the inevitable and speedy result will be the downfall of our domestic manufactures. And what will be the effect of diminishing the demand for labour amongst the masses congregated together in our manufacturing districts? Will morals be improved as degrading poverty advances? Will education spread, when wages become lower? Will manners become more civilized, and will religion penetrate the masses when discontent has taken the place of prosperity, and when ease and comfort have given place to despair?[41]

◆§Graham's gloomy tenacity steadied the ragged government forces. The House divided first on the government's proposal that the daytime hours of labor for the protected categories be limited to twelve, rejecting it by a vote of 186 to 183. Ashley had won by a narrow margin. Graham called immediately for a vote on Ashley's amendment to substitute "ten" for "twelve" in the clause. Members who had previously voted "no," against the government, now voted "yes" for Ashley's amendment, while the government's supporters now voted "no." But in the confusion occasioned by successive rapid votes on the two questions five members who had first voted "no" voted "no" a second time. As a result, the House rejected Ashley's motion 188 to 181. The bill was virtually nullified§◆.

March 23rd.—Last night victorious in rejecting Twelve Hours by 186 to 183; defeated attempting Ten Hours, by 181 to 188! Yet the cause is mightily advanced. God, in His wisdom and goodness, demands a little longer trial of faith and patience. The consummation will then arrive, and it will be the more evidently seen to be His own work. House very kind. Charles Buller made an admirable speech. What ignorance of the House, of the country, and of mankind, have the Ministry shown. Feeling is very often far better than logic for a guide to conduct. What a patrimony had Peel: the especial protection of the working classes, and he has cast it away! The majority, in fact, included the larger proportion of manufacturing constituencies, and certainly the best of the Government supporters. The House of Commons never saw, before these events, such an utter resignation of party-feeling on all sides to the assertion of a great act of humanity. The influence of Ministers, used unscrupulously and unsparingly, obtained at last but a majority of seven, and that not in support of their original proposition.[42]

◆§Graham and Peel were determined not to yield. On March 24 Graham acknowledged that his bill was in inextricable confusion and proposed to withdraw it and bring in another. The general expec-

tation of a compromise on eleven hours was quickly disappointed;
Graham announced that the new bill would be a twelve-hours bill
and that the government would accept nothing less.

March 25th.—What a scene in the House last night! The tiptoe
of expectation, every one anticipating an Eleven Hours Bill. I was
prepared to accept it, reserving to myself the power of moving whenever I pleased. It would have settled the question for at least two
years. Graham, I am told, very hostile in Cabinet. Peel for it; determined, however, to resist. Graham notified his opposition, and signified that all who supported me were entering on a course of 'Jack
Cade' legislation. Indecent, foolish, and stupid; but he did himself
thereby irreparable mischief. Consideration of bill, or rather withdrawal of it, deferred till Friday next.

March 26th.—Consultations without end; annoyances of all kinds;
unabated anxiety. Prayed heartily for counsel, wisdom, and understanding.

March 27th.—Resolved to act in conformity with my first impression, and allow withdrawal of Bill. Did so, and Graham pledged himself to bring in a new Bill. I can, therefore, do on *this* what I could
not have done on the old Bill—take a debate and division on the
simple question of ten hours.[43]

During Parliament's Easter recess the excitement of the opera-
tives, already intense, reached unprecedented heights. The ten-hour
day, which they believed won on March 18, they now saw slipping
through their grasp, denied by ministerial intransigence and lost in
Parliamentary confusion. Their protests found expression in a series
of great mass meetings that shook each of the factory cities in
turn.

April 17th.—Well, what next? Can I believe my ears? Old Bonham
informed me (stating, while he did so, that it was almost a breach of
confidence, inasmuch as no hint of any sort or kind was to be given)
that Peel had determined to offer me the Lord Lieutenancy of Ireland, *with almost unlimited powers*, in respect especially of the
Church. It came out very naturally, arising from a conversation in
which we were engaged; he lamenting that my position rendered office impossible, and that such a state of things was a loss to Government in general. Peel, he said, had told him, and Graham confirmed it, that no one in the kingdom could effect such good in

Ireland; no one but myself could grapple with the landlords and the prelates and maintain, against influence, the rights of the working clergy. He had, he added, done wrong in mentioning it; it might have the appearance of wishing to abate opposition by such an offer. He trusted to my saying nothing. No one but himself, Peel, and Graham had any idea of the scheme. I listened in silence and astonishment; a little gratified, *but not at all in doubt.* I quite admitted that I could, probably, do more with the Irish clergy than most men at present. I said no more. He argued, and somewhat urged. Silent, not offended, not puffed-up, not beguiled, *fully resolved never to do or accept any-thing,* however pressed by the strong claims of public necessity and public usefulness, which should, in the least degree, limit my opportunity or control my free action in respect of the Ten Hours Bill. Peel had told him that he *would not even breathe the subject* until after the Factory Bill had been disposed of. God give me a right judgment in all things! O God, grant that I may never be seduced by any worldly motive to abandon truth and mercy and justice! Keep me from all specious patriotism, and alike from all fear of man's reproach![44]

When Graham, on May 3, 1844, brought in his new twelve-hours bill, Ashley announced that he intended to move the insertion of a clause that would limit the labor of young persons to eleven hours a day, or sixty-four a week, until October 1, 1847, and thereafter to ten hours a day, or fifty-eight a week. His enemies leaped to the attack.

May 4th.—I was the direct and indirect target. They fired at me without mercy, and left me, like a portrait of St. Sebastian, shot through and through by their arrows. Had not intended to make any reply; perhaps I felt incompetent, as I always do now. Strong in my cause and conduct, weak in my capacity. Ward's accusation against my knowledge, my statements, my veracity, rendered an answer inevitable. What kind of answer? Not one of declamation, but one of facts, that involved much reading of documents, and at half-past ten at night! Why did not Ward make his attack before? But as a man, wishing to be thought a man of honour, I could not decline the challenge. Alas for my necessity! I began and ended amid cries of 'Question' and 'Divide.' Appeal was in vain. The House had heard Ward and Roebuck, but it would not hear me, and I spouted my papers with a heavy heart, a parched mouth, a feeble voice, a faltering tongue, and a hopeless pertinacity—a spectacle of present and future exultation to those who hate me and seek my confusion.

I am certainly conscious of a decline in physical and mental energy during the last three months; the fact I perceive, I cannot arrive at the cause. I have had no sense of comfort from above; I have seen no pillar of cloud by day or of fire by night; my spirits do not rally; fears seem to have obtained undisputed possession of my whole system; I labour under a notion of solitude without external aid or internal assurance; what or whence is it? I have yet before me another conflict. I am languid, weary, diffident; many assail, and no one defends me; I am utterly without resource; I neither possess nor seek the 'arm of flesh.' I tremble at the prospect. I never felt so forlorn as I do now. What is it? I had an inward conviction of support in every other case; in Collieries, in Education, in Opium; here alone I have never experienced a cheering thought, an invigorating grace. Am I right in my purpose? Is it according to God's will?[45]

Ashley moved his ten-hours clause on May 10 with a speech in which for the first time he regarded his proposal from the commercial point of view. Heretofore he had insisted on treating it as a moral issue, supported by considerations of religion, humanity, and patriotism. In his mind these imperatives overrode any calculation of profit and loss. Now, having exhausted every other argument, he undertook to defend his position against those who predicted disaster to mill-owners and operatives alike. True, he conceded, production would be reduced under a ten-hours act, but not in arithmetical proportion to the reduction of working hours; experience had already shown that the operatives worked better and faster when their hours were reduced. Similarly, the anticipated loss in the value of fixed capital had been exaggerated, since there would be concurrent savings in depreciation, repairs, maintenance, and fuel. The decline in the operatives' wages, which they willingly accepted, would be small; since the adult operatives were paid by the piece rather than by the hour, their loss would be proportionate to the relatively small diminution of production instead of to the diminution of time worked. Finally, the rise in the cost of the finished textiles, Ashley demonstrated, would be insignificant and unlikely to affect the competitive position of British manufactures abroad. Earlier factory legislation, he recalled, had been received with prophesies of disaster similar to those currently heard, but capital was now flowing into the textile industry at a greater rate than ever. The 344 cotton mills that ex-

*isted in 1819 had, by 1839, grown to 1,815—irrefutable testimony to
the vigor of domestic industry.*

*But the commercial objections to the ten-hours bill, Ashley in-
sisted, were after all feeble. They had always been urged but never
verified, and they were refuted by the history of the textile industry.
The moral argument remained the decisive one. The evidence for the
need for reform was overwhelming, but the government refused to
listen. Indeed, by now compelling the House to rescind its previous
votes in favor of ten hours, it established a new ministerial despotism
ominous in its implications though futile for its present objects.*

Sir, it is possible, nay, more, it is probable (for their efforts have
been great), that Her Majesty's Ministers will carry the day; but
for how long?—If they would render their victory a lasting one, they
must extinguish all the sentiments that gave rise to mine. Their
error is stupendous—"Scilicet illo igne, vocem populi, et libertatem
senatûs, et conscientiam humani generis aboleri arbitrabantur."
Could you, simultaneously with your extinction of myself, extinguish
for a while the sense of suffering, or at least all sympathy with it, you
might indeed hope for an inglorious repose, and by the indulgence of
your own ease, heap up, for your posterity, turmoil, anxiety, and
woe. But things will not end here. The question extends with numbers, strengthens with their strength, and rises with their intelligence. The feeling of the country is roused; and, so long as there
shall be voices to complain and hearts to sympathise, you will have
neither honour abroad, nor peace at home, neither comfort for the
present, nor security for the future. But I dare to hope for far
better things—for restored affections, for renewed understanding
between master and man, for combined and general efforts, for large
and mutual concessions of all classes of the wealthy for the benefit of
the common welfare, and specially of the labouring people.—Sir, it
may not be given to me to pass over this Jordan; other and better
men have preceded me, and I entered into their labours; other and
better men will follow me, and enter into mine; but this consolation
I shall ever continue to enjoy—that, amidst much injustice, and
somewhat of calumny, we have at last "lighted such a candle in England as, by God's blessing, shall never be put out."[46]

May 12th.—Sunday. At last a day of repose! Have been in a whirl
by night and day—occupied and anxious all day; sleepless, or if

sleeping, like a drunken man, all night; my head quite giddy, and my heart absolutely fainting; too much to do, in quantity, in variety, and importance. Delivered at last, by God's especial mercy, on Friday night, of my burden, not only *without failure*, as I felt at the time, but also *with honour*, as I learned afterwards. Oh, what trouble, time, and perplexity removed![47]

The debate on Ashley's ten-hours clause, sometimes bitter and violent, continued through May 13. It ended when Peel, reiterating his irrevocable opposition to a ten-hour day on the ground of its danger to the prosperity and security of the country, announced that he would resign if Ashley carried his amendment.

Our duty, *he told the House of Commons*, is to take a comprehensive view of all the great interests, commercial, political, social, and moral, of all classes of this great empire. It is a maxim of distributive justice, a maxim of law, a technical rule, in the administration of justice—"*volenti non fit injuria*"—that injury cannot be done to him who consents to it; but you, deputed to perform the functions of watching the welfare of a great country, you cannot act upon that principle. And it cannot be a greater proof of your possessing attributes appropriate to the duties of legislation, that you revise the maxim "*volenti non fiat injuria*," and you tell the people "We will resist your wishes in order to promote your welfare." "We will discharge the duty assigned to us, on account of our being able to take a more comprehensive and more beneficent view, than you are." I protest, then, against the doctrine, that we are to concede because it is the popular will. If we are satisfied that it is not for the popular interests, then it is our painful but necessary duty to resist. If this House be of a different opinion—if you are satisfied that you must make this great experiment on labour—or if you think concession is inevitable, and that you must give way to the wishes and feelings of the people—be it so! But if you take that course, and if you resolve (as you cannot but do in consistency) to pursue it, you must—I say it with all respect—you must do so under other auspices, and other guides who can trace a clearer and a better way than can the present Administration. The noble Lord says that we ought not to attach so much importance to this question, that it is a question not of principle but of degree, that the majority will be composed of conflicting elements, and that we ought not, therefore, to insist upon acting on our own opinions. I say, that attaching the importance we do to this question, and foreseeing its results it is our duty in this case to act upon and to enforce our opinions. There is no other way in which we can avert that which we believe to be a serious evil. It may be that by the combination to which the noble Lord refers, you may succeed: but there are occasions when it is the duty of a Government to refuse to be the instruments of carrying into effect the decisions of such combinations. I believe this to be one of those cases. I know not what the result may be this night, but this I know, that I shall with a perfectly safe conscience, if the result be unfavourable to my views, retire with perfect satisfaction into a private station, wishing well to the result of your legislation, but for myself prepared to pursue that more rugged but not inglorious path of duty—prepared to resist concession which, though popular, I believe to be injurious, and to consult the public interest at the expense of popular favour.[48]

May 14th.—Last night defeated—utterly, singularly, prodigiously defeated by a majority of 138!! The House seemed aghast, perplexed, astounded. No one could say how, why, and almost *when*. It seemed that 35 or 40 was the highest majority expected. Such is the power and such the exercise of Ministerial influence!

May 15th.—The majority was one to save the Government (even Whigs being reluctant to turn them out just now), not against the question of Ten Hours. Freemantle went from one member to another assuring them of Ministerial danger, and thus each man believed that his own vote was the salvation of the Government.[49]

Graham's second bill passed the House and eventually the Lords without further incident. Despite the failure of the ten-hours campaign and the enormous disappointment of the operatives, the Factory Act of 1844 was in some respects an important advance over the Act of 1833, particularly in its extension of protection to women and in its provisions for improved factory safety and better inspection.

May 16th.—Amply satisfied now that I permitted the withdrawal of the [first] Bill. Should have been defeated by an equal majority, and the question would have been ended for the Session. But what should I have lost? The interval has produced all these public meetings, all the witnesses they exhibited, all the feeling they roused, not only throughout those provinces, but the whole country, and, finally, I have obtained a debate and division on the true issue of the *Ten Hours*, not on a mere technicality. Have I not, moreover, saved the [second] Bill with all its valuable clauses about machinery and female labour? A withdrawal or a vigorous resistance to it would have prompted the Ministers to proceed no further; an amendment, stoutly maintained in committee on the *second Bill*, would have deterred them from the third reading. It is now gone to the House of Lords. O God, prosper it!

'Cast down, but not destroyed.' I feel no abatement of faith, no sinking of hope, no relaxation of perseverance. The stillest and darkest hour of the night just precedes the dawn. 'Though it tarry, wait for it,' believing that God send you a trial, and yet bears you up with a corresponding courage; and, although you may pass not the stream of Jordan, it is something that God has permitted you to wash your feet in the waters of the promised land.[50]

VI

When the victory was finally won, Ashley was temporarily out of Parliament, having resigned his seat over a question of conscience. Since 1841, Peel had been gradually liberalizing British tariffs, tending ever toward free trade at least where manufactured goods were concerned. The Corn Laws, however, which set prohibitively high duties on the importation of foreign grain, were sacrosanct in a Parliament composed largely of landowners. Then in 1845 a potato blight in Ireland and the failure of English crops left no alternative to repeal but a disastrous famine. Braving the fury of the protectionist majority of his own party, Peel in January, 1846, announced his intention to repeal the Corn Laws. Ashley, who had also come to accept the necessity of repeal, was caught in a dilemma. He could not in good conscience vote with Peel in violation of electoral pledges to his county constituents, but neither could he vote against Peel contrary to his own convictions. On January 31 Ashley resigned.

Two days before, however, on January 29, Ashley had introduced a new ten-hours bill, sternly putting aside the suggestion that he postpone the measure, with which he was personally so closely identified, until he would be returned to Parliament. Management of the bill he entrusted to his colleague John Fielden, a cotton-spinner whose works at Oldham were the largest in the country but who had steadfastly supported Sadler and Ashley since 1832. Ashley himself hurried north to explain to the operatives his motives for resigning and to summon them to Fielden's support.

March 2nd.—Manchester. Large and crowded meeting in Town Hall. Operatives in general feel that I have advanced the question by the mode and subject of my retirement. I told them that I had nothing to serve them with but my personal character; that, had I continued in Parliament, while I retained my seat, I should have lost my reputation; holding the opportunity, but throwing away the means to do them service.

March 4th.—Preston. This is hard work. Shall I accomplish it? Would to heaven I were home again! Monday, from London to Manchester, and meeting in the evening; Tuesday, to Preston, and meeting; Wednesday, to dine with Thomas Fielden, and meeting at Ashton; Thursday, to inspect large mad-house, and a meeting at Bolton; Friday, Oldham; Saturday, to Bradford, and dinner with Walker. God grant that Sunday may be quiet! Monday, meeting at Bradford; Tuesday, Halifax; Wednesday, Huddersfield; Thursday, Leeds; Friday, homeward, God be praised. This is the pertinacious, unwearied revolution of a steam-engine!

Not satisfied with myself. Monstrous difficult to find a fresh speech every night, and more difficult, too, to make them run on the soft, conciliatory line; to avoid all exciting topics, and, so that we may attain our end, to leave out, in fact, all our reasons for it! I want to propitiate the masters, and yet encourage the workpeople. 'Soft sawder' to the mill-owners (unless it be skilfully applied) is a damper to the men; and a stirrer to the men is a damper to the mill-owners. Nevertheless, by God's blessing, I have hitherto been passably successful.[51]

Returned to London, Ashley paced the lobby of the House of Commons while the familiar debates were repeated within.

April 29th.—Factory Bill in House of Commons. Waited in lobby. Had not spirit to attend under the gallery. Many things will be stated in debate which no one can refute but myself. Alas! alas!

April 30th.—So Sir James Graham and his colleagues have declared themselves against the Factory Bill. Heartless and dishonest men! The whole debate proceeded, and will proceed, on a lie; on the lie that the Bill is directed to the control of the labour of grown men! Alas! alas! I must have fallen very low, or this proposal would not *now* be treated so contemptuously.[52]

On May 22 the bill was lost. A month later, however, Peel's ministry fell. Peel had carried the repeal of the Corn Laws at the price of a split in his own party. On the very day repeal passed the House of Lords, Tory protectionists joined with the Whigs to defeat the government in the House of Commons. Peel resigned, and the Whigs returned to power under the leadership of Lord John Russell, a consistent supporter of ten-hours bills. In January, 1847, Fielden again introduced a ten-hours bill, now with every prospect of success. Once again Ashley fretted anxiously in the lobby.

Feb. 10th.—Factory Bill is under discussion in the House of Commons. I lingered in the lobby; had not spirit to enter the House; should have been nervously excited to reply, and grieved by inability to do so.

March 1st.—Intense anxiety about Factory Bill. I dream of it by day and by night, and work as though I had charge of the Bill.

March 12.—Lady De Gray observed to me, last night, that I was grown silent, and had lost all my spirits. It is quite true. I have, during the last two or three years, been growing more melancholy and even stupid.[53]

Fifteen years of devoted labor were now rewarded. Public opinion had been aroused and educated; a new government favorable to the measure was in power; and the mill-owners, for once, were apathetic, few mills, in a period of sharp recession, then working more than ten hours a day. On May 3, 1847, Fielden's bill was carried in the Commons and on June 1 in the Lords.

May 18th.—Bill passed second reading in House of Lords by 53 to 11. How can we praise Thee, or thank Thee, O Lord? One step more, and all will be safe.

The Bishops behaved gallantly—13 remained to vote; three spoke, and most effectively: London, Oxford, St. David's: Clarendon (!) and Brougham (!!) in opposition. This will do very much to win the hearts of the manufacturing people to Bishops and Lords—it has already converted the hard mind of a Chartist Delegate.

June 1st.—Six o'clock. News that the Factory Bill has just passed the third reading. I am humbled that my heart is not bursting with thankfulness to Almighty God—that I can find breath and sense to express my joy. What reward shall we give unto the Lord for all the benefits He hath conferred upon us? God, in His mercy, prosper the work, and grant that these operatives may receive the cup of Salvation, and call upon the name of the Lord! Praised be the Lord, praised be the Lord, in Christ Jesus![54]

The long fight was over. Rejoicing swept the factory cities. Everywhere the workingmen hailed Ashley and Fielden with the wildest enthusiasm. For Ashley, however, it was a time for humble thanksgiving and for solemn leave-taking. The cause that, fifteen years before, had sought out the obscure Tory aristocrat and made him its champion had at last triumphed. Prayerfully, devotedly, at the sacrifice of his own ambition and prospects, Ashley had served the men, women, and children who trusted and followed him. But more work, endless work, called in other quarters. The "city of oppression and vice" still stood, and Ashley would labor during the rest of his long life on behalf of its suffering inhabitants. In the midst of the workers' celebrations, Ashley, on June 4, 1847, addressed an earnest farewell to the men of the Short Time Committees.

My good Friends,—Although there is no longer any necessity to name you collectively and as united together for the purpose of obtaining a reduction of the hours of working in factories, I will address a few words to you, in your capacity of representatives of the whole operative body, on questions of the highest and dearest interest.

First, we must give most humble and hearty thanks to Almighty God for the unexpected and wonderful success that has attended our efforts. We have won the great object of all our labours—the Ten Hours Bill has become the law of the land; and we may hope, nay, more, we believe that we shall find in its happy results, a full compensation for all our toils.

But, with success have commenced new duties. You are now in possession of those two hours which you have so long and so ardently desired; you must, therefore, turn them to the best account, to that account which was ever in the minds of your friends and advocates when they appealed to the Legislature on behalf of your rights as immortal beings, as citizens and Christians.

You will remember the principal motive that stimulated your own activity, and the energetic aid of your supporters in Parliament, was the use that might be made of this leisure for the moral improvement of the factory people, and especially the female workers; who will now enjoy far better opportunities both of learning and practising those duties which must be known and discharged if we would have a comfortable, decent, and happy population.

You will experience no difficulty, throughout your several districts, in obtaining counsel or assistance on these subjects. The clergy, the various ministers, the medical men—all who have been so forward and earnest in your cause—will, I am sure, be really delighted to co-operate with your efforts.

I need not, I know, exhort you to an oblivion of past conflicts, and to hearty endeavour for future harmony. I trust that there will be no language of triumph, as though we had defeated an enemy. Let us be very thankful that the struggle is over, and that we can once more combine, not only the interests, but also the feelings, of employer and employed, in a mutual understanding for the comfort and benefit of each other, and for the welfare of the whole community.

I cannot entertain a doubt that you will have anticipated me in this respect; it has been my endeavour from the beginning, to seek and to advise all methods of conciliation; and I can safely declare, that in the periods of the greatest ardour or disappointment, I never heard, either in meetings or from individuals, a single vindictive expression.

Although the final completion of this great measure has been achieved by another, I could not, after so many years of labour, take leave of it altogether without a few words to you of advice and congratulation. To no one could the lot have fallen so happily as to our friend Mr. Fielden. He joined me in 1833 in the introduction of the first Bill, and has been ever since, as you well know, your able, energetic, and unshrinking advocate.

In bidding you farewell, I do not retire from your service. I shall, at all times, hold myself in readiness to aid you in any measures that may conduce to the moral and physical welfare of yourselves and of your children; and I shall, indeed, most heartily pray that it may please God to prosper this consummation of our toils with every public and private blessing.

I remain, your very affectionate friend and servant,

ASHLEY.[55]

CHAPTER 2

John Henry Newman

---- ❧ ----

"Dare not to think you have got to the bottom
of your hearts."

I

I am a Catholic by virtue of my believing in a God; and if I am asked why I believe in a God, I answer that it is because I believe in myself, for I feel it impossible to believe in my own existence (and of that fact I am quite sure) without believing also in the existence of Him, who lives as a Personal, All-seeing, All-judging Being in my conscience.

⚜The generation that John Henry Newman addressed in 1864 must have been startled as by an apparition by that dimly remem-bered voice. The passionate controversies of the Oxford Movement, though long quiescent, were not forgotten. Newman was now a Ro-man Catholic priest of the Oratory, living in relative obscurity near Birmingham. Thirty years before, he had been the brilliant leader of a group of Oxford dons who had disrupted the complacent, somnolent

73

*Church of England by reviving old doctrines and usages that alone,
they believed, could equip it to resist the manifold revolutions of the
age. Revered, trusted, followed by thousands—suspected, condemned,
rejected by thousands more—Newman had discovered, to his inef-
fable pain, that his spiritual home lay not in the national church he
loved but in the alien Church of Rome. Nearly twenty years after
quitting the Anglican church, Newman was thrust again into national prominence by a public impugning of his honesty. His reply
was the* Apologia pro vita sua, *a spiritual autobiography in which
he recounted his religious history and sought to demonstrate that it
was possible for an Englishman of the nineteenth century to profess
honestly and without reservation the doctrines of the Roman church.
Significantly, Newman founded his faith not on reason (which could
neither prove nor disprove articles of faith) nor on the popular
"evidences" from nature (which would never convince the skeptical),
but on the unassailable testimony of conscience to a mind already
predisposed to believe. He was more certain of the existence of God,
Newman wrote, than that he himself had hands and feet*.

Yet, Newman continued, I look out of myself into the
world of men, and there I see a sight which fills me with unspeakable
distress. The world seems simply to give the lie to that great truth,
of which my whole being is so full; and the effect upon me is, in
consequence, as a matter of necessity, as confusing as if it denied
that I am in existence myself. If I looked into a mirror, and did not
see my face, I should have the sort of feeling which actually comes
upon me, when I look into this living busy world, and see no reflection
of its Creator. This is, to me, one of the great difficulties of this absolute primary truth, to which I referred just now. Were it not for
this voice, speaking so clearly in my conscience and my heart, I
should be an atheist, or a pantheist, or a polytheist when I looked
into the world. I am speaking for myself only; and I am far from
denying the real force of the arguments in proof of a God, drawn
from the general facts of human society, but these do not warm me or
enlighten me; they do not take away the winter of my desolation, or
make the buds unfold and the leaves grow within me, and my moral
being rejoice. The sight of the world is nothing else than the
prophet's scroll, full of "lamentations, and mourning, and woe."

To consider the world in its length and breadth, its various history,
the many races of man, their starts, their fortunes, their mutual

alienation, their conflicts; and then their ways, habits, governments, forms of worship; their enterprises, their aimless courses, their random achievements and acquirements, the impotent conclusion of long-standing facts, the tokens so faint and broken, of a superintending design, the blind evolution of what turn out to be great powers or truths, the progress of things, as if from unreasoning elements, not towards final causes, the greatness and littleness of man, his far-reaching aims, his short duration, the curtain hung over his futurity, the disappointments of life, the defeat of good, the success of evil, physical pain, mental anguish, the prevalence and intensity of sin, the pervading idolatries, the corruptions, the dreary hopeless irre-ligion, that condition of the whole race, so fearfully yet exactly de-scribed in the Apostle's words, "having no hope and without God in the world,"—all this is a vision to dizzy and appal; and inflicts upon the mind the sense of a profound mystery, which is absolutely beyond human solution.

What shall be said to this heart-piercing, reason-bewildering fact? I can only answer, that either there is no Creator, or this living society of men is in a true sense discarded from His presence. Did I see a boy of good make and mind, with the tokens on him of a refined nature, cast upon the world without provision, unable to say whence he came, his birth-place or his family connexions, I should conclude that there was some mystery connected with his history, and that he was one, of whom, from one cause or other, his parents were ashamed. Thus only should I be able to account for the contrast between the promise and condition of his being. And so I argue about the world; —if there be a God, *since* there is a God, the human race is impli-cated in some terrible aboriginal calamity. It is out of joint with the purposes of its Creator. This is a fact, a fact as true as the fact of its existence; and thus the doctrine of what is theologically called original sin becomes to me almost as certain as that the world exists, and as the existence of God.

And now, supposing it were the blessed and loving will of the Creator to interfere in this anarchical condition of things, what are we to suppose would be the methods which might be necessarily or naturally involved in His object of mercy? Since the world is in so abnormal a state, surely it would be no surprise to me, if the inter-position were of necessity equally extraordinary—or what is called miraculous. But that subject does not directly come into the scope of my present remarks. Miracles as evidence, involve an argument;

and of course I am thinking of some means which does not immediately run into argument. I am rather asking what must be the face-
to-face antagonist, by which to withstand and baffle the fierce energy
of passion and the all-corroding, all-dissolving scepticism of the intellect in religious inquiries? I have no intention at all to deny, that
truth is the real object of our reason, and that, if it does not attain
to truth, either the premiss or the process is in fault; but I am not
speaking of right reason, but of reason as it acts in fact and con-
cretely in fallen man. I know that even the unaided reason, when
correctly exercised, leads to a belief in God, in the immortality of
the soul, and in a future retribution; but I am considering it actually
and historically; and in this point of view, I do not think I am wrong
in saying that its tendency is towards a simple unbelief in matters
of religion. No truth, however sacred, can stand against it, in the
long run; and hence it is that in the pagan world, when our Lord
came, the last traces of the religious knowledge of former times were
all but disappearing from those portions of the world in which the
intellect had been active and had had a career.

And in these latter days, in like manner, outside the Catholic
Church things are tending, with far greater rapidity than in that old
time from the circumstance of the age, to atheism in one shape or
other. What a scene, what a prospect, does the whole of Europe
present at this day! and not only Europe, but every government and
every civilization through the world, which is under the influence of
the European mind! Especially, for it most concerns us, how sorrowful, in the view of religion, even taken in its most elementary, most
attenuated form, is the spectacle presented to us by the educated
intellect of England, France, and Germany! Lovers of their country
and of their race, religious men, external to the Catholic Church,
have attempted various expedients to arrest fierce wilful human nature in its onward course, and to bring it into subjection. The necessity of some form of religion for the interests of humanity, has been
generally acknowledged: but where was the concrete representative
of things invisible, which could have the force and the toughness
necessary to be a breakwater against the deluge? Three centuries
ago the establishment of religion, material, legal, and social, was
generally adopted as the best expedient for the purpose, in those
countries which separated from the Catholic Church; and for a long
time it was successful; but now the crevices of those establishments
are admitting the enemy. Thirty years ago, education was relied
upon: ten years ago there was a hope that wars would cease for ever,

under the influence of commercial enterprise and the reign of the
useful and fine arts; but will any one venture to say that there is
any thing any where on this earth, which will afford a fulcrum for
us, whereby to keep the earth from moving onwards?

The judgment, which experience passes on establishments or education, as a means of maintaining religious truth in this anarchical
world, must be extended even to Scripture, though Scripture be
divine. Experience proves surely that the Bible does not answer a
purpose, for which it was never intended. It may be accidentally the
means of the conversion of individuals; but a book, after all, cannot
make a stand against the wild living intellect of man, and in this day
it begins to testify, as regards its own structure and contents, to the
power of that universal solvent, which is so successfully acting upon
religious establishments.

Supposing then it to be the Will of the Creator to interfere in
human affairs, and to make provisions for retaining in the world a
knowledge of Himself, so definite and distinct as to be proof against
the energy of human scepticism, in such a case,—I am far from
saying that there was no other way,—but there is nothing to surprise
the mind, if He should think fit to introduce a power into the world,
invested with the prerogative of infallibility in religious matters.
Such a provision would be a direct, immediate, active, and prompt
means of withstanding the difficulty; it would be an instrument suited
to the need; and, when I find that this is the very claim of the Catholic Church, not only do I feel no difficulty in admitting the idea, but
there is a fitness in it, which recommends it to my mind. And thus I
am brought to speak of the Church's infallibility, as a provision,
adapted by the mercy of the Creator, to preserve religion in the
world, and to restrain that freedom of thought, which of course in
itself is one of the greatest of our natural gifts, and to rescue it from
its own suicidal excesses.[1]

*Newman's religious history—which ended, he wrote, in 1845
with his reception into the Roman Catholic church—is the history
of his search for an ecclesiastical authority that could preserve
Christian civilization against the fast-running tides of change.*

II

*Newman was born in the first year of the nineteenth century,
when all Europe was at war with revolutionary France. To con-*

temporaries, who did not perceive or fully understand its long-maturing economic and social causes, the French Revolution was a catastrophe brought about by the unregulated human intellect. Rationalism, divorced from religious first principles, seemed to have been the potent weapon with which the revolutionists had recklessly toppled institutions that had shaped European civilization for a thousand years. In the end France was defeated, and the moribund forms of the Old Order were briefly reimposed upon a changed and changing Europe.

In 1830 revolution again swept across the continent and menaced England. Nowhere were the transforming social forces of the new century more apparent than in England. There the industrial revolution was already far advanced and the old fabric of society rapidly dissolving. A wretched and multiplying urban working class hungered dumbly, and sometimes violently, for a place in a commonwealth that made no provision for them. The rising industrial and commercial middle classes, though largely excluded from political life, were better able than the working class to recognize their interests and better equipped to challenge the monopoly of government enjoyed by the aristocracy and country gentry. Revolution was averted in England by the enfranchisement of the upper middle class and the reform of Parliament in 1832, but the fever for reform was only intensified. In the names of justice, humanity, efficiency, prosperity, progress—but without losing sight of their own material interests—the triumphant middle class set about the transformation of England. Rationalism, whether called Liberalism, Utilitarianism, Political Economy, or Science, was again the creed of innovators.

The young Newman watched the course of events with dismay. Though the cherished old order was fast being swept away, one great pillar remained: the established church. Unfortunately, the Church of England was in no condition to sustain a fundamental contest with the spirit of the age. It was infected by a genteel worldliness, its services neglected, hundreds of cures unfilled, the new working class altogether alienated. Indeed, large portions of the middle and lower classes had long since left the established church to seek a more vigorous religious experience in Methodism and other dissenting sects. Anglicanism was further weakened by division into parties, loosely styled in retrospect the High Church, Low Church, and Broad Church parties. The High Church party preserved the considerable measure of Catholic doctrine and practice that the English

*church had retained when it left the Roman communion in the
sixteenth century, the reformation in England having been in its
initial stage almost entirely political: Henry VIII had simply substituted the royal supremacy for the papal, leaving virtually untouched the "Catholic faith of Christendom." Priests and sacraments,
dogma and liturgy, insistence on the apostolical succession that connected the Anglican church to the primitive catholic church, were the
characteristic "notes" of the High Church party. The Low Church
party, the Evangelicals, represented in the English church the Protestant tradition that had first entered England with the continental
reformers in the sixteenth century and that had received successive
infusions of vigor from the Puritan revolution in the seventeenth
century and the Wesleyan revival in the eighteenth. The Evangelicals
minimized church, priesthood, and sacraments, emphasizing instead
such distinctively Protestant tenets as the ultimate authority in
doctrinal matters of the Bible privately interpreted and the suffi-
ciency for salvation of personal conversion evidenced by a firm sense
of "election" and by good works. The Broad Church party, liberals
and latitudinarians, were always prepared to reinterpret Christian
doctrine in contemporary terms in order to preserve its primary
moral and ethical efficacy. Newman abhorred the liberals as utterly
subversive of all religion, for he could not conceive of religion without dogma. But it was the Evangelicals who seemed to him to present
the gravest danger to the church. Newman deplored the progressive
Protestantization of the Anglican church that he observed in the
preceding three centuries. Bible reading and private judgment, he
was convinced, were inadequate foundations for a Christian's faith;
Protestantism must ever tend toward rationalism and infidelity. Any
revival of the Anglican church, therefore, must be built on the dogmatic and ecclesiastical principles associated with the High Church
party.*

*And a revival was urgent if the church was to be capable of re-
sisting the encroachments of a hostile secular state. Since the sixteenth century, the Anglican church had been avowedly an arm of the
state, its government vested in the crown and ultimately in Parliament. So long as dissenters and Catholics had been excluded from
civil life, the body politic was in theory coextensive with the body
ecclesiastic, and Parliament could be viewed as a lay synod of the
church. But the admission to Parliament after 1829 of dissenters
and Catholics introduced into that body an important element not*

only outside the Anglican church but inveterately hostile to it. The likelihood of government intervention in church affairs seemed heightened, moreover, by popular demonstrations against the bishops who resisted the Reform Bill in the House of Lords. On all sides, indications mounted that the Whig reformers would spare neither the property, the prerogatives, nor the doctrines of the established church.

In 1832 Newman was a Fellow of Oriel College, the most brilliant member of the college that then enjoyed the intellectual primacy of the university. He was also vicar of the church of St. Mary the Virgin in Oxford. Though not actually a part of the university, St. Mary's was virtually transformed into a university institution by the numbers of students and dons who flocked there to hear Newman preach. From its pulpit Newman wielded an influence that in time disturbed and eventually alarmed the university authorities—indeed, two years before, the provost of Newman's own college had attempted to check that influence at Oriel by depriving Newman of his tutorship there. Finally, with his Arians of the Fourth Century, *completed in 1832 and published the next year, Newman attained distinction as a scholar and theologian. This history of the great heretical movement that divided the early church was the first product of Newman's absorption in the history and literature of the patristic period. The church of Augustine, Ambrose, and Leo, pure and vigorous, captivated Newman's imagination. In those distant centuries the great fathers and early councils, beset by heresies on all sides, had elaborated a doctrinal system that for seven centuries had been the creed of all Christians, of the one universal catholic church. Corrupted and added to by the Roman church, discarded in greater or lesser degree by the Protestant churches, this doctrinal system was preserved (Newman theorized) in its primitive integrity in the Anglican church. Thus the Church of England was one with the church founded by Christ Himself. What a contrast, Newman reflected, between that august dignity and the humiliating condition of the English church in 1832&!*

While I was engaged in writing my work upon the Arians, great events were happening at home and abroad, which brought out into form and passionate expression the various beliefs which had so gradually been winning their way into my mind. Shortly before, there had been a Revolution in France; the Bourbons had been dis-

missed: and I believed that it was unchristian for nations to cast off
their governors, and, much more, sovereigns who had the divine right
of inheritance. Again, the great Reform Agitation was going on
around me as I wrote. The Whigs had come into power; Lord Grey
had told the Bishops to set their house in order, and some of the
Prelates had been insulted and threatened in the streets of London.
The vital question was how were we to keep the Church from being
liberalized? there was such apathy on the subject in some quarters,
such imbecile alarm in others; the true principles of Churchmanship
seemed so radically decayed, and there was such distraction in the
Councils of the Clergy. The Bishop of London of the day, an active
and open-hearted man, had been for years engaged in diluting the
high orthodoxy of the Church by the introduction of the Evangelical
body into places of influence and trust. He had deeply offended men
who agreed with myself, by an off-hand saying (as it was reported)
to the effect that belief in the Apostolical succession had gone out
with the Non-jurors. "We can count you," he said to some of the
gravest and most venerated persons of the old school. And the
Evangelical party itself seemed, with their late successes, to have
lost that simplicity and unworldliness which I admired so much in
Milner and Scott. It was not that I did not venerate such men as
the then Bishop of Lichfield, and others of similar sentiments, who
were not yet promoted out of the ranks of the Clergy, but I thought
little of them as a class. I thought they played into the hands of the
Liberals. With the Establishment thus divided and threatened, thus
ignorant of its true strength, I compared that fresh vigorous power
of which I was reading in the first centuries. In her triumphant zeal
on behalf of that Primeval Mystery, to which I had had so great a
devotion from my youth, I recognized the movement of my Spiritual
Mother. "Incessu patuit Dea." The self-conquest of her Ascetics,
the patience of her Martyrs, the irresistible determination of her
Bishops, the joyous swing of her advance, both exalted and abashed
me. I said to myself, "Look on this picture and on that;" I felt
affection for my own Church, but not tenderness; I felt dismay at
her prospects, anger and scorn at her do-nothing perplexity. I
thought that if Liberalism once got a footing within her, it was sure
of the victory in the event. I saw that Reformation principles were
powerless to rescue her. As to leaving her, the thought never crossed
my imagination; still I ever kept before me that there was something
greater than the Established Church, and that that was the Church

Catholic and Apostolic, set up from the beginning, of which she was
but the local presence and organ. She was nothing, unless she was
this. She must be dealt with strongly, or she would be lost. There was
need of a second Reformation.[2]

*But how to proceed? Anxious about the state of the church
but uncertain what course to take, Newman left Oxford in December, 1832, for a tour of the Mediterranean with his friend Hurrell
Froude. In April they were at Rome on their way home when Newman
felt an irresistible impulse to return alone to Sicily. On May 2, alone
except for his Italian servant, he fell critically ill in the Sicilian
mountain village of Leonforte. The significance that Newman attributed to this illness is attested by the long, meticulous account of
it he wrote two years afterward*.

As I lay in bed the first day many thoughts came over me. I felt
God was fighting agst me—& felt at last I knew *why*—it was for self
will. I felt I had been very self willed—that the Froudes had been
agst my coming, so also (at Naples) the Wilberforces—perhaps the
Neales & Andersons—I said to myself Why did no one speak out?
say half a word? Why was I left now to interpret their meaning?
Then I tried to fancy where the Froudes were, & how happy I should
have been with them—in France, or perhaps in England. Yet I felt
& kept saying to myself "I have not sinned against light." And at
one time I had a most consoling overpowering thought of God's
electing love, & seemed to feel I was His. But I believe all my feelings,
painful & pleasant, were heightened by somewhat of delirium, tho'
they still are from God in the way of Providence. Next day the self
reproaching feelings increased. I seemed to see more & more my utter
hollowness. I began to think of all my professed principles, & felt
they were mere intellectual deductions from one or two admitted
truths. I compared myself with Keble, and felt that I was merely
developing his, not my convictions. I know I had *very* clear thoughts
about this then; &, I believe in the main true ones. Indeed this is how
I look on myself; very much (as the illustration goes) as a pane of
glass, which transmit[s] heat being cold itself. I have a vivid perception of the consequences of certain admitted principles, have a
considerable intellectual capacity of drawing them out, have the
refinement to admire them, & a rhetorical or histrionic power to
represent them; and, having no great (i.e. no vivid) love of this

world, whether riches, honors, or any thing else, and some firmness
and natural dignity of character, take the profession of them upon me,
as I might sing a tune which I liked—loving the Truth, but not possessing it—for I believe myself at heart to be nearly hollow—i.e. with
little love, little self denial. I believe I have some faith, that is all—
& as to my sins, they need my possessing no little amount of faith
to set against them & gain their remission. By the bye, this statement
will account for it how I can preach the Truth without thinking
much of myself. Arnold in his letter to Grant about me, accuses me
among others of identifying high excellence with certain peculiarities
of my own—i.e. preaching myself. But to return. Still more serious
thoughts came over me. I thought I had been very self willed about
the Tutorship affair—and now I viewed my whole course as of one
of presumption. It struck me that the 5th of May was just at hand,
which was a memorable day, as being that on which (what we called)
my Ultimatum was sent in to the Provost. On the 3rd anniversary I
sh^{d} be lying on a sick bed in a strange country. Then I bitterly
blamed myself, as disrespectful & insulting to the Provost, my superior. So keenly did I feel this, that I dictated to myself (as it
were) a letter which I was to send (I fixed upon) James (the late
fellow), on my getting to England, stating in strong terms my self
reproach; & I was not to preach at St Mary's or any where for a
length of time as a penitent unworthy to show myself. I recollected
too that my last act on leaving Oxford was to preach a University
Sermon on the character of Saul agst self will. Yet still I said to
myself "I have not sinned against light." (Now, or at Palermo I
thought strongly & retained the thought that my illness came upon
me as having come to the Sacr^{t} in malice and resentment.) I cannot
describe my full misery on this Saturday May 4. My door only
locked (i.e. no mere clasp, but with a key)—my servant was a good
deal away, & thus locked me in. My feelings were acute & nervous in
a high degree. I forced myself up to keep my mind from thinking of
itself, & from leading to that distressing bodily affection which in
such cases follow[s] in my case;—I kept counting the number of
stars, flowers &c. in the pattern of the paper on the walls to occupy
me. Just at this time, (before or after) the miserable whine of
Sicilian beggars was heard outside my door, the staircase communicating with the street. Who can describe the wretchedness of that
low feeble monotonous cry, which went on I cannot say how long,
(I unable to do any thing) till my servant released me after a time.

Now in my lowest distress I was relieved, first by some music from some travelling performers who were passing on (I believe) to Palermo. (N.B. I had seen a *bagpipe* to my surprise between Catania & Paternò.) The music was (I believe) such as harp & clarionet— And now I think it was that my servant proposed a walk. He had talked much of some handsome fountain at the end of the Town— but I put off seeing it, I believe now—& we walked out on the St Filippo road, & then turned up a lane on the south (i.e. the left hand) There I sat down on a bank upon (under?) a fig tree—the leaves I believe were out—& wondered how it s^{hd} be that I was there—it was the evening. I forget what else I thought of or saw. (I think this walk was on this day; yet some how have some times a notion that the ride on the Mule which is to come presently was today.) My servant wished to get me on (I believe) naturally enough—(Febr 6. 1843. We had a speculation about having a *litter* made, on which I might be carried to Palermo.)—he thought me dying; & told me a story about a sick officer he had attended on in Spain, who left him all his baggage & then got well. I did not see the drift of the story at the time. I gave him a direction to write to, if I died (Froude's) but I said "I do not think I shall"—"I have not sinned against light" or "God has still work for me to do." I think the latter.[3]

His illness in Sicily, Newman believed, was providential. By escaping to Sicily rather than returning directly to England, where his duty lay, he had resisted God's purpose. Like more than one prophet, he had first to be purged of self-will in order that God's will might be done. This purging Newman experienced in the lonely, fever-wracked struggle with his destiny in Sicily. Chastened, resolute, he passed an impatient convalescence.

I got to Castro-Giovanni, and was laid up there for nearly three weeks. Towards the end of May I set off for Palermo, taking three days for the journey. Before starting from my inn in the morning of May 26th or 27th, I sat down on my bed, and began to sob bitterly. My servant, who had acted as my nurse, asked what ailed me. I could only answer, "I have a work to do in England."

I was aching to get home; yet for want of a vessel I was kept at Palermo for three weeks. I began to visit the Churches, and they calmed my impatience, though I did not attend any services. I knew nothing of the Presence of the Blessed Sacrament there. At last I got off in an orange boat, bound for Marseilles. We were becalmed a whole week in the Straits of Bonifacio. Then it was that I wrote the lines, "Lead, kindly light," which have since become well known. I was writing verses the whole time of my passage. At length I got to Marseilles, and set off for England. The fatigue of travelling was too much for me, and I was laid up for several days at Lyons. At last I got off again, and did not stop night or day till I reached England, and my mother's house. My brother had arrived from Persia only a few hours before. This was on the Tuesday. The following Sunday, July 14th, Mr. Keble preached the Assize Sermon in the University Pulpit. It was published under the title of "National Apostasy." I have ever considered and kept the day, as the start of the religious movement of 1833.[4]

III

The stage on which what is called the Oxford movement ran through its course had a special character of its own, unlike the circumstances in which other religious efforts had done their work, *recalled Richard Church, Dean of St. Paul's, who had entered Oxford in 1833*. The scene of Jansenism had been a great capital, a brilliant society, the precincts of a court, the cells of a convent, the studies and libraries of the doctors of the Sorbonne, the council chambers of the Vatican. The scene of Methodism had been English villages and country towns, the moors of Cornwall, and the collieries of Bristol, at length London fashionable chapels. The scene of this new movement was as like as it could be in our modern world to a Greek *polis*, or an Italian self-centered city of the Middle Ages. Oxford stood by itself in its meadows by the rivers, having its relations with all England, but, like its sister at Cambridge, living a life of its own, unlike that of any other spot in England, with its privileged powers, and exemptions from the general law, with its special mode of government and police, its usages and tastes and traditions, and even costume, which the rest of England looked at from the outside, much interested but much puzzled, or knew only by transient visits. And Oxford was as proud and jealous of its own ways as Athens or Florence; and like them it had its quaint fashions of polity; its democratic Convocation and its oligarchy; its social ranks; its discipline, severe in theory and usually lax in fact; its self-governed bodies and corporations within itself; its faculties and colleges, like the guilds and "arts" of Florence; its internal rivalries and discords; its "sets" and factions. Like these, too, it professed a special recognition of the supremacy of religion; it claimed to be a home of worship and religious training, *Dominus illuminatio mea*, a claim too often falsified in the habit and tempers of life. It was a small sphere, but it was a conspicuous one; for there was much strong and energetic character, brought out by the aims and conditions of University life; and though moving in a separate orbit, the influence of the famous place over the outside England, though imperfectly understood, was recognised and great. These conditions affected the character of the movement, and of the conflicts which it caused. Oxford claimed to be eminently the guardian of "true religion and sound learning"; and therefore it was eminently the place where religion should be recalled to its purity and strength, and also the place where there ought to be the most vigilant jealousy against the perversions and corruptions of religion. Oxford was a place where every one knew his neighbour, and measured him, and was more or less friendly or repellent; where the customs of life brought men together every day and all day, in converse or discussion; and where every fresh statement or every new step taken furnished endless material for speculation or debate, in common rooms or in the afternoon walk. And for this reason, too, feelings were apt to be more keen and intense and personal than in the larger scenes of life; the man who was disliked or distrusted was so close to his neighbours that he was more irritating than if he had been obscured by a crowd; the man who attracted confidence and kindled enthusiasm, whose voice was continually in men's ears, and whose private conversation and life was something ever new in its sympathy and charm, created in those about him not mere admiration, but passionate friendship, or unreserved discipleship. And these feelings passed from individuals into parties; the small factions of a limited area. Men struck blows and loved and hated in those days in Oxford as they hardly did on the wider stage of London politics or general religious controversy.[5]

⚜*In that calm, self-contained community, Keble's sermon on "National Apostasy" made no immediate stir, though it set in motion forces that shortly aroused the university to unprecedented commotion. A few months before, the Whigs had brought into Parlia-*

*ment an Irish Church Temporalities Bill which would cut off certain
revenues of the established church in Ireland and reorganize the
Irish bishoprics, suppressing ten sees. For the Whigs, the bill was
a minimal concession to the Catholic Irish, whose taxes supported
the church of their English landlords. To Newman and others of the
High Church party, however, the bill was the first move in the
spoliation of the established church. If there was to be a decisive
conflict between church and state, they agreed, let it begin here.
Keble's famous sermon, on a text from the Book of Samuel, was
preached in St. Mary's to a convocation of judges. Just as the
Israelites had rejected the kingship of God by importuning Samuel
to appoint a human king over them, Keble warned the assembled
magistrates, so might a Christian nation be guilty of apostasy if it
expelled God's church from its high and integral place in the national life.*

The case is at least possible, of a nation, having for centuries
acknowledged, as an essential part of its theory of government, that,
as a Christian nation, she is also a part of Christ's church, and
bound, in all her legislation and policy, by the fundamental rules of
that Church—the case is, I say, conceivable, of a government and
people, so constituted, deliberately throwing off the restraint, which
in many respects such a principle would impose on them, nay, dis-
avowing the principle itself; and that, on the plea, that other states,
as flourishing or more so in regard to wealth and dominion, do well
enough without it. Is not this desiring, like the Jews, to have an
earthly king over them, when the Lord their God is their King? Is
it not saying in other words, "We will be as the heathen, the families
of the countries," the aliens to the Church of our Redeemer?

To such a change, whenever it takes place, the immediate impulse
will probably be given by some pretence of danger from without,—
such as, at the time now spoken of, was furnished to the Israelites
by an incursion of the children of Ammon; or by some wrong or
grievance in the executive government, such as the malversation of
Samuel's sons, to whom he had deputed his judicial functions. Pre-
tences will never be hard to find; but, in reality, the movement will
always be traceable to the same decay or want of faith, the same
deficiency in Christian resignation and thankfulness, which leads so
many, as individuals, to disdain and forfeit the blessings of the
Gospel. Men not impressed with religious principles attribute their

ill success in life,—the hard times they have to struggle with,—to anything rather than their own ill-desert: and the institutions of the country, ecclesiastical and civil, are always at hand to bear the blame of whatever seems to be going amiss. Thus, the discontent in Samuel's time, which led the Israelites to demand a change of constitution, was discerned by the Unerring Eye, though perhaps little suspected by themselves, to be no better than a fresh development of the same restless, godless spirit, which had led them so often into idolatry. "They have not rejected thee, but they have rejected Me, that I should not reign over them. According to all the works, which they have done since the day that I brought them up out of Egypt even unto this day, wherewith they have forsaken Me, and served other Gods, so do they also unto thee."

The charge might perhaps surprise many of them, just as, in other times and countries, the impatient patrons of innovation are surprised, at finding themselves rebuked on religious grounds. Perhaps the Jews pleaded the express countenance, which the words of their Law, in one place, seemed, by anticipation, to lend to the measure they were urging. And so, in modern times, when liberties are to be taken, and the intrusive passions of men to be indulged, precedent and permission, or what sounds like them, may be easily found and quoted for everything. But Samuel, in God's Name, silenced all this, giving them to understand, that in His sight the whole was a question of motive and purpose, not of ostensible and colourable argument;— in His sight, I say, to Whom we, as well as they, are nationally responsible for much more than the soundness of our deductions as matter of disputation, or of law; we are responsible for the meaning and temper in which we deal with His Holy Church, established among us for the salvation of our souls.[6]

For Newman, just recovered from desperate illness and newly returned to his beloved university, Keble's words had the exhilarating effect of a call to arms in a holy cause. I had the exultation of health restored, and home regained. While I was at Palermo and thought of the breadth of the Mediterranean, and the wearisome journey across France, I could not imagine how I was ever to get to England; but now I was amid familiar scenes and faces once more. And my health and strength came back to me with such a rebound, that some friends at Oxford, on seeing me, did not well know that it was I, and hesitated before they spoke to me. And I had the con-

sciousness that I was employed in the work which I had been dreaming about, and which I felt to be so momentous and inspiring. I had
a supreme confidence in our cause; we were upholding that primitive
Christianity which was delivered for all time by the early teachers of
the Church, and which was registered and attested in the Anglican
formularies and by the Anglican divines. That ancient religion had
well nigh faded away out of the land, through the political changes
of the last 150 years, and it must be restored. It would be in fact a
second Reformation:—a better reformation, for it would be a return
not to the sixteenth century, but to the seventeenth. No time was to
be lost, for the Whigs had come to do their worst, and the rescue
might come too late. Bishopricks were already in course of suppres-
sion; Church property was in course of confiscation; Sees would soon
be receiving unsuitable occupants. We knew enough to begin preaching upon, and there was no one else to preach. I felt as on a vessel,
which first gets under weigh, and then clears out the deck, and stores
away luggage and live stock into their proper receptacles.[7]

*Late in July, a small group of Newman's colleagues, men pos-
sessed by a sense of imminent danger to the church, met to discuss
a course of action in its defense. Newman, who was absent from the
meeting, was disappointed to learn that the older, more cautious
members of the group preferred some sort of national association,
centered in London, to bolder schemes. Living movements, Newman
was convinced, did not come of committees. He preferred instead a
direct and vigorous propaganda campaign among the clergy emanat-
ing from Oxford, the intellectual center of the church. To this end
he conceived a series of tracts—a propaganda medium rarely associated with High Church opinions—that would not merely alert the
clergy to the immediate danger of the liberal assault but call them
back to the ancient dignity of their vocation and enlist them in the
new reformation. On September 9, 1833, appeared Number 1 of
"Tracts for the Times," entitled by its author with deceptive diffidence* Thoughts on the Ministerial Commission, Respectfully addressed to the Clergy.

I am but one of yourselves,—a Presbyter, *Newman wrote*;
and therefore I conceal my name, lest I should take too much on
myself by speaking in my own person. Yet speak I must; for the
times are very evil, yet no one speaks against them. . . .

Now then let me come at once to the subject which leads me to address you. Should the Government and Country so far forget their God as to cast off the Church, to deprive it of its temporal honors and substance, *on what* will you rest the claim of respect and attention which you make upon your flocks? Hitherto you have been upheld by your birth, your education, your wealth, your connexions; should these secular advantages cease, on what must CHRIST's Ministers depend? Is not this a serious practical question? We know how miserable is the state of religious bodies not supported by the State. Look at the Dissenters on all sides of you, and you will see at once that their Ministers, depending simply upon the people, become the *creatures* of the people. Are you content that this should be your case? Alas! can a greater evil befal Christians, than for their teachers to be guided by them, instead of guiding? How can we "hold fast the form of sound words," and "keep that which is committed to our trust," if our influence is to depend simply on our popularity? Is it not our very office to *oppose* the world? can we then allow ourselves to *court* it? to preach smooth things and prophesy deceits? to make the way of life easy to the rich and indolent, and to bribe the humbler classes by excitements and strong intoxicating doctrine? Surely it must not be so;—and the question recurs, on *what* are we to rest our authority, when the State deserts us?

CHRIST has not left His Church without claim of its own upon the attention of men. Surely not. Hard Master He cannot be, to bid us oppose the world, yet give us no credentials for so doing. There are some who rest their divine mission on their own unsupported assertion; others, who rest it upon their popularity; others, on their success; and others, who rest it upon their temporal distinctions. This last case has, perhaps, been too much our own; I fear we have neglected the real ground on which our authority is built,—OUR APOSTOLICAL DESCENT.

We have been born, not of blood, nor of the will of the flesh, nor of the will of man, but of God. The Lord JESUS CHRIST gave His Spirit to His Apostles; they in turn laid their hands on those who should succeed them; and these again on others; and so the sacred gift has been handed down to our present Bishops, who have appointed us as their assistants, and in some sense representatives.

Now every one of us believes this. I know that some will at first deny they do; still they do believe it. Only, it is not sufficiently practically impressed on their minds. They *do* believe it; for it is the doctrine of the Ordination Service, which they have recognised as truth in the most solemn season of their lives. In order, then, not to prove, but to remind and impress, I entreat your attention to the words used when you were made Ministers of CHRIST's Church.

The office of Deacon was thus committed to you: "Take thou authority to execute the office of a Deacon in the Church of GOD committed unto thee: In the name," &c.

And the priesthood thus:

"Receive the HOLY GHOST, for the office and work of a Priest, in the Church of GOD, now committed unto thee by the imposition of our hands. Whose sins thou dost forgive, they are forgiven; and whose sins thou dost retain, they are retained. And be thou a faithful dispenser of the Word of GOD, and of His Holy Sacraments: In the name," &c.

These, I say, were words spoken to us, and received by us, when we were brought nearer to God than at any other time of our lives. I know the grace of ordination is contained in the laying on of hands, not in any form of words;—yet in our own case, (as has ever been usual in the Church,) words of blessing have accompanied the act. Thus we have confessed before GOD our belief, that through the Bishop who ordained us, we received the HOLY GHOST, the power to bind and to loose, to administer the Sacraments, and to preach. Now *how* is he able to give these great gifts? *Whence* is his right? Are these words idle, (which would be taking GOD's name in vain,) or do they express merely a wish, (which surely is very far below their meaning,) or do they not rather indicate that the Speaker is conveying a gift? Surely they can mean nothing short of this. But whence, I ask, his right to do so? Has he any right, except as having received the power from those who consecrated him to be a Bishop? He could not give what he had never received. It is plain then that he but *transmits;* and that the Christian Ministry is a *succession.* And if we trace back the power of ordination from hand to hand, of course we shall come to the Apostles at last. We know we do, as a plain historical fact; and therefore all we, who have been ordained Clergy, in the very form of our ordination acknowledged the doctrine of the APOSTOLICAL SUCCESSION.

And for the same reason, we must necessarily consider none to be *really* ordained who have not *thus* been ordained. For if ordination is a divine ordinance, it must be necessary; and if it is not a divine ordinance, how dare we use it? Therefore all who use it, all of *us,* must consider it necessary. As well might we pretend the Sacraments are not necessary to Salvation, while we make use of the offices of the Liturgy; for when GOD appoints means of grace, they are *the* means.

I do not see how any one can escape from this plain view of the subject, except, (as I have already hinted,) by declaring, that the words do not mean all that they say. But only reflect what a most unseemly time for random words is that, in which Ministers are set apart for their office. Do we not adopt a Liturgy, *in order* to hinder inconsiderate idle language, and shall we, in the most sacred of all services, write down, subscribe, and use again and again forms of speech, which have not been weighed, and cannot be taken strictly?

Therefore, my dear Brethren, act up to your professions. Let it not be said that you have neglected a gift; for if you have the Spirit of the Apostles on you, surely this *is* a great gift. "Stir up the gift of GOD which is in you." Make much of it. Show your value of it. Keep it before your minds as an honorable badge, far higher than that secular respectability, or cultivation, or polish, or learning, or rank, which gives you a hearing with the many. Tell *them* of your gift. The times will soon drive you to do this, if you mean to be still any thing. But wait not for the times. Do not be compelled, by the world's forsaking you, to recur as if unwillingly to the high source of your authority. Speak out now, before you are forced, both as glorying in your privilege, and to ensure your rightful honor from your people. A notion has gone abroad, that they can take away your power. They think they have given and can take it away. They think it lies in the Church property, and they know that they have politically the power to confiscate that property. They have been deluded into a notion that present palpable usefulness, produceable results, acceptableness to your flocks, that these and such like are the tests of your Divine commission. Enlighten them in this matter. Exalt our Holy Fathers, the Bishops, as the Representatives of the Apostles, and the Angels of the Churches; and magnify your office, as being ordained by them to take part in their Ministry.

But, if you will not adopt my view of the subject, which I offer to you, not doubtingly, yet (I hope) respectfully, at all events, CHOOSE YOUR SIDE. To remain neuter much longer will be itself to take a part. *Choose* your side; since side you shortly must, with one or other party, even though you do nothing. Fear to be of those, whose line is decided for them by chance circumstances, and who may perchance find themselves with the enemies of CHRIST, while they think but to remove themselves from worldly politics. Such abstinence is impossible in troublous times. HE THAT IS NOT WITH ME, IS AGAINST ME, AND HE THAT GATHERETH NOT WITH ME SCATTERETH ABROAD.[8]

More tracts followed quickly in the next months, most of them written by Newman himself, the remainder by his friends at Oxford under his editorship. Throughout the university, into the important churches and foundations of the large cities, into the most distant rural parsonages the tracts found their way, their circulation ever widening. When, in 1834, they began to be collected and published in volumes, they achieved a popular audience far wider than the academic and clerical community. Newman, however, was less interested in winning a large public than he was in reaching and agitating the clergy, and in this he was at once successful. Oxford divided immediately and passionately over the tracts. Evangelicals saw in them a revival of popery, liberals saw a return to superstition and obscurantism. For Newman and his friends—the Apostolicals or Tractarians, as they came to be called—the meaning of the tracts was simple. They were intended to compel men to face the logic and consequences of their opinions. Did Christians really believe the doctrines they professed? If they did, was not the claim of these doctrines to govern every department of life, private and public, of transcendent priority? To this bold challenge, bold men in the High Church party responded enthusiastically. Timid or uncertain men shrank from Newman's uncompromising logic and aggressive tone.

To an old friend who wrote complaining of Tract No. 1, Newman replied without apology. Your letters are always acceptable; and do not fancy one is less so which happens to be objurgatory. Faithful are the blows of a friend, and surely I may be antecedently sure that I require them in many respects. As to our present doings, we are set off, and with God's speed we will go forward, through evil report and good report, through real and supposed blunders. We are as men climbing a rock, who tear clothes and flesh, and slip now and then, and yet make progress (so be it!), and are careless that bystanders criticise, so that their cause gains while they lose. We are set out, and we have funds for the present; we, like the widow's cruse, shall not fail. This then is our position: connected with no association, answerable to no one except God and His Church, committing no one, bearing the blame, doing the work. I trust I speak sincerely in saying I am willing that it be said I go too far, so that I push on the cause of truth some little way. Surely it is energy that gives edge to any undertaking, and energy is ever incautious and exaggerated. I do not say this to excuse such defects, or as conscious of having them myself, but as a consolation and explanation to those who love me, but are sorry at some things I do. Be it so; it is well to fall if you kill your adversary. Nor can I wish anyone a happier lot than to be himself unfortunate, yet to urge on a triumphant cause; like Laud and Ken in their day, who left a name which after ages censure or pity, but whose works do follow them. Let it be the lot of those I love to live in the heart of one or two in each succeeding generation, or to be altogether forgotten, while they have helped forward the truth.[9]

IV

⮑For fifteen years the Tractarians dominated the intellectual life of Oxford. Men who were students there in the 1830s and 1840s, whatever their opinions of the Oxford Movement, testify as one to its influence. Late in life the caustic Mark Pattison dismissed as a morbid aberration the movement in which he had been a zealous participant. More sympathetic writers, on the other hand, attributed to it a wholesome elevation of the moral and intellectual tone of the university, a new seriousness of inquiry and purpose among hitherto indolent young men. There was not, John Campbell Shairp affirmed, a reading man uninfluenced by it. Only the younger undergraduates at one extreme and the older fellows and heads of houses at the other were impervious to it. The latter group, the governing oligarchy of the university, watched the movement's progress among the junior tutors and fellows with apprehension. They were repelled by the Tractarians' enthusiasm, suspicious of their tendency, perhaps jealous of the young men whom the movement was raising to prominence.

For the Tractarians were unquestionably the new and coming men. Newman himself was thirty-two when the movement started. Of the three men closest to him in the origin and conduct of the Oxford Movement—the unworldly John Keble, the brilliant and paradoxical Hurrell Froude, the learned Edward Pusey—only Keble was significantly his senior. Keble had attained a unique eminence at Oriel when Newman was elected to his fellowship there; Froude, two years younger than Newman, and Pusey, a year older, were elected to Oriel *fellowships after Newman. Around Newman gathered the Tractarian party, young tutors and fellows of Oriel, Balliol, and Trinity, Newman's undergraduate college, earnest students from all parts of the university who happily acknowledged their discipleship to the rising celebrity at Oriel. However much Newman owed to Keble, Froude, and Pusey for their contributions to his intellectual development, the Oxford Movement was undeniably the product of his genius, impelled forward by his energy and indelibly stamped by his personality*.

When I entered at Oxford, *Hurrell Froude's younger brother, James Anthony Froude, recalled*, John Henry Newman was beginning to be famous. The responsible authorities were watching him with anxiety; clever men were looking with interest and curiosity on the apparition among them of one of those persons of indisputable genius who was likely to make a mark upon his time. His appearance was striking. He was above the middle height, slight and spare. His head was large, his face remarkably like that of Julius Caesar. The forehead, the shape of the ears and nose, were almost the same. The lines of the mouth were very peculiar, and I should say exactly the same. I have often thought of the resemblance, and believed that it extended to the temperament. In both there was an original force of character which refused to be moulded by circumstances, which was to make its own way, and become a power in the world; a clearness of intellectual perception, a disdain for conventionalities, a temper imperious and wilful, but along with it a most attaching gentleness, sweetness, singleness of heart and purpose. Both were formed by nature to command others; both had the faculty of attracting to themselves the passionate devotion of their friends and followers; and in both cases, too, perhaps the devotion was rather due to the personal ascendancy of the leader than to the cause which he represented. It was Caesar, not the principles of the empire, which overthrew Pompey and the constitution. *Credo in Newmannum* was a common phrase at Oxford, and is still unconsciously the faith of nine-tenths of the English converts to Rome.[10]

Professor Shairp, who entered Oxford in 1840, in later years pondered the phenomenon of Newman's eminence. The influence he had gained, apparently without setting himself to seek it, was something altogether unlike anything else in our time. A mysterious veneration had by degrees gathered round him, till now it was almost as though some Ambrose or Augustine of elder ages had reappeared. He himself tells how one day, when he was an undergraduate, a friend with whom he was walking in the Oxford street cried out eagerly, 'There's Keble!' and with what awe he looked at him! A few years, and the same took place with regard to himself. In Oriel Lane light-hearted undergraduates would drop their voices and whisper, 'There's Newman!' when, head thrust forward, and gaze fixed as though on some vision seen only by himself, with swift, noiseless step he glided by. Awe fell on them for a moment, almost as if it had been some apparition that had passed. For his inner circle of friends, many of them younger men, he was said to have a quite romantic affection, which they returned with the most ardent devotion and the intensest faith in him. But to the outer world he was a mystery. What were the qualities that inspired these feelings? There was of course learning and refinement, there was genius, not indeed of a philosopher, but of a subtle and original thinker, an unequalled edge of dialectic, and these all glorified by the imagination of a poet. Then there was the utter unworldliness, the setting at naught of all things which most men prize, the tamelessness of soul, which was ready to essay the impossible. Men felt that here was

> 'One of that small transfigured band
> Which the world cannot tame.'

It was this mysteriousness which, beyond all his gifts of head and heart, so strangely fascinated and overawed,—that something about him which made it impossible to reckon his course and take his bearings, that soul-hunger and quenchless yearning which nothing short of the eternal could satisfy. This deep and resolute ardour, this tenderness yet severity of soul, were no doubt an offence not to be forgiven by older men, especially by the wary and worldly-wise; but in these lay the very spell which drew to him the hearts of all the younger and the more enthusiastic.[11]

Though Newman denied that the Tractarians were a party, it was inevitable that they should be so regarded by the rest of the university when they marshaled their strength in convocation to restrict the influence of an heretical professor of divinity or to seek the election of one of their number to the professorship of poetry. If he could not rid his followers of the stigma of party, Newman could truthfully deny that he himself had ever sought to be or in fact ever was an effective party leader.

I was not the person to take the lead of a party; I never was, from first to last, more than a leading author of a school; nor did I ever wish to be any thing else. This is my own account of the matter, and I say it, neither as intending to disown the responsibility of what was done, nor as if ungrateful to those who at that time made more of me than I deserved, and did more for my sake and at my bidding than I realized myself. I am giving my history from my own point of sight, and it is as follows :—I had lived for ten years among my personal friends; the greater part of the time, I had been influenced, not influencing; and at no time have I acted on others, without their acting upon me. As is the custom of a University, I have lived with my private, nay, with some of my public, pupils, and with the junior fellows of my College, without form or distance, on a footing of equality. Thus it was through friends, younger, for the most part, than myself, that my principles were spreading. They heard what I said in conversation, and told it to others. Undergraduates in due time took their degree, and became private tutors themselves. In this new *status*, in turn, they preached the opinions which they had already learned themselves. Others went down to the country, and became curates of parishes. Then they had down from London parcels of the Tracts, and other publications. They placed them in the shops of local booksellers, got them into newspapers, introduced them to clerical meetings, and converted more or less their Rectors and their brother curates. Thus the Movement, viewed with relation to myself, was but a floating opinion; it was not a power. It never would have been a power, if it had remained in my hands. Years after, a friend, writing to me in remonstrance at the excesses, as he thought them, of my disciples, applied to me my own verse about St. Gregory Nazianzen, "Thou couldst a people raise, but couldst not rule." At the time that he wrote to me, I had special impediments in the way of such an exercise of power; but at no time could I exercise over others that authority, which under the circumstances was imperatively required. My great principle ever was, Live and let live. I never had the staidness or dignity necessary for a leader. To the last I never recognized the hold I had over young men. Of late years I have read and heard that they even imitated me in various ways. I was quite unconscious of it, and I think my immediate friends knew too well how disgusted I should be at the news, to have the heart to tell me.[12]

᭭§*Within Oxford itself, Newman's prominence derived less from the tracts or his ascendancy over a circle of intimate friends than*

*from his Sunday afternoon sermons preached at St. Mary's. New-
man was perhaps the greatest preacher of the age. The impression he
made upon his hearers was ineffaceable, and the literature of reminis-
cence about them, often composed a generation or more after the
authors had left Oxford, is considerable. Though a Scotch Presby-
terian, John Campbell Shairp bore witness to the profound impression made by Newman's sermons&.*

The centre from which his power went forth was the pulpit of St.
Mary's, with those wonderful afternoon sermons. Sunday after Sunday, month by month, year by year, they went on, each continuing
and deepening the impression the last had made. As the afternoon
service at St. Mary's interfered with the dinner-hour of the colleges,
most men preferred a warm dinner without Newman's sermon to a
cold one with it, so the audience was not crowded—the large church
little more than half-filled. The service was very simple,—no pomp,
no ritualism; for it was characteristic of the leading men of the
movement that they left these things to the weaker brethren. Their
thoughts, at all events, were set on great questions which touched
the heart of unseen things. About the service, the most remarkable
thing was the beauty, the silver intonation, of Mr. Newman's voice,
as he read the Lessons. It seemed to bring new meaning out of the
familiar words. Still lingers in memory the tone with which he read,
'But Jerusalem which is above is free, which is the mother of us all.'
When he began to preach, a stranger was not likely to be much
struck, especially if he had been accustomed to pulpit-oratory of the
Boanerges sort. Here was no vehemence, no declamation, no show of
elaborate argument, so that one who came prepared to hear a 'great
intellectual effort' was almost sure to go away disappointed. Indeed,
I believe that if he had preached one of his St. Mary's sermons before
a Scotch town congregation, they would have thought the preacher
a 'silly body.' The delivery had a peculiarity which it took a new
hearer some time to get over. Each separate sentence, or at least each
short paragraph, was spoken rapidly, but with great clearness of
intonation; and then at its close there was a pause, lasting for nearly
half a minute; then another rapidly but clearly spoken sentence, followed by another pause. It took some time to get over this, but, that
once done, the wonderful charm began to dawn on you. The look and
bearing of the preacher were as of one who dwelt apart, who, though
he knew his age well, did not live in it. From his seclusion of study,

and abstinence, and prayer, from habitual dwelling in the unseen, he seemed to come forth that one day of the week to speak to others of the things he had seen and known. Those who never heard him might fancy that his sermons would generally be about apostolical succession or rights of the Church, or against Dissenters. Nothing of the kind. You might hear him preach for weeks without an allusion to these things. What there was of High Church teaching was implied rather than enforced. The local, the temporary, and the modern were ennobled by the presence of the catholic truth belonging to all ages that pervaded the whole. His power showed itself chiefly in the new and unlooked-for way in which he touched into life old truths, moral or spiritual, which all Christians acknowledge, but most have ceased to feel—when he spoke of 'Unreal Words,' of 'The Individuality of the Soul,' of 'The Invisible World,' of a 'Particular Providence;' or again, of 'The Ventures of Faith,' 'Warfare the Condition of Victory,' 'The Cross of Christ the Measure of the World,' 'The Church a Home for the Lonely.' As he spoke, how the old truth became new! how it came home with a meaning never felt before! He laid his finger —how gently, yet how powerfully!—on some inner place in the hearer's heart, and told him things about himself he had never known till then. Subtlest truths, which it would have taken philosophers pages of circumlocution and big words to state, were dropt out by the way in a sentence or two of the most transparent Saxon. What delicacy of style yet what calm power! how gentle yet how strong! how simple yet how suggestive! how homely yet how refined! how penetrating yet how tender-hearted! If now and then there was a forlorn undertone which at the time seemed inexplicable, if he spoke of 'many a sad secret which a man dare not tell lest he find no sympathy,' of 'secrets lying like cold ice upon the heart,' of 'some solitary incommunicable grief,' you might be perplexed at the drift of what he spoke, but you felt all the more drawn to the speaker. To call these sermons eloquent would be no word for them; high poems they rather were, as of an inspired singer, or the outpourings as of a prophet, rapt yet self-possessed. And the tone of voice in which they were spoken, once you grew accustomed to it, sounded like a fine strain of unearthly music. Through the stillness of that high Gothic building the words fell on the ear like the measured drippings of water in some vast dim cave. After hearing these sermons you might come away still not believing the tenets peculiar to the High Church system; but you would be harder than most men, if you did not feel more than ever ashamed of coarseness, selfishness, worldliness, if you did not feel the things of faith brought closer to the soul.[13]

Newman's Sunday afternoon sermons were pastoral sermons, addressed as much to the hearts of his congregation as to their intellects. To change hearts, to move men to embrace the Christian life with wholehearted commitment, was his object. Most often his subjects were illustrative of those darkly fateful doctrines stressed by St. Paul, St. Augustine, and John Calvin that complacent moderns ignored or reduced to platitudes but that for Newman were literally, dreadfully, urgently true. "The Religion of the Day," preached in 1832, is characteristic of Newman's sermons in its rejection of merely conventional morality, its solemn warning against shallow optimism. As ever, the world is the unrelenting enemy of the spirit, but never more seductive or corrupting than when it seems most to reflect the beneficent influence of religion.

In every age of Christianity, since it was first preached, there has been what may be called a *religion of the world*, which so far imitates the one true religion, as to deceive the unstable and unwary. The world does not oppose religion *as such*. I may say, it never has opposed it. In particular, it has, in all ages, acknowledged in one sense or other the Gospel of Christ, fastened on one or other of its characteristics, and professed to embody this in its practice; while by neglecting the other parts of the holy doctrine, it has, in fact, distorted and corrupted even that portion of it which it has exclusively put forward, and so has contrived to explain away the whole;—for he who cultivates only one precept of the Gospel to the exclusion of the rest, in reality attends to no part at all. Our duties *balance* each other; and though we are too sinful to perform them all perfectly, yet we may in some measure be performing them all, and preserving the balance on the whole; whereas, to give ourselves only to this or that commandment, is to incline our minds in a wrong direction, and at length to pull them down to the earth, which is the aim of our adversary, the Devil.

What is the world's religion now? It has taken the brighter side of the Gospel,—its tidings of comfort, its precepts of love; all darker, deeper views of man's condition and prospects being comparatively forgotten. This is the religion *natural* to a civilized age, and well has Satan dressed and completed it into an idol of the Truth. As the reason is cultivated, the taste formed, the affections and sentiments refined, a general decency and grace will of course spread over the face of society, quite independently of the influence of Revelation. That beauty and delicacy of thought, which is so attractive in books, then extends to the conduct of life, to all we have, all we do, all we are. Our manners are courteous; we avoid giving pain or offence; our words become correct; our relative duties are carefully performed. Our sense of propriety shows itself even in our domestic arrangements, in the embellishments of our houses, in our amusements, and so also in our religious profession. Vice now becomes unseemly and hideous to the imagination, or, as it is sometimes familiarly said, "out of taste." Thus elegance is gradually made the test and standard of virtue, which is no longer thought to possess an intrinsic claim on our hearts, or to exist, *further than* it leads to the quiet and comfort of others. Conscience is no longer recognized as an independent arbiter of actions, its authority is explained away; partly it is superseded in the minds of men by the so-called moral sense, which is regarded merely as the love of the beautiful; partly by the rule of expediency, which is forthwith substituted for it in the details of conduct. Now conscience is a stern, gloomy principle; it tells us of guilt and of prospective punishment. Accordingly, when its terrors disappear, then disappear also, in the creed of the day, those fearful images of Divine wrath with which the Scriptures abound. They are explained away. Every thing is bright and cheerful. Religion is pleasant and easy; benevolence is the chief virtue; intolerance, bigotry, excess of zeal, are the first of sins. Austerity is an absurdity;— even firmness is looked on with an unfriendly, suspicious eye. On the other hand, all open profligacy is discountenanced; drunkenness is accounted a disgrace; cursing and swearing are vulgarities. Moreover, to a cultivated mind, which recreates itself in the varieties of literature and knowledge, and is interested in the ever-accumulating discoveries of science, and the ever-fresh accessions of information, political or otherwise, from foreign countries, religion will commonly seem to be dull, from want of novelty. Hence excitements are eagerly sought out and rewarded. New objects in religion, new systems and plans, new doctrines, new preachers, are necessary to satisfy that craving which the so-called spread of knowledge has created. The mind becomes morbidly sensitive and fastidious; dissatisfied with things as they are, desirous of change *as such*, as if alteration must of itself be a relief.

Here I will not shrink from uttering my firm conviction, that it would be a gain to this country, were it vastly more superstitious, more bigoted, more gloomy, more fierce in its religion, than at present it shows itself to be. Not, of course, that I think the tempers of mind herein implied desirable, which would be an evident absurdity; but I think them infinitely more desirable and more promising than a heathen obduracy, and a cold, self-sufficient, self-wise tranquillity. Doubtless, peace of mind, a quiet conscience, and a cheerful countenance are the gift of the Gospel, and the sign of a Christian; but the same effects (or, rather, what appear to be the same) may arise from very different causes. Jonah slept in the storm,—so did our Blessed Lord. The one slept in an evil security: the Other in the "peace of God which passeth all understanding." The two states cannot be confounded together, they are perfectly distinct; and as distinct is the calm of the man of the world from that of the Christian. Now take the case of the sailors on board the vessel; they cried to Jonah, "What meanest thou, O sleeper?"—so the Apostles said to Christ, "Lord, we perish." This is the case of the superstitious; they stand between the false peace of Jonah and the true peace of Christ; they are better than the one, though far below the Other. Applying this to the present religion of the educated world, full as it is of security and cheerfulness, and decorum, and benevolence, I observe that these appearances may arise either from a great deal of religion, or from the absence of it; they may be the fruits of shallowness of mind and a blinded conscience, or of that faith which has peace with God through our Lord Jesus Christ. And if this alternative be proposed, I might leave it to the common sense of men to decide (if they could get themselves to think seriously) to which of the two the temper of the age is to be referred. For myself I cannot doubt, seeing what I see of the world, that it arises from the sleep of Jonah; and it is therefore but a dream of religion, far inferior in worth to the well-grounded alarm of the superstitious, who are awakened and see their danger, though they do not attain so far in faith as to embrace the remedy of it.

Think of this, I beseech you, my brethren, and lay it to heart, as far as you go with me, as you will answer for having heard it at the last day. I would not willingly be harsh; but knowing "that the world lieth in wickedness," I think it highly probable that you, so far as you are in it (as you must be, and we all must be in our degree), are, most of you, partially infected with its existing error, that shallowness of religion, which is the result of a blinded conscience; and, therefore, I speak earnestly to you. Believing in the existence of a general plague in the land, I judge that you probably have your share in the sufferings, the voluntary sufferings, which it is spreading among us. The fear of God is the beginning of wisdom; till you see Him to be a consuming fire, and approach Him with reverence and godly fear, as being sinners, you are not even in sight of the strait gate. I do not wish you to be able to point to any particular time when you renounced the world (as it is called), and were converted; this is a deceit. Fear and love must go together; always fear, always love, to your dying day. Doubtless;—still you must know what it is to sow in tears here, if you would reap in joy hereafter. Till you know the weight of your sins, and that not in mere imagination, but in practice, not so as merely to confess it in a formal phrase of lamentation, but daily and in your heart in secret, you cannot embrace the offer of mercy held out to you in the Gospel, through the death of Christ. Till you know what it is to fear with the terrified sailors or the Apostles, you cannot sleep with Christ at your Heavenly Father's feet. Miserable as were the superstitions of the dark ages, revolting as are the tortures now in use among the heathen of the East, better, far better is it, to torture the body all one's days, and to make this life a hell upon earth, than to remain in a brief tranquillity here, till the pit at length opens under us, and awakens us to an eternal fruitless consciousness and remorse. Dare not to think you have got to the bottom of your hearts; you do not know what evil lies there. How long and earnestly must you pray, how many years must you pass in careful obedience, before you have any right to lay aside sorrow, and to rejoice in the Lord? In one sense, indeed, you may take comfort from the first; for, though you dare not yet anticipate you are in the number of Christ's true elect, yet from the first you know He desires your salvation, has died for you, has washed away your sins by baptism, and will ever help you; and this thought must cheer you while you go on to examine and review your lives, and to turn to God in self-denial. But, at the same time, you never can be sure of salvation, while you are here; and therefore you must always fear while you hope. Your knowledge of your sins increases with your view of God's mercy in Christ. And this is the true Christian state, and the nearest approach to Christ's calm and placid sleep in the tempest;—not perfect joy and certainty in heaven, but a deep resignation to God's will, a surrender of ourselves, soul and body, to Him; hoping indeed, that we shall be saved, but fixing our eyes more earnestly on Him than on ourselves; that is, acting for His glory, seeking to please Him, devoting ourselves to Him in all manly obedience and strenuous good works; and, when we do look within, thinking of ourselves with a certain abhorrence and contempt as being sinners, mortifying our flesh, scourging our appetites, and composedly awaiting that time when, if we be worthy, we shall be stripped of our present selves, and new made in the kingdom of Christ.[14]

V

The Oxford Movement, hastily begun, with little organization and embracing diverse personalities and views, nevertheless quickly reached out beyond the sheltered quadrangles of the university and made itself felt in the country at large.

From beginnings so small, *Newman recounted*, from elements of thought so fortuitous, with prospects so unpromising, the Anglo-Catholic party suddenly became a power in the National Church, and an object of alarm to her rulers and friends. Its originators would have found it difficult to say what they aimed at of a practical kind: rather, they put forth views and principles, for their own sake, because they were true, as if they were obliged to say them; and, as they might be themselves surprised at their earnestness in uttering them, they had as great cause to be surprised at the success which attended their propagation. And, in fact, they could only say that those doctrines were in the air; that to assert was to prove, and that to explain was to persuade; and that the Movement in which they were taking part was the birth of a crisis rather than of a place. In a very few years a school of opinion was formed, fixed in its principles, indefinite and progressive in their range; and it extended itself into every part of the country. If we inquire what the world thought of it, we have still more to raise our wonder; for, not to mention the excitement it caused in England, the Movement and its party-names were known to the police of Italy and to the backwoodsmen of America. And so it proceeded, getting stronger and stronger every year, till it came into collision with the Nation, and that Church of the Nation, which it began by professing especially to serve.[15]

To Hurrell Froude, Newman wrote in July, 1835: What you say about our opuscula is very encouraging. I am astonished to see how they take. As to my sermons, Williams has lately been inquiring in London, and been told they are selling as well as they can sell, and when he pressed to know which volume most, they would not tell, only answer they both were, &c. I do verily believe a spirit is abroad at present, and we are but blind tools, not knowing whither we are going. I mean, a flame seems arising in so many places as to show no mortal incendiary is at work, though this man or that may have more influence in shaping the course or modifying the nature of the flame. I have, at present, some misgivings whether I have not been too bold in the June Magazine on the subject of Monachism. You saw it, and it is only my confidence in this unseen agitator which bears me up. I doubt whether I am not burdening my well-wishers with too heavy a load when I oblige them to take up and defend these opinions too.[16]

The tracts and sermons were not Newman's only productions in those busy years. In 1836 he published Romanism and Popular Protestantism, *in which he pointed out, in answer to critics who accused the Tractarians of Romanizing tendencies, what he believed to be an unbridgeable cleavage between the Roman and Anglican systems. To provide Anglicans with the beginnings of a sound and consistent theology, he published in 1837 the* Prophetical Office of the Church; *here, drawing upon the great seventeenth-century Anglican divines, he elaborated the theory of the Via Media or Middle Way, a catholic Anglicanism that was neither Roman nor Protestant. Besides these labors, Newman assumed in 1838 the editorship of the church periodical, the* British Critic. *From other members of the movement too there flowed a growing stream of historical, theological, and controversial works.*

Newman wrote to John Bowden on March 19, 1838: I have not seen Williams's 'Cathedral,' but I fear it will be obscure. However, everyone has his line. To be sure, what a mass of Catholic literature is now being poured upon the public! Have you seen Palmer's book? It is quite overcoming—his reading—and makes one feel quite ashamed. It will do a great deal of good, for just at this moment we need ballast. Then again, Froude's in an opposite direction, as if marking out the broad *limits* of Anglicanism and the differences of opinion which are allowable in it. Then Woodgate's Sermons, which began yesterday with a bold, uncompromising statement of the Doctrine of Tradition, and of the difference between the Catholic and Rationalistic spirit, which comes from a certain pamphlet. I hope to do something with my forthcoming Lectures, and there are to come Keble's Papers on Mysticism (read at the Theological) in the next (5th) volume, viz. No. 89 of the Tracts. (By-the-bye, have you seen Williams's most valuable Tract 80?) Then your 'Hildebrand'; then Froude's 'Becket, &c.' which is now ready; and besides all this, the 'British Critic.' But one must not exult too much. What I fear is the *now* rising generation at Oxford, Arnold's youths. Much depends on how they turn out.[17]

&§*The rising fortunes of the Movement were marked by an ever-increasing storm of criticism, echoed in the press and even carried into Parliament. It was to be expected that the doughty liberal, Thomas Arnold, pillar of the Broad Church, should damn the "Oxford conspirators"; the fanatical, superstitious, persecuting—indeed, dishonest—temper Arnold attributed to them was the very antithesis of that manly Christian character he sought to inculcate in the boys at Rugby School. But leaders of the High Church party, eminent prelates, comfortable and cautious clergymen, also drew back in alarm from the Tractarians, dreading the unsettling of customary practices, beliefs, and attitudes. Significantly, when the Bishop of Oxford, Newman's own ecclesiastical superior, felt moved to allude to the Tractarians in a pastoral letter, or "charge," to the clergy of his diocese, he did so in carefully balanced terms of praise and warning*§&.

A ragged paper came to me this morning, &§*Newman wrote to James Mozley on August 10, 1838*§&, with great portions cut out —parts, however, remained, else it could not have come. I will extract for your edification a sentence or two. 'The Debate [in Parliament] was rendered remarkable for bringing before the notice of the country, through Lord Morpeth, a sect of damnable and detestable heretics of late sprung up in Oxford; a sect which evidently affects Popery, and merits the heartiest condemnation of all true Christians. We have paid a good deal of attention to these gentry, and by the grace of God we shall show them up, and demonstrate that they are a people to be abhorred of all faithful men. We do not hesitate to say that they are criminally heterodox,' &c. That they are *what?* Do you know that Lord Morpeth went out of his way to mention my name? The paper in question is the 'Dublin Record.'

Bliss, in the 'Oxford Herald,' has called us all, Froude inclusive, 'amiable and fanciful men.' The Bishop delivers his Charge next Tuesday. 'Frazer's Magazine,' I am told, has opened on us. We must expect a volley from the whole Conservative press. I can fancy the Old Duke sending down to ask the Heads of Houses whether we cannot be silenced.[18]

To Keble, on August 14: I am just come away from hearing the Bishop's Charge, and certainly I am disappointed in the part in which he spoke of us.

He said he must allude to a remarkable development, both in matters of discipline and of doctrine, in one part of his Diocese; that he had had many anonymous letters, charging us with Romanism; that he had made inquiries; that, as far as discipline went, he found nothing to find fault with—one addition of a clerical vestment there had been, but that had been discontinued (alluding to Seager); but this he would say, that, in the choice of alternatives, he had rather go back to what is obsolete, in order to enforce the Rubric, than break it in order to follow the motley fashions now prevailing. Next, as to doctrine, he had found many most excellent things in the 'Tracts for the Times' (this was the only book he referred to), and most opportune and serviceable; but for some words and expressions he was sorry, as likely to lead *others* into error; he feared more for the disciples than for the masters, and he conjured those who were concerned in them to beware lest, &c.

Now does it not seem rather hard that he should publicly attack things in the Tracts without speaking to me about them privately? Again, what good does it do to fling an indefinite suspicion over them, when in the main they be orthodox? Then again, it seems hard that those who work, and who while working necessarily commit mistakes, instead of being thanked for that work, which others do *not* do, are blamed. It is very comfortable to do nothing and to criticise.[19]

Despite the attacks of its enemies and the confusion and uncertainty of those who might have been expected to be its friends, the Oxford Movement was vigorous and rising. In the spring of 1839, *Newman related*, my position in the Anglican Church was at its height. I had supreme confidence in my controversial *status*, and I had a great and still growing success, in recommending it to others. I had in the foregoing autumn been somewhat sore at the Bishop's Charge, but I have a letter which shows that all annoyance had passed from my mind. In January, if I recollect aright, in order to meet the popular clamour against myself and others, and to satisfy the Bishop, I had collected into one all the strong things which they, and especially I, had said against the Church of Rome, in order to [secure] their insertion among the advertisements appended to our publications. Conscious as I was that my opinions in religion were not gained, as the world said, from Roman sources, but were, on the contrary, the birth of my own mind and of the circumstances in which I had been placed, I had a scorn of the imputations which were heaped upon me. It was true that I held a large bold system of religion, very unlike the Protestantism of the day, but it was the concentration and adjustment of the statements of great Anglican authorities, and I had as much right to do so as the Evangelical party had, and more right than the Liberal, to hold their own respective doctrines.[20]

VI

At the height of his success, in the midst of a summer of quiet study, the ground on which Newman stood suddenly crumbled beneath his feet.

The Long Vacation of 1839 began early. There had been a great many visitors to Oxford from Easter to Commemoration; and Dr. Pusey and myself had attracted attention, more, I think, than any former year. I had put away from me the controversy with Rome for more than two years. In my Parochial Sermons the subject had never been introduced: there had been nothing for two years, either in my Tracts or in the British Critic, of a polemical character. I was returning, for the Vacation, to the course of reading which I had many years before chosen as especially my own. I have no reason to suppose that the thoughts of Rome came across my mind at all. About the middle of June I began to study and master the history of the Monophysites. I was absorbed in the doctrinal question. This was from about June 13th to August 30th. It was during this course of reading that for the first time a doubt came upon me of the tenable-ness of Anglicanism. I recollect on the 30th of July mentioning to a friend, whom I had accidentally met, how remarkable the history was; but by the end of August I was seriously alarmed.

I have described in a former work, how the history affected me. My stronghold was Antiquity; now here, in the middle of the fifth century, I found, as it seemed to me, Christendom of the sixteenth and the nineteenth centuries reflected. I saw my face in that mirror, and I was a Monophysite. The Church of the *Via Media* was in the position of the Oriental communion, Rome was, where she now is; and the Protestants were the Eutychians. Of all passages of history, since history has been, who would have thought of going to the sayings and doings of old Eutyches, that *delirus senex,* as (I think) Petavius calls him, and to the enormities of the unprincipled Dioscorus, in order to be converted to Rome!

Now let it be simply understood that I am not writing controversially, but with the one object of relating things as they happened to me in the course of my conversion. With this view I will quote a passage from the account, which I gave in 1850, of my reasonings and feelings in 1839:

"It was difficult to make out how the Eutychians or Monophysites were heretics, unless Protestants and Anglicans were heretics also; difficult to find arguments against the Tridentine Fathers, which did not tell against the Fathers of Chalcedon; difficult to condemn the Popes of the sixteenth century, without condemning the Popes of the fifth. The drama of religion, and the combat of truth and error, were ever one and the same. The principles and proceedings of the Church now, were those of the Church then; the principles and proceedings of heretics then, were those of Protestants now. I found it so,—almost fearfully; there was an awful similitude, more awful, because so silent and unimpassionate, between the dead records of the past and the feverish chronicle of the present. The shadow of the fifth century was on the sixteenth. It was like a spirit rising from the troubled waters of the old world, with the shape and lineaments of the new. The Church then, as now, might be called peremptory and stern, resolute, overbearing, and relentless; and heretics were shifting, changeable, reserved, and deceitful, ever courting civil power, and never agreeing together except by its aid; and the civil power was ever aiming at comprehensions, trying to put the invisible out of view, and substituting expediency for faith. What was the use of continuing the controversy, or defending my position, if, after all,

I was forging arguments for Arius or Eutyches, and turning devil's advocate against the much-enduring Athanasius and the majestic Leo? Be my soul with the Saints! and shall I lift up my hand against them? Sooner may my right hand forget her cunning, and wither outright, as his who once stretched it out against a prophet of God! Anathema to a whole tribe of Cranmers, Ridleys, Latimers, and Jewels! perish the names of Bramhall, Ussher, Taylor, Stillingfleet, and Barrow from the face of the earth, ere I should do aught but fall at their feet in love and in worship, whose image was continually before my eyes, and whose musical words were ever in my ears and on my tongue!"

Hardly had I brought my course of reading to a close, when the Dublin Review of that same August was put into my hands, by friends who were more favourable to the cause of Rome than I was myself. There was an Article in it on the "Anglican Claim" by Bishop Wiseman. This was about the middle of September. It was on the Donatists, with an application to Anglicanism. I read it, and did not see much in it. The Donatist controversy was known to me for some years, as I have instanced above. The case was not parallel to that of the Anglican Church. St. Augustine in Africa wrote against the Donatists in Africa. They were a furious party who made a schism within the African Church, and not beyond its limits. It was a case of Altar against Altar, of two occupants of the same See, as that between the Non-jurors in England and the Established Church; not the case of one Church against another, as Rome against the Oriental Monophysites. But my friend, an anxiously religious man, now, as then, very dear to me, a Protestant still, pointed out the palmary words of St. Augustine, which were contained in one of the extracts made in the Review, and which had escaped my observation. "Securus judicat orbis terrarum" ["The judgment of the world is sure"]. He repeated these words again and again, and, when he was gone, they kept ringing in my ears. "Securus judicat orbis terrarum;" they were words which went beyond the occasion of the Donatists: they applied to that of the Monophysites. They gave a cogency to the Article, which had escaped me at first. They decided ecclesiastical questions on a simpler rule than that of Antiquity; nay, St. Augustine was one of the prime oracles of Antiquity; here then Antiquity was deciding against itself. What a light was hereby thrown upon every controversy in the Church! not that, for the moment, the multitude may not falter in their judgment,—not that, in the Arian hurricane, Sees more than can be numbered did not bend before its fury, and fall off from St. Athanasius,—not that the crowd of Oriental Bishops did not need to be sustained during the contest by the voice and eye of St. Leo; but that the deliberate judgment, in which the whole Church at length rests and acquiesces, is an infallible prescription and a final sentence against such portions of it as protest and secede. Who can account for the impressions which are made on him? For a mere sentence, the words of St. Augustine, struck me with a power which I never had felt from any words before. To take a familiar instance, they were like the "Turn again Whittington" of the chime; or, to take a more serious one, they were like the "Tolle, lege,—Tolle, lege," of the child, which converted St. Augustine himself. "Securus judicat orbis terrarum!" By those great words of the ancient Father, the theory of the *Via Media* was absolutely pulverized.[21]

⊷§*Badly shaken, Newman revealed his state of mind to only two of his closest friends. On September 22 he confessed to Frederic Rogers*§⊶: Since I wrote to you, I have had the first real hit from Romanism which has happened to me. R.W., who has been passing through, directed my attention to Dr. Wiseman's article in the new 'Dublin.' I must confess it has given me a stomach-ache. You see the whole history of the Monophysites has been a sort of alternative. And now comes this dose at the end of it. It does certainly come upon one that we are not at the bottom of things. At this moment we have sprung a leak; and the worst of it is that those sharp fellows, Ward, Stanley, and Co. will not let one go to sleep upon it. *Curavimus Babylonem et non curata* was an awkward omen. I have not said so much to anyone.

I seriously think this is a most uncomfortable article on every account, though of course it is *ex parte*. I think I shall get Keble to answer it. As to Pusey, I am curious to see how it works with him.

And now, *carissime*, good-bye. It is no laughing matter. I will not blink the question, so be it; but you don't suppose I am a madcap to take up notions suddenly—only there is an uncomfortable vista opened which was closed before. I am writing upon my first feelings.[22]

⊷§*Henry Wilberforce recalled a walk with Newman in the New Forest soon after*§⊶. It was in the beginning of October, 1839, that he made the astounding confidence, mentioning the two subjects which had inspired the doubt, the position of S. Leo in the Monophysite controversy, and the principle, *"securus judicat orbis terrarum"* in that of the Donatists. He added that he felt confident that when he returned to his rooms and was able fully and calmly to consider the whole matter, he should see his way completely out of the difficulty. But, he said, I cannot conceal from myself, that for the first time since I began the study of theology, a vista has been opened before me, to the end of which I do not see. He was walking in the New Forest, and he borrowed the form of his expression from the surrounding scenery. His companion, upon whom such a fear came like a thunderstroke, expressed his hope that Mr. Newman might die rather than take such a step. He replied, with deep earnestness, that he had thought if ever the time should come when he was in serious danger, of asking his friends to pray, that, if it was not indeed the will of God, he might be taken away before he did it.[23]

Other friends who were not admitted into Newman's confidence nevertheless sensed his painful perplexity. Isaac Williams, his curate at St. Mary's, related of this period: Nothing had as yet impaired my friendship with Newman. We lived daily very much together; but I had a secret uneasiness, not from anything said or implied, but from a want of repose about his character, that I thought he would start into some line different from Keble and Pusey, though I knew not in what direction it would be. Often after walking together, when leaving him, have I heard a deep secret sigh which I could not interpret. It seemed to speak of weariness of the world, and of aspirations for something he wished to do and had not yet done. Of the putting out of Church principles he often spoke as of an experiment which he did not know whether the Church of England would bear, and knew not what would be the issue. In looking back, most intimately as I was united with him, I cannot remember when my prayer for him was not rather that he might be preserved from error and the dangers to which he was exposed from his peculiar temperament, than for his perfection, and that I might follow his example, as would have been my prayer with regard to John Keble and Pusey.[24]

Newman's confidence drained from him. For the first time he seemed to feel the full burden of his responsibilities. The duty of preaching to impressionable young men when his own convictions were unsettled, of leading others in a movement that daily encountered increasing hostility from the university authorities, weighed heavily upon him. Letters to his beloved sister Jemima recorded his new mood.

On November 17, 1839: As to the Vice-Chancellor I should not wonder if my situation got unpleasant at St. Mary's. Had I my will, I should like giving up preaching. Only it is more than probable that any person I appointed would be liked less than myself. My greatest encouragement is the number of weekly communicants, and that among the M.A.'s. The Undergraduates are few, which I am glad of, the B.A.'s more, and the M.A.'s more. This morning I had forty-three altogether, in the dark even. This shows, one trusts, a steady growth of seriousness among the clergy of the place, and that the change, whatever it is to be, is not from the *Undergraduates*, which would be very objectionable if it could be helped. But the prospect is gloomy. The Heads of Houses are getting more and more uneasy. I should not wonder if the Bishop got uneasy, in which case I suppose I should resign the living; and I expect the country clergy will be getting uneasy. Then the question of the Fathers is getting more and more anxious. For certain persons will not find in them just what they expected. People seem to have thought they contained nothing but the doctrines of Baptismal Regeneration, Apostolical Succession, Canonicity of Scripture, and the like. Hence many have embraced the principle of appeal to them with this view. Now they are beginning to be undeceived. I never can be surprised at *individuals* going off to Romanism, but that is not my chief fear, but a schism in the Church: that is, those two parties who have hitherto got on together as they could, from the times of Puritanism downward, gathering up into clear, direct, tangible forces, and colliding. Our Church is not at one with itself, there is no denying it. However, as I never have felt elation when matters were promising, so I do not (I trust) feel despondency or trouble now when they threaten. I do really trust, if it may be said without presumption, that we are brought forward for a purpose, and we may leave the matter to Him who directs all things well. One thing seems plain, if it did not before, that *temporal* prospects we (personally) have none. I could fancy things going so far as to make me resign even my fellowship.[25]

On February 25, 1840 : I have got very sluggish about writing, for various reasons: first, I am so busy; next, my hand is so tired; and, thirdly, I am somehow desponding about the state of things, and this disinclines me to exert myself.

Everything is miserable. I expect a great attack upon the Bible —indeed, I have long expected it. At the present moment indications of what is coming gather. Those wretched Socialists on the one hand, then Carlyle on the other—a man of first-rate ability, I suppose, and quite fascinating as a writer. His book on the 'French Revolution' is most taking (to me). I had hoped he might have come round right, for it was easy to see he was not a believer; but they say he has settled the wrong way. His view is that Christianity has good in it, or is good *as far as it goes*, which, when applied to Scripture, is, of course, a picking and choosing of its contents. Then, again, you have Arnold's school, such as it is (I do hope he will be frightened back), giving up the inspiration of the Old Testament, or of all Scripture (I do not say Arnold himself does). Then you have Milman, clenching his 'History of the Jews' by a 'History of Christianity' which they say is worse; and just in the same line. Then you have all your political economists, who *cannot* accept (it is impossible) the Scripture rules about almsgiving, renunciation of wealth, self-denial, &c., and then your geologists, giving up parts of the Old Testament. All these and many more spirits seem uniting and forming into something shocking.

But this is not all. I begin to have serious apprehensions lest any religious body is strong enough to withstand the league of evil but the Roman Church. At the end of the first millenary it withstood the fury of Satan, and now the end of the second is drawing on. It has *tried* strength; what is *has* endured during these last centuries! and it is stronger than ever. We on the other hand have never been tried and come out of trial without practical concessions. I cannot see that we *can* receive the assault of the foe. We are divided among ourselves, like the Jews in their siege. So that it seems to me as if there were coming on a great encounter between infidelity and Rome, and that we should be smashed between them. Certainly the way that good principles have shot up is wonderful; but I am not clear that they are not tending to Rome—not from any necessity in the principles themselves, but from the much greater proximity between Rome and us than between infidelity and us, and that in a time of trouble we naturally look about for allies.[26]

᪐§*Attached to the parish of St. Mary's was the hamlet of Littlemore, some fifteen miles outside of Oxford. In 1836 Newman had
built a chapel there for the inhabitants of the place. Now he moved
there to escape the pressures of the university and to recover if he
could, in the exercise of simple pastoral duties, a measure of serenity*§᪐.

᪐§*From Littlemore he wrote to Jemima on April 1, 1840*§᪐: I
am getting on here; the children are improving in their singing. I
have had the audacity to lead them and teach them some new tunes.
Also I have rummaged out a violin and strung it, and on Mondays
and Thursdays have begun to *lead* them with it, a party of between
twenty and thirty great and little in the schoolroom. I am catechiz-
ing them in church, too, and have got them so far that they take an
interest in it. I have only one girl as much as ten, and not two more
than eight or nine, except some Sunday scholars. I have effected a
great reform (for the time) in the girls' hands and faces. Lectured
with unblushing effrontery on the necessity of their keeping their
work clean, and set them to knit stockings.

Also I have drawn up a sort of liturgy for School Prayers, varying
with the seasons, on a hint I gained from some printed prayers, &c.,
done by some ladies in Sussex.

I think I shall be a good deal here in future.[27]

᪐§*But there was no escape from responsibility, particularly as
the criticisms of the Romish affectations of some of the more zealous
younger adherents of the movement, which he had long ignored, began to be borne in upon him*§᪐. At that time, ᪐§*Newman recorded
in the* Apologia*§᪐, I thought little of such an evil, but the new
thoughts, which had come on me during the Long Vacation, on the
one hand made me comprehend it, and on the other took away my
power of effectually meeting it. A firm and powerful control was
necessary to keep men straight; I never had a strong wrist, but at the
very time, when it was most needed, the reins had broken in my
hands. With an anxious presentiment on my mind of the upshot of
the whole inquiry, which it was almost impossible for me to conceal
from men who saw me day by day, who heard my familiar conversation, who came perhaps for the express purpose of pumping me, and
having a categorical *yes* or *no* to their questions,—how could I expect to say any thing about my actual, positive, present belief, which

would be sustaining or consoling to such persons as were haunted already by doubts of their own? Nay, how could I, with satisfaction to myself, analyze my own mind, and say what I held and what I did not? or say with what limitations, shades of difference, or degrees of belief, I held that body of opinions which I had openly professed and taught? how could I deny or assert this point or that, without injustice to the new view, in which the whole evidence for those old opinions presented itself to my mind?[28]

What he must do, Newman knew, was to integrate his new ideas with the theory of the Via Media he had been upholding until now. The Middle Way was supposed to be the way of the primitive church, before Protestant subtractions or Roman additions to the creed of the Fathers. The Tractarians justified the Anglican position by appealing to antiquity; Rome replied that its universality proved it to be the one true church—and it was the overwhelming force of this claim that Newman was now compelled to acknowledge. The Anglican church did indeed seem to be estranged from the largest single Christian communion, from the great body of Christians over the world. If the Via Media was to be saved, Newman must demonstrate that the Anglican church was as legitimate a descendant in England of the primitive catholic church as was the Roman church on the Continent, that its apparent estrangement was a superficial matter attributable to local peculiarities and did not extend to those fundamental doctrines that Anglicanism shared with Rome. This was the purpose of the famous Tract 90.

The Apologia continues: Anglicanism claimed to hold that the Church of England was nothing else than a continuation in this country, (as the Church of Rome might be in France or Spain,) of that one Church of which in old times Athanasius and Augustine were members. But, if so, the doctrine must be the same; the doctrine of the Old Church must live and speak in Anglican formularies, in the 39 Articles. Did it? Yes, it did; that is what I maintained; it did in substance, in a true sense. Man had done his worst to disfigure, to mutilate, the old Catholic Truth, but there it was, in spite of them, in the Articles still. It was there, but this must be shown. It was a matter of life and death to us to show it. And I believed that it could be shown; I considered that those grounds of justification, which I gave above, when I was speaking of Tract 90, were sufficient

for the purpose; and therefore I set about showing it at once. This
was in March, 1840, when I went up to Littlemore. And, as it was a
matter of life and death with us, all risks must be run to show it.
When the attempt was actually made, I had got reconciled to the
prospect of it, and had no apprehensions as to the experiment; but
in 1840, while my purpose was honest, and my grounds of reason
satisfactory, I did nevertheless recognize that I was engaged in an
experimentum crucis. I have no doubt that then I acknowledged to
myself that it would be a trial of the Anglican Church, which it had
never undergone before,—not that the Catholic sense of the Articles
had not been held or at least suffered by their framers and promul-
gators, and was not implied in the teaching of Andrewes or Bever-
idge, but that it had never been publicly recognized, while the interpretation of the day was Protestant and exclusive. I observe also,
that, though my Tract was an experiment, it was, as I said at the
time, "no *feeler*," the event showed it; for, when my principle was
not granted, I did not draw back, but gave up. I would not hold
office in a Church which would not allow my sense of the Articles.
My tone was, "This is necessary for us, and have it we must and
will, and, if it tends to bring men to look less bitterly on the Church
of Rome, so much the better."[29]

VII

*Tract 90 was published on February 27, 1841. In this long,
subtly reasoned, and intricately argued production, Newman attempted to demonstrate that the basic formularies of the Anglican
church, those Thirty-nine Articles adopted by the Anglican clergy
in 1562, were susceptible to—were "tolerant" of—a Catholic interpretation. Now it was true that some of the doctrines most essential to Newman were not even mentioned in the Articles, as for
example the reservation of ministerial functions to those who had
been episcopally ordained—a doctrine fundamental to an episcopal
system and antithetical to the spiritual egalitarianism of Protestants.
But the Articles were not a body of divinity, Newman argued; they
were in large part protests against specific Roman abuses; they did
not mention any of the doctrines which the reformers held in common with Rome. The Articles were in fact so ambiguous as to be
susceptible to many interpretations. It was obvious that such ambiguity was deliberate, that the authors of the Articles, while seek-*

*ing to establish Reformation principles in England, had not wanted
to exclude from the Anglican communion Catholics who were willing
to accept the royal supremacy. Their tolerance of Catholic views,
Newman pointed out, was evidenced by their approval of the two
books of* Homilies, *which, like* The Book of Common Prayer, *preserved the Catholic origins of the English church. Newman maintained, therefore, that a Catholic interpretation of the Articles was
as legitimate as any other. He had a right, he insisted, to interpret
the Articles not according to the particular beliefs of their authors
but according to the beliefs of the Catholic church, so long as the
words of the Articles did not expressly exclude those beliefs.*

*Newman's view, if not unprecedented, was admittedly extreme, and
the difficulties to be surmounted were considerable. Thus in his commentary on Article XI, which asserted the distinctively Protestant
doctrine of justification by faith, Newman had to argue that the
language of the Article did not exclude belief in the efficacy of sacraments and good works.*

Article xi.—"That we are justified by Faith only, is a most wholesome doctrine."

The Homilies add that Faith is the sole *means*, the sole *instrument*
of justification. Now, to show briefly what such statements imply,
and what they do not.

1. They do *not* imply a denial of *Baptism* as a means and an instrument of justification; which the Homilies elsewhere affirm, as will
be shown incidentally in a later section.

The instrumental power of Faith cannot interfere with the instrumental power of Baptism; because Faith is the sole justifier, not in
contrast to *all* means and agencies whatever, (for it is not surely
in contrast to our LORD's merits, or GOD's mercy,) but to all other
graces. When, then, Faith is called the sole instrument, this means
the sole *internal* instrument, not the sole instrument of any kind.

There is nothing inconsistent, then, in Faith being the sole instrument of justification, and yet Baptism also the sole instrument,
and that at the same time, because in distinct senses; an inward instrument in no way interfering with an outward instrument, Baptism
may be the hand of the giver, and Faith the hand of the receiver.

Nor does the sole instrumentality of Faith interfere with the doctrine of *Works* being a means also. And that it is a mean, the

Homily of Alms-deeds declares in the strongest language, as will also be quoted in Section 11.

An assent to the doctrine that Faith alone justifies, does not at all preclude the doctrine of Works justifying also. If, indeed, it were said that Works justify in *the same sense* as Faith only justifies, this would be a contradiction in terms; but Faith only may justify in one sense—Good Works in another:—and this is all that is here maintained. After all, does not CHRIST only justify? How is it that the doctrine of Faith justifying does not interfere with our LORD's being the sole Justifier? It will, of course, be replied, that our LORD is the *meritorious cause,* and Faith the *means;* that Faith justifies in a different and subordinate sense. As, then, CHRIST justifies *in the sense* in which He justifies alone, yet Faith also justifies in its own sense; so Works, whether moral or ritual, may justify us in their own respective senses, though in the sense in which Faith justifies, it only justifies. The only question is, *What* is that sense in which Works justify, so as not to interfere with Faith only justifying? It may, indeed, turn out on inquiry, that the sense alleged will not hold, either as being unscriptural, or for any other reason; but, whether so or not, at any rate the apparent inconsistency of language should not startle persons; nor should they so promptly condemn those who, though they do not use *their* language, use St. James's. Indeed, is not this argument the very weapon of the Arians, in their warfare against the SON OF GOD? They said, "CHRIST is not GOD, because the FATHER is called the *'Only* GOD.' "

2. Next we have to inquire *in what sense* Faith only does justify. In a number of ways, of which here two only shall be mentioned.

First, it is the pleading or impenetrating principle, or constitutes our *title* to justification; being analogous among the graces to Moses' lifting up his hands on the Mount, or the Israelites eyeing the Brazen Serpent,—actions which did not merit GOD's mercy, but *asked* for it. A number of means go to effect our justification. We are justified by CHRIST alone, in that He has purchased the gift; by Faith alone, in that Faith asks for it; by Baptism alone, for Baptism conveys it; and by newness of heart alone, for newness of heart is the life of it.

And secondly, Faith, as being the beginning of perfect or justifying righteousness, is taken for what it tends towards, or ultimately will be. It is said by anticipation to be that which it promises; just as one might pay a labourer his hire before he began his work. Faith working by love is the seed of divine graces, which in due time will be brought forth and flourish—partly in this world, fully in the next.[30]

Many have naturally supposed, *Isaac Williams related*, that it was the condemnation of the Tract No. 90, by the Heads of Houses, which gave his sensitive mind the decided turn to the Church of Rome. But I remember circumstances which indicated it was not so. He talked to me of publishing a tract on the Thirty-nine Articles, and at the same time said things in favour of the Church of Rome, which quite startled and alarmed me, and I was afraid he would express the same in this tract, with no idea (as his manner was) of the sensation it would occasion. After endeavouring to dissuade him from it, I said, "Well, at all events let me see it first." On returning after the vacation, he said, "I have written that tract after all, but you have no need to be alarmed, for I have got John Keble to look it over, and he says nothing against it." Very true; but he had not the reasons for apprehension that I had. Yet, still, the sensation and the strong and bitter opposition it excited seemed to take Newman quite by surprise. I remember well being with him when Ward came into his room, on the day of its publication, and said, "There is an immense demand for that tract, and it is creating a tremendous stir, I find from Parker's shop." Newman walked with me at the time of the condemnation of it, much depressed. And he wrote to apologize for it to Dr. Jelf, partly unsaying it. This also was his manner; he was carried away first of all by his own mind, but afterwards, from a very amiable and good feeling, wished to do away with the uneasiness occasioned.[31]

Tract 90 threw Oxford into an uproar. Whatever arguments might have been brought against it in detail were lost in the outrage of the anti-Tractarians who vehemently denounced the tract as dishonest and immoral. By oversubtle reasoning, they felt, the tract overturned the very obvious meaning and intention of the Articles and provided Newman's followers with grounds for evading the plain obligations they had incurred by subscribing to them. Newman's surprise and momentary despair, which was soon succeeded by a calm confidence, were expressed in letters written in the next few days.

To Jemima on March 9: I have got into what may prove a serious mess here. I have just published a Tract (90) which I did not feel likely to attract attention. I sent it to Keble before publishing;

he, too, made no remark upon it. But people are taking it up very warmly—thanks, I believe, entirely to Golightly. ⚜§On March 12§⚜: I fear I am clean dished. The Heads of Houses are at this very moment concocting a manifesto against me. Do not think I fear for my cause. We have had too great a run of luck.[32]

⚜§To Frederic Rogers on March 21§⚜: Carissime,—Church has told you the scrape I have got into. Yet though my own infirmity mixes with everything I do, I trust you would approve of my *position* much; I now am in my right place, which I have long wished to be in, which I did not know how to attain, and which has been brought about without my intention, I hope I may say providentially, though I am perfectly aware at the same time that it is a rebuke and punishment for my secret pride and sloth. I do not think, indeed, I have not had one misgiving about what I have done, though I have done it in imperfection; and, so be it, all will turn out well. I cannot anticipate what will be the result of it in this place or elsewhere as regards *myself*. Somehow I do not fear for the *cause*.[33]

⚜§On March 15 the Hebdomadal Board, composed of the Heads of Houses, acting hastily but decisively, condemned Tract 90, resolving "That modes of interpretation, such as are suggested in the said Tract, evading rather than explaining the sense of the Thirty-nine Articles, and reconciling subscription to them with the adoption of errors which they are designed to counteract, defeat the object, and are inconsistent with the due observance of the [university] statutes." Though without theological authority, the judgment possessed sufficient weight to signal the doom of the Tractarian party at Oxford, where every student was required to subscribe to the Thirty-nine Articles as a condition of matriculation§⚜.*

⚜§Newman, who had not been permitted to defend his position before the Board, observed to John Bowden on March 15§⚜: The Heads, I believe, have just done a violent act: they have said that my interpretation of the Articles is an *evasion*. Do not think that this will pain me. You see no *doctrine* is censored, and my shoulders shall manage to bear the charge.

If you knew all, or when you know, you will see that I have asserted a great principle, and I ought to suffer for it; that the Articles are to be interpreted, not according to the meaning of the writers, but (as far as the wording will admit) according to the sense of the Catholic Church.[34]

Not the Heads of Houses but the Bishop of Oxford, Newman's ecclesiastical superior, possessed the theological authority to censure doctrine. This the bishop did not do, merely asking that publication of the tracts cease. Newman's "great principle" remained intact.

To Jemima, March 30: The tract affair is settled on these terms, which others may think a disappointment, but to me is a very fair bargain. I am now publishing a letter to the Bishop at his wish, stating that he wishes the tracts to be discontinued, and he thinks No. 90 objectionable as tending to disturb the Church. I am quite satisfied with the bargain I have got, if this is all—as I suppose it will be.[35]

To Keble, April 1: I am sanguine about my letter to the Bishop, which was out yesterday. I have spoken quite what I feel; yet I think I have managed to wedge in a good many bits of Catholicism, which *now* come out with the Bishop's sanction. How odd it is that one should be *able* to act from the heart, yet from the head too; yet I think I have been honest—at least I hope so.[36]

Again to Keble, the same day: I write a second note about your projected pamphlet. I am not at all sure that our game, if I may use the word, is not to let the matter drop at present. We have got the principle of our interpretation admitted, in that it has not been condemned. Do not let us provoke opposition. Numbers will be taking advantage silently and quietly of the admission for their own benefit. It will soon be *assumed* as a matter of course.[37]

To Keble on April 10: I add more words about your pamphlet. My view is this: that we should make good and complete the *argumentative* ground of our interpretation of the Articles and then leave it to work. If that has not been yet done, as perhaps it has not, and your pamphlet is on it, let it come out; but *protests* and *authorities*, or *numbers*, these let us *altogether discard.*

I cannot help thinking this is right.

As to the Bishops, the one thing they fear is a *disturbance*—

1. Either a secession to Rome.
2. Or a division within.

For this reason I am sure they cannot like the Hebdomadal Act. We may do anything if we keep from disturbance. The more we can yield, the better policy. We can gain anything by giving way.[38]

The impact of Tract 90 spread outward from Oxford in ever widening circles. The outrage of the Oxford authorities was shared by bishops in dioceses across the country. In charges to their clergy they condemned Tract 90, one after another, through 1841, 1842, and 1843.

To James Hope, Newman wrote on October 17, 1841 : As to the Bishops' Charges, this too must be remembered, that they have no direct authority except in their own dioceses. A Bishop's word is to be obeyed, not as to doctrine, but as a part of discipline; only in Synod do they prescribe doctrine. There is nothing to hinder anyone in the Oxford diocese maintaining just the negative of what these particular Bishops have said. Till the truth is *silenced* among us, I do not see that Catholic minds need be in a difficulty.

Having said this, I will go on candidly to own that the said Charges are very serious matters; as virtually silencing portions of the truth in particular dioceses, and as showing that it is not impossible that our Church *may* lapse into heresy. I cannot deny that a great and anxious *experiment* is going on, whether our Church be or be not Catholic; the issue may not be in our day. But I must be plain in saying that, if it does issue in Protestantism, I shall think it my duty, if alive, to leave it. This does not seem much to grant, but it is much, supposing such an event to be at our doors, for one naturally tries to make excuses then, whereas one safely pledges oneself to what is distant. I trust it not only is distant, but never to be. But the way to hinder it is to be prepared for it.

I fear I must say that I am beginning to think that the only way to keep in the English Church is steadily to contemplate and act upon the possibility of leaving it. Surely the Bishops ought to be brought to realise what they are doing.

But still, on the whole, I hope better things. At all events, I am sure that, to leave the English Church, unless something very flagrant happens, must be the work of years.[39]

◄§"Something very flagrant" happened immediately—the announcement that Great Britain and Prussia had agreed to establish an Anglican bishop in Jerusalem, where there were no Anglicans, in order to introduce the influence of those Protestant powers into the Turkish Empire where France and Russia already enjoyed special privileges as protectors of Roman Catholic and Orthodox minorities. This cynical employment of the Anglican church as a political instrument dealt the final blow to Newman's hopes for its regeneration. It was now clear that the vision of a Catholic Anglican church was a bookish theory.

In February 1842 Newman gave up his rooms at Oriel and moved permanently to Littlemore. He still retained his Oriel fellowship and, though with an increasingly troubled conscience, his position at St. Mary's, where he continued to preach every Sunday§►.

◄§To Jemima, February 6§►: I am going up to Littlemore [i.e. for good] and my books are all in motion—part gone; the rest in a day or two. It makes me very downcast.[40]

◄§To Jemima, February 15§►: I am in Oxford only on Saturday evening and Sunday morning. My books are all up, but not my bookcases. You may think it makes me somewhat downcast, but I don't know how I frightened you. For some years, as is natural, I have felt that I am out of place at Oxford, as customs are. Every one almost is my junior. And then, added to this, is the hostility of the Heads, who are now taking measures to keep the men from St. Mary's. But I think I have made up my mind, unless something very much out of the way happens, to anticipate them by leaving off preaching at St. Mary's. I shall tell no one. My being up here is an excuse, and I can at any time begin again. But I think my preaching is a cause of *irritation,* and, for what I know, any moment they may do something against me at St. Mary's, and I would rather anticipate this.[41]

◄§To Jemima, February 21§►: I have several things that puzzle me about St. Mary's pulpit. One special thing is this, which I have felt for years: is it right to be preaching to those who are not, in any sense, my charge, and whose legitimate guardians, the Heads of Houses, wish them not to be preached to? This seems to me a *view,*

to which others might be added, cogent also. But, as you say, there
are great difficulties on the other side. Of course, I shall not pledge
myself to anything for the future.[42]

VIII

*Around Newman at Littlemore gathered a small group of his
more zealous adherents in a semimonastic community devoted to
study, reflection, and religious exercise. The existence of such a
group, its mysterious activities and intentions, excited the most intense interest among friends and enemies alike at the university.*

After Tract 90 the Protestant world would not let me alone; they
pursued me in the public journals to Littlemore. Reports of all
kinds were circulated about me. "Imprimis, why did I go up to
Littlemore at all? For no good purpose certainly; I dared not tell
why." Why, to be sure, it was hard that I should be obliged to say
to the Editors of newspapers that I went up there to say my prayers;
it was hard to have to tell the world in confidence, that I had a certain doubt about the Anglican system, and could not at that moment
resolve it, or say what would come of it; it was hard to have to
confess that I had the thought of giving up my Living a year or two
before, and that this was a first step to it. It was hard to have to
plead, that, for what I knew, my doubts would vanish, if the newspapers would be so good as to give me time and let me alone. Who
would ever dream of making the world his confidant? yet I was considered insidious, sly, dishonest, if I would not open my heart to the
tender mercies of the world. But they persisted: "What was I doing
at Littlemore?" Doing there? have I not retreated from you? have
I not given up my position and my place? am I alone, of Englishmen,
not to have the privilege to go where I will, no questions asked? am
I alone to be followed about by jealous prying eyes, who note down
whether I go in at a back door or at the front, and who the men are
who happen to call on me in the afternoon? Cowards! if I advanced
one step, you would run away; it is not you that I fear: "Di me
terrent, et Jupiter hostis." It is because the Bishops still go on
charging against me, though I have quite given up: it is that secret
misgiving of heart which tells me that they do well, for I have neither
lot nor part with them: this it is which weighs me down. I cannot
walk into or out of my house, but curious eyes are upon me. Why will

you not let me die in peace? Wounded brutes creep into some hole
to die in, and no one grudges it them. Let me alone, I shall not trouble
you long. This was the keen heavy feeling which pierced me, and, I
think, these are the very words that I used to myself. I asked, in the
words of a great motto, "Ubi lapsus? quid feci?" One day when I
entered my house, I found a flight of Undergraduates inside. Heads
of Houses, as mounted patrols, walked their horses round those poor
cottages. Doctors of Divinity dived into the hidden recesses of that
private tenement uninvited, and drew domestic conclusions from
what they saw there. I had thought that an Englishman's house was
his castle; but the newspapers thought otherwise.[43]

*By now Newman knew that there was no place for him in the
Anglican church. Each new bishop's charge underlined the utter
condemnation and rejection of the Via Media by an irremediably
Protestantized church. But conversion to the Church of Rome was
still impossible. How alien Rome was to an Englishman and Oxonian!
How repellent those doctrines he had abominated since childhood—
the idolatrous veneration of the Virgin and the saints, the unhistori-
cal primacy of the Roman see, the arrogant claim to infallibility.
He would wait, all the while studying, thinking, and praying, for a
resolution of his quandary one way or another. To some of the young
men around him who strained to embrace the Roman church he
urged patience, wielding what authority he possessed to compel them
to wait two, three years, by which time their seriousness of purpose
might be sufficiently tested—and perhaps his own mind made
clear*.

*In August 1843, one of his followers deserted. To Keble, New-
man wrote on August 25*: I have just received a letter from Lockhart, one of my inmates, who has been away for three weeks, saying
that he is on the point of joining the Church of Rome, and is in retreat under Dr. Gentili of Loughborough. You may fancy how sick
it makes me.[44]

To Jemima on August 28: Perhaps you know already from
your proximity to Loughborough that Lockhart, who has been living
here with me for a year past, has, at Dr. Gentili's at that place,
conformed to the Church of Rome.

It has taken us all by surprise. When he came here I took a

promise of him that he would remain quiet for three years, otherwise I would not receive him.

This occurrence will very likely fix the time of my resigning St. Mary's, for he has been teaching in our school till he went away.

These are reasons enough to make me give up St. Mary's, but, were there no other, this feeling would be sufficient, that I am not so zealous a defender of the established and existing system of religion as I ought to be for such a post.[45]

To Jemima on August 31: I am sorry to put you to such pain. Your letter and ——'s to you, would have brought me to many tears unless I had so hard a heart. You must take what I do in faith at least; if not, I fear I cannot find a better way of consoling you.

I wonder my late letters have not prepared you for this. Have you realised that three years since I wished to do it; and that I have said so in print, and that then only a friend prevented me?

It has been determined on since Lent. All through Lent I and another kept it in mind; and then, for safety, I said I would not act till October, though we both came to one view. October is coming!

No time is '*the*' time. You may have thought as you read, 'three years ago it would not have mattered.' Will three years hence be easier? The question is, *Ought* it to be done?

My dearest Jemima, my circumstances are not of my making. One's duty is to act *under* circumstances. Is it a light thing to give up Littlemore? Am I not providing dreariness for myself? If others, whom I am pierced to think about, because I cannot help them, suffer, shall not I suffer in my own way?

Everything that one does honestly, sincerely, with prayer, with advice, must turn to good. In what am I not likely to be as good a judge as another? In the consequences? True, but is not this what I have been ever protesting against? the going by expedience, not by principle? My sweetest Jemima, of whom I am quite unworthy, rather pray that I may be directed aright, rather pray that something may occur to hinder me if I am wrong, then take the matter into your own hands.[46]

To James Mozley on September 1: I thought you would know already the prospect of my leaving St. Mary's without my speaking to you of a subject which was *but* in prospect, and which (as you may think) makes me very sick. I have been thinking of it these three, I may say four, years, nor do I act without advice.

Really it is no personal feeling or annoyance under which I do it. I hope I am right in speaking openly to you, which I have not done but to a very few, but now I will tell you the real cause—which others besides those to whom I have said it may guess—but which (as far as I recollect) I have only told to Rogers, H. Wilberforce, R. Wilberforce, and Keble. Tom may suspect it and Copeland, so may Church and Marriott. Indeed, I cannot name the limit of surmisers.

The truth then is, I am not a good son enough of the Church of England to feel I can in conscience hold preferment under her. I love the Church of Rome too well.

Now please *burn this*, there's a good fellow, for you sometimes let letters lie on your mantelpiece.[47]

On September 18, Newman formally resigned St. Mary's. The next Sunday he preached his last sermon there, and the following day, Monday, September 25, took leave of his congregation at Littlemore at a special service commemorating the seventh anniversary of the consecration of the chapel. The church was crowded with friends from Oxford who understood that this day's sermon would be Newman's last in the parish, though few foresaw that it would be his last as an Anglican. Newman's subject was "The Parting of Friends." Movingly he recalled the memorable friendships and partings recorded in the Bible, all of which he viewed as memorial and tokens of the parting of Jesus from his disciples when his work was done. Even as Jesus mourned over the country and city which had rejected him, so Newman apostrophized the Church of England in a bitter confession of defeat and despair.

O mother of saints! O school of the Wise! O nurse of the heroic! of whom went forth, in whom have dwelt, memorable names of old, to spread the truth abroad, or to cherish and illustrate it at home! O thou, from whom surrounding nations lit their lamps! O virgin of Israel! wherefore dost thou now sit on the ground and keep silence, like one of the foolish women who were without oil on the coming of the Bridegroom? Where is now the ruler in Sion, and the doctor in the Temple, and the ascetic on Carmel, and the herald in the wilderness, and the preacher in the market-place? where are thy "effectual fervent prayers," offered in secret, and thy alms and good works coming up as a memorial before God? How is it, O once holy place, that "the land mourneth, for the corn is wasted, the new wine is dried up, the oil languisheth, . . . because joy is withered away from the sons of men?" "Alas for the day! . . . how do the beasts groan! the herds of cattle are perplexed, because they have no pasture, yea, the flocks of sheep are made desolate." "Lebanon is ashamed and hewn down; Sharon is like a wilderness, and Bashan and Carmel shake off their fruits." O my mother, whence is this unto thee, that thou hast good things poured upon thee and canst not keep them, and bearest children, yet darest not own them? why hast thou not the skill to use their services, nor the heart to rejoice in their love? how is it that whatever is generous in purpose, and tender or deep in devotion, thy flower and thy promise, falls from thy bosom and finds no home within thine arms? Who hath put this note upon thee, to have "a miscarrying womb, and dry breasts," to be strange to thine own flesh, and thine eye cruel towards thy little ones? Thine own offspring, the fruit of thy womb, who love thee and would toil for thee, thou dost gaze upon with fear, as though a portent, or thou dost loathe as an offence;—at best thou dost but endure, as if they had no claim but on thy patience, self-possession, and vigilance, to be rid of them as easily as thou mayest. Thou makest them "stand all the day idle," as the very condition of thy bearing with them; or thou biddest them be gone, where they will be more welcome; or thou sellest them for nought to the stranger that passes by. And what wilt thou do in the end thereof?

Finally, his leave-taking: And, O my brethren, O kind and affectionate hearts, O loving friends, should you know any one whose lot it has been, by writing or by word of mouth, in some degree to help you thus to act; if he has ever told you what you knew about yourselves, or what you did not know; has read to you your wants or feelings, and comforted you by the very reading; has made you feel that there was a higher life than this daily one, and a brighter world than that you see; or encouraged you, or sobered you, or opened a way to the inquiring, or soothed the perplexed; if what he has said or done has ever made you take interest in him, and feel well inclined towards him; remember such a one in time to come, though you hear him not, and pray for him, that in all things he may know God's will, and at all times he may be ready to fulfil it.[48]

IX

One by one, Newman's ties with the Anglican church were parting. He had removed himself from Oxford; he had resigned St. Mary's; friends who would not follow his now apparent course began to withdraw from him. Most important, he had now grasped the intellectual principle that was to resolve his final doubts and carry him into the Roman church—the principle of the development, the historical evolution, of doctrine. Purgatory, transubstantiation, the worship of saints—these and other Roman doctrines and practices were surely not elaborated in the primitive church. But might they not be necessary developments from the primitive doctrine? Assuming a divine guidance, might not the Roman church, in a truly historical sense, be closer to the primitive church than was the Anglican?

And thus I was led on to a further consideration. I saw that the principle of development not only accounted for certain facts, but was in itself a remarkable philosophical phenomenon, giving a character to the whole course of Christian thought. It was discernible from the first years of the Catholic teaching up to the present day, and gave to that teaching a unity and individuality. It served as a sort of test, which the Anglican could not exhibit, that modern Rome was in truth ancient Antioch, Alexandria, and Constantinople, just as a mathematical curve has its own law and expression.

And thus again I was led on to examine more attentively what I doubt not was in my thoughts long before, viz. the concatenation of argument by which the mind ascends from its first to its final religious idea; and I came to the conclusion that there was no medium, in true philosophy, between Atheism and Catholicity, and that a perfectly consistent mind, under those circumstances in which it finds itself here below, must embrace either the one or the other. And I hold this still: I am a Catholic by virtue of my believing in a God; and if I am asked why I believe in a God, I answer that it is because I believe in myself, for I feel it impossible to believe in my own existence (and of that fact I am quite sure) without believing also in the existence of Him, who lives as a Personal, All-seeing, All-judging Being in my conscience. Now, I dare say, I have not expressed myself with philosophical correctness, because I have not given myself to the study of what others have said on the subject; but I think I have a strong true meaning in what I say which will stand examination.

Moreover, I came to the conclusion which I have been stating, on reasoning of the same nature, as that which I had adopted on the subject of development of doctrine. The fact of the operation from first to last of that principle of development is an argument in favour of the identity of Roman and Primitive Christianity; but as there is a law which acts upon the subject-matter of dogmatic theology, so is there a law in the matter of religious faith. In the third part of this narrative I spoke of certitude as the consequence, divinely intended and enjoined upon us, of the accumulative force of certain given reasons which, taken one by one, were only probabilities. Let it be recollected that I am historically relating my state of mind, at the period of my life which I am surveying. I am not speaking theologically, nor have I any intention of going into controversy, or of defending myself; but speaking historically of what I held in 1843–4, I say, that I believed in a God on a ground of probability, that I believed in Christianity on a probability, and that I believed in Catholicism on a probability, and that all three were about the same kind of probability, a cumulative, a transcendent probability, but still probability; inasmuch as He who made us, has so willed that in mathematics indeed we arrive at certitude by rigid demonstration, but in religious inquiry we arrive at certitude by accumulated probabilities,—inasmuch as He who has willed that we should so act, cooperates with us in our acting, and thereby bestows on us a certitude which rises higher than the logical force of our conclusions. And thus I came to see clearly, and to have a satisfaction in seeing, that, in being led on into the Church of Rome, I was proceeding, not by any secondary grounds of reason, or by controversial points in detail but was protected and justified, even in the use of those secondary arguments, by a great and broad principle. But, let it be observed, that I am stating a matter of fact, not defending it; and if any Catholic says in consequence that I have been converted in a wrong way, I cannot help that now.[49]

≈§Newman's course was now a lonely one. Two letters to James Mozley suggest the painful estrangement between these friends§≈.

≈§On November 23, 1843, from Oriel§≈ : Will you dine here in the Common-Room at half-past 5 on Monday? I have nothing to tempt you, but I want to see your face: it is so long since we met.

You cannot tell how much I have been anxious about you, as to what you heard not so long ago. After your father and mother and my own aunt, you have been uppermost in my thoughts. I fear your so-called indisposition is really mental disgust—nothing bodily. Gladly, my dear James, would I say anything to relieve you, but I can only say I wish to do so, if there is any good in that; nothing more.

For myself, I have so long divested myself of hopes for the future, if I ever had them, that I seem to have nothing to grieve for, except the grief of others.[50]

On November 24: Your note made my heart ache—it is the simple truth, so I may say it. I don't know whether it will comfort you, yet I hope it may (as *omne ignotum pro magnifico*), to tell you that my present feelings are not new, nor have they come upon me gradually, nor from disgust and despair, nor have they been indulged.

Last summer four years (1839) it came strongly upon me, from reading first the Monophysite controversy, and then turning to the Donatist, that we were external to the Catholic Church. I have never got over this. I did not, however, yield to it at all, but wrote an article in the 'British Critic' on the Catholicity of the English Church, which had the effect of quieting me for two years. Since this time two years the feeling has revived and gradually strengthened. I have all along gone against it and think I ought to do so still. I am now publishing sermons, which speak more confidently about our position than I inwardly feel, but I think it right and do not care for seeming inconsistent.

I trust you may quite rely on my not admitting despair or disgust, or giving way to feelings *which I wish otherwise*, though, from the experience of the last four years, I do not think they are likely to be otherwise.[51]

A note to John Bowden is dated February 21, 1844: Half-past 10 A.M. I am just up, having a bad cold; the like necessity has not happened to me (except twice in January) in my memory. This winter has been very trying here. But you may think you have been in my thoughts long before rising—of course you are continually, as you well know. I could not come to see you, there were so many difficulties in the way, and (though I shall pain you by saying so)

I am not worthy of friends. With my opinions, to the full of which I dare not confess, I feel like a guilty person with others, though I trust I am not so. People kindly think that I have much to bear externally—disappointment, slander, &c. No, I have nothing to bear but the anxiety which I feel for my friends' anxiety for me, and perplexity.[52]

Lonely and melancholy, he wrote to Jemima on August 13, 1844: I do fancy I am getting changed. I go into Oxford, and find myself out of place. Everything seems to say to me, 'This is not your home.' The college seems strange to me, and even the college servants seem to look as if I were getting strange to them. I cannot tell whether it is fancy or not, but to myself I seem changing. I am so much more easily touched than I used to be. Reading St. Wolstan's Life just now almost brought tears to my eyes. What a very mysterious thing the mind is! Yet nothing that my feelings suggest to me is different from what has been engraven more or less strongly on my reason long ago.[53]

To Jemima on November 24: I have gone through a great deal of pain, and have been very much cut up. The one predominant distress upon me has been this unsettlement of mind I am causing. This is a thing that has haunted me day by day. And for days I had a literal pain in and about my heart, which I suppose at any moment I could bring on again. I have been overworked lately. The translation of St. Athanasius is, I am glad to say, just coming to an end, and I shall (so be it) relax. I suppose I need it. This has been a very trying year.

Besides the pain of unsettling people, of course I feel the loss I am undergoing in the good opinion of my friends and well-wishers, though I can't tell how much I feel this. It is the shock, surprise, terror, forlornness, disgust, scepticism to which I am giving rise; the differences of opinion, division of families—all this it is that makes my heart ache.

I cannot make out that I have any motive but a sense of indefinite risk to my soul in remaining where I am. A clear conviction of the substantial identity of Christianity and the Roman system has now been on my mind for a full three years. It is more than five years since the conviction first came on me, though I struggled against it and overcame it. I believe all my feelings and wishes are against

change. I have nothing to draw me elsewhere. I hardly ever was at a
Roman service; even abroad I knew no Roman Catholics. I have no
sympathies with them as a party. I am giving up everything. I am
not conscious of any resentment, disgust, or the like, to repel me
from my present position; and I have no dreams whatever—far from
it indeed. I seem to be throwing myself away.

Unless something occurs which I cannot anticipate I have no intention of any early step even now. But I cannot but think—though
I can no more realise it than being made Dean of Ch. Ch. or Bishop
of Durham—that some day it will be, and at a definite distance of
time. As far as I can make out I am in the state of mind which
divines call *indifferentia*, inculcating it as a duty to be set on nothing,
but to be willing to take whatever Providence wills. How *can* I at my
age and with my past trials be set upon nothing? I really don't think
I am. What keeps me here is the desire of giving every chance for
finding out if I am under the power of a delusion. Various persons
have sent me very kind letters, and I really trust that many are
bearing me in mind in their prayers.[54]

*A final resolution seemed near in the spring of 1845. Dis-
traught, Jemima wrote to him on March 13*: You imagine rightly
in thinking the communication at the end of your letter would give
me a great deal of pain. I can think of nothing else since, and yet
seem to be without the power of writing to you. Yet I can hardly
say why it is so, for I am far from taken by surprise; indeed, I have
been dreading to hear something of this sort for some time past. You
have sufficiently warned me of it. Yet I have so much sanguineness in
my composition that I always hope the worst misfortunes may be
averted till they are irremediable. And what can be worse than this?
It is like hearing that some dear friend must die. I cannot shut my
eyes to this overpowering event that threatens any longer. What the
consequences may be I know not. O dear John, can you have thought
long enough before deciding on a step which, with its probable effects,
must plunge so many into confusion and dismay? I know what you
will answer—that nothing but the risk of personal salvation would
lead you to it; and I quite believe it. I know you have all along had
the greatest regard for others, and acted upon it for some time past.
But think what must be our feelings who cannot entertain your view,
but can only deplore it as a grievous mistake! And I feel bitterly
how many good sort of people would not do you justice, but judge

you very hardly indeed. It is a real pain and grief to think of you as severed from us, as it were, by your own sentence. I am much afraid, dear John, you may be taken by surprise by what I say, and expect I shall receive this event more easily. Indeed I cannot; it is to me the great proof of the badness of this world and the unfortunate times we live in, that such a one as you should take the line you have taken. Pray excuse the incoherence of this letter. I am afraid it is very strange, and does not express one small portion of my feelings. Our poor distracted Church seems to me in pieces, and there is no one to help her, and her children's sympathies seem all drawn off another way. And how sad it is to me that I cannot say these things to you without your thinking me in error and in the wrong way, and not to have found the true way! Is there not enough in the world to make one weary of it, to all who try to see things as they really are? I am so afraid I have said wrong things, as well as not said what I intended; but I am really writing in great trouble and discomfort. Pray forgive me if I have not been as considerate as I ought to be, and wish earnestly to be, for I know your trial must be great indeed.[55]

Newman replied on March 15: I have just received your very painful letter, and wish I saw any way of making things easier to you or to myself.

If I went by what I wished, I should complete my seven years of waiting. Surely more than this, or as much, cannot be expected of me—cannot be right in me to give at my age. How life is going! I see men dying who were boys, almost children, when I was born. Pass a very few years, and I am an old man. What means of judging can I have more than I have? What maturity of mind am I to expect? If I am right to move at all, surely it is high time not to delay about it longer. Let me give my strength to the work, not my weakness— years in which I can profit the cause which calls me, not the dregs of life. Is it not like a death-bed repentance to put off what one feels one ought to do?

As to my convictions, I can but say what I have told you already, that I cannot at all make out *why* I should determine on moving, except as thinking I should offend God by not doing so. I cannot make out what I am *at* except on this supposition. At my time of life men love ease. I love ease myself. I am giving up a maintenance [his Oriel fellowship] involving no duties, and adequate to all my wants. What in the world am I doing this for (I ask *myself* this), except that I think I am called to do so? I am making a large income by my sermons. I am, to say the very least, risking this; the chance is that my sermons will have no further sale at all. I have a good name with many; I am deliberately sacrificing it. I have a bad name with more; I am fulfilling all their worst wishes, and giving them their most coveted triumph. I am distressing all I love, unsettling all I have instructed or aided. I am going to those whom I do not know, and of whom I expect very little. I am making myself an outcast, and that at my age. Oh, what can it be but a stern necessity which causes this?

Pity me, my dear Jemima.[56]

The final move was not made until the fall. On October 8 he addressed similar notes to Jemima and a number of friends.

My dear Jemima,—I must tell you what will pain you greatly, but I will make it as short as you would wish me to do.

This night Father Dominic, the Passionist, sleeps here. He does not know of my intention, but I shall ask him to receive me into what I believe to be the One Fold of the Redeemer.

This will not go till all is over.[57]

The troubled pilgrimage was ended. Doubts were finally at rest, uncertainty and hesitation finished. Newman was about to embrace a new life, and must take leave of the old.

I left Oxford for good on Monday, February 23, 1846. On the Saturday and Sunday before, I was in my House at Littlemore simply by myself, as I had been for the first day or two when I had originally taken possession of it. I slept on Sunday night at my dear friend's, Mr. Johnson's, at the Observatory. Various friends came to see the last of me; Mr. Copeland, Mr. Church, Mr. Buckle, Mr. Pattison, and Mr. Lewis. Dr. Pusey too came to take leave of me; and I called on Dr. Ogle, one of my very oldest friends, for he was my private Tutor, when I was an Undergraduate. In him I took leave of my first College, Trinity, which was so dear to me, and which held on its foundation so many who have been kind to me both when I was a boy, and all through my Oxford life. Trinity had never been unkind to me. There used to be much snapdragon growing on the walls opposite my freshman's rooms there, and I had for years taken it as the emblem of my own perpetual residence even unto death in my University.

On the morning of the 23rd I left the Observatory. I have never seen Oxford since, excepting its spires, as they are seen from the railway.[58]

CHAPTER 3

Elizabeth Barrett Browning

---------- ❊ ----------

*"None are so bold as the timid, when
they are fairly roused"*

I

I have lived only inwardly; or with *sorrow*, for a strong emotion, *Elizabeth Barrett wrote to Robert Browning*. Before this seclusion of my illness, I was secluded still, and there are few of the youngest women in the world who have not seen more, heard more, known more, of society, than I, who am scarcely to be called young now. I grew up in the country—had no social opportunities, had my heart in books and poetry, and my experience in reveries. My sympathies drooped towards the ground like an untrained honeysuckle—and but for *one*, in my own house—but of this I cannot speak. It was a lonely life, growing green like the grass around it. Books and dreams were what I lived in—and domestic life only seemed to buzz gently around, like the bees about the grass. And so time passed, and passed—and afterwards, when my illness came and I seemed to stand at the edge of the world with all done,

139

and no prospect (as appeared at one time) of ever passing the threshold of one room again; why then, I turned to thinking with some bitterness (after the greatest sorrow of my life had given me room and time to breathe) that I had stood blind in this temple I was about to leave—that I had seen no Human nature, that my brothers and sisters of the earth were *names* to me, that I had beheld no great mountain or river, nothing in fact. I was as a man dying who had not read Shakespeare, and it was too late! do you understand? And do you also know what a disadvantage this ignorance is to my art? Why, if I live on and yet do not escape from this seclusion, do you not perceive that I labour under signal disadvantages —that I am, in a manner, as a *blind poet?* Certainly, there is a compensation to a degree. I have had much of the inner life, and from the habit of self-consciousness and self-analysis, I make great guesses at Human nature in the main. But how willingly I would as a poet exchange some of this lumbering, ponderous, helpless knowledge of books, for some experience of life and man.[1]

II

From the tightly closed window of her room at the back of the house, Elizabeth Barrett could look out in the winter of 1845 upon the rooftops and chimneys of the other substantial houses that lined Wimpole Street. That constricted view and the walls of the room had been for more than three years the physical boundaries of her world, even while her fame as a poet spread through England and to America. There, an invalid and timid recluse, she passed her quiet days, receiving a few close friends, diverted occasionally by her younger brothers and sisters, visited briefly in the evenings by her affectionate but sternly authoritarian father. Always frail and sickly, she had been prostrated by a serious illness in 1838 and by the death two years later of a cherished brother. Now, at 39, her life seemed over, the future promising at best years of sheltered seclusion and absolute dependence.

Into that sealed room on January 10, 1845, like a gust of fresh spring air, came a letter from a fellow poet. Robert Browning, six years her junior, had no comparable reputation. Only a small circle of admirers discerned in Paracelsus *and his other early poems and plays the emergence of a dramatic poet of the first rank, and he was reduced to publishing his current work in a series of pamphlets, the*

Bells and Pomegranates, *paid for by his father. But Elizabeth Bar-rett was one of that small circle. Browning's portrait, sweetly, darkly handsome, hung in her room beside those of Wordsworth and Tenny-son. In "Lady Geraldine's Courtship," contained in her recently pub-lished two volumes of* Poems, *she had mentioned his name with per-ceptive praise. Delighted by this rare evidence of appreciation, and encouraged to write by a mutual friend, Browning poured out his own admiration for Elizabeth's poetry.*

I love your verses with all my heart, dear Miss Barrett,—and this is no off-hand complimentary letter that I shall write,—what-ever else, no prompt matter-of-course recognition of your genius, and there a graceful and natural end of the thing. Since the day last week when I first read your poems, I quite laugh to remember how I have been turning and turning again in my mind what I should be able to tell you of their effect upon me, for in the first flush of delight I thought I would this once get out of my habit of purely passive enjoyment, when I do really enjoy, and thoroughly justify my admiration—perhaps even, as a loyal fellow-craftsman should, try and find fault and do you some little good to be proud of hereafter!—but nothing comes of it all—so into me has it gone, and part of me has it become, this great living poetry of yours, not a flower of which but took root and grew— Oh, how different that is from lying to be dried and pressed flat, and prized highly, and put in a book with a proper account at top and bottom, and shut up and put away . . . and the book called a 'Flora,' besides! After all, I need not give up the thought of doing that, too, in time; be-cause even now, talking with whoever is worthy, I can give a reason for my faith in one and another excellence, the fresh strange music, the affluent language, the exquisite pathos and true new brave thought; but in this addressing myself to you—your own self, and for the first time, my feeling rises altogether. I do, as I say, love these books with all my heart—and I love you too. Do you know I was once not very far from seeing—really seeing you? Mr. Kenyon said to me one morning 'Would you like to see Miss Barrett?' then he went to announce me,—then he returned . . . you were too un-well, and now it is years ago, and I feel as at some untoward passage in my travels, as if I had been close, so close, to some world's wonder in chapel or crypt, only a screen to push and I might have entered, but there was some slight, so it now seems, slight and just sufficient bar to admission, and the half-opened door shut, and I went home my thousands of miles, and the sight was never to be? [2]

❧"I had a letter from Browning the poet last night, which threw me into ecstasies," Elizabeth wrote to a correspondent; "—Browning, the author of 'Paracelsus,' and king of the mystics." Eagerly she replied to Browning's letter the next day❧.

I thank you, dear Mr. Browning, from the bottom of my heart. You meant to give me pleasure by your letter—and even if the object had not been answered, I ought still to thank you. But it is thoroughly answered. Such a letter from such a hand! Sympathy is dear—very dear to me: but the sympathy of a poet, and of such a poet, is the quintessence of sympathy to me! Will you take back my gratitude for it?—agreeing, too, that of all the commerce done in the world, from Tyre to Carthage, the exchange of sympathy for gratitude is the most princely thing!

For the rest you draw me on with your kindness. It is difficult to get rid of people when you once have given them too much pleasure —*that* is a fact, and we will not stop for the moral of it. What I was going to say—after a little natural hesitation—is, that if ever you emerge without inconvenient effort from your 'passive state,' and will *tell* me of such faults as rise to the surface and strike you as important in my poems, (for of course, I do not think of troubling you with criticism in detail) you will confer a lasting obligation on me, and one which I shall value so much, that I covet it at a distance. I do not pretend to any extraordinary meekness under criticism and it is possible enough that I might not be altogether obedient to yours. But with my high respect for your power in your Art and for your experience as an artist, it would be quite impossible for me to hear a general observation of yours on what appear to you my master-faults, without being the better for it hereafter in some way. I ask for only a sentence or two of general observation—and I do not ask even for *that*, so as to tease you—but in the humble, low voice, which is so excellent a thing in women—particularly when they go a-begging! The most frequent general criticism I receive, is, I think, upon the style, 'if I *would* but change my style'! But *that* is an objection (isn't it?) to the writer bodily? Buffon says, and every sincere writer must feel, that '*Le style c'est l'homme;*' a fact, however, scarcely calculated to lessen the objection with certain critics.

Is it indeed true that I was so near to the pleasure and honour of making your acquaintance? and can it be true that you look back upon the lost opportunity with any regret? *But*—you know—if you had entered the 'crypt,' you might have caught cold, or been tired to death, and *wished* yourself 'a thousand miles off;' which would have been worse than travelling them. It is not my interest, however, to put such thoughts in your head about its being 'all for the best;' and I would rather hope (as I do) that what I lost by one chance I may recover by some future one. Winters shut me up as they do dormouse's eyes; in the spring, *we shall see:* and I am so much better that I seem turning round to the outward world again. And in the meantime I have learnt to know your voice, not merely from the poetry but from the kindness in it. Mr. Kenyon often speaks of you—dear Mr. Kenyon!—who most unspeakably, or only speakably with tears in my eyes,—has been my friend and helper, and my book's friend and helper! critic and sympathiser, true friend of all hours! You know him well enough, I think, to understand that I must be grateful to him.

I am writing too much,—and notwithstanding that I am writing too much, I will write of one thing more. I will say that I am your debtor, not only for this cordial letter and for all the pleasure which came with it, but in other ways, and those the highest: and I will say that while I live to follow this divine art of poetry, in proportion to my love for it and my devotion to it, I must be a devout admirer and student of your works. This is in my heart to say to you—and I say it.[3]

From Browning, Monday, Jan. 13, 1845: I just shall say, in as few words as I can, that you make me very happy, and that, now the beginning is over, I dare say I shall do better, because my poor praise, number one, was nearly as felicitously brought out, as a certain tribute to no less a personage than Tasso, which I was amused with at Rome some weeks ago, in a neat pencilling on the plaister-wall by his tomb at Sant' Onofrio—'Alla cara memoria—di —(please fancy solemn interspaces and grave capital letters at the new lines) di—Torquato Tasso—il Dottore Bernardini—offriva— il seguente Carme—*O tu'*—and no more, the good man, it should seem, breaking down with the overload of love here! But my 'O tu'— was breathed out most sincerely, and now you have taken it in gracious part, the rest will come after. Only,—and which is why I

write now—it looks as if I have introduced some phrase or other
about 'your faults' so cleverly as to give exactly the opposite meaning to what I meant, which was, that in my first ardour I had thought
to tell you of *everything* which impressed me in your verses, down,
even, to whatever 'faults' I could find—a good earnest, when I had
got to *them*, that I had left out not much between—as if some Mr.
Fellows were to say, in the overflow of his first enthusiasm of rewarded adventure: 'I will describe you all the outer life and ways of
these Lycians, down to their very sandal-thongs,' whereto the be-
corresponded one rejoins—'Shall I get next week, then, your disserta-
tion on sandal-thongs'? Yes, and a little about the 'Olympian Horses,'
and God-charioteers as well!

What 'struck me as faults,' were not matters on the removal of
which, one was to have—poetry, or high poetry,—but the very
highest poetry, so I thought, and that, to universal recognition. For
myself, or any artist, in many of the cases there would be a positive
loss of time, peculiar artist's pleasure—for an instructed eye loves to
see where the brush has dipped twice in a lustrous colour, has lain in-
sistingly along a favourite outline, dwelt lovingly in a grand shadow;
for these 'too muches' for the everybody's picture are so many helps
to the making out the real painter's picture as he had it in his brain.
And all of the Titian's Naples Magdalen must have once been golden
in its degree to justify that heap of hair in her hands—the *only*
gold effected now!

But about this soon—for night is drawing on and I go out, yet
cannot, quiet at conscience, till I repeat (to *myself*, for I never said
it to you, I think) that your poetry must be, cannot but be, infinitely
more to me than mine to you—for you *do* what I always wanted,
hoped to do, and only seem now likely to do for the first time. You
speak out, *you*,—I only make men and women speak—give you truth
broken into prismatic hues, and fear the pure white light, even if it
is in me, but I am going to try; so it will be no small comfort to have
your company just now, seeing that when you have your men and
women aforesaid, you are busied with them, whereas it seems bleak,
melancholy work, this talking to the wind (for I have begun)—yet
I don't think I shall let *you* hear, after all, the savage things about
Popes and imaginative religions that I must say.

See how I go on and on to you, I who, whenever now and then
pulled, by the head and hair, into letter-writing, get sorrowfully on
for a line or two, as the cognate creature urged on by stick and

string, and then come down 'flop' upon the sweet haven of page one,
line last, as serene as the sleep of the virtuous! You will never more,
I hope, talk of 'the honour of my acquaintance,' but I will joyfully
wait for the delight of your friendship, and the spring, and my
Chapel-sight after all!⁴

№*From Elizabeth, Wednesday, Jan. 15, 1845* : The fault was
clearly with me and not with you.

When I had an Italian master, years ago, he told me that there
was an unpronounceable English word which absolutely expressed me,
and which he would say in his own tongue, as he could not in mine
—'*testa lunga.*' Of course, the signor meant *headlong!*—and now I
have had enough to tame me, and might be expected to stand still in
my stall. But you see I do not. Headlong I was at first, and headlong
I continue—precipitously rushing forward through all manner of
nettles and briars instead of keeping the path; guessing at the meaning of unknown words instead of looking into the dictionary—tearing
open letters, and never untying a string,—and expecting everything
to be done in a minute, and the thunder to be as quick as the lightning. And so, at your half word I flew at the whole one, with all its
possible consequences, and wrote what you read.

In art, however, I understand that it does not do to be headlong,
but patient and laborious—and there is a love strong enough, even
in me, to overcome nature. I apprehend what you mean in the criticism you just intimate, and shall turn it over and over in my mind
until I get practical good from it. What no mere critic sees, but
what you, an artist, know, is the difference between the thing desired
and the thing attained, between the idea in the writer's mind and the
εἴδωλον cast off in his work. All the effort—the quick'ning of the
breath and beating of the heart in pursuit, which is ruffling and injurious to the general effect of a composition; all which you call
'insistency,' and what many would call superfluity, and which *is* su-
perfluous in a sense—*you* can pardon, because you understand. The
great chasm between the thing I say, and the thing I would say, would
be quite dispiriting to me, in spite even of such kindnesses as yours,
if the desire did not master the despondency. 'Oh for a horse with
wings!' It is wrong of me to write so of myself—only you put your
finger on the root of a fault, which has, to my fancy, been a little
misapprehended. I do not *say everything I think* (as has been said

of me by master-critics) but I *take every means to say what I think,* which is different!—or I fancy so!

In one thing, however, you are wrong. Why should you deny the full measure of my delight and benefit from your writings? I could tell you why you should not. You have in your vision two worlds, or to use the language of the schools of the day, you are both subjective and objective in the habits of your mind. You can deal both with abstract thought and with human passion in the most passionate sense. Thus, you have an immense grasp in Art; and no one at all accustomed to consider the usual forms of it, could help regarding with reverence and gladness the gradual expansion of your powers. Then you are 'masculine' to the height—and I, as a woman, have studied some of your gestures of language and intonation wistfully, as a thing beyond me far! and the more admirable for being beyond.

But I break in on myself out of consideration for you. I might have done it, you will think, before. I vex your 'serene sleep of the virtuous' like a nightmare. Do not say 'No.' I am *sure* I do! As to the vain parlance of the world, I did not talk of the 'honour of your acquaintance' without a true sense of honour, indeed; but I shall willingly exchange it all (and *now*, if you please, at this moment, for fear of worldly mutabilities) for the 'delight of your friendship.'[5]

From Browning, Monday night, Jan. 27, 1845: Your books lie on my table here, at arm's length from me, in this old room where I sit all day: and when my head aches or wanders or strikes work, as it now or then will, I take my chance for either green-covered volume, as if it were so much fresh trefoil to feel in one's hands this winter-time,—and round I turn, and, putting a decisive elbow on three or four half-done-with 'Bells' of mine, read, read, read, and just as I have shut up the book and walked to the window, I recollect that you wanted me to find faults there, and that, in an unwise hour, I engaged to do so. Meantime, the days go by (the whitethroat is come and sings now) and as I would not have you 'look down on me from your white heights' as promise breaker, evader, or forgetter, if I could help: and as, if I am very candid and contrite, you may find it in your heart to write to me again—who knows?—I shall say at once that the said faults cannot be lost, must be *somewhere*, and shall be faithfully brought you back whenever they turn up,—as people tell one of missing matters. I am rather exacting, myself, with my own gentle audience, and get to say spiteful things about them when they

are backward in their dues of appreciation—but really, *really*—
could I be quite sure that anybody as good as—I must go on, I suppose, and say—as myself, even, were honestly to feel towards me as
I do, towards the writer of 'Bertha,' and the 'Drama,' and the
'Duchess,' and the 'Page,' and—the whole two volumes, I should be
paid after a fashion, I know.

See now, how, of that 'Friendship' you offer me (and here Juliet's
word rises to my lips)—I feel sure once and for ever. I have got
already, I see, into this little pet-handwriting of mine (not anyone
else's) which scratches on as if theatrical copyists (ah me!) and
BRADBURY AND EVANS' READER were not! But you shall get something better than this nonsense one day, if you will have patience
with me—hardly better, though, because this does me real good, gives
real relief, to write. After all, you know nothing, next to nothing of
me, and that stops me. Spring is to come, however!

If you hate writing to me as I hate writing to nearly everybody, I
pray you never write—if you do, as you say, care for anything I
have done. I will simply assure you, that meaning to begin work in
deep earnest, *begin* without affectation, God knows—I do not know
what will help me more than hearing from you,—and therefore, if
you do not so very much hate it, I know I *shall* hear from you—and
very little more about your 'tiring me.'[6]

From Elizabeth, Monday, Feb. 3, 1845: Why how could I
hate to write to you, dear Mr. Browning? Could you believe in such
a thing? If nobody likes writing to everybody (except such professional letter writers as you and I are *not*), yet everybody likes writing to somebody, and it would be strange and contradictory if I
were not always delighted to hear from *you* and to write to *you*, this
talking upon paper being as good a social pleasure as another, when
our means are somewhat straitened. As for me, I have done most of
my talking by post of late years—as people shut up in dungeons take
up with scrawling mottoes on the walls. Not that I write to many in
the way of regular correspondence, as our friend Mr. Horne predi-
cates of me in his romance (which is mere romancing!), but that there
are a few who will write and be written to by me without a sense of
injury. Dear Miss Mitford, for instance. You do not know her, I
think, personally, although she was the first to tell me (when I was
very ill and insensible to all the glories of the world except poetry)
of the grand scene in 'Pippa Passes.' *She* has filled a large drawer in

this room with delightful letters, heart-warm and soul-warm, . . . driftings of nature (if sunshine could drift like snow), and which, if they should ever fall the way of all writing, into print, would assume the folio shape as a matter of course, and take rank on the lowest shelf of libraries, with Benedictine editions of the Fathers, χ.τ.λ. I write this to you to show how I can have pleasure in letters, and never think them too long, nor too frequent, nor too illegible from being written in little 'pet hands.' I can read any MS. except the writing on the pyramids. And if you will only promise to treat me *en bon camarade*, without reference to the conventionalities of 'ladies and gentlemen,' taking no thought for your sentences (nor for mine), nor for your blots (nor for mine), nor for your blunt speaking (nor for mine), nor for your badd speling (nor for mine), and if you agree to send me a blotted thought whenever you are in the mind for it, and with as little ceremony and less legibility than you would think it necessary to employ towards your printer—why, *then*, I am ready to sign and seal the contract, and to rejoice in being 'articled' as your correspondent. Only *don't* let us have any constraint, any ceremony! *Don't* be civil to me when you feel rude,— nor loquacious when you incline to silence,—nor yielding in the manners when you are perverse in the mind. See how out of the world I am! Suffer me to profit by it in almost the only profitable circumstance, and let us rest from the bowing and the courtesying, you and I, on each side. You will find me an honest man on the whole, if rather hasty and prejudging, which is a different thing from prejudice at the worst. And we have great sympathies in common, and I am inclined to look up to you in many things, and to learn as much of everything as you will teach me. On the other hand you must prepare yourself to forbear and to forgive—will you? While I throw off the ceremony, I hold the faster to the kindness.[7]

III

§*A sudden warm day in February heralded the still-distant spring. "Wednesday morning—Spring!" Browning wrote at the head of his letter on February 26*: Real warm Spring, dear Miss Barrett, and the birds know it; and in Spring I shall see you, surely see you—for when did I once fail to get whatever I had set my heart upon? As I ask myself sometimes, with a strange fear.[8]

From Elizabeth, Thursday, Feb. 27, 1845: Yes, but, dear Mr. Browning, I want the spring according to the new 'style' (mine), and not the old one of you and the rest of the poets. To me unhappily, the snowdrop is much the same as the snow—it feels as cold underfoot—and I have grown sceptical about 'the voice of the turtle,' the east winds blow so loud. April is a Parthian with a dart, and May (at least the early part of it) a spy in the camp. *That* is my idea of what you call spring; mine, in the *new style!* A little later comes my spring; and indeed after such severe weather, from which I have just escaped with my life, I may thank it for coming at all. How happy you are, to be able to listen to the 'birds' without the commentary of the east wind, which, like other commentaries, spoils the music.[9]

From Browning, Saturday night, March 1, 1845: I seem to find of a sudden—surely I knew before—anyhow, I *do* find now, that with the octaves on octaves of quite new golden strings you enlarged the compass of my life's harp with, there is added, too, such a tragic chord, that which you touched, so gently, in the beginning of your letter I got this morning, 'just escaping' &c. But if my truest heart's wishes avail, as they have hitherto done, you shall laugh at East winds yet, as I do! See now, this sad feeling is so strange to me, that I must write it out, *must*, and you might give me great, the greatest pleasure for years and yet find me as passive as a stone used to wine libations, and as ready in expressing my sense of them, but when I am pained, I find the old theory of the uselessness of communicating the circumstances of it, singularly untenable. I have been 'spoiled' in this world—to such an extent, indeed, that I often *reason* out—make clear to myself—that I might very properly, so far as myself am concerned, take any step that would peril the whole of my future happiness—because the past is gained, secure, and on record; and, though not another of the old days should dawn on me, I shall not have lost my life, no! Out of all which you are—please—to make a sort of sense, if you can, so as to express that I have been deeply struck to find a new real unmistakable sorrow along with these as real but not so new joys you have given me.[10]

From Elizabeth, Wednesday, March 5, 1845: But I did not mean to strike a 'tragic chord;' indeed I did not! Sometimes one's melancholy will be uppermost and sometimes one's mirth,—the world goes round, you know—and I suppose that in that letter of mine the melancholy took the turn. As to 'escaping with my life,' it was just a phrase—at least it did not signify more than that the sense of mortality, and discomfort of it, is peculiarly strong with me when east winds are blowing and waters freezing. For the rest, I am *essentially better*, and have been for several winters; and I feel as if it were intended for me to live and not die, and I am reconciled to the feeling. Yes! I am satisfied to 'take up' with the blind hopes again, and have them in the house with me, for all that I sit by the window.

You are not to think—whatever I may have written or implied— that I lean either to the philosophy or affectation which beholds the world through darkness instead of light, and speaks of it wailingly. Now, may God forbid that it should be so with me. I am not desponding by nature, and after a course of bitter mental discipline and long bodily seclusion, I come out with two learnt lessons (as I sometimes say and oftener feel),—the wisdom of cheerfulness—and the duty of social intercourse. Anguish has instructed me in joy, and solitude in society; it has been a wholesome and not unnatural reaction. And altogether, I may say that the earth looks the brighter to me in proportion to my own deprivations. The laburnum trees and rose trees are plucked up by the roots—but the sunshine is in their places, and the root of the sunshine is above the storms. What we call Life is a condition of the soul, and the soul must improve in happiness and wisdom, except by its own fault. These tears in our eyes, these faintings of the flesh, will not hinder such improvement.

And I do like to hear testimonies like yours, to *happiness*, and I feel it to be a testimony of a higher sort than the obvious one. Still, it is obvious too that you have been spared, up to this time, the great natural afflictions, against which we are nearly all called, sooner or later, to struggle and wrestle—or your step would not be 'on the stair' quite so lightly. And so, we turn to you, dear Mr. Browning, for comfort and gentle spiriting! Remember that as you owe your unscathed joy to God, you should pay it back to His world. And I thank you for some of it already.

Also, writing as from friend to friend—as you say rightly that we are—I ought to confess that of one class of griefs (which has been called too the bitterest), I know as little as you. The cruelty of the world, and the treason of it—the unworthiness of the dearest; of these griefs I have scanty knowledge. It seems to me from my personal experience that there is kindness everywhere in different proportions,

and more goodness and tenderheartedness than we read of in the mor-
alists. People have been kind to *me*, even without understanding me,
and pitiful to me, without approving of me:—nay, have not the very
critics tamed their beardom for me, and roared delicately as sucking
doves, on behalf of me? I have no harm to say of your world, though
I am not of it, as you see. And I have the cream of it in your friendship, and a little more, and I do not envy much the milkers of the
cows.

How kind you are!—how kindly and gently you speak to me!
Some things you say are very touching, and some, surprising; and
although I am aware that you unconsciously exaggerate what I can
be to you, yet it is delightful to be broad awake and think of you as
my friend.[11]

From Elizabeth, Thursday, March 20, 1845: Whenever I
delay to write to you, dear Mr. Browning, it is not, be sure, that I
take my 'own good time,' but submit to my own bad time. It was kind
of you to wish to know how I was, and not unkind of me to suspend
my answer to your question—for indeed I have not been very well,
nor have had much heart for saying so. This implacable weather!
this east wind that seems to blow through the sun and moon! who can
be well in such a wind? Yet for me, I should not grumble. There has
been nothing very bad the matter with me, as there used to be—I
only grow weaker than usual, and learn my lesson of being mortal, in
a corner—and then all this must end! April is coming. There will be
both a May and a June if we live to see such things, and perhaps,
after all, we may. And as to seeing *you* besides, I observe that you
distrust me, and that perhaps you penetrate my morbidity and guess
how when the moment comes to see a living human face to which I
am not accustomed, I shrink and grow pale in the spirit. Do you?
You are learned in human nature, and you know the consequences of
leading such a secluded life as mine—notwithstanding all my fine
philosophy about social duties and the like—well—if you have such
knowledge or if you have it not, I cannot say, but I do say that I will
indeed see you when the warm weather has revived me a little, and
put the earth 'to rights' again so as to make pleasures of the sort
possible. For if you think that I shall not *like* to see you, you are
wrong, for all your learning. But I shall be afraid of you at first—
though I am not, in writing thus. You are Paracelsus, and I am a

recluse, with nerves that have been all broken on the rack, and now hang loosely, quivering at a step and breath.[12]

"Surely," Browning implored on May 3, "the wind that sets my chestnut-tree dancing, all its baby-cone-blossoms, green now, rocking like fairly castles on a hill in an earthquake,—that is South West, surely!" But Elizabeth hesitated still.

From Elizabeth, Tuesday, May 6, 1845: Shall I have the courage to see you soon, I wonder! If you ask me, I must ask myself. But oh, this make-believe May—it can't be May after all! If a southwest wind sate in your chestnut tree, it was but for a few hours—the east wind 'came up this way' by the earliest opportunity of succession. As the old 'mysteries' showed 'Beelzebub with a bearde,' even so has the east wind had a 'bearde' of late, in a full growth of bristling exaggerations—the English spring-winds have excelled themselves in evil this year; and I have not been down stairs yet.—*But* I am certainly stronger and better than I was—that is undeniable —and I *shall* be better still. You are not going away soon—are you? In the meantime you do not know what it is to be . . . a little afraid of Paracelsus.[13]

From Browning, Tuesday morning, May 13, 1845: 'If you ask me, I must ask myself'—that is, when I am to see you—I will *never* ask you! You do *not* know what I shall estimate that permission at,—nor do I, quite—but you do—do not you? know so much of me as to make my 'asking' worse than a form—I do not 'ask' you to write to me—not *directly* ask, at least.

I will tell you—I ask you *not* to see me so long as you are unwell, or mistrustful of—

No, no, that is being too grand! Do see me when you can, and let me not be only writing myself, Yours, R.B.[14]

From Elizabeth, Thursday, May 15, 1845: But how 'mistrustfulness'? And how 'that way'? What have I said or done, *I*, who am not apt to be mistrustful of anybody and should be a miraculous monster if I began with *you!* What can I have said, I say to myself again and again.

One thing, at any rate, I have done, 'that way' or this way! I have made what is vulgarly called a 'piece of work' about little; or seemed to make it. Forgive me. I am shy by nature:—and by position and experience, . . . by having had my nerves shaken to excess, and by leading a life of such seclusion, . . . by these things together and by others besides, I have appeared shy and ungrateful to you. Only not mistrustful. You could not mean to judge me so. Mistrustful people do not write as I write, surely! for wasn't it a Richelieu or Mazarin (or who?) who said that with five lines from anyone's hand, he could take off his head for a corollary? I think so.

Well!—but this is to prove that I am not mistrustful, and to say, that if you care to come to see me you can come; and that it is my gain (as I feel it to be) and not yours, whenever you do come. You will not talk of having come afterwards I know, because although I am 'fast bound' to see one or two persons this summer (besides your-self, whom I receive of choice and willingly) I *cannot* admit visitors in a general way—and putting the question of health aside, it would be unbecoming to lie here on the sofa and make a company-show of an infirmity, and hold a beggar's hat for sympathy. I should blame it in another woman—and the sense of it has had its weight with me sometimes.

For the rest, . . . when you write 'that *I* do not know how you would value, &c. *nor yourself quite*,' you touch very accurately on the truth, . . . and *so* accurately in the last clause, that to read it, made me smile 'tant bien que mal.' Certainly you cannot 'quite know,' or know at all, whether the least straw of pleasure can go to you from knowing me otherwise than on this paper—and I, for my part, 'quite know' my own honest impression, dear Mr. Browning, that none is likely to go to you. There is nothing to see in me; nor to hear in me —I never learnt to talk as you do in London; although I can admire that brightness of carved speech in Mr. Kenyon and others. If my poetry is worth anything to any eye, it is the flower of me. I have lived most and been most happy in it, and so it has all my colours; the rest of me is nothing but a root, fit for the ground and the dark. And if I write all this egotism, . . . it is for shame; and because I feel ashamed of having made a fuss about what is not worth it; and because you are extravagant in caring so for a permission, which will be nothing to you afterwards. Not that I am not touched by your caring so at all! I am deeply touched now; and presently, . . . I shall understand. Come then. There will be truth and simplicity for you in any case; and a friend. And do not answer this—I do not write it as a fly trap for compliments. Your spider would scorn me for it too much.[15]

&*At three o'clock on Tuesday, May 20, Browning called at No. 50 Wimpole Street and was led up to Elizabeth's room on the second floor. His visit lasted an hour and a half*&.

&*That night he wrote to her in delicious anxiety*& : I trust to you for a true account of how you are—if tired, if not tired, if I did wrong in any thing,—or, if you please, *right* in any thing—(only, not one more word about my 'kindness,' which, to get done with, I will grant is exceptive)—but, let us so arrange matters if possible, —and why should it not be—that my great happiness, such as it will be if I see you, as this morning, from time to time, may be obtained at the cost of as little inconvenience to you as we can contrive. For an instance—just what strikes me—they all say here I speak very loud—(a trick caught from having often to talk with a deaf relative of mine). And did I stay too long?

I will tell *you* unhesitatingly of such 'corrigenda'—nay, I will again say, do not humiliate me—*do not* again,—by calling me 'kind' in that way.

I am proud and happy in your friendship—now and ever. May God bless you![16]

&*From Elizabeth, Wednesday morning, May 21, 1845*& : Indeed there was nothing wrong—how could there be? And there was everything right—as how should there not be? And as for the 'loud speaking,' I did not hear any—and, instead of being worse, I ought to be better for what was certainly (to speak it, or be silent of it,) happiness and honour to me yesterday.

Which reminds me to observe that you are so restricting our vocabulary, as to be ominous of silence in a full sense, presently. First, one word is not to be spoken—and then, another is not. And why? Why deny me the use of such words as have natural feelings belonging to them—and how can the use of such be 'humiliating' to *you?* If my heart were open to you, you could see nothing offensive to you in any thought there or trace of thought that has been there —but it is hard for you to understand, with all your psychology (and to be reminded of it I have just been looking at the preface of some poems by some Mr. Gurney where he speaks of 'the reflective wisdom of a Wordsworth and the profound psychological utterances of a Browning') it is hard for you to understand what my mental position is after the peculiar experience I have suffered, and what τί ἐμοὶ καὶ σοί a sort of feeling is irrepressible from me to you, when, from the height of your brilliant happy sphere, you ask, as you did ask, for personal intercourse with me. What words but 'kindness' . . . but 'gratitude'—but I will not in any case be *un*kind and *un*grateful, and do what is displeasing to you. And let us both leave the subject with the words—because we perceive in it from different points of view; we stand on the black and white sides of the shield; and there is no coming to a conclusion.

But you will come really on Tuesday—and again, when you like and can together—and it will not be more 'inconvenient' to me to be pleased, I suppose, than it is to people in general—will it, do you think? Ah—how you misjudge! Why it must obviously and naturally be delightful to me to receive you here when you like to come, and it cannot be necessary for me to say so in set words.[17]

Browning's natural exuberance could not now be checked. He had gone to Wimpole Street prepared to fall in love with the writer of the poems and letters he already loved, and he had done so promptly. On May 21, in a letter later destroyed, he declared his love to Elizabeth.

From Elizabeth, Friday evening, May 23, 1845: I intended to write to you last night and this morning, and could not,—you do not know what pain you give me in speaking so wildly. And if I disobey you, my dear friend, in speaking, (I for my part) of your wild speaking, I do it, not to displease you, but to be in my own eyes, and before God, a little more worthy, or less unworthy, of a generosity from which I recoil by instinct and at the first glance, yet conclusively; and because my silence would be the most disloyal of all means of expression, in reference to it. Listen to me then in this. You have said some intemperate things . . . fancies,—which you will not say over again, nor unsay, but *forget at once*, and *for ever, having said at all;* and which (so) will die out between *you and me alone*, like a misprint between you and the printer. And this you will do *for my sake* who am your friend (and you have none truer)—and this I ask, because it is a condition necessary to our future liberty of intercourse. You remember—surely you do—that I am in the most excep-

tional of positions; and that, just *because of it*, I am able to receive
you as I did on Tuesday; and that, for me to listen to 'unconscious
exaggerations,' is as unbecoming to the humilities of my position, as
unpropitious (which is of more consequence) to the prosperities of
yours. Now, if there should be one word of answer attempted to this;
or of reference; *I must not . . . I will not see you again*—and you
will justify me later in your heart. So for my sake you will not say
it—I think you will not—and spare me the sadness of having to
break through an intercourse just as it is promising pleasure to me;
to me who have so many sadnesses and so few pleasures. You will!—
and I need not be uneasy—and I shall owe you that tranquillity, as
one gift of many. For, that I have much to receive from you in all
the free gifts of thinking, teaching, master-spirits, . . . *that*, I
know!—it is my own praise that I appreciate you, as none can
more. Your influence and help in poetry will be full of good and
gladness to me—for with many to love me in this house, there is no
one to judge me . . . *now*. Your friendship and sympathy will be
dear and precious to me all my life, if you indeed leave them with me
so long or so little. Your mistakes in me . . . which *I* cannot mistake
(—and which have humbled me by too much honouring—)I put away
gently, and with grateful tears in my eyes; because *all that hail* will
beat down and spoil crowns, as well as 'blossoms.'[18]

⮕§*Alarmed at Elizabeth's reaction to his declaration, Browning
labored lengthily, clumsily, to explain it away. From Browning, Saturday morning, May 24, 1845*§⮕ : Don't you remember I told you,
once on a time, that you 'knew nothing of me'? whereat you de-
murred—but I meant what I said, and knew it was so. To be grand
in a simile, for every poor speck of a Vesuvius or a Stromboli in my
microcosm there are huge layers of ice and pits of black cold water
—and I make the most of my two or three fire-eyes, because I know
by experience, alas, how these tend to extinction—and the ice grows
and grows—still this last is true part of me, most characteristic
part, *best* part perhaps, and I disown nothing—only,—when you
talked of '*knowing* me'! Still, I am utterly unused, of these late years
particularly, to dream of communicating anything about *that* to another person (all my writings are purely dramatic as I am always
anxious to say) that when I make never so little an attempt, no
wonder if I *bungle* notably—'language,' too, is an organ that never
studded this heavy heavy head of mine. Will you not think me very

brutal if I tell you I could almost smile at your misapprehension of
what I meant to write?—Yet I *will* tell you, because it will undo the
bad effect of my thoughtlessness, and at the same time exemplify the
point I have all along been honestly earnest to set you right upon
. . . my real inferiority to you; just that and no more. I wrote to
you, in an unwise moment, on the spur of being again 'thanked,' and,
unwisely writing just as if thinking to myself, said what must have
looked absurd enough as seen apart from the horrible counterbalanc-
ing never-to-be-written *rest of me*—by the side of which, could it be
written and put before you, my note would sink to its proper and
relative place, and become a mere 'thank you' for your good opinion
—which I assure you is far too generous—for I really believe you
to be my superior in many respects, and feel uncomfortable till *you*
see that, too—since I hope for your sympathy and assistance, and
frankness is everything in such a case. I do assure you, that had you
read my note, *only* having '*known*' so much of me as is implied in
having inspected, for instance, the contents, merely, of that fatal and
often-referred-to 'portfolio' [containing his unpublished poems]
there (*Dii meliora piis!*), you would see in it, (the note not the portfolio) the blandest utterance ever mild gentleman gave birth to. But
I forgot that one may make too much noise in a silent place by playing the few notes on the 'ear-piercing fife' which in Othello's regi-
mental band might have been thumped into decent subordination by
his 'spirit-stirring drum'—to say nothing of gong and ophicleide.
Will you forgive me, on promise to remember for the future, and be
more considerate? Not that you must too much despise me, neither;
nor, of all things, apprehend I am attitudinizing à la Byron, and giving you to understand unutterable somethings, longings for Lethe
and all that—far from it! I never committed murders, and sleep the
soundest of sleeps—but 'the heart is desperately wicked,' that is
true, and though I dare not say 'I know' mine, yet I have had signal
opportunities, I who began life from the beginning, and can forget
nothing (but names, and the date of the battle of Waterloo), and
have known good and wicked men and women, gentle and simple, shaking hands with Edmund Kean and Father Mathew, you and—Ottima!
Then, I had a certain faculty of self-consciousness, years and years
ago, at which John Mill wondered, and which ought to be improved
by this time, if constant use helps at all—and, meaning, on the whole,
to be a Poet, if not *the* Poet . . . for I am vain and ambitious some
nights,—I do myself justice, and dare call things by their names to

myself, and say boldly, this I love, this I hate, this I would do, this I would not do, under all kinds of circumstances,—and talking (thinking) in this style *to myself*, and beginning, however tremblingly, in spite of conviction, to write in this style *for myself*—on the top of the desk which contains my 'Songs of the Poets—no. 1 M.P.,' I wrote,—what you now forgive, I know! Because I am, from my heart, sorry that by a foolish fit of inconsideration I should have given pain for a minute to you, towards whom, on every account, I would rather soften and 'sleeken every word as to a bird.'[19]

From Elizabeth, Sunday, May 25, 1845 : I owe you the most humble of apologies dear Mr. Browning, for having spent so much solemnity on so simple a matter, and I hasten to pay it; confessing at the same time (as why should I not?) that I am quite as much ashamed of myself as I ought to be, which is not a little. You will find it difficult to believe me perhaps when I assure you that I never made such a mistake (I mean of overseriousness to indefinite compliments), no, never in my life before—indeed my sisters have often jested with me (in matters of which they were cognizant) on my supernatural indifference to the superlative degree in general, as if it meant nothing in grammar. I usually know well that 'boots' may be called for in this world of ours, just as you called for your's; and that to bring '*Bootes*,' were the vilest of mal-à-pro-posities. Also, I should have understood 'boots' where you wrote it, in the letter in question; if it had not been for *the relation of two things* in it—and now I perfectly seem to see *how* I mistook that relation; ('*seem to see*;' because I have not looked into the letter again since your last night's commentary, and will not—) inasmuch as I have observed before in my own mind, that a good deal of what is called obscurity in you, arises from a habit of very subtle association; so subtle, that you are probably unconscious of it, . . . and the effect of which is to throw together on the same level and in the same light, things of likeness and unlikeness—till the reader grows confused as I did, and takes one for another. I may say however, in a poor justice to myself, that I wrote what I wrote so unfortunately, *through reverence for you*, and not at all from vanity on my own account . . . although I do feel palpably while I write these words here and now, that I might as well leave them unwritten; for that no man of the world who ever lived in the world (not even *you*) could be expected to believe them, though said, sung, and sworn.

So I here enclose to you your letter back again, as you wisely desire; although you never could doubt, I hope, for a moment, of its safety with me in the completest of senses: and then, from the heights of my superior . . . stultity, and other qualities of the like order, . . . I venture to advise you . . . however (to speak of the letter critically, and as the dramatic composition it is) it is to be admitted to be very beautiful, and well worthy of the rest of its kin in the portfolio, . . . 'Lays of the Poets,' or otherwise, . . . I venture to advise you to burn it at once. And then, my dear friend, I ask you (having some claim) to burn at the same time the letter I was fortunate enough to write to you on Friday, and this present one—don't send them back to me; I hate to have letters sent back—but burn them for me and never mind Mephistopheles. After which friendly turn, you will do me the one last kindness of forgetting all this exquisite nonsense, and of refraining from mentioning it, by breath or pen, *to me or another*. Now I trust you so far:—you will put it with the date of the battle of Waterloo—and I, with every date in chronology; seeing that I can remember none of them. And we will shuffle the cards, and take patience, and begin the game again, if you please —and I shall bear in mind that you are a dramatic poet, which is not the same thing, by any means, with *us* of the primitive simplicities, who don't tread on cothurns nor shift the mask in the scene. And I will reverence you both as 'a poet' and as '*the* poet'; because it is no false 'ambition,' but a right you have—and one which those who live longest, will see justified to the uttermost.[20]

IV

Though Browning now became a regular weekly visitor, the correspondence with Elizabeth continued. They had far more to say to one another than could be communicated at their brief meetings. They wrote of work in progress, earnestly discussed the poet's craft, gossiped about literary celebrities. Elizabeth's letters, graceful, clear, sometimes intensely poignant, reflected that inner world in which she dwelt as much by choice as by necessity. Browning's, characteristically cheerful but at times tortuous and obscure, spoke more of the external world in which he moved easily, an attractive and sought-after young man. That a man of Browning's genius should prefer an invalid's room to that "brilliant happy sphere" seemed incredible to Elizabeth. In their interviews she drew her caution

*closely about her, remembering his dangerous impetuosity. Browning,
she believed, was enamored of an ideal and would soon tire of the
pallid reality. There was indeed a large measure of romanticism in
Browning's view of Elizabeth, but there was also an awareness of her
as a woman with qualities of mind and spirit akin to his own, com-
plementary to his own and therefore necessary to his wholeness.
Browning was truly in love. For the present he dutifully accepted the
role of friend that Elizabeth assigned him, but it was impossible in
his letters and his bearing to suppress altogether his feeling for her.
And almost against her will Elizabeth responded, gradually, as her
trust in him grew, opening to him compartments of her life and feeling that she had kept closed to others.*

*Elizabeth's health was a continuing source of anxiety to Browning.
He urged her to leave her room, to venture outside every fair summer
day. As her strength returned he encouraged her to think about
passing the next winter in Italy where she might completely recover
her health. Only gradually did Browning become aware that Elizabeth was a prisoner less of her illness than of her strange, dominating
father. A widower for nearly twenty years, Edward Barrett held his
adult children about him with a jealous passion bordering on the
pathological. He ruled his family absolutely, consulting no one, announcing his will abruptly, compelling obedience even by physical
force. In July he mentioned to an aunt sending Elizabeth to Malta
or Alexandria for the winter in the company of a brother and sister
—"though in every case, I suppose, I should not be much consulted,"
she acknowledged to Browning. But weeks passed, no decision was
forthcoming, and Mr. Barrett was unapproachable. Apparently he
was unwilling to disrupt his domestic arrangements on Elizabeth's
behalf. Helpless to appeal, Elizabeth faced another winter confined
to her room, where the cold and fog and the merciless east wind
would surely endanger the precarious gains of the past summer. Such
a paternal despotism, eccentric even by Victorian standards, was
incomprehensible to Browning.*

~§*From Elizabeth, Friday, Aug. 22, 1845*§~: You must not, you
must not, make an unjust opinion out of what I said to-day. I have
been uncomfortable since, lest you should—and perhaps it would
have been better if I had not said it apart from all context in that
way; only that you could not long be a friend of mine without knowing and seeing what so lies on the surface. But then, . . . as far as I

am concerned, . . . no one cares less for a 'will' than I do (and this
though I never had one, . . . in clear opposition to your theory
which holds generally nevertheless) for a will in the common things of
life. Every now and then there must of course be a crossing and
vexation—but in one's mere pleasures and fantasies, one would rather
be crossed and vexed a little than vex a person one loves . . . and it
is possible to get used to the harness and run easily in it at last; and
there is a side-world to hide one's thoughts in, and the word 'literature' has, with me, covered a good deal of liberty as you must see . . .
real liberty which is never enquired into—and it has happened
throughout my life by an accident (as far as anything is accident)
that my own sense of right and happiness on any important point of
overt action, has never run contrariwise to the way of obedience required of me . . . while in things not exactly *overt*, I and all of us are
apt to act sometimes up to the limit of our means of acting, with
shut doors and windows, and no waiting for cognisance or permission. Ah—and that last is the worst of it all perhaps! to be forced
into concealments from the heart naturally nearest to us; and forced
away from the natural source of counsel and strength!—and then,
the disingenuousness—the cowardice—the 'vices of slaves'!—and
everyone you see . . . all my brothers, . . . constrained *bodily* into
submission . . . apparent submission at least . . . by that worst and
most dishonouring of necessities, the necessity of *living*, everyone of
them all, except myself, being dependent in money-matters on the
inflexible will . . . do you see? But what you do *not* see, what you
cannot see, is the deep tender affection behind and below all those
patriarchal ideas of governing grown up children 'in the way they
must go!' and there never was (under the strata) a truer affection
in a father's heart . . . no, nor a worthier heart in itself . . . a heart
loyaller and purer, and more compelling to gratitude and reverence,
than his, as I see it! The evil is in the system—and he simply takes it
to be his duty to rule, and to make happy according to his own views
of the propriety of happiness—he takes it to be his duty to rule like
the Kings of Christendom, by divine right. But he loves us through
and through it—and *I*, for one, love *him!* and when, five years ago,
I lost what I loved best in the world beyond comparison and rivalship
. . . far better than himself as he knew . . . for everyone who knew
me could not choose but know what was my first and chiefest affection
. . . when I lost *that*, . . . I felt that he stood the nearest to me on
the closed grave . . . or by the unclosing sea . . . I do not know

which nor could ask. And I will tell you that not only he has been kind and patient and forbearing to me through the tedious trial of this illness (far more trying to standers by than you have an idea of perhaps) but that he was generous and forebearing in that hour of bitter trial, and never reproached me as he might have done and as my own soul has not spared—never once said to me then or since, that if it had not been for *me*, the crown of his house would not have fallen. He *never did* . . . and he might have said it, and more—and I could have answered nothing. Nothing, except that I had paid my own price—and that the price I paid was greater than his *loss* . . . his !! For see how it was ; and how, 'not with my hand but heart,' I was the cause or occasion of that misery—and though not with the intention of my heart but with its weakness, yet the *occasion*, any way !

They sent me down you know to Torquay—Dr. Chambers saying that I could not live a winter in London. The worst—what people call the worst—was apprehended for me at that time. So I was sent down with my sister to my aunt there—and he, my brother whom I loved so, was sent too, to take us there and return. And when the time came for him to leave me, *I*, to whom he was the dearest of friends and brothers in one . . . the only one of my family who . . . well, but I cannot write of these things ; and it is enough to tell you that he was above us all, better than us all, and kindest and noblest and dearest to *me*, beyond comparison, any comparison, as I said— and when the time came for him to leave me I, weakened by illness, could not master my spirits or drive back my tears—and my aunt kissed them away instead of reproving me as she should have done; and said that *she* would take care that I should not be grieved . . . *she !* . . . and so she sate down and wrote a letter to Papa to tell him that he would 'break my heart' if he persisted in calling away my brother—As if hearts were broken *so !* I have thought bitterly since that my heart did not break for a good deal more than *that !* And Papa's answer was—burnt into me, as with fire, it is—that 'under such circumstances he did not refuse to suspend his purpose, but that he considered it to be *very wrong in me to exact such a thing.*' So there was no separation *then:* and month after month passed—and sometimes I was better and sometimes worse—and the medical men continued to say that they would not answer for my life . . . they ! if I were agitated—and so there was no more talk of a separation. And once *he* held my hand, . . . how I remember ! and said that he 'loved me better than them all and that he *would not* leave me . . . till I was well,' he said! how I remember *that!* And ten days from that day the boat had left the shore which never returned; never—and he *had* left me! gone! For three days we waited—and I hoped while I could—oh—that awful agony of three days! And the sun shone as it shines to-day, and there was no more wind than now; and the sea under the windows was like this paper for smoothness—and my sisters drew the curtains back that I might see for myself how smooth the sea was, and how it could hurt nobody—and other boats came back one by one.

Remember how you wrote in your 'Gismond'

> What says the body when they spring
> Some monstrous torture-engine's whole
> Strength on it? No more says the soul.

and you never wrote anything which *lived* with me more than *that*. It is such a dreadful truth. But you knew it for truth, I hope, by your genius, and not by such proof as mine—I, who could not speak or shed a tear, but lay for weeks and months half conscious, half unconscious, with a wandering mind, and too near to God under the crushing of His hand, to pray at all. I expiated all my weak tears before, by not being able to shed then one tear—and yet they were forbearing—and no voice said 'You have done this.'

Do not notice what I have written to you, my dearest friend. I have never said so much to a living being—I never *could* speak or write of it. I asked no question from the moment when my last hope went: and since then, it has been impossible for me to speak what was in me. I have borne to do it to-day and to you, but perhaps if you were to write—so do not let this be noticed between us again—*do not!* And besides there is no need! I do not reproach myself with such acrid thoughts as I had once—I *know* that I would have died ten times over for *him*, and that therefore though it was wrong of me to be weak, and I have suffered for it and shall learn by it I hope; *remorse* is not precisely the word for me—not at least in its full sense. Still you will comprehend from what I have told you how the spring of life must have seemed to break within me *then*; and how natural it has been for me to loathe the living on—and to lose faith (even without the loathing), to lose faith in myself . . . which I have done on some points utterly. It is not from the cause of illness—no. And you will comprehend too that I have strong reasons for being grate-

ful to the forbearance. . . . It would have been *cruel,* you think, to
reproach me. Perhaps so! yet the kindness and patience of the de-
sisting from reproach, are positive things all the same.[21]

   *This opening of her heart to Browning was a testimony of her
love for him, and Browning recognized it as such. When a few days
later he delayed replying to a subsequent note and Elizabeth wrote
anxiously to inquire if he were offended by something she had written,
Browning cast aside the restraint she had imposed on him.*

   From Browning, Saturday, Aug. 30, 1845: Can you understand me *so,* dearest friend, after all? Do you see me—when I am
away, or with you—'taking offence' at words, 'being vexed' at words,
or deeds of yours, even if I could not immediately trace them to
their source of entire, pure kindness; as I have hitherto done in every
smallest instance?

I believe in *you* absolutely, utterly—I believe that when you bade
me, that time, be silent—that such was your bidding, and I was
silent—dare I say I think you did not know at that time the power
I have over myself, that I could sit and speak and listen as I have
done since? Let me say now—*this only once*—that I loved you from
my soul, and gave you my life, so much of it as you would take,—
and all that is *done,* not to be altered now: it was, in the nature of
the proceeding, wholly independent of any return on your part. I
will not think on extremes you might have resorted to; as it is, the
assurance of your friendship, the intimacy to which you admit me,
now, make the truest, deepest joy of my life—a joy I can never think
fugitive while we are in life, because I KNOW, as to me, I *could* not
willingly displease you,—while, as to you, your goodness and understanding will always see to the bottom of involuntary or ignorant
faults—always help me to correct them. I have done now. If I
thought you were like other women I have known, I should say so
much!—but—(my first and last word—I *believe* in you!)—what you
could and would give me, of your affection, you would give nobly and
simply and as a giver—you would not need that I tell you—(*tell
you!*)—what would be supreme happiness to me in the event—however distant—

I repeat . . . I call on your justice to remember, on your intelligence to believe . . . that this is merely a more precise stating the
first subject; to put an end to any possible misunderstanding—to

prevent your henceforth believing that because I *do not write*, from thinking too deeply of you, I am offended, vexed &c. &c. I will never recur to this, nor shall you see the least difference in my manner next Monday: it is indeed, always before me . . . how I know nothing of you and yours. But I think I ought to have spoken when I did—and to speak clearly . . . or more clearly what I do, as it is my pride and duty to fall back, now, on the feeling with which I have been in the meantime—Yours—God bless you—[22]

From Elizabeth, Sunday, Aug. 31, 1845: You, who profess to believe in me, do yet obviously believe that it was only merely silence, which I required of you on one occasion—and that if I had 'known your power over yourself,' I should not have minded . . . no! In other words you believe of me that I was thinking just of my own (what shall I call it for a motive base and small enough?) my own scrupulousness . . . freedom from embarrassment! of myself in the least of me; in the tying of my shoestrings, say!—so much and no more! Now this is so wrong, as to make me impatient sometimes in feeling it to be your impression: I asked for silence—but *also* and chiefly for the putting away of . . . you know very well what I asked for. And this was sincerely done, I attest to you. You wrote once to me . . . oh, long before May and the day we met: that you 'had been so happy, you should be now justified to yourself in taking any step most hazardous to the happiness of your life—but if you were justified, could *I* be therefore justified in abetting such a step,—the step of wasting, in a sense, your best feelings . . . of emptying your water gourds into the sand? What I thought then I think now—just what any third person, knowing you, would think, I think and feel. I thought too, at first, that the feeling on your part was a mere generous impulse, likely to expend itself in a week perhaps. It affects me and has affected me, very deeply, more than I dare attempt to say, that you should persist *so*—and if sometimes I have felt, by a sort of instinct, that after all you would not go on to persist, and that (being a man, you know) you might mistake, a little unconsciously, the strength of your own feeling; you ought not to be surprised; when I felt it was more advantageous and happier for you that it should be so. *In any case*, I shall never regret my own share in the events of this summer, and your friendship will be dear to me to the last. You know I told you so—not long since. And as to what you say otherwise, you are right in thinking that I would not hold by unworthy motives in avoiding to speak what you had any claim to hear. But what could I speak that would not be unjust to you? Your life! if you gave it to me and I put my whole heart into it; what should I put but anxiety, and more sadness than you were born to? What could I give you, which it would not be ungenerous to give? Therefore we must leave this subject—and I trust you to leave it without one word more; (too many have been said already—but I could not let your letter pass quite silently . . . as if I had nothing to do but to receive all as matter of course *so!*) while you may well trust *me* to remember to my life's end, as the grateful remember; and to feel, as those do who have felt sorrow (for where these pits are dug, the water will stand), the full price of your regard. May God bless you, my dearest friend.[23]

From Browning, Saturday morning, Sept. 13, 1845 : I have read your letter again and again. I will tell you—no, not *you*, but any imaginary other person, who should hear what I am going to avow; I would tell that person most sincerely there is not a particle of fatuity, shall I call it, in that avowal; cannot be, seeing that from the beginning and at this moment I never dreamed of winning your *love*. I can hardly write this word, so incongruous and impossible does it seem; such a change of our places does it imply—nor, next to that, though long after, *would* I, if I *could*, supplant one of any of the affections that I know to have taken root in you—*that* great and solemn one, for instance. I feel that if I could get myself *remade*, as if turned to gold, I WOULD not even then desire to become more than the mere setting of *that* diamond you must always wear. The regard and esteem you now give me, in this letter, and which I press to my heart and bow my head upon, is all I can take and all too embarrassing, using *all* my gratitude. And yet, with that contented pride in being infinitely your debtor as it is, bound to you for ever as it is; when I read your letter with all the determination to be just to us both; I dare not so far withstand the light I am master of, as to refuse seeing that whatever is recorded as an objection to your disposing of that life of mine I would give you, has reference to some supposed good in that life which your accepting it would destroy (of which fancy I shall speak presently)—I say, wonder as I may at this, I cannot but find it there, surely there. I could no more 'bind *you* by words,' than you have bound me, as you say—but if I misunderstand you, one assurance to that effect will be but too intelligible to me—

but, as it *is*, I have difficulty in imagining that while one of so many reasons, which I am not obliged to repeat to myself, but which any one easily conceives; while *any one* of those reasons would impose silence on me *for ever* (for, as I observed, I love you as you now are, and *would* not remove one affection that is already part of you,)— *would* you, being able to speak *so*, only say *that you* desire not to put 'more sadness than I was born to,' into my life?—that you 'could give me only what it were ungenerous to give'?

Have I your meaning here? In so many words, is it on my account that you bid me 'leave this subject'? I think if it were so, I would for once call my advantages round me. I am not what your generous self-forgetting appreciation would sometimes make me out—but it is not since yesterday, nor ten nor twenty years before, that I began to look into my own life, and study its end, and requirements, what would turn to its good or its loss—and I *know*, if one may know anything, that to make that life yours and increase it by union with yours, would render me *supremely happy*, as I said, and say, and feel. My whole suit to you is, in that sense, *selfish*—not that I am ignorant that *your* nature would most surely attain happiness in being conscious that it made another happy—but *that best, best end of all*, would, like the rest, come from yourself, be a reflection of your own gift.

Dearest, I will end here—words, persuasion, arguments, if they were at my service I would not use them—I believe in you, altogether have faith in you—in you. I will not think of insulting by trying to reassure you on one point which certain phrases in your letter might at first glance seem to imply—you do not understand me to be living and labouring and writing (and *not* writing) in order to be successful in the world's sense? I even convinced the people *here* what was my true 'honourable position in society,' &c. &c. therefore I shall not have to inform *you* that I desire to be very rich, very great; but not in reading Law gratis with dear foolish old Basil Montagu, as he ever and anon bothers me to do;—much less—enough of this nonsense.

'Tell me what I have a claim to hear': I can hear it, and be as grateful as I was before and am now—your friendship is my pride and happiness. If you told me your love was bestowed elsewhere, and that it was in my power to serve you *there*, to serve you there would still be my pride and happiness. I look on and on over the prospect of my love, it is all *on*wards—and all possible forms of unkindness

. . . I quite laugh to think how they are *behind* . . . cannot be encountered in the route we are travelling! I submit to you and will obey you implicitly—obey what I am able to conceive of your least desire, much more of your expressed wish. But it was necessary to make this avowal, among other reasons, for one which the world would recognize too. My whole scheme of life (with its wants, material wants at least, closely cut down) was long ago calculated—and it supposed *you*, the finding such an one as you, utterly impossible—because in calculating one goes upon *chances*, not on providence—how could I expect you? So for my own future way in the world I have always refused to care—any one who can live a couple of years and more on bread and potatoes as I did once on a time, and who prefers a blouse and a blue shirt (such as I now write in) to all manner of dress and gentlemanly appointment, and who can, if necessary, groom a horse not so badly, or at all events would rather do it all day long than succeed Mr. Fitzroy Kelly in the Solicitor-Generalship,—such an one need not very much concern himself beyond considering the lilies how they grow. But now I see you near this life, all changes—and at a word, I will do all that ought to be done, that every one used to say could be done, and let 'all my powers find sweet employ' as Dr. Watts sings, in getting whatever is to be got—not very much, surely. I would print these things, get them away, and do this now, and go to you at Pisa with the news—at Pisa where one may live for some £100 a year—while, lo, I seem to remember, I *do* remember, that Charles Kean offered to give me 500 of those pounds for any play that might suit him—to say nothing of Mr. Colburn saying confidentially that he wanted more than his dinner 'a novel on the subject of *Napoleon*'! So may one make money, if one does not live in a house in a row, and feel impelled to take the Princess's Theatre for a laudable development and exhibition of one's faculty.

Take the sense of all this, I beseech you, dearest—all you shall say will be best—I am yours—

Yes, Yours ever. God bless you for all you have been, and are, and will certainly be to me, come what He shall please![24]

From Elizabeth, postmarked Sept. 16, 1845: I scarcely know how to write what is to be written nor indeed why it is to be written and to what end. I have tried in vain—and you are waiting to hear from me. I am unhappy enough even where I am happy—but ungrateful nowhere—and I thank you from my heart—profoundly from the depths of my heart . . . which is nearly all I can do.

One letter I began to write and asked in it how it could become me to speak at all if *'from the beginning and at this moment you never dreamed of'* . . . and there, I stopped and tore the paper; because I felt that you were too loyal and generous, for me to bear to take a moment's advantage of the same, and bend down the very flowering branch of your generosity (as it might be) to thicken a little the fence of a woman's caution and reserve. You will not say that you have not acted as if you 'dreamed'—and I will answer therefore to the general sense of your letter and former letters, and admit at once that I *did* state to you the difficulties most difficult to myself . . . though not all . . . and that if I had been worthier of you I should have been proportionably less in haste to 'bid you leave that subject.' I do not understand how you can seem at the same moment to have faith in my integrity and to have doubt whether all this time I may not have felt a preference for another . . . which you are ready 'to serve,' you say. Which is generous in you—but in *me*, where were the integrity? Could you really hold me to be blameless, and do you think that true-hearted women act usually so? Can it be necessary for me to tell you that I could not have acted so, and did not? And shall I shrink from telling you besides . . . you, who have been generous to me and have a right to hear it . . . and have spoken to me in the name of an affection and memory most precious and holy to me, in this same letter . . . that neither now nor formerly has any man been to my feelings what you are . . . and that if I were different in some respects and free in others by the providence of God, I would accept the great trust of your happiness, gladly, proudly, and gratefully; and give away my own life and soul to that end. I *would* do it . . . *not, I do* . . . observe! it is a truth without a consequence; only meaning that I am not all stone—only proving that I am not likely to consent to help you in wrong against yourself. You see in me what is not:—*that*, I know: and you overlook in me what is unsuitable to you . . . *that* I know, and have sometimes told you. Still, because a strong feeling from some sources is self-vindicating and ennobling to the object of it, I will not say that, if it were proved to me that you felt this for me, I would persist in putting the sense of my own unworthiness between you and me—not being heroic, you know, nor pretending to be so. But something worse than even a sense of unworthiness, *God* has put between us! and judge yourself if to beat your thoughts against the immovable marble of it, can be anything but pain and vexation of spirit, waste and wear of spirit to you . . . judge! The present is here to be seen . . . speaking for itself! and the best future you can imagine for me, what a precarious thing it must be . . . a thing for making burdens out of . . . only not for your carrying, as I have vowed to my own soul. As dear Mr. Kenyon said to me to-day in his smiling kindness . . . 'In ten years you may be strong perhaps'—or 'almost strong'! that being the encouragement of my best friends! What would he say, do you think, if he could know or guess . . . ! what *could* he say but that you were . . . a poet!—and I . . . still worse! *Never* let him know or guess!

And so if you are wise and would be happy (and you have excellent practical sense after all and should exercise it) you must leave me— these thoughts of me, I mean . . . for if we might not be true friends for ever, I should have less courage to say the other truth. But we may be friends always . . . and cannot be so separated, that your happiness, in the knowledge of it, will not increase mine. And if you will be persuaded by me, as you say, you will be persuaded *thus* . . . and consent to take a resolution and force your mind at once into another channel. Perhaps I might bring you reasons of the class which you tell me 'would silence you for ever.' I might certainly tell you that my own father, if he knew that you had written to me *so*, and that I had answered you—*so*, even, would not forgive me at the end of ten years—and this, from none of the causes mentioned by me here and in no disrespect of your name and your position . . . though he does not over-value poetry even in his daughter, and is apt to take the world's measures of the means of life . . . but for the singular reason that he never *does* tolerate in his family (sons or daughters) the development of one class of feelings. Such an objection I could not bring to you of my own will—it rang hollow in my ears—perhaps I thought even too little of it:—and I brought to you what I thought much of, and cannot cease to think much of equally. Worldly thoughts, these are not at all, nor have been: there need be no soiling of the heart with any such:—and I will say, in reply to some words of yours, that you cannot despise the gold and gauds of the world more than I do, and should do even if I found a use for them. And if I *wished* to be very poor, in the world's sense of poverty, I *could not*, with three or four hundred a year of which no living will can dispossess me. And is it not the chief good of money, the being free from the need of thinking of it? It seems so to me.

The obstacles then are of another character, and the stronger for being so. Believe that I am grateful to you—*how* grateful, cannot be shown in words nor even in tears . . . grateful enough to be truthful in all ways. You know I might have hidden myself from you —but I would not: and by the truth told of myself, you may believe in the earnestness with which I tell the other truths—of you . . . and of this subject. The subject will not bear consideration—it breaks in our hands. But that God is stronger than we, cannot be a bitter thought to you but a holy thought . . . while He lets me, as much as I can be anyone's, be only yours.[25]

From Browning, Tuesday night, Sept. 16, 1845: I do not know whether you imagine the precise effect of your letter on me— very likely you do, and write it just for that—for I conceive *all* from your goodness. But before I tell you what is that effect, let me say in as few words as possible what shall stop any fear—though only for a moment and on the outset—that you have been misunderstood, that the goodness *outside*, and round and over all, hides all or any thing. I understand you to signify to me that you see, at this present, insurmountable obstacles to that—can I speak it—entire gift, which I shall own, was, while I dared ask it, above my hopes— and wishes, even, so it seems to me . . . and yet could not but be asked, so plainly was it dictated to me, by something quite out of those hopes and wishes. Will it help me to say that once in this Aladdin-cavern I knew I ought to stop for no heaps of jewel-fruit on the trees from the very beginning, but go on to the lamp, *the* prize, the last and best of all? Well, I understand you to pronounce that at present you believe this gift impossible—and I acquiesce entirely—I submit wholly to you; repose on you in all the faith of which I am capable. Those obstacles are solely for *you* to see and to declare . . . had *I* seen them, be sure I should never have mocked you or myself by affecting to pass them over . . . what *were* obstacles, I mean: but you *do* see them, I must think,—and perhaps they strike me the more from my true, honest unfeigned inability to imagine what they are,—not that I shall endeavour. After what you *also* apprise me of, I know and am joyfully confident that if ever they cease to be what you now consider them, you who see now *for me*, whom I implicitly trust in to see for me; you will *then*, too, see and remember me, and how I trust, and shall then be still trusting. And until you so see, and so inform me, I shall never utter a word—for that would involve the vilest of implications. I thank God—I *do* thank him, that in this whole matter I have been, to the utmost of my power, not unworthy of his introducing you to me, in this respect that, being no longer in the first freshness of life, and having for many years now made up my mind to the impossibility of loving any woman . . . having wondered at this in the beginning, and fought not a little against it, having acquiesced in it at last, and accounted for it all to myself, and become, if anything, rather proud of it than sorry . . . I say, when real love, making itself at once recognized as such, *did* reveal itself to me at last, I *did* open my heart to it with a cry—nor care for its overturning all my theory—nor mistrust its effect upon a mind set in ultimate order, so I fancied, for the few years more—nor apprehend in the least that the new element would harm what was already organized without its help. Nor have I, either, been guilty of the more pardonable folly, of treating the new feeling after the pedantic fashions and instances of the world. I have not spoken when *it* did not speak, because 'one' might speak, or has spoken, or *should* speak, and 'plead' and all that miserable work which after all, I may well continue proud that I am not called to attempt. *Here* for instance, *now* . . . 'one' should despair; but 'try again' first, and work blindly at removing those obstacles (—if I saw them, I should be silent, and only speak when a month hence, ten years hence, I could bid you look where they *were*)—and 'one' would do all this, not for the *play-acting's* sake, or to 'look the character' . . . (*that* would be something quite different from folly . . .) but from a not unreasonable anxiety lest by too sudden a silence, too complete an acceptance of your will; the earnestness and endurance and unabatedness . . . the *truth*, in fact, of what had already been professed, should get to be questioned—But I believe that you believe me—And now that all is clear between us I will say, what you will hear, without fearing for me or yourself, that I am utterly contented . . . ('grateful' I have done with . . . it must go—) I accept what you give me, what those words deliver to me, as —not all I asked for . . . as I said . . . but as more than I ever hoped for,—*all*, in the best sense, that I deserved.[26]

From Elizabeth, Wednesday evening, Sept. 17, 1845: But one word before we leave the subject, and then to leave it finally; but

I cannot let you go on to fancy a mystery anywhere, in obstacles or the rest. You deserve at least a full frankness; and in my letter I meant to be fully frank. I even told you what was an absurdity, so absurd that I should far rather not have told you at all, only that I felt the need of telling you all: and no mystery is involved in that, except as an 'idiosyncrasy' is a mystery. But the 'insurmountable' difficulty is for you and everybody to see; and for me to feel, who have been a very by-word among the talkers, for a confirmed invalid through months and years, and who, even if I were going to Pisa and had the best prospects possible to me, should yet remain liable to relapses and stand on precarious ground to the end of my life. Now that is no mystery for the trying of 'faith'; but a plain fact. But *don't* let us speak of it.

And for all the rest I thank you—believe that I thank you . . . and that the feeling is not so weak as the word. That *you* should care at all for *me* has been a matter of unaffected wonder to me from the first hour until now—and I cannot help the pain I feel sometimes, in thinking that it would have been better for you if you never had known me. I had done *living*, I thought, when you came and sought me out! and why? and to what end? *That*, I cannot help thinking now. Perhaps just that I may pray for you—which were a sufficient end. If you come on Saturday I trust you to leave this subject untouched,—as it must be indeed henceforth.[27]

From Browning, Thursday morning, Sept. 18, 1845: But you, too, will surely want, if you think me a rational creature, *my* explanation—without which all that I have said and done would be pure madness, I think. It *is* just 'what I see' that I *do* see,—or rather it has proved, since I first visited you, that the reality was infinitely worse than I know it to be . . . for at, and after writing of *that first letter*, on my first visit, I believed—through some silly or misapprehended talk, collected at second hand too—that your complaint was of quite another nature—a spinal injury irremediable in the nature of it. Had it been *so*—now speak for *me*, for what you hope I am, and say how *that* should affect or neutralize what you *were*, what I wished to associate with myself in you? But *as you now are:* —then if I had married you seven years ago, and this visitation came now first, I should be 'fulfilling a pious duty,' I suppose, in enduring what could not be amended—a pattern to good people in not running away . . . for where were *now* the use and the good and the profit and—

I desire in this life (with very little fluctuation for a man and too a weak one) to live and just write out certain things which are in me, and so save my soul. I would endeavour to do this if I were forced to 'live among lions' as you once said—but I should best do this if I lived quietly with myself and with you. That you cannot dance like Cerito does not materially disarrange this plan—nor that I might (beside the perpetual incentive and sustainment and consolation) get, over and above the main reward, the incidental, particular and unexpected happiness of being allowed when not working to rather occupy myself with watching you, than with certain other pursuits I might be otherwise addicted to—*this*, also, does not constitute an obstacle, as I see obstacles.

But *you* see them—and I see *you*, and know my first duty and do it resolutely if not cheerfully.

As for referring again, till leave by word or letter—you will see—[28]

V

The apparent impasse at which they had arrived was now suddenly dissolved by the abrupt severing of those ties of affection and obligation that bound Elizabeth to her father. Though Mr. Barrett's silence on the question of Malta boded ill for any similar projects, Elizabeth, at the urging of Browning and her brothers and sisters, had initiated a plan for passing the winter at Pisa. All of course depended on Mr. Barrett's consent, but surely, if he loved her as she believed he did, he could not refuse.

From Elizabeth, Wednesday morning, Sept. 17, 1845: I write one word just to say that it is all over with Pisa; which was a probable evil when I wrote last, and which I foresaw from the beginning—being a prophetess, you know. I cannot tell you now how it has all happened—*only do not blame me*, for I have kept my ground to the last, and only yield when Mr. Kenyon and all the world see that there is no standing. I am ashamed almost of having put so much earnestness into a personal matter—and I spoke face to face and quite firmly—so as to pass with my sisters for the 'bravest person in the house' without contestation.

Sometimes it seems to me as if it *could not* end so—I mean, that

the responsibility of such a negative must be reconsidered . . . and
you see how Mr. Kenyon writes to me. Still, as the matter lies, . . .
no Pisa! And, as I said before, my prophetic instincts are not likely
to fail, such as they have been from the beginning.[29]

Later that day Elizabeth wrote again : Papa has been walking to and fro in this room, looking thoughtfully and talking leisurely—and every moment I have expected I confess, some word
(that did not come) about Pisa. Mr. Kenyon thinks it cannot end
so—and I do sometimes—and in the meantime I do confess to a little
'savageness' also—at heart! All I asked him to say the other day,
was that he was not displeased with me—*and he wouldn't*; and for
me to walk across his displeasure spread on the threshold of the door,
and moreover take a sister and brother with me, and do such a thing
for the sake of going to Italy and securing a personal advantage,
were altogether impossible, obviously impossible! So poor Papa is
quite in disgrace with me just now—if he would but care for *that!*[30]

From Elizabeth, Wednesday, Sept. 24, 1845 : I have spoken
again, and the result is that we are in precisely the same position;
only with bitterer feelings on one side. If I go or stay they *must* be
bitter: words have been said that I cannot easily forget, nor remember without pain; and yet I really do almost smile in the midst of
it all, to think how I was treated this morning as an undutiful
daughter because I tried to put on my gloves . . . for there was no
worse provocation. At least he complained of the undutifulness and
rebellion (!!!) of everyone in the house—and when I asked if he
meant that reproach for *me*, the answer was that he meant it for all
of us, one with another. And I could not get an answer. He would
not even grant me the consolation of thinking that I sacrificed what
I supposed to be good, to *him*. I told him that my prospects of health
seemed to me to depend on taking this step, but that through my
affection for him, I was ready to sacrifice those to his pleasure if he
exacted it—only it was necessary to my self-satisfaction in future
years, to understand definitely that the sacrifice *was* exacted by him
and *was* made to him, . . . and not thrown away blindly and by a
misapprehension. And he would not answer *that*. I might do my own
way, he said—*he* would not speak—*he* would not say that he was not
displeased with me, nor the contrary:—I had better do what I liked:
—for his part, he washed his hands of me altogether.

And so I have been very wise—witness how my eyes are swelled with annotations and reflections on all this! The best of it is that now George himself admits I can do no more in the way of speaking, . . . I have no spell for charming the dragons, . . . and allows me to be passive and enjoins me to be tranquil, and not 'make up my mind' to any dreadful exertion for the future. Moreover he advises me to go on with the preparations for the voyage, and promises to state the case himself at the last hour to the 'highest authority;' and judge finally whether it be possible for me to go with the necessary companionship.

Well!—and what do you think? Might it be desirable for me to give up the whole? Tell me. I feel aggrieved of course and wounded —and whether I go or stay that feeling must last—I cannot help it. But my spirits sink altogether at the thought of leaving England *so* —and then I doubt about Arabel and Stormie . . . and it seems to me that I *ought not* to mix them up in a business of this kind where the advantage is merely personal to myself. On the other side, George holds that if I give up and stay even, there will be displeasure just the same, . . . and that, when once gone, the irritation will exhaust and smooth itself away—which however does not touch my chief objection. Would it be better . . . more *right* . . . to give it up? Think for me. Even if I hold on to the last, at the last I shall be thrown off—*that* is my conviction. But . . . shall I give up *at once?* Do think for me.[31]

From Browning, Thursday, Sept. 25, 1845: You have said to me more than once that you wished I might never know certain feelings *you* had been forced to endure. I suppose all of us have the proper place where a blow should fall to be felt most—and I truly wish *you* may never feel what I have to bear in looking on, quite powerless, and silent, while you are subjected to this treatment, which I refuse to characterize—so blind is it *for* blindness. I think I ought to understand what a father may exact, and a child should comply with; and I respect the most ambiguous of love's caprices if they give never so slight a clue to their all-justifying source. Did I, when you signified to me the probable objections—you remember what— to myself, my own happiness,—did I once allude to, much less argue against, or refuse to acknowledge those objections? For I wholly sympathize, however it go against me, with the highest, wariest, pride and love for you, and the proper jealousy and vigilance they entail

—but now, and here, the jewel is not being over guarded, but ruined, cast away. And whoever is privileged to interfere should do so in the possessor's own interest—all common sense interferes—all rationality against absolute no-reason at all. And you ask whether you ought to obey this no-reason? I will tell you: all passive obedience and implicit submission of will and intellect is by far too easy, if well considered, to be the course prescribed by God to Man in this life of probation—for they *evade* probation altogether, though foolish people think otherwise. Chop off your legs, you will never go astray; stifle your reason altogether and you will find it is difficult to reason ill. 'It is hard to make these sacrifices!'—not so hard as to lose the reward or incur the penalty of an Eternity to come; 'hard to effect them, then, and go through with them'—*not* hard, when the leg is to be *cut off*,—that it is rather harder to keep it quiet on a stool, I know very well. The partial indulgence, the proper exercise of one's faculties, there is the difficulty and problem for solution, set by that Providence which might have made the laws of Religion as indubitable as those of vitality, and revealed the articles of belief as certainly as that condition, for instance, by which we breathe so many times in a minute to support life. But there is no reward proposed for the feat of breathing, and a great one for that of believing —consequently there must go a great deal more of voluntary effort to this latter than is implied in the getting absolutely rid of it at once, by adopting the direction of an infallible church, or private judgment of another—for all our life is some form of religion, and all our action some belief, and there is but one law, however modified, for the greater and the less. In your case I do think you are called upon to do your duty to yourself; that is, to God in the end. Your own reason should examine the whole matter in dispute by every light which can be put in requisition; and every interest that appears to be affected by your conduct should have its utmost claims considered—your father's in the first place; and that interest, not in the miserable limits of a few days' pique or whim in which it would seem to express itself; but in its whole extent . . . the *hereafter* which all momentary passion prevents him seeing . . . indeed, the *present* on either side which everyone else must see. And this examination made, with whatever earnestness you will, I do think and am sure that on its conclusion you should act, in confidence that a duty has been performed . . . *difficult*, or how were it a duty? Will it *not* be infinitely harder to act so than to blindly adopt his pleasure, and die under it? Who can *not* do that?

I fling these hasty rough words over the paper, fast as they will fall—knowing to whom I cast them, and that any sense they may contain or point to, will be caught and understood, and presented in a better light. The hard thing . . . this is all I want to say . . . is to act on one's own best conviction—not to abjure it and accept another will, and say '*there* is my plain duty'—easy it is, whether plain or no!

How 'all changes!' When I first knew you—you know what followed. I supposed you to labour under an incurable complaint—and, of course, to be completely dependent on your father for its commonest alleviations; the moment after that inconsiderate letter, I reproached myself bitterly with the selfishness apparently involved in any proposition I might then have made—for though I have never been at all frightened of the world, nor mistrustful of my power to deal with it, and get my purpose out of it if once I thought it worth while, yet I could not but feel the consideration, of *what* failure would *now* be, paralyse all effort even in fancy. When you told me lately that 'you could never be poor'—all my solicitude was at an end—I had but myself to care about, and I told you, what I believed and believe, that I can at any time amply provide for that, and that I could cheerfully and confidently undertake the removing of *that* obstacle. Now again the circumstances shift—and you are in what I should wonder at as the veriest slavery—and I who *could* free you from it, I am here scarcely daring to write . . . though I know you must feel for me and forgive what forces itself from me . . . what retires so mutely into my heart at your least word . . . what *shall not* be again written or spoken, if you so will . . . that I should be made happy beyond all hope of expression by. Now while I *dream*, let me once dream! I would marry you now and thus—I would come when you let me, and go when you bade me—I would be no more than one of your brothers—'*no more*'—that is, instead of getting to-morrow for Saturday, I should get Saturday as well—two hours for one—when your head ached I should be *here*. I deliberately choose the realization of that dream (—of sitting simply by you for an hour every day) rather than any other, excluding you, I am able to form for this world, or any world I know—And it will continue but a dream.

You understand that I see you to-morrow, Friday, as you propose. You know what I am, what I would speak, and all I would do.[32]

From Elizabeth, Friday evening, Sept. 26, 1845: I had your letter late last night, everyone almost, being out of the house by an accident, so that it was left in the letter-box, and if I had wished to answer it before I saw you, it had scarcely been possible.

But it will be the same thing—for you know as well as if you saw my answer, what it must be, what it cannot choose but be, on pain of sinking me so infinitely below not merely your level but my own, that the depth cannot bear a glance down. Yet, though I am not made of such clay as to admit of my taking a base advantage of certain noble extravagances (and that I am not I thank God for your sake), I will say, I must say, that your words in this letter have done me good and made me happy, . . . that I thank and bless you for them, . . . and that to receive such a proof of attachment from *you*, not only overpowers every present evil, but seems to me a full and abundant amends for the merely personal sufferings of my whole life. When I had read that letter last night I *did* think so. I looked round and round for the small bitternesses which for several days had been bitter to me, and I could not find one of them. The tear-marks went away in the moisture of new, happy tears. Why, how else could I have felt? how else do you think I could? How would any woman have felt . . . who could feel at all . . . hearing such words said (though 'in a dream' indeed) by such a speaker?

And now listen to me in turn. You have touched me more profoundly than I thought even *you* could have touched me—my heart was full when you came here to-day. Henceforward I am yours for everything but to do you harm—and I am yours too much, in my heart, ever to consent to do you harm in that way. If I could consent to do it, not only should I be less loyal . . . but in one sense, less yours. I say this to you without drawback and reserve, because it is all I am able to say, and perhaps all I *shall* be able to say. However this may be, a promise goes to you in it that none, except God and your will, shall interpose between you and me, . . . I mean, that if He should free me within a moderate time from the trailing chain of this weakness, I will then be to you whatever at that hour you shall choose . . . whether friend or more than friend . . . a friend to the last in any case. So it rests with God and with you—only in the meanwhile you are most absolutely free . . . 'unentangled' (as they call it) by the breadth of a thread—and if I did not know that you considered yourself so, I would not see you any more, let the effort cost me what it might. You may force me to *feel:* . . . but you cannot force me to *think* contrary to my first thought . . . that it were better for you to forget me at once in one relation. And if better for *you*, can it be bad for *me?* which flings me down on the stone-pavement of the logicians.[33]

Supported by Browning's love and counsel, Elizabeth continued to plan to go abroad. But though she professed to be resolute, an enervating pessimism spread through her and paralyzed her will. It was already late in the season for easy travel; ships were booked up; more than anything else, the weight of her father's displeasure bore her down. Edward Barrett said nothing, but he discontinued his nightly visits to Elizabeth's room when they would talk and pray together—visits that Elizabeth treasured as evidence of her father's special love for her. In the end Edward Barrett had his way.

From Elizabeth, Monday, Oct. 13, 1845: Do not be angry with me—do not think it my fault—but *I do not go to Italy* . . . it has ended as I feared. What passed between George and Papa there is no need of telling: only the latter said that 'I might go if I pleased, but that going it would be under his heaviest displeasure.' George, in great indignation, pressed the question fully: but all was vain . . . and I am left in this position . . . to go, if I please, with his displeasure over me, (which after what you have said and after what Mr. Kenyon has said, and after what my own conscience and deepest moral convictions say aloud, I would unhesitatingly do at this hour!) and necessarily run the risk of exposing my sister and brother to that same displeasure . . . from which risk I shrink and fall back and feel that to incur it, is impossible. Dear Mr. Kenyon has been here and we have been talking—and he sees what I see . . . that I am justified in going myself, but not in bringing others into difficulty. The very kindness and goodness with which they desire me (both my sisters) 'not to think of them,' naturally makes me think more of them. And so, tell me that I am not wrong in taking up my chain again and acquiescing in this hard necessity. The bitterest 'fact' of all is, that I had believed Papa to have loved me more than he obviously does: but I never regret knowledge . . . I mean I never would *un*know anything . . . even were it the taste of the apples by the Dead sea—and this must be accepted like the rest. In the meantime your letter comes—and if I could seem to be very unhappy after reading it . . . why it would be 'all pretence' on my part, believe me. Can you care for me so much . . . *you?* Then *that* is light enough to account for all the shadows, and to make them almost unregarded—the shadows of the life behind.[34]

VI

&§*The brief rebellion was over. Elizabeth returned resignedly— perhaps with relief—to her familiar routine, the courage of summer giving way to renewed apathy, hopelessness, and self-abasement. Another autumn, another long winter lay ahead. Not until the next spring or summer, Browning knew, could he hope to liberate her from the mysterious thralldom that held her prisoner in her room. Meanwhile the regular visits continued—and the letters.*

Early in January Browning cautiously suggested that she begin to consider some course of action that would end the intolerable state of affairs in which they were drifting. "So begin thinking,—as for Spring, as for a New Year, as for a new life&§."

&§*From Elizabeth, Friday morning, Jan. 16, 1846*&§: I will think as you desire: but I have thought a great deal, and there are certainties which I know; and I hope we *both* are aware that nothing can be more hopeless than our position in some relations and aspects, though you do not guess perhaps that the very approach to the subject is shut up by dangers, and that from the moment of a suspicion entering *one* mind, we should be able to meet never again in this room, nor to have intercourse by letter through the ordinary channel. I mean, that letters of yours, addressed to me here, would infallibly be stopped and destroyed—if not opened. Therefore it is advisable to hurry on nothing—on these grounds it is advisable. What should I do if I did not see you nor hear from you, without being able to feel that it was for your happiness? What should I do for a month even? And then, I might be thrown out of the window or its equivalent—I look back shuddering to the dreadful scenes in which poor Henrietta was involved who never offended as I have offended . . . years ago which seem as present as to-day. She had forbidden the subject to be referred to until that consent was obtained—and at a word she gave up all—at a word. In fact she had no true attachment, as I observed to Arabel at the time—a child never submitted more meekly to a revoked holiday. Yet how she was made to suffer. Oh, the dreadful scenes! and only because she had seemed to feel a little. I told you, I think, that there was an obliquity—an eccentricity, or something beyond—on one class of subjects. I hear how her knees were made to ring upon the floor, now! she was carried out of the room in strong hysterics, and I, who rose up to follow her, though I was quite well at that time and suffered only by sympathy, fell flat down upon my face in a fainting-fit. Arabel thought I was dead.

I have tried to forget it all—but now I must remember—and throughout our intercourse *I have remembered.* It is necessary to remember so much as to avoid such evils as are inevitable, and for this reason I would conceal nothing from you. Do *you* remember, besides, that there can be no faltering on my 'part,' and that, if I should remain well, which is not proved yet, I will do for you what you please and as you please to have it done. But there is time for considering!

Only . . . as you speak of 'counsel,' I will take courage to tell you that my *sisters know.* Arabel is in most of my confidences, and being often in the room with me, taxed me with the truth long ago— she saw that I was affected from some cause—and I told her. We are as safe with both of them as possible . . . and they thoroughly understand that *if there should be any change it would not be your fault* . . . I made them understand that thoroughly. From themselves I have received nothing but the most smiling words of kindness and satisfaction (I thought I might tell you so much), they have too much tenderness for me to fail in it now. My brothers, it is quite necessary not to draw into a dangerous responsibility. I have felt that from the beginning, and shall continue to feel it—though I hear and can observe that they are full of suspicions and conjectures, which are never unkindly expressed. I told you once that we held hands the faster in this house for the weight over our heads. But the absolute *knowledge* would be dangerous for my brothers: with my sisters it is different, and I could not continue to conceal from *them* what they had under their eyes; and then, Henrietta is in a like position. It was not wrong of me to let them know it?—no?[35]

At the end of January Browning declared that he would claim his bride "at the summer's end." They would go to Italy for a year or two.

From Elizabeth, Friday morning, Jan. 30, 1846: Let it be this way, ever dearest. If in the time of fine weather, I am not ill, . . . *then . . . not now . . .* you shall decide, and your decision shall be duty and desire to me, both—I will make no difficulties. Remember, in the meanwhile, that I *have* decided to let it be as you shall choose . . . *shall* choose. That I love you enough to give you up 'for your good,' is proof (to myself at least) that I love you enough for any other end:—but you thought *too much of me in the last letter.* Do not mistake me. I believe and trust in all your words—only you are generous unawares, as other men are selfish.

For Italy . . . you are right. We should be nearer the sun, as you say, and further from the world, as I think—out of hearing of the great storm of gossiping, when 'scirocco is loose.' Even if you liked to live altogether abroad, coming to England at intervals, it would be no sacrifice for me—and whether in Italy or England, we should have sufficient or more than sufficient means of living, without modifying by a line that 'good free life' of yours which you reasonably praise—which, if it had been necessary to modify, *we must have parted,* . . . because I could not have borne to see you do it; though, that you once offered it for my sake, I never shall forget.[36]

As often as Browning urged Elizabeth to fix upon a definite plan of action, as often did she procrastinate and return the responsibility to him. At the beginning of March he complained impatiently of her unwillingness to commit herself to him without reservation and accused her of seeking some "security" of his intentions first.

From Elizabeth, Sunday, March 1, 1846: And for myself, it was my compromise with my own scruples, that you should not be 'chained' to me, not in the merest metaphor, that you should not seem to be bound, in honour or otherwise, so that if you stayed with me it should be your free choice to stay, not the *consequence* of a choice so many months before. That was my compromise with my scruples, and not my doubt of your affection—and least of all, was it an intention of trifling with you sooner or later that made me wish to suspend all *decisions* as long as possible. I have decided (for me) to let it be as you shall please—now I told you that before. Either we will live on as we are, until an obstacle arises,—for indeed I do not look for a 'security' where you suppose, and the very appearance of it *there*, is what most rebuts me—or I will be yours in the obvious way, to go out of England the next half-hour if possible. As to the steps to be taken (or not taken) before the last step, we must think of those. The worst is that the only question is about a *form*. Virtually the evil is the same all round, whatever we do. Dearest, it was plain to see yesterday evening when he came into this room for a moment at seven o'clock, before going to his own to dress for dinner . . . plain to see, that he was not altogether pleased at finding you here in the morning. There was no pretext for objecting gravely— but it was plain that he was not pleased. Do not let this make you uncomfortable, he will forget all about it, and I was not *scolded*, do you understand. It was more manner, but my sisters thought as I did of the significance:—and it was enough to prove to me (if I had not known) what a desperate game we should be playing if we depended on a yielding nerve *there*.[37]

◆§*In June, an unseasonably cold day reminded Browning of the approaching end of summer. Suddenly apprehensive about the dangers of autumnal travel, he begged Elizabeth to decide whether she would go early or late—to decide and spare him the necessity of exercising his will over her*§◆.

◆§*From Elizabeth, Saturday, June 27, 1846*§◆: How shall I say more than I have said and you know? *Do* you not know, you who will not will 'over' me, that I *cannot* will against you, and that if you set yourself seriously to take September for October, and August for September, it is all at an end with me and the calendar? Still, seriously . . . there is time for deciding, is there not? . . . even if I grant to you, which I do at once, that the road does not grow smoother for us by prolonged delays. The single advantage perhaps of delay is, that in the summer I get stronger every week and fitter to travel—and then, it never was thought of before (that I have heard) to precede September *so*. Last year, was I not ordered to leave England in October, and *permitted* to leave it in November? Yet I agree, November and perhaps October might be late—might be running a risk through lingering . . . in our case; and you will believe me when I say I should be loth to run the risk of being forced to the further delay of a year—the position being scarcely tenable. Now for September, it generally passes for a hot month—it ripens the peaches—it is the figtime in Italy. Well—nobody decides for

September nevertheless. The end of August is nearer—and at any rate we can consider, and observe the signs of the heavens and earth in the meanwhile—there is so much to think of first; and the end, remember, is only too frightfully easy. Also you shall not have it on your conscience to have killed me, let ever so much snow fall in September. If the sea should be frozen over, almost we might go by the land—might we not? and apart from fabulous ports, there are the rivers—the Seine, the Soane, the Rhone—which might be cheaper than the sea and the steamers; and *would*, I almost should fancy. These are things among the multitude, to think of, and you shall think of them, dearest, in your wisdom. Oh—there is time—full time.[38]

During July and August the advantages and disadvantages of alternative routes to Italy were canvassed. Meanwhile others of Elizabeth's friends urged an Italian winter upon her and offered plans of their own for getting her there—plans that Elizabeth turned aside noncommittally. Nevertheless her secret was beginning to be guessed. Late in August, with their plans still unmade but with a sense of the imminence of some decision, the lovers resolved to see each other less often in order to avert the suspicions of friends and relatives.

From Browning, Friday, Aug. 28, 1846: I altogether agree with you—it is best to keep away—we cannot be too cautious now at the 'end of things.' I am prepared for difficulties enough, without needing to cause them by any rashness or wilfulness of my own. I really expect, for example, that out of the various plans of these sympathising friends and relations some one will mature itself sufficiently to be directly proposed to you, for your acceptance or refusal contingent on your father's approbation; the shortness of the remaining travelling season serving to compel a speedy development. Or what if your father, who was the first to propose, or at least talk about, a voyage to Malta or elsewhere, when you took no interest in the matter comparatively, and who perhaps chiefly found fault with last year's scheme for its not originating with himself . . . what if he should again determine on some such voyage now that you are apparently as obedient to his wishes as can be desired? Would it be strange, not to say improbable, if he tells you some fine morning that your passage is taken to Madeira, or Palermo? Because, all the attempts in the world cannot hide the truth from the mind, any more than all five fingers before the eyes keep out the sun at noon-day: you see a red through them all—and your father must see your improved health and strength, and divine the opinion of everybody round him as to the simple proper course for the complete restoration of them. Therefore be prepared, my own Ba![39]

From Elizabeth, Friday evening, Aug. 28, 1846: Dearest, I have had all your thoughts by turns, or most of them . . . and each one has withered away without coming to bear fruit. Papa seems to have no more idea of my living beyond these four walls, than of a journey to Lapland. I confess that I thought it possible he might propose the country for the summer, or even Italy for the winter, in a 'late remark'—but no, 'nothing' and there is not a possibility of either word, as I see things. My brothers 'wish that something could be arranged'—a wish which I put away quietly as often as they bring it to me. And for my uncle and aunt, they have been talking to me to-day—and she with her usual acuteness in such matters, observing my evasion, said, 'Ah Ba, you have arranged your plans more than you would have us believe. But you are right not to tell us—indeed I would rather not hear. Only *don't be rash—that* is my only advice to you.'

While we were talking, Papa came into the room. My aunt said, 'How well she is looking'—'Do you think so?' he said. 'Why, do not *you* think so? Do you pretend to say that you see no surprising difference in her?'—'Oh, I don't know,' he went on to say. 'She is mumpish, I think.' Mumpish!

'She does not talk,' resumed he—

'Perhaps she is nervous'—my aunt apologised—I said not one word . . . When birds have their eyes out, they are apt to be mumpish.

Mumpish! The expression proved a displeasure. Yet I am sure that I have shown as little sullenness as was possible. To be very talkative and vivacious under such circumstances as those of mine, would argue insensibility, and was certainly beyond my power.

I told her gently afterwards that she had been wrong in speaking of me at all—a wrong with a right intention,—as all her wrongness must be. She was very sorry to have done it, she said, and looked sorry.

Poor Papa!—Presently I shall be worse to him than 'mumpish'

even. But *then*, I hope, he will try to forgive me, as I have forgiven him, long ago.[40]

Again Browning sensed her dread of taking action, and complained.

From Elizabeth, Sunday, Aug. 30, 1846: Seriously, I don't want to make unnecessary delays. It is a horrible position, however I may cover it with your roses and thoughts of you—and far worse to myself than to you, inasmuch that what is painful to you once a week, is to me so continually. To hear the voice of my father and meet his eye makes me shrink back—to talk to my brothers leaves my nerves all trembling . . . and even to receive the sympathy of my sisters turns into sorrow and fear, lest they should suffer through their affection for me. How I can look and sleep as well as I do, is a miracle exactly like the rest—or would be, if the love were not the deepest and strongest thing of all, and did not hold and possess me overcomingly.[41]

From Browning, Sunday morning, Aug. 30, 1846: I wonder what I shall write to you, Ba—I could suppress my feelings here, as I do on other points, and say nothing of the hatefulness of this state of things which is prolonged so uselessly. There is the point—show me one good reason, or show of reason, why we gain anything by deferring our departure till next week instead of to-morrow, and I will bear to perform yesterday's part for the amusement of Mr. Kenyon a dozen times over without complaint. But if the cold plunge *must* be taken, all this shivering delay on the bank is hurtful as well as fruitless. I *do* understand your anxieties, dearest—I take your fears and make them mine, while I put my own natural feeling of quite another kind away from us both, succeeding in *that* beyond all expectation. There is no amount of patience or suffering I would not undergo to relieve you from these apprehensions. But if, on the whole, you really determine to act as we propose in spite of them,—why, a new leaf is turned over in our journal, an old part of our adventure done with, and a new one entered upon, altogether distinct from the other. Having once decided to go to Italy with me, the next thing to decide is on the best means of going—or rather, there is just this connection between the two measures, that by the success or failure of the last, the first will have to be justified or condemned.

You tell me you have decided to go—then, dearest, you will be prepared to go earlier than you promised yesterday—by the end of September at very latest. In proportion to the too probable excitement and painful circumstances of the departure, the greater amount of advantages should be secured for the departure itself. How can I take you away in even the beginning of October? We shall be a fortnight on the journey—with the year, as everybody sees and says, a full month in advance . . . cold mornings and dark evenings already. Everybody would cry out on such folly when it was found that we let the favourable weather escape, in full assurance that the Autumn would come to us unattended by any one beneficial circumstance.

My own dearest, I am wholly your own, for ever, and under every determination of yours. If you find yourself unable, or unwilling to make this effort, tell me so and plainly and at once—I will not offer a word in objection,—I will continue our present life, if you please, so far as may be desirable, and wait till next autumn, and the next and the next, till providence end our waiting. It is clearly not for me to pretend to instruct you in your duties to God and yourself; . . . enough, that I have long ago chosen to accept your decision. If, on the other hand, you make up your mind to leave England now, you will be prepared by the end of September.

I should think myself the most unworthy of human beings if I could employ any arguments with the remotest show of a tendency to *frighten* you into a compliance with any scheme of mine. Those methods are for people in another relation to you. But you love me, and, at lowest, shall I say, wish me well—and the fact is too obvious for me to commit any indelicacy in reminding you, that in any dreadful event to our journey of which I could accuse myself as the cause,— as of this undertaking to travel with you in the worst time of year when I could have taken the best,—in the case of your health being irretrievably shaken, for instance . . . the happiest fate I should pray for would be to live and die in some corner where I might never hear a word of the English language, much less a comment in it on my own wretched imbecility,—to disappear and be forgotten.

So that must not be, for all our sakes. My family will give me to you that we may be both of us happy . . . but for such an end—no! Dearest, do you think all this earnestness foolish and uncalled for? —that I might know you spoke yesterday in mere jest,—as yourself said, 'only to hear what I would say'? Ah but consider, my own Ba, the way of our life, as it is, and is to be—a word, a simple word from you, is not as a word is counted in the world—the word between us is different—I am guided by your will, which a word shall signify to me. Consider that just such a word, so spoken, even with that lightness, would make me lay my life at your feet at any minute. Should we gain anything by my trying, if I could, to deaden the sense of hearing, dull the medium of communication between us; and procuring that, instead of this prompt rising of my will at the first intimation from yours, the same effect should only follow after fifty speeches, and as many protestations of complete serious desire for their success on your part, accompanied by all kinds of acts and deeds and other evidence of the same?

At all events, God knows I have said this in the deepest, truest love of you. I will say no more, praying you to forgive whatever you shall judge to need forgiveness here,—dearest Ba!

My friend Pritchard tells me that Brighton is not to be thought of under ordinary circumstances as a point of departure for Havre. Its one packet a week from Shoreham cannot get in if the wind and tide are unfavourable. There is the greatest uncertainty in consequence . . . as I have heard before—while, of course, from Southampton, the departures are calculated punctually. He considers that the least troublesome plan, and the cheapest, is to go from London to Havre . . . the voyage being so arranged that the river passage takes up the day and the sea-crossing the night—you reach Havre early in the morning and get to Paris by four o'clock, perhaps, in the afternoon . . . in time to leave for Orleans and spend the night there, I suppose.[42]

From Elizabeth, Monday night, Aug. 31, 1846: I have not given you reason to *doubt me* or my inclination to accede to any serious wish of yours relating to the step before us. On the contrary I told you in so many words in July, that, if you really wished to go in August rather than in September, I would make no difficulty—to which you answered, remember, that *October or November would do as well.* Now *is* it fair, ever dearest, that you should turn round on me so quickly, and call in question my willingness to keep my engagement for years, if ever? Can I help it, if the circumstances around us are painful to both of us? Did I not keep repeating, from the beginning, that they *must* be painful? Only you could not believe, you see, until you felt the pricks. And when all is done, and the doing shall be the

occasion of new affronts, sarcasms, every form of injustice, will you
be any happier then, than you are now that you only imagine the
possibility of them? I tremble to answer that question—even to myself—! As for myself, though I cannot help feeling pain and fear, in
encountering what is to be encountered, and though I sometimes fear,
in addition, for *you*, lest you should overtask your serenity in bearing
your own part in it, . . . yet certainly I have never wavered for a
moment from the decision on which all depends. I might fill up your
quotations from 'Prometheus,' and say how no evil takes me unaware,
having foreseen all from the beginning—but I have not the heart for
filling up quotations. I mean to say only, that I never wavered from
the promise I gave freely; and that I will keep it freely at any time
you choose—that is, within a week of any time you choose. As to a
light word . . . why now, dear, judge me in justice! If I had written
it, there might have been more wrong in it—but I spoke it lightly to
show it was light, and in the next breath I told you that it was a jest.
Will you not forgive me a word so spoken, Robert? will you rather
set it against me as if habitually I threw to you levities in change for
earnest devotion?—you imply *that* of me. Or you *seem* to imply it—
you did not mean, you could not, a thought approaching to unkindness,—but it looks like *that* in the letter, or *did*, this morning. And
all the time, you pretended not to know very well, . . . (dearest!)
. . . that what you made up your mind to wish and ask of me, I had
not in my power to say 'no' to. Ah, you *knew* that you had only to
make up your mind, and to see that the thing was possible. So if
September shall be possible, let it be September. I do not object nor
hold back. To sail from the Thames has not the feasibility—and
listen why! All the sailing or rather steaming from London begins
early; and I told you how out of the question it was, for me to leave
this house early. I could not, without involving my sisters. Arabel
sleeps in my room, on the sofa, and is seldom out of the room before
nine in the morning—and for me to draw her into a ruinous confidence, or to escape without a confidence at that hour, would be
equally impossible. Now see if it is my fancy, my whim! And as for
the expenses, *they* are as nearly equal as a shilling and two sixpences
can be—the expense of the sea-voyage from London to Havre, and
of the land and sea voyage, through Southampton . . . *or* Brighton.
But of course what you say of Brighton, keeps us to Southampton,
of those two routes. We can go to Southampton and meet the
packet . . . take the river-steamer to Rouen, and proceed as rapidly

as your programme shows. You are not angry with me, dearest, dearest? I did not mean any harm.[43]

From Elizabeth, Tuesday, Sept. 1, 1846: If we go to South-ampton, we go straight from the railroad to the packet, without en-tering any hotel—and if we do *so, no* greater expense is incurred than by the long water-passage from London. Also, we reach Havre alike in the morning, and have the day before us for Rouen, Paris and Orleans. Thereupon nothing is lost by losing the early hour for the departure. Then, if I accede to your *idée fixe* about the marriage! Only do not let us put a long time between that and the setting out, and do not you come here afterwards—let us go away as soon as possible afterwards at least. You are afraid for me of my suffering from the autumnal cold when it is yet far off—while *I* (observe this!) while *I* am afraid for myself, of breaking down under quite a differ-ent set of causes, in nervous excitement and exhaustion. I belong to that pitiful order of weak women who cannot command their bodies with their souls at every moment, and who sink down in hysterical disorder when they ought to act and resist. Now I think and believe that I shall take strength from my attachment to you, and so go through to the end what is before us; but at the same time, knowing myself and fearing myself, I do desire to provoke the 'demon' as little as possible, and to be as quiet as the situation will permit. Still, where things *ought* to be done, they of course *must* be done. Only we should consider whether they really *ought* to be done—not for the sake of the inconvenience to me, but of the consequence to both of us.

Do I frighten you, ever dearest? Oh no—I shall go through it, if I keep a breath of soul in me to live with. I shall go through it, as certainly as that I love you. I speak only of the accessory circum-stances, that they may be kept as smooth as is practicable.[44]

VII

From Elizabeth, Wednesday night, Sept. 9, 1846: Dearest, you are a prophet, I suppose—there can be no denying it. This night, an edict has gone out, and George is to-morrow to be on his way to take a house for a month either at Dover, Reigate, Tunbridge, . . . Papa did 'not mind which,' he said, and 'you may settle it among you!!' but he 'must have this house empty for a month in order to its cleaning'—we are to go therefore and not delay.

Now!—what *can* be done? It is possible that the absence may be longer than for a month, indeed it is probable—for there is much to do in painting and repairing, here in Wimpole Street, more than a month's work they say. Decide, after thinking. I am embarrassed to the utmost degree, as to the best path to take. If we are taken away on Monday . . . what then?

Of course I decline to give any opinion and express any preference,—as to places, I mean. It is not for my sake that we go:—if *I* had been considered at all, indeed, we should have been taken away earlier, . . . and not certainly now, when the cold season is at hand. And so much the better it is for me, that I have not, obviously, been thought of.

Therefore decide! It seems quite too soon and too sudden for us to set out on our Italian adventure now—and perhaps even we could not compass—

Well—but you must think for both of us. It is past twelve and I have just a moment to seal this and entrust it to Henrietta for the morning's post.

I will do as you wish—understand.[45]

From Browning, Thursday, Sept. 10, 1846: 'I will do as you wish—understand'—then I understand you are in earnest. If you *do* go on Monday, our marriage will be impossible for another year—the misery! You see what we have gained by waiting. We must be *married directly* and go to Italy. I will go for a licence to-day and we can be married on Saturday. I will call to-morrow at 3 to arrange everything with you. We can leave from Dover &c., *after* that,—but otherwise, impossible! Inclose the ring, or a substitute—I have not a minute to spare for the post.

A few hours later: I broke open your sealed letter and added the postscript just now. The post being thus saved, I can say a few words more leisurely.

I will go to-morrow, I think, and not to-day for the licence—there are fixed hours I fancy at the office—and I might be too late. I will also make the arrangement with my friend for Saturday, if we should want him,—as we shall, in all probability—it would look suspiciously to be unaccompanied. We can arrange to-morrow.

Your words, first and last, have been that you 'would not fail me'— you will not.

And the marriage over, you can take advantage of circumstances and go early or late in the week, as may be practicable. There will be facilities in the general packing &c.,—your own measures may be taken unobserved. Write short notes to the proper persons,—promising longer ones, if necessary.

See the *tone* I take, the way I write to *you* . . . but it is all through you, in the little brief authority you give me,—and in the perfect belief of your truth and firmness—indeed, I do not consider this an extraordinary occasion for proving those qualities—this conduct of your father's is quite characteristic.

Otherwise, too, the departure with its bustle is not unfavourable. If you hesitated, it would be before a little hurried shopping and letter-writing! I expected it, and therefore spoke as you heard yesterday. *Now your* part must begin. It may as well begin and end, both, *now* as at any other time. I will bring you every information possible to-morrow.

It seems as if I should insult you if I spoke a word to confirm you, to beseech you, to relieve you from your promise, if you claim it.[46]

From Elizabeth, Thursday, Sept. 10, 1846: Dearest, I write one word, and have one will which is yours. At the same time, do not be precipitate—we shall not be taken away on Monday, no, nor for several days afterward. George has simply gone to look for houses—going to Reigate first.

Oh yes—come to-morrow. And then, you shall have the ring . . . soon enough and safer.[47]

Robert Browning and Elizabeth Barrett were married in St. Marylebone Parish Church at eleven o'clock on Saturday morning, September 12. The only witnesses were a cousin of Browning's and Elizabeth's maid, Wilson, who was to accompany them to Italy. Immediately after the ceremony they parted, Elizabeth removing her ring and going for a preannounced visit to the house of a friend, where her sisters found her and took her home.

From Browning, 1:00 P.M., Saturday, Sept. 12, 1846: You will only expect a few words—what will those be? When the heart is full it may run over, but the real fulness stays within.

You asked me yesterday 'if I should repent?' Yes—my own Ba,—I could wish all the past were to do over again, that in it I might somewhat more,—never so little more, conform in the outward homage to the inward feeling. What I have professed . . . (for I have performed nothing) seems to fall short of what my first love required even—and when I think of *this* moment's love . . . I could repent, as I say.

Words can never tell you, however,—form them, transform them anyway,—how perfectly dear you are to me—perfectly dear to my heart and soul.

I look back, and in every one point, every word and gesture, every letter, every *silence*—you have been entirely perfect to me—I would not change one word, one look.

My hope and aim are to preserve this love, not to fall from it—for which I trust to God who procured it for me, and doubtlessly can preserve it.

Enough now, my dearest, dearest, own Ba! You have given me the highest, completest proof of love that ever one human being gave another. I am all gratitude—and all pride (under the proper feeling which ascribes pride to the right source) all pride that my life has been so crowned by you.

God bless you prays your very own R.

I will write to-morrow of course. Take every care of *my life* which is in that dearest little hand; try and be composed, my beloved.

Remember to thank Wilson for me.[48]

From Elizabeth, 4:30 P.M., Saturday, Sept. 12, 1846 : Ever dearest, I write a word that you may read it and know how all is safe so far, and that I am not slain downright with the day—oh, *such a day!* I went to Mr. Boyd's directly, so as to send Wilson home the faster—and was able to lie quietly on the sofa in his sitting-room downstairs, before he was ready to see me, being happily engaged with a medical councillor. Then I was made to talk and take Cyprus wine,—and, my sisters delaying to come, I had some bread and butter for dinner, to keep me from looking too pale in their eyes. At last they came, and with such grave faces! Missing me and Wilson, they had taken fright,—and Arabel had forgotten at first what I told her last night about the fly. I kept saying, 'What nonsense, . . . what fancies you do have to be sure,' . . . trembling in my heart with every look they cast at me. And so, to complete the bravery, I went on with them in the carriage to Hampstead . . . as far as the heath, —and talked and looked—now you shall praise me for courage—or rather you shall love me for the love which was the root of it all. How necessity makes heroes—or heroines at least! For I did not sleep all last night, and when I first went out with Wilson to get to the fly-stand in Marylebone Street I staggered so, that we both were afraid for the fear's sake,—but we called at a chemist's for sal volatile and were thus enabled to go on. I spoke to her last night, and she was very kind, very affectionate, and never shrank for a moment. I told her that always I should be grateful to her.

You—how are you? how is your head, ever dearest?

It seems all like a dream! When we drove past that church again, I and my sisters, there was a cloud before my eyes. Ask your mother to forgive me, Robert. If *I* had not been there, *she* would have been there, perhaps.

And for the rest, if either of us two is to suffer injury and sorrow for what happened there to-day—I pray that it may all fall upon *me!* Nor should I suffer the most pain *that* way, as I know, and God knows.[49]

From Elizabeth, Sunday, Sept. 13, 1846: My own beloved, if ever you should have reason to complain of me in things voluntary and possible, all other women would have a right to tread me under-foot, I should be so vile and utterly unworthy. There is my answer to what you wrote yesterday of wishing to be better to me . . . you! What could be better than lifting me from the ground and carrying me into life and the sunshine? I was yours rather by right than by gift (yet by gift also, my beloved!) ; for what you have saved and renewed is surely yours. All that I am, I owe you—if I enjoy any-thing now and henceforth, it is through you. You know this well. Even as *I*, from the beginning, knew that I had no power against you, . . . or that, if I *had*, it was for your sake.

Dearest, in the emotion and confusion of yesterday morning, there was yet room in me for one thought which was not a feeling—for I thought that, of the many, many women who have stood where I stood, and to the same end, not one of them all perhaps, not one per-haps, since that building was a church, has had reasons strong as mine, for an absolute trust and devotion towards the man she mar-ried,—not one! And then I both thought and felt, that it was only just, for them, . . . those women who were less happy, . . . to have that affectionate sympathy and support and presence of their nearest relations, parent or sister . . . which failed to *me*, . . . needing it less through being happier!

All my brothers have been here this morning, laughing and talking, and discussing this matter of the leaving town,—and in the room, at the same time, were two or three female friends of ours, from Herefordshire—and I did not *dare* to cry out against the noise, though my head seemed splitting in two (one half for each shoulder), I had such a morbid fear of exciting a suspicion. Trippy too being one of them, I promised to go to see her to-morrow and dine in her drawing-room if she would give me, for dinner, some bread and butter. It was like having a sort of fever. And all in the midst, the bells began to ring. 'What bells are those?' asked one of the provincials. 'Marylebone Church bells' said Henrietta, standing behind my chair.

And now . . . while I write, having escaped from the great din, and sit here quietly,—comes . . . who do you think?—Mr. Kenyon.

He came with his spectacles, looking as if his eyes reached to their rim all the way round; and one of the first words was, '*When did you see Browning?*' And I think I shall make a pretension to presence of mind henceforward; for, though *certainly* I changed colour and he saw it, I yet answered with a tolerably quick evasion, . . . 'He was here on Friday'—and leapt straight into another subject, and left him gazing fixedly on my face. Dearest, he saw something, but not all. So we talked, talked. He told me that the 'Fawn of Sertorius,' (which I refused to cut open the other day,) was ascribed to Landor—and he told me that he meant to leave town again on Wednesday, and would see me once before then. On rising to go away, he mentioned your name a second time . . . 'When do you see Browning again?' To which I answered that I did not know.

Is not *that* pleasant? The worst is that all these combinations of things make me feel so bewildered that I cannot make the necessary arrangements, as far as the letters go. But I must break from the dream-stupor which falls on me when left to myself a little, and set about what remains to be done.

A house near Watford is thought of now—but, as none is concluded on, the removal is not likely to take place in the middle of the week even, perhaps.

I sit in a dream, when left to myself. I cannot believe, or understand. Oh! but in all this difficult, embarrassing and painful situation, I look over the palms to Troy—I feel happy and exulting to belong to you, past every opposition, out of sight of every will of man— none can put us asunder, now, at least. I have a right now openly to love you, and to hear other people call it *a duty*, when I do, . . . knowing that if it were a sin, it would be done equally. Ah—*I* shall not be first to leave off *that*—see if I shall! May God bless you, ever and ever dearest! Beseech for me the indulgence of your father and mother, and ask your sister to love me. I feel so as if I had slipped down over the wall into somebody's garden—I feel ashamed. To be grateful and affectionate to them all, while I live, is all that I can do, and it is too much a matter of course to need to be promised. Promise it however for your very own Ba whom you made so happy with the dear letter last night. But say in the next how you are— and how your mother is.

I did hate so, to have to take off the ring! You will have to take the trouble of putting it on again, some day.[50]

From Elizabeth, Monday evening, Sept. 14, 1846: In the meantime, there seems so much to do, that I am frightened to look towards the heaps of it. As to accoutrements, everything has been arranged as simply as possible that way—but still there are neces- sities—and the letters, the letters! I am paralysed when I think of having to write such words as . . . 'Papa, I am married; I hope you will not be too displeased.' Ah, poor Papa! You are too sanguine if you expect any such calm from him as an assumption of indifference would imply. To the utmost, he will be angry,—he will cast me off as far from him. Well—there is no comfort in such thoughts. How I felt to-night when I saw him at seven o'clock, for the first time since Friday, and the event of Saturday! He spoke kindly too, and asked me how I was. Once I heard of his saying of me that I was 'the purest woman he ever knew,'—which made me smile at the moment, or laugh I believe, outright, because I understood perfectly what he meant by *that*—viz—that I had not troubled him with the iniquity of love affairs, or any impropriety of seeming to think about being married. But now the whole sex will go down with me to the perdition of faith in any of us. See the effect of my wickedness!—'Those women!'

But we will submit, dearest. I will put myself under his feet, to be forgiven a little, . . . enough to be taken up again into his arms. I love him—he is my father—he has good and high qualities after all: he is my father *above* all. And *you*, because you are so generous and tender to me, will let me, you say, and help me to try to win back the alienated affection—for which, I thank you and bless you,—I did not thank you enough this morning. Surely I may say to him, too, . . . 'With the exception of this act, I have submitted to the least of your wishes all my life long. Set the life against the act, and forgive me, for the sake of the daughter you once loved.' Surely I may say *that*,—and then remind him of the long suffering I have suffered,—and entreat him to pardon the happiness which has come at last.

And *he* will wish in return, that I had died years ago! For the storm will come and endure. And at last, perhaps, he will forgive us —it is my hope.

It is best, I continue to think, that you should not come here—best for *you*, because the position, if you were to try it, would be less tolerable than ever—and best for both of us, that in case the whole truth were ever discovered (I mean, of the previous marriage) we might be able to call it simply an act in order to security. I don't know how to put my feeling into words, but I do seem to feel that it would be better, and less offensive to those whom we offend at any rate, to avoid all possible remark on this point. It seems better to a sort of instinct I have.[51]

From Elizabeth, postmarked Sept. 17, 1846: Dearest, the general departure from this house takes place on Monday—and the house at Little Bookham is six miles from the nearest railroad, and a mile and a half from Leatherhead where a coach runs. Now you are to judge. Certainly if I go with you on Saturday I shall not have half the letters written—you, who talk so largely of epic poems, have not the least imagination of my state of mind and spirits. I began to write a letter to Papa this morning, and could do nothing but cry, and looked so pale thereupon, that everybody wondered what could be the matter. Oh—quite well I am now, and I only speak of myself in that way to show you how the inspiration is by no means sufficient for epic poems. Still, I may certainly write the necessary letters, . . . and do the others on the road . . . could I, do you think? I would rather have waited—indeed rather—only it may be difficult to leave Bookham . . . yet *possible*—so tell me what you would have me do.

Wilson and I have a light box and a carpet bag between us—and I will be docile about the books, dearest. Do you take a desk? Had I better not, I wonder?

Then for the box and carpet bag . . . Remember that we cannot take them out of the house with us. We must send them the evening before—Friday evening, if we went on Saturday . . . and where? Have you a friend anywhere, to whose house they might be sent, or could they go direct to the railroad office—and what office? In that case they should have your name on them, should they not?[52]

From Browning, Thursday, Sept. 17, 1846: My only sweetest, I will write just a word to catch the earlier post,—time pressing. Bless you for all you suffer . . . I *know* it though it would be very needless to call your attention to the difficulties. I know much, if not all, and can only love and admire you,—not help, alas!

Surely these difficulties will multiply, if you go to Bookham—the way will be to leave at once. The letters may easily be written during the journey . . . at Orléans, for example. But now,—you propose *Saturday* . . . nothing leaves Southampton according to *to-day's* advertisement till *Tuesday* . . . the days seemed changed to *Tuesdays* and *Fridays*. To-morrow at $8\frac{1}{4}$ P.M. and Friday [Tuesday] the 22, $10\frac{1}{4}$. Provoking! I will go to town directly to the railway office and enquire particularly—getting the time-table also. Under these circumstances, we have only the choice of Dieppe (as needing the shortest diligence-journey)—or the Sunday morning Havre-packet, at 9 A.M.—which you do not consider practicable: though it would, I think, take us the quickliest out of all the trouble. I will let you know all particulars in a note to-night . . . it shall reach you to-night.[53]

From Browning, 5 P.M., Thursday, Sept. 17, 1846: My own Ba, I believe, or am sure the mistake has been mine—in the flurry I noted down the departures from *Havre*—instead of *Southampton*. You must either be at the Vauxhall Station by *four* o'clock —so as to arrive in 3 hours and a half at Southampton and leave by $8\frac{1}{4}$ P.M.—or must go by the Sunday Boat,—or *wait* till Tuesday. Dieppe is impossible, being too early. You must decide—and let me know directly. To-morrow *is* too early—yet one . . . that is, *I*— could manage.[54]

From Browning, 7:30 P.M., Thursday, Sept. 17, 1846: My own Ba—forgive my mistaking! I had not enough confidence in my own correctness. The advertisement of the Tuesday and Friday Boats is of the South of England Steam Company. The Wednesday and Saturday is that of the *South Western*. There must be then *two* companies, because on the Southampton Railway Bill it is expressly stated that there are departures for Havre on all four days. Perhaps you have seen my blunder. In that case, you can leave by 1-$12\frac{1}{2}$ as you may appoint—[55]

From Elizabeth, postmarked Sept. 18, 1846: Dearest take this word, as if it were many. I am so tired—and then it shall be the right word.

Sunday and Friday are impossible. On Saturday I will go to you, if you like—with half done, . . . nothing done . . . scarcely. Will you come for me to Hodgson's? or shall I meet you at the station? At what o'clock should I set out, to be there at the hour you mention?

Also, for the boxes . . . we cannot carry them out of the house, you know, Wilson and I. They must be sent on Friday evening to the Vauxhall Station, 'to be taken care of.' Will the people keep them carefully? Ought someone to be spoken to beforehand? If we sent them to New Cross, they would not reach you in time.

Hold me my beloved—with your love. It is very hard—But Saturday seems the only day for us. Tell me if you think so indeed.[56]

From Browning, 11:30 a.m., Friday, Sept. 18, 1846: How thankful I am you have seen my blunder—I took the other company's days for the South Western's changed. What I shall write now is with the tables before me (of the Railway) and a transcript from *to-day's* advertisement in the *Times*.

The packet will leave to-morrow evening, from the Royal Pier, Southampton at *nine*. We leave Nine Elms, Vauxhall, at *five*—to arrive at *eight*. Doors close *five* minutes before. I will be at Hodgson's *from* half-past three to *four precisely* when I shall hope you can be ready. I shall go to Vauxhall, apprise them that luggage is coming (yours) and send *mine* there—so that we both shall be unencumbered and we can take a cab or coach from H's.

Never mind your scanty preparations . . . we can get everything at Leghorn,—and the new boats carry parcels to Leghorn on the 15th of every month, remember—so can bring what you may wish to send for.[57]

From Elizabeth, Friday night, Sept. 18, 1846: At from half-past three to four, then—four will not, I suppose, be too late. I will not write more—*I cannot*. By to-morrow at this time, I shall have *you* only, to love me—my beloved!

You *only!* As if one said *God only*. And we shall have *Him* beside, I pray of Him.

I shall send to your address at New Cross your Hanmer's poems— and the two dear books you gave me, which I do not like to leave here and am afraid of hurting by taking them with me. Will you ask *our* Sister to put the parcel into a drawer, so as to keep it for us?

Your letters to me I take with me, let the 'ounces' cry out aloud, ever so. I *tried* to leave them, and I could not. That is, they would not be left: it was not my fault—I will not be scolded.

Is this my last letter to you, ever dearest? Oh—if I loved you less . . . a little, little less.

Why I should tell you that our marriage was invalid, or ought to be; and that you should by no means come for me to-morrow. It is dreadful . . . dreadful . . . to have to give pain here by a voluntary act—for the first time in my life.

Remind your mother and father of me affectionately and gratefully—and your Sister too! Would she think it too bold of me to say *our* Sister, if she had heard it on the last page?

Do you pray for me to-night, Robert? Pray for me, and love me, that I may have courage, feeling both—

Your own
Ba.

The boxes are *safely sent*. Wilson has been perfect to me. And *I* . . . calling her 'timid,' and afraid of her timidity! I begin to think that none are so bold as the timid, when they are fairly roused.[58]

CHAPTER 4

Dante Gabriel Rossetti

———————— ❧ ————————

"Why should we go on talking about the visionary vanities
of half-a-dozen boys?"

I

Cheyne Walk, ❧*recalled the novelist Hall Caine of an autumn*
afternoon in 1880❧, was unknown to me at the time of my first visit
to Rossetti, except as the locality in which men and women eminent in
literature were residing. George Eliot, after her marriage with Mr.
Cross, had lately come to No. 4; while at No. 5 in the second street
to the westward Carlyle was still living, and a little beyond Cheyne
Row stood the modest cottage wherein Turner died. Rossetti's house
was No. 16. It seemed to be the oldest house in the Walk, and the
exceptional size of its gate piers and the height and weight of its
gate and railings suggested to my eye that perhaps at some period
it had stood alone, commanding as grounds a large part of the space
occupied by the houses on either side.

The house itself was a plain Queen Anne erection, much mutilated
by the introduction of unsightly bow windows, the brick work falling

into decay, the paint in need of renewal, the windows dull with the dust of months, the sills bearing more than the suspicion of cobwebs, the angles of the steps to the porch and the untrodden flags of the little court leading up to them overgrown with moss and weed, while round the walls and up the reveals of door and windows were creeping the tangled branches of the wildest ivy that ever grew untouched by shears.

Such was the exterior of the house of the poet-painter when I walked up to it on the autumn evening of my earliest visit, and the interior of the house, when with trembling heart I first stepped over the threshold, seemed to be at once like and unlike the outside. The hall had a puzzling look of equal nobility and shabbiness, for the floor was paved with white marble, which was partly covered by a strip of worn-out cocoa-nut matting. Three doors led out of the hall, one at each side and one in front, and two corridors opened into it, but there was no sign of a staircase, and neither was there any daylight, except the little that was borrowed from a fanlight which looked into the porch.

I took note of these things in the few minutes I stood waiting in the hall, and if I had to sum up my first impressions of the home of Rossetti, I should say it looked like a house that no woman had ever dwelt in, a house inhabited by a man who had once felt a vivid interest in life, but was now living from day to day.

Very soon Rossetti came to me through the doorway in front, which proved to be the entrance to his studio. Holding out both hands and crying "Hulloa," he gave me that cheery, hearty greeting which I have come to recognise as belonging to him alone, perhaps, of all the men I have ever known. Leading the way into the studio, he introduced me to his brother William, who was there on one of the evening visits which, at intervals of a week, he made then with unfailing regularity.

I should have described Rossetti, at that time, as a man who looked quite ten years older than his actual age (fifty-two), of full middle height and inclining to corpulence, with a round face that ought, one thought, to be ruddy but was pale; with large gray eyes that had a steady introspective look and were surmounted by broad protrusive brows, and divided by a clearly pencilled ridge over the nose, which was well cut and had breathing nostrils resembling the nostrils of a high-bred horse.

His mouth and chin were hidden beneath a heavy moustache and an abundant beard which had once been mixed black-brown and auburn, but were now thickly streaked with gray. His forehead was large, round, without protuberances, and very gently receding to where thin black curls began to roll round to the ears. I thought his head and face singularly noble, and from the eyes upward full of beauty.

His dress was not conspicuous, being rather negligent than eccentric, and only remarkable for a straight sack coat (his "painting coat") buttoned close to the throat, descending at least to the knees, and having large perpendicular pockets, in which he kept his hands almost constantly while he walked to and fro. His voice, even in the preliminary courtesies of conversation, was, I thought, the richest I had ever heard. It was a deep, full barytone, with easy modulations and undertones of infinite softness and sweetness, yet capable, as I speedily found, of almost illimitable compass.

The studio was a large irregular room, structurally puzzling to one who saw it for the first time. Over the fireplace and at either side of it hung a number of drawings in chalk, chiefly studies of female heads, all very beautiful, and all by Rossetti himself. Easels of various size, some very large, bearing partially painted pictures, stood at irregular angles nearly all over the floor, leaving room only for a few pieces of furniture—a large sofa, under a holland cover, somewhat baggy and soiled, two low easy chairs, similarly apparelled, a large bookcase with a glass front, surmounted by a yellow copy of the Stratford bust of Shakespeare, two carved cabinets, and a little writing desk and cane-bottomed chair in the corner, near a small window which was heavily darkened by the thick foliage of the trees that grew in the garden beyond.

He had pulled a huge canvas into a position in which it could be seen, and it was then I saw, for the first time, the painter's most important picture, "Dante's Dream." The effect produced upon me by that wonderful work, so simple in its scheme, so conventional in its composition, yet so noble in its feeling and so profound in its emotion, has probably been repeated a thousand times since in minds more capable of appreciating the technical qualities of the painter's art; but few or none can know what added power of appeal the great picture had as I saw it then, under the waning light of an autumn afternoon, in the painter's studio, so full of the atmosphere of the picture itself, and with the painter beside it, so clearly a man out of another age.

"Does your work take much out of you in physical energy?" I asked.

"Not my painting, certainly," said Rossetti, "though in earlier years it tormented me more than enough. Now I paint by a set of unwritten but clearly defined rules, which I could teach to any man as systematically as you could teach arithmetic."

"Still," I said, "there's a good deal in a picture like this beside what you can do by rule—eh?"

I laughed, he laughed, and then he said, as nearly as I can remember:

"Conception, no doubt; but beyond that, not much. Painting, after all, is the craft of a superior carpenter. The part of a picture that is not mechanical is often trivial enough." And then, with the suspicion of a twinkle in his eye, he added:

"I shouldn't wonder, now, if you imagine that one comes down in a fine frenzy every morning to daub canvas."

More laughter on both sides, and then I said I certainly imagined that a superior carpenter would find it hard to paint another "Dante's Dream," which I considered the best example I had yet seen of the English school.

"Friendly nonsense," replied my frank host; "there is now no English school whatever."

"Well," I said, "if you deny the name to others who lay more claim to it, will you not at least allow it to the three or four painters who started with you in life—the pre-Raphaelites, you know?"

"Not at all, unless it is to Brown, and he's more French than English, Hunt and Jones have no more claim to it than I have. Pre-Raphaelites! A group of young fellows who couldn't draw!" With this came one of his full-chested laughs, and then quickly behind it:

"As for all the prattle about pre-Raphaelitism, I confess to you I am weary of it, and long have been. Why should we go on talking about the visionary vanities of half-a-dozen boys? We've all grown out of them, I hope, by now."[1]

II

By 1880 the Pre-Raphaelite brothers of thirty years before, ardent fellow seekers after life and truth and beauty, had long since

gone their separate ways. Dante Gabriel Rossetti lived in morbid iso-
lation, painting his glorious, idealized women. Broken in health, his
mind intermittently deranged, dependent on drugs for his tormented
sleep, he had only two years to live. William Michael Rossetti—civil
servant, art critic, and literary biographer—still hovered near, as
always devotedly serving his famous brother. John Everett Millais,
the onetime child prodigy of the Academy schools and future
president of the Royal Academy, enjoyed in 1880 enormous popu-
larity, his expert, sentimental pictures and fashionable portraits
earning him the princely income of £40,000 a year. The sculptor
Thomas Woolner, too, had become famous and wealthy for his busts
and medallions of eminent contemporaries. Fortune thus far had
been less kind to William Holman Hunt, who alone persevered in
proud devotion to the Pre-Raphaelite creed, his rigid integrity per-
mitting him to complete relatively few paintings. Like William Ros-
setti, Frederick George Stephens had forsaken practice for criticism
and now wrote regularly on art for The Athenæum. *James Collinson,*
religiously perplexed, had early abandoned painting, lived briefly in
a Jesuit college, then married and disappeared from view. None of
the survivors was in sympathy with the new generation of artists who
derived their inspiration from the French impressionists. The
younger men in turn despised the "subject pictures" of the English
school, not least the languid, etherealized women, the moral and re-
ligious allegories, the medieval costume pieces that in the public
mind had come to represent Pre-Raphaelitism.

Of all the Brotherhood, Rossetti's fame was to prove the most en-
during. Taken separately, his powers as painter or as poet would
have been sufficient to establish him in the front rank of his con-
temporaries; their combination in one man placed him in a class
apart. Rossetti had at times attempted deliberately to subordinate
his poetic genius to his artistic, but his poetry was his more perfect
achievement, excelled among Victorian verse only by that of Tenny-
son and Browning. His painting, though brilliant in design and color,
was technically faulty and of limited range, Rossetti never having
been willing to master the difficult elements of his craft. But both as
painter and poet, Rossetti had attracted brilliant disciples, among
them William Morris, Edward Burne-Jones, and Algernon Swin-
burne. And with Rossetti alone did the rising generation of artists
acknowledge any measure of kinship, though more for his poetry than

for his painting, and perhaps more for his passionate, rebellious, pathetically wrecked life than for either.

Rossetti died in 1882. To the aging men who had been the companions of his youth, that mysterious, fascinating figure, ambiguous and disturbing enough when close at hand, was already obscured by time, estrangements, and varied fortunes. Yet upon all their lives Rossetti had left ineffaceable impressions.

Holman Hunt's recollections of Rossetti went back to 1848, when Hunt was twenty-one and his romantic painting, "The Eve of Saint Agnes," hung high and unregarded in the exhibition rooms of the Royal Academy :

Rossetti came up to me, repeating with emphasis his praise, and loudly declaring that my picture of "The Eve of St. Agnes" was the best in the collection. Probably the fact that the subject was taken from Keats made him the more unrestrained, for I think no one had ever before painted any subject from this still little-known poet. Rossetti frankly proposed to come and see me. Before this I had been only on nodding terms with him in the schools, to which he came but rarely and irregularly. He had always attracted there a following of clamorous students, who, like Millais' throng, were rewarded with original sketches. Rossetti's subjects were of a different class from Millais, not of newly culled facts, but of knights rescuing ladies, of lovers in mediaeval dress, illustrating stirring incidents of romantic poets; in manner they resembled Gilbert's book designs. His flock of impatient petitioners had always barred me from approaching him. Once indeed I had found him alone, perched on some steps stretched across my path, drawing in his sketchbook a single female figure from the gates of Ghiberti. I had recently been attentively drawing some of the groups for their expression and arrangement, and I told Rossetti then how eloquent the Keeper had been in his comments on seeing me at work. Thus chatting and dilating on these quattrocento epochal masterpieces and their fascinating merits gave us subject for a few minutes' talk; but our common enthusiasm for Keats brought us into intimate relations.

A few days more, and Rossetti was in my studio. I showed him all my pictures and studies, even those I had put aside for the nonce, which, at the stage I had entered upon of advance by leaps and bounds, often involved final abandonment; for in youth a month, and even a day in some cases, is an age in which, for all inventive pur-

pose, the past acts as a sepulchre to its idea. My last designs and experiments I rejoiced to display before a man of his poetic instincts;
and it was pleasant to hear him repeat my propositions and theories
in his own richer phrase. I showed him my new picture of "Rienzi,"
in the painting of which at the outset I was putting in practice the
principle of rejection of conventional dogma, and pursuing that of
direct application to Nature for each feature, however humble a part
of foreground or background this might be. I justified the doing of
this thoroughly as the only sure means of eradicating the stereo-
typed tricks of decadent schools, and of any conventions not recommended by experienced personal judgment.

While engaged on the question of the practice of painting, he confessed to me that he was very disheartened about his position. He
had, some short time ago, applied to Madox Brown to take him as a
pupil. This the established artist had generously agreed to do on
terms of amity. In accordance with all sound precedent, the master
had set him to copy a painting of his own of two cherub angels
watching the crown of thorns, and this he had managed to finish.
The next task was a study of still life from a group of bottles and
other objects which happened to be lying about in the studio. This
discipline Rossetti had found so abhorrent that it had tormented his
soul beyond power of endurance. Thus disheartened, he had given up
painting for the time and had turned for counsel to Leigh Hunt, asking him to read his small collection of poems, and to tell him whether
he might not hope to rely upon poetry for his bread. "The heart
knoweth its own bitterness." My namesake had replied about the
verses in the most appreciative manner, but implored him, if he had
any prospect whatever as a painter, on no account to give it up,
since the fortunes of an unfriended poet in modern days were too
pitiable to be risked. Rossetti had thus been again driven to painting.
In subsequent visits I learnt that he had not returned to Brown, but
had been working alone at the studio of Hancock, a sculptor fellow-
student, and there he had broken down again. "Was it necessary," he
asked plaintively, "to go again to still life?" I assured him of my
great deference to the judgment of his master, adding that although,
in ordinary cases, I should prescribe the same course to any pupil,
for him I should try whether the object might not be gained by leaving him to choose one of his recent designs, and that with the composition put upon canvas, the painting should be begun with the still
life. I believed that invested with vital interest as links in an idea to

be welded together, he would find each day's labour interesting and instructive until he had acquired sufficient proficiency to paint the figures in the picture. This suggestion he accepted with unbounded delight, and wanted at once to put it in practice, asking whether he might come and be directed in my studio. For many reasons it was then impossible to agree to this proposal, principally because I had already a professed painting pupil, whose family had conjured me to help him, and it would have been impossible to do my own work with two *habitués* together; but I promised to come to him, and explain all from time to time as he progressed.[2]

Rossetti was persistent, and in a few months he and Hunt shared a studio in Cleveland Street. There they were visited by the poet-painter William Bell Scott, whom Rossetti had long admired and to whom he had sent a collection of his own early poems.

A day or two later, *Scott recalled*, I found Gabriel (who was never called by any other name than Gabriel by his relatives and intimate friends) and his fellow-artist, who was no other than Holman Hunt, whose studio it was: a room not very commodious for two, furnished with the then inevitable lay-figure in all its loveliness. They were both working in the quite novel manner of elaboration as yet untalked of, kept secret apparently, but which even next year began to make a noise in the world and to raise a critical clamour, principally through the work of Millais. Unprepared for any peculiar character, I looked upon these two as following their lights and imitating the early manner so well known and much beloved by me in the early performances of the Low Countries I had then lately seen in the Belgian Galleries. Holman Hunt's picture was the "Oath of Rienzi over the Body of his Brother," designed with every modern advantage in composition and expression. I saw at once he was an educated artist, and a very skilful one; still there was the Flemish elaboration of the primitive days: his lay-figure was mounted on a table, kneeling, and I was made to observe that the chain mail in his picture was articulated perfectly, and as an armourer would construct it, every ring holding four other rings in its grasp—a miracle of elaboration.

Rossetti, the man I had come to see, was painting a subject wholly in the spirit of the poems which had reached me under a cover inscribed "Songs of the Art-Catholic." It was "The Girlhood of the

Virgin." I thought at the first moment: "He is an Italian, a Roman-ist of course, worshipping that young Nazarene, the 'mother of the body of Christ,' painting her and St. Anne from his own sister and mother; and here was St. Joseph without any joinery work, he had apparently turned *vigneron*—a prettier trade; and here too was really the third person of the Trinity—not the symbolic dove with outspread wings that we moderns see in Masonic diplomas and what not, but a natural dove, only within a nimbus, sitting on the vine." The propensity to laugh was strong in a Scotchman who had ab-sorbed in juvenile years the *Philosophical Dictionary*. But admira-tion of this daring performance of a boy turning what was naturally a lyrical subject into a picture, and this his first adventure in paint-ing, was something quite new. I saw at once that he had possibly never before used even a piece of chalk. He was painting in oils with water-colour brushes, as thinly as in water-colour, on canvas which he had primed with white till the surface was as smooth as card-board, and every tint remained transparent. I saw at once, too, that he was not an orthodox boy, but acting purely from the aesthetic motive: the mixture of genius and dilettantism of both men shut me up for the moment, and whetted my curiosity for all the year till I should see them again.[3]

Though Rossetti professed himself to be Hunt's pupil, Hunt —one year Rossetti's senior—received scant deference from the younger man. Rossetti proceeded to paint and criticize independ-ently. Hunt's life was made difficult, moreover, by the hosts of Ros-setti's friends, who might arrive hungry and inquisitive at any hour and lounge about until dawn. Rossetti's own temperamental nature and undisciplined habits sometimes reduced the diligent Hunt to despair.

The doubt more than once returned to me whether Gabriel, after all, would ever discipline himself steadily enough to become a pro-ficient painter, for when he had been so constant to his canvas as to secure a certain advance, some new invention would become his idol, and to this he would devote himself so passionately that his main task was apparently in danger of being forgotten. When he had fairly got entangled in a new design he would refuse the attraction of home, meals, out of door engagements, or bed, and sit through the night, sleeping where he sat for an hour at the time, recommencing his work when he woke. He ate whatever was at hand when hunger suggested, and when time came for bed on the second night he would ask me to leave him; in the morning I would find him still at his engrossing task. "The Girlhood of the Virgin" was a composition with but little intricacy in it, and therefore a penitential return to the easel soon made up for truancy. There was a special trial, however, in store not to be lightly passed by, for when he advanced to the painting of the child angel, for whom he had four or more models in succession, an untried one ever promising to be more manageable than the last, he increasingly lost patience. The unsteadiness of one mild little girl so overtried his temper that he revealed his irritation beyond bounds, storming wildly, overthrowing his tools and stamping about, until the poor child sobbed and screamed with fright, clinging to her conductress, much too alarmed to listen to any comfort he repentantly offered her. After this scene, which had raised clouds of dust and destroyed my tranquillity of mind, further work that day was out of the question. This was one of sundry experiences which caused the doubt whether his real enthusiasm for art would survive the needful pressure of self denying labour; I thereupon invited him to go out walking with me, and in the shining wintry sun, on the broad walk of Regent's Park, bade him consider the certain consequences of action such as his, and argued that indulging all his humours would be fatal to his prospects of becoming a painter. This he had an undoubted right to give up for himself, but he must not destroy my chance of getting my picture done, since its completion was a very vital matter to me. I added that his want of self control affected my power of work more than he imagined, and that unless he could observe a calmer demeanour we must separate at once, whereas I could assure him that latterly, when he had made good progress, I had hoped not only that he would learn all that he desired, and bring his picture to a conclusion in the fulness of time, but that he might do so early enough to appear with Millais and myself at the next Academy Exhibition. He took my remonstrance in the best possible spirit, and assured me that he would put an effectual curb upon his impatience for the future. He held to his promise manfully, and with a fresh model for the angel brought this part of his work to an end.[4]

Sometimes Rossetti would take Hunt to his family's home in Portland Street for dinner. To the penniless youths, the straitened

circumstances of the Rossetti household were opulence itself. Pre-
siding over the home was Gabriel's mother, a woman of English and
Italian extraction, strong in her quiet dignity. Gabriel's father was
a poet whose songs celebrating the Italian revolutionary movement
had caused his exile from his native country. In former years he had
earned a meager living as a teacher of Italian, but now, aged and in
failing health, he occupied himself with eccentric studies of Dante.
The support of the family thus devolved upon Gabriel's younger
brother, William, a clerk in the Inland Revenue Office. There were, in
addition, two sisters: the elder, Maria, possessed her mother's calm,
practical strength; the younger was Christina, intensely, mystically
religious, whose later fame as a poet would rival Gabriel's. Hunt's
account of the Rossetti family is touched with affection and re-
spect.

To be a guest at the dinner-table of the Rossettis was a pleasure
full of novel interest to me. I was invited soon after their son came
to my studio. The old gentleman was then relinquishing the use of
English. He was beginning to be an invalid whose sight needed protection by a projecting shade. Gabriel has left an excellent drawing
of him at a slightly later date. The mother was the gentle and pre-
siding matron we see Saint Ann to be in "The Girlhood of the
Virgin." The elder sister was overflowing with attention to all, expressing interest in each individually, and Miss Christina was exactly
the pure and docile-hearted damsel that her brother portrayed God's
Virgin pre-elect to be. The father arose to receive me from a group
of foreigners around the fire, all escaped revolutionists from the
Continent, and addressed me in English in a few words of welcome
as "Mr. Madox Brown," a slip on which his eldest daughter rated
him pleasantly. He was so engrossed in a warm discussion going on
that some minutes afterwards he again made the same mistake. The
conversation was in Italian, but occasionally merged into French,
with the obvious purpose of taking into the heat of the conference
refugees unfamiliar with the former language. The tragic passions
of the group around the fire did not in the slightest degree involve
either the mother, the daughters, or the sons, except when the latter
explained that the objects of the severest denunciations were Bomba,
Pio Nono, and Metternich, or, in turn, Count Rosso and his memory;
with these execrated names were uttered in different tones those of
Mazzini, Garibaldi, and Louis Napoleon, who had once been a visitor

at the house. The hearth guests took it in turn to discourse, and no one had delivered many phrases ere the excitement of speaking made him rise from his chair, advance to the centre of the group, and there gesticulate as I had never seen people do except upon the stage. What I knew then of French was only by reading, and I was surprised to discover that it helped me scarcely at all to follow the native tongue spoken excitedly and quickly. Each orator evidently found difficulty in expressing his full anger, but when passion had done its measure in work and gesture, so that I as a stranger felt pained at not being able to join in practical sympathy, the declaimer went back to his chair, and while another was taking up the words of mourning and appeal to the too tardy heavens, the predecessor kept up the refrain of sighs and groans. When it was impossible for me to ignore the distress of the alien company, Gabriel and William shrugged their shoulders, the latter with a languid sign of com-miseration, saying it was generally so. As the dinner was being put on the table some of the strangers persisted, despite invitation, in going; some still stayed round the fire declaring solemnly that they had dined.

It was a novelty to me to begin dinner with maccaroni, and there were other dishes and dressings not usual at English tables, but in all respects we had an excellent meal. Our circle conversed in Eng-lish; the father talked with his friends from the hearth, and at the end of each course he got up and joined them, until he was once more called to the head of the table by the appearance of a new dish. At the conclusion of the meal the brothers and I saw the remainder of the company established at dominoes and chess before the arrival of the other members for the P.R.B. meeting upstairs.[5]

Hunt's description of the youthful Rossetti owes its meticulous detail to the painter's practiced eye.

Rossetti is before my mind's eye now, as daily communion with him at the most impressionable period of life made him appear. Imagine, then, a young man of decidedly Southern breed and aspect, about five feet seven in height, with long brown hair touching his shoulders, not caring to walk erect, but rolling carelessly as he slouched along, pouting with parted lips, searching with dreaming eyes; the openings large and oval; grey eyes, looking directly only when arrested by external interest, otherwise gazing listlessly about,

the iris not reaching the lower lid, the ball of the eye somewhat prominent by its fulness, although not by lack of depth in the orbits; the
lids above and below tawny coloured. His nose was aquiline, delicate,
with a depression from the frontal sinus shaping the bridge; the
nostrils full, the brow rounded and prominent, and the line of the
jaw angular and marked, while still uncovered with beard. His shoulders were not square, and only just masculine in shape. His singu-
larity of gait depended upon his width of hip, which was unusual.
Altogether he was a lightly built man, with delicate hands and feet;
although neither weak nor fragile in constitution, he was altogether
unaffected by athletic exercise. He was careless in his dress, which
was, as then not very unusual with professional men, black and of
evening cut. So indifferent was he to the accepted requirements of
society, that he would allow spots of mud to remain dry on his clothes
for several days. He wore a brown overcoat, and, with his pushing
stride and careless exclamations, a special scrutiny would have been
needed to discern the refinement and tenderness that dwelt in the
breast of the defiant youth; but any one who approached and addressed him was struck with surprise to find all critical impressions
dissipated in a moment, for the language of the painter was wealthy
and polished, and he proved to be courteous, gentle, and winsome,
generous in compliment, rich in interest in the pursuits of others,
while he talked much about his own, and in every respect, as far as
could be shown by outward manner, a cultured gentleman.[6]

&*William Bell Scott testified to the mysterious fascination that
Rossetti exerted on those who knew him*&.

During these weeks, &*Scott recalled of a period when Rossetti
was his guest in Newcastle*&, I began to feel some sort of fascination about the personality of D.G.R., that makes one accept certain
peculiarities in him. I found all his intimate associates did so, placing
him in a position different from themselves, a dangerous position to
the man whose temperament takes advantage of it. He was at this
age just getting out of boyhood, and in transition; in the course of
my experience of him he has changed his entire moral nature and
views of life; but this fascination giving him a sort of supremacy,
he has never changed. With regard to his poetry, the spirit that had
made him choose "Songs of the Art-Catholic" as a general title died
out. He had never thought of pietistic matters except as a sentiment,

theology being altogether ignored by him. This was a state of mind entirely new to me, a Scotchman, whose boyhood had been passed with the Shorter Catechism and the New Testament in my hand. He had no idea of the changed position of the historical forms or cosmogony of religion by geological and other discoveries; and, indeed, was himself not sure that the earth really moved round the sun! "Our senses did not tell us so, at any rate, and what then did it matter whether it did move or not?" What Dante knew was enough for him. He then remembered Galileo, another Italian, and gave in! It might matter in a scientific way, oh yes![7]

Late in life, the eminent John Millais thought of Rossetti with an irritation belying the genuine fondness that had united the young painters of the Pre-Raphaelite Brotherhood. It was true, of course, that Millais had never succumbed to Rossetti's influence to the degree that the others had; Millais was too practical-minded, too thoroughly English, to be susceptible to Rossetti's Latin genius.

I doubt very much, *he recounted testily to his son*, whether any man ever gets the credit of being quite square and above-board about his life and work. The public are like sheep. They follow each other in admiring what they don't understand, and rarely take a man at what he is worth. If you affect a mysterious air, and are clever enough to conceal your ignorance, you stand a fair chance of being taken for a wiser man than you are; but if you talk frankly and freely of yourself and your work, as you know I do, the odds are that any silly rumour you may fail to contradict will be accepted as true. That is just what has happened to me. The papers are good enough to speak of me as a typical English artist; but because in my early days I saw a good deal of Rossetti—the mysterious and un-English Rossetti—they assume that my Pre-Raphaelite impulses in pursuit of light and truth were due to him. All nonsense! My pictures would have been exactly the same if I had never seen or heard of Rossetti. I liked him very much when we first met, believing him to be (as perhaps he was) sincere in his desire to further our aims— Hunt's and mine—but I always liked his brother William much better. D.G.R., you must understand, was a queer fellow, and impossible as a boon companion—so dogmatic and so irritable when opposed. His aims and ideals in art were also widely different from ours, and it was not long before he drifted away from us to follow his own peculiar fancies. What they were may be seen from his subsequent works. They were highly imaginative and original, and not without elements of beauty, but they were not Nature. At last, when he presented for our admiration the young women who have since become the type of Rossettianism, the public opened their eyes in amazement. 'And this,' they said, 'is Pre-Raphaelitism!' It was nothing of the sort. The Pre-Raphaelites had but one idea—to present on canvas what they saw in Nature; and such productions as these were absolutely foreign to the spirit of their work.[8]

❧*The faithful William did not attempt to gloss over Gabriel's complexities*❧.

My brother was essentially a man of the artistic, not the ethical, type. From day to day and from year to year his mind was occupied much more with ideas of art—and in especial how to paint good pictures, and write good poems, in both of which efforts he was as fastidious in execution as he was free and energetic in invention—than with rigid or nice considerations of morals or conduct. None the less, his moral sense was just, if somewhat elastic. He prized rectitude, disliked and shunned meanness, and understood, and mostly conformed to, the fine impulses of honour. He appreciated the generous far more than the regulative virtues. It may indeed be said that he was replete with generosity of mind, feeling, and act. The very core of his character was self-will, which easily shelved into wilfulness. As his self-will was sustained by very high powers of intellect and of performance, he was not only a leader but a dominator all his life long. On that footing he was easy and agreeable; any other footing would have been troublesome to himself, and not long to be pursued by others. He would do and say odd things, unreasonable things, and wrongful things. This was in his nature—and, until he was reduced to subjection (not a facile performance, nor accomplished by any one), he would persist in this, *car tel est mon vouloir*. In thought, deed, manner, and speech, there was nothing of the precisian about him. If there had been somewhat at times, that would have been all the better. Not scrupulosity was his, nor moveless fixity of principle; but warmth and breadth of feeling and of perception. He was impetuous and impatient, but by no means difficult to get on with if one approached him from the right side. He could be managed too, but not driven. Nothing in him stands clearer to my mind than his total freedom from pretence, pretension, attitudinizing, and "tall talk." He impressed you certainly as a man of genius, but not in the least as one who made his genius his stalkinghorse. People of all kinds liked him, and, on seeing him close, loved him. And I could not fix upon one who genuinely disliked him, though there were assuredly several who got ruffled and angry, and of these some may even, on occasion, have dogged him with a certain animosity.[9]

III

The foundations of Pre-Raphaelitism had been laid by Hunt and Millais before Rossetti became their companion. Whatever intellectual basis the school possessed was Hunt's creation; Millais, ever pliant and agreeable, accepted Hunt's lead as affording an opportunity for novelty, for breaking away from the conventionalism entrenched in the schools of the Royal Academy and for making a name for himself all the sooner. There was no light or selfish motive in Hunt. For him, art had a moral function; it was to be the handmaiden of religion. The stale conventions of the popular painters of the day, the pretentious attitudinizing or the trivial sentiment of their subjects, were alike offensive to him. Art, he believed, should communicate moral ideas, not only through elevating subject matter but by the integrity of the means by which its final effect was achieved—by its fidelity to nature, its humble concern for truth in every detail. The other Pre-Raphaelites took up Hunt's ideas with greater or less sincerity. For them, the Brotherhood was largely a social convenience, and its rebellion against the Academy a high-spirited lark. Hunt alone persisted to the end of his life in rigorous devotion to his ideal.

The founding of the Pre-Raphaelite Brotherhood Hunt assigned to a meeting of himself, Millais, and Rossetti in September, 1848.

The companionship of Rossetti and myself, *Hunt recalled*, soon brought about a meeting with Millais, at whose house one night we found a book of engravings of the frescoes in the Campo Santo at Pisa. It was probably the finding of this book at this special time which caused the establishment of the Pre-Raphaelite Brotherhood. Millais, Rossetti, and myself were all seeking for some sure ground, some starting-point for our art which would be secure, if it were ever so humble. As we searched through this book of engravings, we found in them, or thought we found, that freedom from corruption, pride, and disease for which we sought. Here there was at least no trace of decline, no conventionality, no arrogance. Whatever the imperfection, the whole spirit of the art was simple and sincere—was, as Ruskin afterwards said, "eternally and unalterably true." Think what a revelation it was to find such work at such a moment, and to recognize it with the triple enthusiasm of our three spirits. If Newton could say of his theory of gravitation, that his conviction of its truth increased tenfold from the moment in which he got one other person to believe in it, was it wonderful that, when we three saw, as it were, in a flash of lightning, this truth of art, it appealed to us almost with the force of a revolution? Neither then nor afterwards did we affirm that there was not much healthy and good art after the time of Raphael; but it appeared to us that afterwards art was so frequently tainted with this canker of corruption that it was only in the earlier work we could find with certainty absolute health. Up to a definite point the tree was healthy; above it, disease began: side by side with life there appeared death. Think how different were the three temperaments which saw this clearly. I may say plainly of myself, that I was a steady and even enthusiastic worker, trained by the long course of early difficulties and opposition of which I have told the story, and determined to find the right path for my art. Rossetti, with his spirit alike subtle and fiery, was essentially a proselytizer, sometimes to an almost absurd degree, but possessed, alike in his poetry and painting, with an appreciation of beauty of the most intense quality. Millais, again, stood in some respects midway between us, showing a rare combination of extraordinary artistic faculty with an amount of sterling English common-sense. And, moreover, he was in these early days, beyond almost any one with whom I have been acquainted, full of a generous, quick enthusiasm; a spirit on fire with eagerness to seize whatever he saw to be good, which shone out in every line of his face, and made it, as Rossetti once said, look sometimes like the face of an angel. All of us had our qualities, though it does not come within the scope of this paper to analyze them fully. They were such as rather helped than embarrassed us in working together.[10]

News of the incipient revolution in art Rossetti communicated at once to Ford Madox Brown, his onetime teacher and, throughout his life, his closest friend. Brown was then twenty-six, a widower embittered by his unremitting struggle against poverty.

Somewhere about then—I dare say it was in '48, as you say,

❧*Brown recalled many years later*❧, Rossetti came to me laughing, or at least more or less joking, about some discovery of Hunt's. It turned out that they were the reproductions of Orcagna's frescoes at Pisa—though, by the way, they say they're not by Orcagna now. I told him it was all nonsense to laugh at them, they were the finest things in the world, and he'd far better go and look at them again; and, of course, he said just what I did after he'd thought about it.

As to the name Pre-Raphaelite, when they began talking about the early Italian masters, I naturally told them of the German P.R.'s, and either it pleased them or not, I don't know, but they took it. I don't know, for one thing, whether they ever asked me to become a P.R.B.; I suppose they did; but I never could have to do with societies—they're bound to end in cliquishness; besides, I was a good deal older than they were.

Of course it was Rossetti who kept things going by his talking, or it wouldn't have lasted as long as it did, and really he talked them into founding it.[11]

❧*Whoever may actually have founded the Pre-Raphaelite Brotherhood, its distinctive characteristics—indeed, the name Brotherhood itself—were Rossetti's contribution: an almost conspiratorial society of young men dedicated to a secret canon of art and signing their works with the cryptic initials "P.R.B." Rossetti promptly enlisted three recruits of his own choosing: James Collinson, a painting student of limited promise; Thomas Woolner, a penniless student of sculpture; and his brother William, who passed his days in a government office and his nights at a drawing school. Not to be outdone, Hunt introduced his former painting pupil, Frederick George Stephens, who had not yet completed a picture, and membership in the society was hastily fixed at seven. Millais, the most practical though the youngest member, saw shrewdly enough that the Brotherhood was little more than a joke. But it was an amiable joke, for its true justification was the companionship it afforded to impecunious art students lacking any place in the society of the city. At once the Brotherhood became the nucleus of a larger group of friends and sympathizers, young painters, poets, and sculptors who shared the Brothers' enthusiasm for new styles, new ideas, new experiences*❧.

As soon as the Præraphaelite Brotherhood was formed, ❧*William Rossetti recorded*❧, it became a focus of boundless companionship, pleasant and touching to recall. We were really like brothers, continually together, and confiding to one another all experiences bearing upon questions of art and literature, and many affecting us as individuals. We dropped using the term "Esquire" on letters, and substituted "P.R.B." I do not exaggerate in saying that every member of the fraternity was just as much intent upon furthering the advance and promoting the interests of his "Brothers" as his own. There were monthly meetings, at the houses or studios of the various members in succession; occasionally a moonlight walk or a night on the Thames. Beyond this, but very few days can have passed in a year when two or more P.R.B.'s did not foregather for one purpose or another. The only one of us who could be regarded as moderately well off, living *en famille* on a scale of average comfort, was Millais; others were struggling or really poor. All that was of no account. We had our thoughts, our unrestrained converse, our studies, aspirations, efforts, and actual doings; and for every P.R.B. to drink a cup or two of tea or coffee, or a glass or two of beer, in the company of other P.R.B.'s, with or without the accompaniment of tobacco (without it for Dante Rossetti, who never smoked at all), was a heart-relished luxury, the equal of which the flow of long years has not often presented, I take it, to any one of us. Those were the days of youth; and each man in the company, even if he did not project great things of his own, revelled in poetry or sunned himself in art. Hunt, to my thinking, was the most sagacious talker; Woolner the most forceful and entertaining; Dante Rossetti the most intellectual. Such men could not be mere plodders in conversation: but all—to their credit be it spoken—were perfectly free-and-easy, and wholly alien from anything approaching to affectation, settled self-display, or stilted "tall talk."[12]

That the record of those conversations should not be altogether lost, it was soon decided to appoint one of their number a secretary. The assignment went to William Rossetti, who, though a conscientious novice at drawing and poetry, was nevertheless concerned to justify by service his association with so select a group of creative spirits. In time it was further decided that the secretary should keep a daily journal of Pre-Raphaelite proceedings.

In May 1849, *William recalled*, it was settled that I, as Secretary to the Brotherhood, or its only non-professional member, should keep a Diary of the proceedings of the Society, and of the art-work of the several P.R.B.'s so far as that came within my cognizance. This I proceeded to do; and up to 8 April 1850 I kept the Diary without the omission of a day.[13]

Tuesday [May] 15th [1849].—At Millais's—Hunt, Stephens, Collinson, Gabriel, and myself. Gabriel brought with him his design of *Dante drawing the figure of an Angel* on the first anniversary of Beatrice's death which he completed in the course of the day, and intends for Millais. Millais has done some figures of the populace in his design of *The Abbey at Caen* since last night, and has also continued painting on the beard in the head of Ferdinand listening to Ariel, being that of Stephens. He says he has begun his "Castle-moat" poem and is to continue it after we left (one o'clock). The plan of writing this diary was fixed, and will, I am in hopes, be steadily persevered in. We minutely analysed such defects as there are in Patmore's *River* from Gabriel's recitation; who also read his poem (in process) intended as introductory to the *Vita Nuova*.

Thursday 17th.—Millais called on us in the evening. He has gone on with his Caen Nunnery design, and has put in some fat men, finding his general tendency to be towards thin ones. He is also progressing with his poem (the Castle-moat subject).

Saturday 19th.—Hunt is getting on with his *Monk succoured by the ancient Britons* in time of persecution. Woolner has done four of his heads commissioned by Cottingham—Raphael, Michelangelo, Titian, and Leonardo—and is engaged on Vandyck. I understand that the *Court Journal*, speaking of a picture by one Walters that has been rejected, exclaims against the injustice, considering that such works as Hunt's ["Rienzi"] and Millais's ["Lorenzo and Isabella"], which can have been admitted only for charity, are hung.

Wednesday 23rd.—Hunt has completed his design of the Ancient Britons and Monk, and has resumed the one from *Isabella*, "He knew whose gentle hand was at the latch." Millais has made considerable progress with the *Caen Nunnery*, having put-in the greater part of the populace. He says his poem is considerably advanced, and that he will work hard on it to-night. He having informed us, almost as soon as we entered, that he had been reading Patmore's *Woodman's Daughter* and *Sir Hubert*, and had found several faults of diction etc. therein, we proceeded to a most careful dissection, and really the amount of improvable is surprisingly small—as he also agreed in thinking. In the course of conversation, Millais said that he had thoughts of painting a hedge (as a subject) to the closest point of imitation, with a bird's nest—a thing which has never been attempted. Another subject he has in his eye is a river-sparrow's nest, built, as he says they are, between three reeds; the bird he describes as with its head always on one side, "a body like a ball, and thin legs like needles." He intends soon to set about his subject from Patmore, Sir Hubert and Mabel, "as she issues from the trees."[14]

Holman Hunt has left a description of one of the almost nightly gatherings of the Brotherhood at this period.

Once, in a studio conclave, some of us drew up a declaration that there was no immortality for humanity except that which was gained by man's own genius or heroism. We were still under the influence of Voltaire, Gibbon, Byron, and Shelley, and we could leave no corners or spaces in our minds unsearched and unswept. Our determination to respect no authority that stood in the way of fresh research in art seemed to compel us to try what the result would be in matters metaphysical, denying all that could not be tangibly proved. We agreed that there were different degrees of glory in great men, and that these grades should be denoted by one, two, or three stars. Ordinary children of men fulfilled their work by providing food, clothing, and tools for their fellows; some, who did not engage in the labour of the earth, had allowed their minds to work without the ballast of common-sense, and some of these had done evil, but the few far-seeing ones revealed to us vast visions of beauty. Where these dreams were too profound for our sight to fathom, our new iconoclasm dictated that such were too little substantial for human trust; for of spiritual powers we for the moment felt we knew nothing, and we saw no profit in relying upon a vision, however beautiful it might be.

Arguing thus, Gabriel wrote out the following manifesto of our absence of faith in immortality, save in that perennial influence exercised by great thinkers and workers:—

We, the undersigned, declare that the following list of Immortals constitutes the whole of our Creed, and that there exists no other Immortality than what is centered in their names and in the names of their contemporaries, in whom this list is reflected:—

Jesus Christ****
The Author of Job***
Isaiah
Homer**
Pheidias
Early Gothic Architects
Cavalier Pugliesi
Dante**
Boccaccio*
Rienzi
Ghiberti
Chaucer**
Fra Angelico*
Leonardo da Vinci**
Spenser
Hogarth
Flaxman
Hilton
Goethe**
Kosciusko
Byron
Wordsworth
Keats**
Shelley**
Haydon
Cervantes
Joan of Arc
Mrs. Browning*
Patmore*

Raphael*
Michael Angelo
Early English Balladists
Giovanni Bellini
Georgioni
Titian
Tintoretto
Poussin
Alfred**
Shakespeare***
Milton
Cromwell
Hampden
Bacon
Newton
Landor**
Thackeray**
Poe
Hood
Longfellow*
Emerson
Washington**
Leigh Hunt
Author of *Stories after Nature*
Wilkie
Columbus
Browning**
Tennyson*

William Rossetti publishes an expression of Gabriel's astonishment made in his last years that men should assume that he denied
an after life, seeing that what he had painted and written ought to
convince them of his belief in immortality. For my part, it may be
pointed out that not many weeks after the signing of the document
I was designing my "Christian" picture ["Christian Missionaries
Pursued by Druids"] to honour the obedience to Christ's command
that His doctrine should be preached to all the world at the expense,
if need be, of life itself.[15]

Continuing from William Rossetti's journal: Monday, July 13th.—In the evening Gabriel and I went to Woolner's with the view of seeing [William] North (whom, however, we did not find at home) about a project for a monthly sixpenny magazine for which four or five of us would write and one make an etching, each subscribing a guinea, and thus becoming a proprietor. The full discussion of the subject is fixed for to-morrow, at Woolner's.

Tuesday 14th.—We went to Woolner's to settle on our contemplated magazine. The title is to be *Monthly Thoughts in Literature and Art*, with a sonnet on the wrapper.

Wednesday 15th.—It was proposed that the magazine should be increased to forty pages, two etchings, and 1*s.* each No. I wrote the first eight lines of a sonnet for the wrapper, to be considered with others.

Thursday 16th.—Gabriel made a study, from a girl whom Collinson recommended to him, for the head of the angel in his picture ["The Girlhood of Mary Virgin"], which head he means to do over again.

Friday 17th.—Gabriel began painting the head of the angel; and he wrote two stanzas of a French song, *La Soeur Morte*.

Sunday 19th.—Hunt has taken his Rienzi picture to Brown's study, and is engaged giving it some finishing touches. At Ewell he made a study (in colour) of a cornfield. I finished my sonnet, begun on the 15th, with reference to the wrapper of the proposed magazine. In the morning Gabriel worked a good deal on the angel's head, and wrote the concluding stanza of his French song.

Thursday 26th.—I composed a sonnet a few lines of which had come into my head yesterday, entitled *For the General Oppression of the better by the worse Cause in July 1849.*

Wednesday, September 12th.—After writing a letter to Woolner I sat down to think as to a subject for a poem, and without much trouble invented one, but it is as yet very incomplete and meagre. I composed 21 lines of it in blank verse.

Thursday 20th.—Gabriel writes that a printer named Haynes, a friend of Hancock, has introduced him to Aylott and Jones the publishers, who are quite willing to publish the *Monthly Thoughts*, on condition of a percentage of ten on the sale; and that Deverell is making enquiries as to the equity of this demand.

Sunday 23rd.—A letter arrived from Woolner, informing me that, as difficulties in keeping back the ardour of our new proprietors begin to rise up, he and Gabriel have determined on at once making me Editor, and that the prospectus has been sent off to the printer's with my name accordingly, and the title altered to *Thoughts towards Nature* (Gabriel's idea), to obviate the many objections that have been made to the old title; that he was to dine to-day with Patmore, who had read his poems, and praised them so much that he won't tell me what he said. I answered him, pointing out several reasons why I think the proposal of publishing my name as Editor should be well reflected on before being carried out.

Tuesday 25th.—I had a letter from Gabriel in answer to my last to Woolner. He says that the words "Conducted by Artists," recently proposed to be inserted in the title of our magazine, are now to be left out; and that therefore, as he thinks, there is no further ground for arguing the question of my name being published as Editor; that a definite agreement has been made with Aylott and Jones, the publishers, and that the prospectus is now being printed; that the 1st No. will not appear till December; that he wrote the preceding night to W. B. Scott, requesting his co-operation; and that Patmore has seen and appears much pleased with the prospectus, and has given us a little poem named *The Seasons* for our 1st No., but with the proviso that his name shall not transpire, as he means to keep it back in all instances till the appearance of his new volume. He praised Woolner's poems immensely, saying however that they were sometimes slightly over-passionate, and generally "sculpturesque" in character. Gabriel and Hunt are to start shortly for the continent.[16]

Though only a few years older than the Brothers, the poet Coventry Patmore enjoyed an established literary reputation and was, indeed, already a Pre-Raphaelite "Immortal." His association with the Brotherhood opened up new and wider social opportunities for them. Patmore introduced them to Tennyson, and, in the crisis of their fortunes, it was Patmore who summoned Ruskin to their defense.

Soon after I was first married, *Patmore recalled*, and before I had published anything but my little volume of 1844, Thomas Woolner introduced himself to me and made me known to his P.R.B.

friends, Millais, Holman Hunt, Gabriel Rossetti, and others, who claimed me as the poetical representative of their principles and got me to give two or three articles to the 'Germ.' I don't think that either by theory or practice I had any particular claim to be regarded as a P.R.B. However, their mistake was very lucky for me, since they were all most interesting persons to know, and one or two of them became close and life-long friends.

I was intimate with the Præ-Raphaelites when we were little more than boys together. They were all very simple, pure-minded, ignorant, and confident. Millais was looked upon as in some sort the leader, but this I fancy was partly because he always had more command of money than the others, who were very poor. They could not even have printed the 'Germ' without assistance. I well remember Millais triumphantly flourishing before my eyes a cheque for £150 which he got for 'The Return of the Dove to the Ark.' Once I was at a gathering of the Brethren and their friends, when Holman Hunt produced forty sketches, and said that any one might have them for a pound apiece. I suppose that a hundred pounds apiece would scarcely have bought them a short time afterwards. About this time Rossetti sold a little drawing of a girl and boy dancing before Borgia for £5. Lord Houghton commissioned me to try if I could get it for £100 a little while after.

Holman Hunt attracted me personally more than any of the other Præ-Raphaelites. He was heroically simple and constant in his purpose of primarily serving religion by his art, and had a Quixotic notion that it was absolutely obligatory upon him to redress every wrong that came under his notice. This mistake sometimes brought him into serious trouble, and more than once into danger of his life.

Rossetti was in manners, mind, and appearance completely Italian. He had very little knowledge of or sympathy with English Literature; and always gave me the impression of tensity rather than intensity.

Woolner was and is a brilliant talker and letter-writer. He has greatly injured his worldly prospects by his habit of always saying, in the strongest words, what is uppermost in his mind; but he is nearly always right. Millais' conversation and personality were not striking, except as being in strong contrast with his vigour and refinement as an artist. From the beginning he felt and exhibited a boyish delight in worldly success and popularity.[17]

Again from William Rossetti's journal: Friday [September] 28th:—Gabriel left yesterday morning with Hunt for the continent.

Wednesday 10th.—A letter came from Gabriel, who gives me an elaborate criticism of my blank-verse poem, and sends me five sonnets he has written—the first suggested by hearing the bells while ascending to the summit of Notre Dame; the second written leaning against the July Column, and musing on the Place de la Bastille; the third concerning "the rate of locomotion which the style of the Old Masters induces in Hunt and himself at the Louvre"; the fourth on a picture by Giorgione, of two naked women and two men with musical instruments; the fifth excited by the disgust he experienced at witnessing the cancan at Valentino's. In reference to this last scene, he declares Gavarni to be "a liar and the father of it." He has been to see the working of the Gobelins tapestries, which has so altered his ideas concerning the matter that he says he shall probably make an entirely new design for Kate the Queen, when he is prepared to paint the subject.

Thursday, 1st November.—In the morning Gabriel [newly returned] called on Millais, and saw a design he has made of the Holy Family. Christ, having pricked his hand with a nail (in symbol of the nailing to the cross), is being anxiously examined by Joseph, who is pulling his hand backwards, while he, unheeding this, kisses the Virgin with his arm round her neck. Millais thinks of painting this for the Exhibition.

Tuesday 6th.—Looked over a house in Cheyne Walk, Chelsea [the house eventually occupied by Rossetti in his last years], with which they [Hunt and Rossetti], and Stephens who was with them, were greatly taken. It is capable of furnishing four good studios, with a bedroom, and a little room that would do for a library, attached to each. There is also an excellent look-out on the river. The rent, £70. In the evening, we all (except Millais) congregated at Woolner's, and discussed the matter. Gabriel, Hunt, and myself, think of going at once, and Stephens and Collinson would join after April. We think likewise of getting Deverell. "P.R.B." might be written on the bell, and stand for "please ring the bell" to the profane. Among other subjects, we spoke of not admitting anything at all referring to politics or religion into our magazine.

Thursday 8th.—Deverell will manage to join us at once in the house at Chelsea; but on reflection the expense begins to look rather formidable.

Friday 9th.—As the feasibility of taking the Chelsea house looks very questionable now, considering the expense, Gabriel and Hunt spent all the early part of the day looking for lodgings and studios about Chelsea, Brompton, etc.

Saturday 10th.—Gabriel found a studio at No. 72 Newman Street. The rent asked is £30, but he succeeded in bringing it down to £28. He is to see further about it to-morrow.

Monday 12th.—Woolner has been hard at work these two days on his new figure in sculpture, which he has blocked out in clay. Patmore called on him yesterday, and talked of my poem, in which he finds a most objectionable absence of moral dignity, all the characters being puny and destitute of elevation. He means nevertheless to read it through again, that he may be able to judge of it in detail without looking so much to the scope—or want of scope. These are very much the objections that we had all foreseen, and acquiesce in.

Monday 19th.—To-night was a P.R.B. meeting at Millais's, at which we were all present with the exception of Woolner. Millais means to make the spirits in the air [in his "Ferdinand lured by Ariel"] half human and half like birds. His brother has begun painting a little from still life etc., and Millais intends to get him to do landscape-pieces. We discussed two or three points concerning the magazine. First, that of advertising; and it was unanimously considered that, as anything of the kind would, to be effective, swallow up some £10 or £15 without doubt, it will be as well to drop it altogether. In the second place, as regards the big "P.R.B." printed at the head of the prospectus. To this Hunt now most strenuously objects.

Thursday 22nd.—Patmore, Cross, Millais, Gabriel, and myself, were at Woolner's; Hunt did not appear. A long argument was maintained concerning poetry—Patmore professing that Burns is a greater poet than Tennyson, in which opinion Tennyson himself fully concurs. Patmore instanced, as a line of unsurpassable beauty, "With joy unfeigned brothers and sisters meet," from *The Cotter's Saturday Night*. He says that Tennyson is the greatest *man* he ever came in contact with, far greater in his life than in his writing— perfectly sincere and frank, never paying uncandid compliments. Browning takes more pains to please, and is altogether much more a man of the world. Patmore thinks that Browning does not value himself at so high a point as he is rated by Gabriel and me. Patmore holds the age of narrative poetry to be passed for ever, and thinks that probably none such will again appear; he considers *Peter Bell,* though most vexatiously imperfect, to be the opening of a new era. He looks on the present race of poets as highly "self-conscious" in comparison with their predecessors, but yet not sufficiently so for the only system now possible—the psychological. The conversation taking a religious turn, he said that the devil is the only being purely reasoning and analytic, and *therefore* is the devil; and he would have every man hold to the faith he is born in, as, if he attempts to get beyond its bounds, he will be far more likely to be a rebel than a seeker after truth, and should not attempt to pull down without having something to build anew. He thinks Millais's picture far better than anything Keats ever did, and that he is adapted to usher in a new style which will eventually educate the people into taste, and make his works some day as popular and saleable as Barraud's *We Praise Thee, O God.* One of the chief curses of the day he considers to be that every one is critical. Of the poets of this and the last generation he says that they are "all nerves and no hearts." We had some talk of ghosts, to a belief in which Patmore does not see any obstacles. Millais related a singular story on the subject he heard at Oxford, and Woolner some experiences of his own immediate relations and friends. Millais, as we walked home, unburdened himself of his observations and conclusions, and declared that, if he had seen Patmore's hand alone cut off, he could have sworn to it as that of a man of genius. His sayings concerning Burns, Keats, Tennyson, etc., are bitter in his belly as wormwood. Gabriel and I sat up to read the *Cotter's Saturday Night,* and failed to realize to our apprehensions its extraordinary excellence.[18]

~§*Gabriel's obscure title for the prospective Pre-Raphaelite magazine, "Thoughts towards Nature," had never been accepted by all concerned without reservation. The painter William Cave Thomas was particularly exercised over the problem of finding a suitable name and submitted to William Rossetti, as secretary to the P.R.B., a list of sixty-one possible titles, all of them preferable to "Thoughts towards Nature"*§~.

As your brother Gabriel was speaking of christening the journal, I've sent you all that I can think of, which may perhaps suggest

something to you or yours which may be much better than anything
I've thought of.

It is an important matter. There is something in a name.

Yours W.C.T.

Several words expressing Progress—

The Accelerator
The Precursor!!!
The Advent
The Harbinger!!!
The Innovator

————

Modest titles

The Print	First Thoughts
The Atom	Earnest Thoughts
The Ant	Accumulator
The Lantern	The Aspirant
The Adventurer	
The Student	————
The Scholar	The Expansive
The Chalice	The United Arts
The Casket	The Mirror of Nature
The Repertory	The Anti-Archeologist
The Investigator	The Circle
The Enterprise	The Sphere
The Lustre	The Prism
The Illuminator	
The Appeal	
The Die	
The Mould	
The Principle	

The number of Notes of Admiration represent my notion of the
value of each. Five being the highest value.

W.C.T.

The Sower!!!!!
The Progressist!!!!
The Seed!!!!!

Aspects of Nature!!!!
The Guide to Nature!!
The Prospective!!
The View
The Alert
The Opinion
The Mediator!!!
The Reflector
The Effort
The Attempt
Aspirations towards Truth!!!
The Truthseeker!!!
The Dawn
The Well
The Spring
The Fountain
The Dawn

The Messenger
The Chariot
The Wheel
The Spur
The Goad
The Bud
The Acorn

The first four names are the best.
The Germ—Qy better than Seed[19]

From William Rossetti's journal: Saturday [November] 25th.—Gabriel began making a sketch for *The Annunciation*. The Virgin is to be in bed, but without any bedclothes on, an arrangement which may be justified in consideration of the hot climate; and the angel Gabriel is to be presenting a lily to her. The picture, and its companion of the Virgin's Death [never painted], will be almost entirely white.

Monday 10th.—We talked about the magazine, and are quite unanimous in considering that the first number must appear; but all except Stephens and myself are somewhat inclined to drop it after that, whether successful or not. We are also disposed to abide by the title *Thoughts towards Nature*, notwithstanding Cave Thomas's proposal of *The Seed*. We debated the propriety of having an article explanatory of the principles in Art of the P.R.B.; but, as so many papers in the first number are to treat of Art, and as the point will necessarily be brought forward incidentally, it is not thought needful.

Saturday 15th.—We settled to print the magazine with George Tupper. An objection was raised by Stephens to the publication of his name, and it was arranged that the question should be submitted to the arbitration of the P.R.B. On making out a list of the materials actually at our disposal, we find that we have enough for the second and half of the third numbers, by making a somewhat different arrangement from that at first contemplated.

Wednesday 19th.—I delivered to George Tupper Woolner's poem and Patmore's *Seasons*, with which we will make a beginning; but he warns me that we must get our materials together with all possible speed, as, next week being Christmas week, it is almost impracticable to get his people to work. In the evening we had a meeting in Gabriel's study, where, besides the whole P.R.B., the two Tuppers, Deverell, Hancock, and Cave Thomas, as being persons interested in the magazine, were present. The latter brought the commencement of an opening address he is writing for No. 1. Ford Brown came in at a late hour, and showed us a sonnet which he has composed on *The Love of Beauty*, and which we will find room for in the first number. It was proposed by Woolner, and carried without opposition except a very strong one by myself, that our names should not be published; and another point in which all present came to the vote was the title to be finally adopted. *The Seed* was set aside in favour of *The Germ*; and this was near being superseded by *The Scroll* (also Thomas's invention), but was finally fixed on by six to four.

Saturday 29th.—Millais says he has begun his picture from the childhood of Christ, and is going to have a bed in the carpenter's shop he paints from, so as to be able to set to work early in the morning.

Monday 31st.—To-day before noon fifty copies of *The Germ* were in the hands of the Publishers; I took home with me twelve.

1850.—Tuesday, January 1st.—This was the day appointed (in lieu of yesterday, which was found unsuitable) for our first anniversary meeting at Stephens's—fixed on the last day of 1848 for the last day of each succeeding year. Millais and Woolner were prevented from attending. We settled to what magazines and newspapers to send *The Germ*, and to what private gentlemen and authors—viz.: Sir Robert Peel, Lord John Russell.

Monday 7th.—Deverell called on Gabriel, and told him that the porter at Somerset House, who supplies the School of Design Students with stationery &c., would be very likely to get off some of *The Germ*; and it is arranged to let him have fifty, on the understanding that, if he succeeds with the whole number, he is to have 10s., in which case we might probably try it on with another fifty. Hunt, in coming to Gabriel, sold twelve copies out of nineteen; and I left three with a bookseller on trial.

Tuesday 8th.—George Tupper suggested to me the great propriety of sending about *The Germ* to the principal Club-houses. I accordingly made out a list of twenty-one, which I gave to the Publisher.

Friday 11th.—All the P.R.B. was at Ford Brown's, with several others, to induct him properly into his new rooms in Newman Street. Millais has been knocked up these two or three days with colds caught at his carpenter's shop. He has thrown up the commission for his *Ferdinand and Ariel*, as Mr. Wethered, among other things on which they did not come to terms perfectly satisfactory to Millais, expressed some doubts of the greenness of his fairies, and wished to have them more sylph-like. Stephens says he has by this time disposed of thirty *Germs*.

Wednesday 16th.—I had a letter from Stephens, giving me a list of the subscribers he has obtained, and suggesting that we need not print so many as 700 copies of No. 2: 300 would, he thinks, suffice. In answering him I concurred in the reasonableness of the suggestion, but consider that 400 will not be too much.

Thursday 17th.—George Tupper advises that 500 copies should be published of the 2nd No., to which I agreed.

Monday 21st.—By enquiry at the Publisher's I learn that he has sold 120 or 130 copies, which is at least as good as I looked for.

Wednesday 30th.—I left with the Publisher a list of twenty-five newspapers, magazines, &c., to which No. 2 is to be sent. He tells me that he has sold some 70 copies of No. 1—not 120 or 130, as I heard some time back.

Thursday 31st.—Appeared No. 2 of *The Germ*. George Tupper gave me his bill for No. 1, amounting, on a scale even below his original estimate, to £19 1s. 6d., from which he will deduct five per cent. for discount, leaving £18 2s. 6d. It now becomes a most momentous question whether we shall be in a position to bring out a 3rd No. The chance seems but very doubtful—quite beyond a doubt, unless No. 2 sells much better than its predecessor, and of this we see but little likelihood.

Saturday 2nd.—In the evening we had a full P.R.B. meeting at

Gabriel's. We consulted about *The Germ*, and are unanimously of opinion that it will not reach another No. Calculating the number of copies sold among ourselves as ninety-five (not I think more than in fact) and by the publisher as seventy (from which profits we shall have to deduct some few personal expenses, which can scarcely amount to 15*s.*) it seems that the expense to each of us beyond the receipts will be £1 15*s.* 5¼*d.* This is a kind of experiment that won't bear repetition more than once or twice. The next meeting is fixed for Monday at Millais's.

Saturday 9th.—I saw the publisher about the sale of the 2nd *Germ*, and am informed that some forty copies or so have sold, and that the 1st No. also continues to go off every now and then. This is the last knockdown blow. We certainly cannot attempt a 3rd No.

Saturday 16th.—George Tupper called on me in the morning, and said that he and his brother, looking with regret at the *Germ* failure, propose to carry it on at their own risk for a No. or two longer, to give it a fair trial; when it would have a better chance of success, through their being able to send about the subscribers' copies, to advertise by posters, &c. This I consider a very friendly action on their part. I wrote at his request to convene all the hitherto proprietors, and saw the publisher about the sale of Nos. 1 and 2. It appears from what he says that he must have sold not much less than 100 of the 1st, but the 2nd he states goes off less well. All the P.R.B.'s came to Gabriel's study at night to talk the matter over.[20]

The young poet William Allingham, newly introduced to the Brothers and their friends at this time, recorded in his diary the events of an evening passed with the P.R.B.

London, Friday, July 19.—With Woolner, two Rossettis, and Buchanan Reid in omnibus to Chelsea, to Holman Hunt's lodging, large first-floor room looking on river, near the old church. Deverell —much talk on pictures, etc.; we have coffee and fruit; some lie on the floor smoking.

Elegiac poem—'To N. P. Rogers, Esq., in Heaven.' Painter proposing to call his picture 'Gil Blas about to endeavour to assume an air of unconcern while waiting on the robbers in their cave'—a very subtle shade of expression. 'Bring some milk from the pantry.'— Tipsy man in reply: 'Is it done up in paper or lying about loose?'

Hunt's picture of 'Claudio and Isabella'; he has to be at the Royal Academy every morning now at seven, copying for somebody. As it was now late, and his guests showed no wish to depart, Hunt lay down on three chairs for a nap; but they only made merry of his drowsiness, proposed to sit on him, etc., and so the time lounged on till dawn was broad upon the river and its trailing barges, and D. G. Rossetti (usual Captain on such occasions and notorious night-bird) uprooted himself at last from some cushion or easy-chair and all departed, after three o'clock, save myself, to whom Hunt kindly offered a spare bed.[21]

IV

The first Pre-Raphaelite paintings—Rossetti's "Girlhood of Mary Virgin," Millais' "Lorenzo and Isabella," Hunt's "Rienzi"— were shown to the public in the spring of 1849. Millais and Hunt exhibited at the Royal Academy; Rossetti, who perhaps feared a rejection by the Academy of his first serious effort, selected the Free Exhibition at Hyde Park Corner, where any artist who paid the hanging fee could show his work. Among the conventionally dark and classical works of the other exhibitors, the Pre-Raphaelite paintings were conspicuous for their brilliant colors, their romantic themes, the incongruous precision with which every detail of those imagined scenes was photographically reproduced. On each painting the artist's signature was followed by the unexplained initials "P.R.B." The pictures inspired little comment, though that generally favorable. Encouraged, the Brothers threw themselves into their work for the next year's exhibitions.

[Rossetti] was painting his "Annunciation," Millais was progressing with his "Carpenter's Shop," and I with my "Druid" picture, *Hunt related of the spring of 1850*, each anxious to improve the position that we had gained last year at the Exhibition, when suddenly a newspaper in its gossiping column published a spirited paragraph revealing the true meaning of the initials of P.R.B. on our pictures, about which there had been hitherto only the most preposterous guesses. It held the whole body up to derision. The effect of the announcement proved how much our intention of secrecy had been wise. The younger members of the profession, our forerunners, had nearly to a man declared themselves hostile to us, and the bitterness had grown wilder and wider. Now with the exposure of our "wicked" designs an almost universal fury was excited against us; far and near it seemed as if the honour of Raphael were the dearest feeling existing in the bosom of Englishmen, and in our imputed hostility to this master we had put ourselves outside the pale of toleration. We knew that some one of our body had played traitor, and at the next meeting, when we insisted upon a searching investigation being made, Gabriel avowed that little Munro had persisted for long in beseeching him to tell the riddle, till, under pledge of secrecy, the mysterious monogram had been explained. By comparing dates it became evident that the sculptor must have hurried away to Angus Reach, the writer, with intelligence of the dire meaning in the initials, so immediately did the announcement appear.[22]

Apprehensively, the Brothers readied their new paintings for exhibition. Rossetti this time selected the Portland Gallery, Hunt and Millais the Royal Academy. Because the exhibition at the Portland Gallery opened two weeks before that at the Academy, Rossetti received the first critical assault on the newly discovered Pre-Raphaelite conspiracy.

But what shall we say, *demanded* The Athenæum's *exasperated critic in his review of the Portland Gallery Exhibition*, of a work hanging by the side of Mr. Newenham's historical picture—which we notice less for its merits than as an example of the perversion of talent which has recently been making too much way in our school of Art and wasting the energies of some of our most promising aspirants? We allude to the *Ecce Ancilla Domini* of Mr. D. G. Rossetti (225). Here, a certain amount of talent is distorted from its legitimate course by a prominent crotchet. Ignoring all that has made the art great in the works of the greatest masters, the school to which Mr. Rossetti belongs would begin the work anew, and accompany the faltering steps of its earliest explorers. This is archæology turned from all its legitimate uses, and made into a mere pedant. Setting at nought all the advanced principles of light and shade, colour and composition,—these men, professing to look only to Nature in its truth and simplicity, are the slavish imitators of artistic inefficiency. Granted that in these early masters there is

occasionally to be seen all that is claimed for them of divine expression and sentiment, accompanied by an earnestness and devotion of
purpose which preserved their productions from oblivion;—are such
qualities inconsistent with all subsequent progress in historical excellence,—or do these crotchet-mongers propose that the Art should
begin and end there? The world will not be led to that deduction by
such puerilities as the one before us; which, with the affectation of
having done a great thing, is weakness itself. An unintelligent imitation of the mere technicalities of old Art—golden glories, fanciful
scribblings on the frames, and the other infantine absurdities—constitutes all its claim. A certain expression in the eyes of the ill-drawn
face of the Virgin affords a gleam of something high in intention,—
but it is still not the true inspiration. The face of the Angel is
insipidity itself. One arm of the Virgin is well drawn; and there is
careful, though timid, workmanship in the inferior and accessorial
part of the work,—but this is in many places where it would have
been better left out. Yet, with this we have exhausted all the praise
due, in our opinion, to a work evidently thrust by the artist into the
eye of the spectator more with the presumption of a teacher than in
the modesty of a hopeful and true aspiration after excellence.[23]

*Rossetti recoiled, wounded, from the critical onslaught, deter-
mined never again to show his paintings in public. By the time the
exhibition at the Royal Academy opened its doors, the bold front of
the Pre-Raphaelite Brotherhood was already crumbling.*

*The Royal Academy Exhibition opened on May 3. At seven o'clock
that morning Hunt and Millais were admitted at the students' entrance and bounded up the stairs to view their pictures hanging together in the first large room. It was the first time Hunt had seen
Millais' "Carpenter Shop".*

I was dumb for some moments, when Millais suddenly uttered in
undertone, "It's the most beastly thing I ever saw. Come away!"
"My dear fellow," I returned, "the picture is truly marvellous. It
is indeed! But it is so many sided that I really don't know how to
express myself till I have taken it all in."
I had scarcely arrested the impatient self-judge when two tall
fellow-students of vain-glorious mien rollicked into the room, and,
seeing us standing there, walked between the picture and ourselves,
courting our regard as they looked at Millais' work, and then turned

and laughed in our faces. Before they moved another step, Millais had advanced, and putting his hand on the shoulder of the least imbecile, said to him, "Do you know what you are doing? *Don't you see that if you were to live to the age of Methuselah both of you, and you were to improve every day of your life more than you will in the whole course of it, you would never be able to achieve any work fit to compare with that picture.*"

"But we did not say anything," they each pleaded with a pitiable affectation of innocence.

"No, but you did this, you laughed at my painting, and you did so defiantly in my face, so that you should not be surprised at my telling you that you were egregious fools."

They slunk away crestfallen.[24]

    The reviews were unanimous in condemnation. Mr. Millais and his imitators, *The Times declared*, are attempting to engraft themselves on the wildest and most uncouth productions of the early German school with a marked affectation of indifference to everything we are accustomed to seek and to admire. Mr. Millais's principal picture (518) is, to speak plainly, revolting. The attempt to associate the Holy Family with the meanest details of a carpenter's shop, with no conceivable omission of misery, of dirt, and even disease, all finished with the same loathsome minuteness, is disgusting; and with a surprising power of imitation this picture serves to show how far mere imitation may fall short by dryness and conceit of all dignity and truth. The picture of Ariel and Ferdinand (504), by the same artist, is less offensive in point of subject and feeling, but scarcely more pardonable in style. We do not want to see Ariel and the spirits of the Enchanted Isle in the attitudes and shapes of green goblins, or the gallant Ferdinand twisted like a posture-master by Albert Durer. These are mere caprices of genius; but whilst we condemn them as deplorable examples of perverted taste, we are not insensible to the power they indicate over some of the most curious spells of art. Mr. Hunt's picture of "The Fugitive Druids" (553) has a good deal of originality in its conception and careful handling in some of the figures, but it sins by the same intolerable pedantry which seems to brave the first laws of space and ease.[25]

Apropos of aberrations, *Blackwood's Magazine sneered*, we have a word to say, which may as well be said here as elsewhere. Af-

fectation, however, is a more suitable word for the mountebank proceedings of a small number of artists, who, stimulated by their own
conceit, and by the applause of a few foolish persons, are endeavouring to set up a school of their own. We allude to the pre-Raphaelites.
Let not Messrs Millais, Hunt, Rossetti, & Co. suppose, because we
give them an early place in this imperfect review of the exhibitions,
that we concede to them an undue importance. As to admiration, we
shall presently make them aware how far we entertain that feeling
toward them. Meanwhile, let them not plume themselves on a place
amongst men of genius. Just as well might they experience an exalta-
tion of their horns, because their absurd and pretentious productions
get casually hung next to pictures by Landseer or Webster. It appears they have got into their wise heads certain notions that the
ideal of expression is to be found in the works of the artists who
flourished previously to Raphael. And they have accordingly set to
work to imitate those early masters, not only in the earnestness of
purpose visible in their productions, but in their errors, crudities,
and imperfections—renouncing, in fact, the progress that since then
has been made ; rejecting the experience of centuries, to revert for
models, not to art in its prime, but to art in its uncultivated infancy.
And a nice business they make of it. Regardless of anatomy and
drawing, they delight in ugliness and revel in diseased aspects. Mr
Dante Rossetti, one of the high-priests of this retrograde school,
exhibits at the Portland Gallery. Messrs Millais and Hunt favour the
saloons of the Academy. Ricketty children, emaciation and deformity
constitute their chief stock in trade. They apparently select bad
models, and then exaggerate their badness till it is out of all nature.
We can hardly imagine anything more ugly, graceless, and unpleasant than Mr. Millais' picture of Christ in the carpenter's shop. Such
a collection of splay feet, puffed joints, and misshapen limbs was
assuredly never before made within so small a compass. We have
great difficulty in believing a report that this unpleasing and atrociously affected picture has found a purchaser at a high price. Another specimen, from the same brush, inspires rather laughter than
disgust. A Ferdinand of most ignoble physiognomy is being lured by
a pea-green monster intended for Ariel ; whilst a row of sprites, such
as it takes a Millais to devise, watch the operation with turquoise
eyes. It would occupy more room than the thing is worth to expose
all the absurdity and impertinence of this work. Mr Hunt's picture

of a Christian Missionary sheltered from Druid pursuit is in as ridiculous taste as any of the group.[26]

Even the lordly Charles Dickens devoted a leading article in his magazine, Household Words, *to a tasteless tirade against the Brotherhood*.

In the fifteenth century, a certain feeble lamp of art arose in the Italian town of Urbino. This poor light, Raphael Sanzio by name, better known to a few miserably mistaken wretches in these later days, as Raphael (another burned at the same time, called Titian), was fed with a preposterous idea of Beauty—with a ridiculous power of etherealising, and exalting to the very Heaven of Heavens, what was most sublime and lovely in the expression of the human face divine on Earth—with the truly contemptible conceit of finding in poor humanity the fallen likeness of the angels of GOD, and raising it up again to their pure spiritual condition. This very fantastic whim effected a low revolution in Art, in this wise, that Beauty came to be regarded as one of its indispensable elements. In this very poor delusion, Artists have continued until this present nineteenth century, when it was reserved for some bold aspirants to "put it down."

The Pre-Raphael Brotherhood, Ladies and Gentlemen, is the dread Tribunal which is to set this matter right. Walk up, walk up; and here, conspicuous on the wall of the Royal Academy of Art in England, in the eighty-second year of their annual exhibition, you shall see what this new Holy Brotherhood, this terrible Police that is to disperse all Post-Raphael offenders, has "been and done!"

You come—in this Royal Academy Exhibition, which is familiar with the works of WILKIE, COLLINS, ETTY, EASTLAKE, MULREADY, LESLIE, MACLISE, TURNER, STANFIELD, LANDSEER, ROBERTS, DANBY, CRESWICK, LEE, WEBSTER, HERBERT, DYCE, COPE, and others who would have been renowned as great masters in any age or country —you come, in this place, to the contemplation of a Holy Family. You will have the goodness to discharge from your minds all Post-Raphael ideas, all religious aspirations, all elevating thoughts; all tender, awful, sorrowful, ennobling, sacred, graceful, or beautiful associations; and to prepare yourselves, as befits such a subject— Pre-Raphaelly considered—for the lowest depths of what is mean, odious, repulsive, and revolting.

You behold the interior of a carpenter's shop. In the foreground of that carpenter's shop is a hideous, wry-necked, blubbering, red-headed boy, in a bed-gown; who appears to have received a poke in the hand, from the stick of another boy with whom he has been playing in an adjacent gutter, and to be holding it up for the contemplation of a kneeling woman, so horrible in her ugliness, that (supposing it were possible for any human creature to exist for a moment with that dislocated throat) she would stand out from the rest of the company as a Monster, in the vilest cabaret in France, or the lowest ginshop in England. Two almost naked carpenters, master and journeyman, worthy companions of this agreeable female, are working at their trade; a boy, with some small flavor of humanity in him, is entering with a vessel of water; and nobody is paying any attention to a snuffy old woman who seems to have mistaken that shop for the tobacconist's next door, and to be hopelessly waiting at the counter to be served with half an ounce of her favourite mixture. Wherever it is possible to express ugliness of feature, limb, or attitude, you have it expressed. Such men as the carpenters might be undressed in any hospital where dirty drunkards, in a high state of varicose veins, are received. Their very toes have walked out of Saint Giles's.

This, in the nineteenth century, and in the eighty-second year of the annual exhibition of the National Academy of Art, is the Pre-Raphael representation to us, Ladies and Gentlemen, of the most solemn passage which our minds can ever approach. This, in the nineteenth century, and in the eighty-second year of the annual exhibition of the National Academy of Art, is what Pre-Raphael Art can do to render reverence and homage to the faith in which we live and die! Consider this picture well. Consider the pleasure we should have in a similar Pre-Raphael rendering of a favourite horse, or dog, or cat; and, coming fresh from a pretty considerable turmoil about "desecration" in connexion with the National Post Office, let us extol this great achievement, and commend the National Academy![27]

The cruelty of the attack on Millais stunned the artist's parents. Up to this time, Millais' brilliant career had been marked by universal praise, by medals, prizes, and prophecies of greatness. Now with grief and incredulity his mother spread the reviews before Holman Hunt:

The father meanwhile was walking about with a cane in his hand, which he switched, making it whistle in the air, and breaking out into indignation, clenching his fist and swearing that if he knew where to find the anonymous brood of abusers he would drag them out into the street and thrash them within an inch of their lives. And in his heat he meant what he said. "Ah," continued Mrs. Millais, "the pity is he ever altered his style, he would never have provoked this outrageous malice had he not changed. His manner was admired by every one. I say let every one keep his own style. His was right for him. Yours, Hunt, is quite right for you; an excellent manner, I call it. It is the forming yourselves into so large a body and all the talking that has done the mischief. I wish that you had never had anything to do with *that* Rossetti."

"Poor Rossetti, how is he to blame in the matter?" I urged. "Jack had quite agreed upon his new course long before Rossetti came here, when in fact Rossetti was not thinking of painting at all. In the Academy Schools I am pretty certain they never spoke ten words together."

"Ah," said Mrs. Millais, "I don't like the look of him; he's a sly Italian, and his forestalling you deceitfully by sending his first picture to an exhibition, where it was seen with your joint insignia upon it, a week before the pictures by you and Jack would appear, was quite un-English and unpardonable, when you had taught him and treated him with great generosity."

When the old lady ceased the father added, "I don't admire his behaviour; he loudly indulges in insulting denunciation of persons who have the right to be treated with respect, and asserts himself generally so as to offend people quite unnecessarily. Moreover, I agree with my wife, his forestalling you in the exhibition of your first pictures, and his letting out of the P.R.B. secret to Munro, was quite unpardonable, and most injurious to the public understanding of your purpose. I am convinced that he makes you many enemies."

"Well," I said, "his conduct with Munro was certainly wrong, but I persuade myself that Rossetti did not steal a march upon us designedly. Rossetti, it is certain, does not hide all his faults; you cannot long remain indifferent to the need of guarding yourself from his rashness, but he has the redeeming grace of genius, so that with common-sense and justice to himself and others, he cannot but make a mark in the world."

The father replied, "I know that you and Jack thought his first picture very good, and of course I could see it was excellent; but it was such an easy design to work out, and yet you had great difficulty to make him finish that. Mrs. Millais does not of course mean that Rossetti influenced you or Jack, who had painted for years, to change your styles; she thinks really that he goes about stirring up ill-feeling towards your principles of art, without doing his part to justify the reform you attempt, and people assume that Rossetti Gothicism is what you are aiming at. If Jack and you had gone on your courses quietly no one would have been offended; now, all the Associate brood are stirred up as in a death struggle. Dickens is their friend, and out of good comradeship has adopted their interest. You see how effectively he uses Rossetti's revelation of the meaning of P.R.B. Dickens has committed a great wrong, and that's what I would tell him if I met him. *He* was treated kindly on his first appearance, and he should have remembered that fact." Growing warm as he thought of the whole phalanx of enemies, he walked about the room bursting forth with, "But there's *one* question I would ask. What is the purpose of this Pre-Raphaelite Brotherhood? I thought there were to be seven of you; why should the fight be left only to you and Jack? Rossetti's picture of 'The Annunciation,' whatever critics may say, is undoubtedly very dainty and chaste, but the principle he carries out is not Pre-Raphaelitism as you and Jack started it. His is church traditional work with gilt aureoles and the conventionalisms of early priesthood, which we did away with at the Reformation. Jack has treated his 'Holy Family' in a strictly natural manner, and you have painted your 'Early Missionary' so, and when the subject was historical that was what, as I understood, you originally intended to do. Rossetti provokes the common-sense of the world, and you suffer his penalties as well as your own. But whatever he produces he ought to exhibit at the Academy to bear fair comparison with you, and take his full share of the fight. Who goes to the Portland Gallery to see pictures?"

I explained that his mediaevalism seemed to me counter to his repeated declarations of purpose, and needed excuse, but this I found in the fact that the "Annunciation" design was a sequence to his last picture which he had made before coming under our special influence, when, in fact, he was inspired by Brown in his Overbeckian phase, and that I had assented to the choice he made of the composition because this essay in painting was scarcely at first regarded by me as more than an experiment. In both cases, however, the expressions revealed such artistic penetration, and the figures had so much individuality about them, that for initial works they seemed not outside the borders of regenerated art, seeing it was desirable to have the utmost variety in our combination. However, I regretted that on account of the rancour of the press, and perhaps also of the non-sale of his "Annunciation," he has finally determined never again to exhibit in public.

"Ah! that accords with my reading of his character," said Mr. Millais. "What's the good of an ally who keeps out of the fight, disowning his friends if they are beaten, and claiming part of the conquest if they win? Then what are the others about? Was not Collinson to have done wonders? Is it a sham to all but you and Jack? The fact is they make the tumult, and raise up the whole country to destroy you. They have all the pleasure of making a fuss and playing the important, while you get the wounds."[28]

Strangely enough, in view of the charges of Romanism frequently directed against the Brotherhood, the first of the members to desert was the Catholic James Collinson.

To Gabriel Rossetti, Collinson wrote on Whitmonday, 1850: I feel that, as a sincere Catholic, I can no longer allow myself to be called a P.R.B. in the brotherhood sense of the term, or to be connected in any way with the magazine. Perhaps this determination to withdraw myself from the Brotherhood is altogether a matter of feeling. I am uneasy about it. I love and reverence God's faith, and I love His holy Saints; and I cannot bear any longer the self-accusation that, to gratify a little vanity, I am helping to dishonour them, and lower their merits, if not absolutely to bring their sanctity into ridicule. I cannot blame any one but myself. Whatever may be my thoughts with regard to their works, I am sure that all the P.R.B.'s have both written and painted conscientiously; it was for me to have judged beforehand whether I could conscientiously, as a Catholic, assist in spreading the artistic opinions of those who are not. I reverence—indeed almost idolize—what I have seen of the Pre-Raphael painters; [and this] chiefly because [they fill] my heart and mind with that divine faith which could alone animate them to give up their intellect and time and labour so as they did, and all for His glory who, they could never forget, was the Eternal, although he had once humbled Himself to the form of man, that man might be clothed with and know and love His divinity. I have been influenced by no one in this matter; and indeed it is not from any angry or jealous feeling that I wish to be no longer a P.R.B., and I trust you will . . . [something torn off], but believe me affectionately yours, James Collinson.

P.S.—Please do not attempt to change my mind.[29]

Sometimes, ✑§*Hunt confessed*§✑, I went stealthily to the Exhibition, hoping to hear some favourable opinion expressed, but as soon as the public arrived at my picture they invariably said, "Oh, this is one of those preposterous Pre-Raphaelite works," and went on to the next without looking again upon the canvas. One fellow-student, some years my senior, told me that he regretted to see me mixed up with this charlatanism, that he perfectly understood that our object was to attract great attention to ourselves by our extravagant work, and that when we had succeeded in making ourselves notorious, which, being undeniably clever fellows, we should soon do, we should paint pictures of real merit. I thereupon wickedly said that he had divined our purpose, and besought him to respect the secret.[30]

V

✑§*Despair possessed the survivors of the critical assault of 1850. Their poverty deepened, their prospects vanished. Rossetti sank into a state of morbid lethargy. Unable to master problems of technique, he began and abandoned painting after painting, turning increasingly to poetry with the certain result that he would have nothing to show in the next year's exhibits. Millais, disenchanted with copying from nature, executed a tactical retreat from Pre-Raphaelite naturalism. Others of the Brotherhood contemplated more strategic retreats: Woolner planned to emigrate to the Australian gold fields, Hunt dreamed of an expedition to the Holy Land where he would paint Biblical pictures of surpassing realism. Stephens in time abandoned painting altogether for criticism. William Rossetti, too, reflecting on his uncertain future in art, seized an opportunity to write without pay for the* Spectator. *At William's urging the Brotherhood made a feeble effort to check the process of disintegration: a code of*

*rules was promulgated to restore the solidarity of old, but the elabo-
rate document was already a dead letter when the faithful secretary
added it to his notebok. In the spring of 1851 Millais and Hunt,
along with Charles Alston Collins, one of the larger Pre-Raphaelite
circle, were again represented at the Royal Academy, though in less
favored places than in the past—Millais by his "Marianna" and
"Return of the Dove to the Ark," Hunt by his "Valentine and
Sylvia." Once more the ferocious critics heaped scorn upon the luck-
less young men. The fortunes of the Pre-Raphaelite Brotherhood
had reached their lowest ebb*.

I had been asked to do illustrations for an edition of Longfellow,
Hunt recalled of those dark days, and I did three drawings,
but the publisher declined them, saying he had made arrangements
with another artist; and no one would have his portrait painted by
me when my name was a proverb of incompetence, and, as it was made
to appear, criminality. I was so reduced in means that once, when I
had a letter written lying before me, I could not tell where to find
a penny for the stamp. Leaning back in the old cushioned chair, I
thrust my hand down behind the seat, and my fingers came in contact
with a coin, which proved to be half-a-crown, and I felt quite rich
for the time. In the midst of this came thunder as out of a clear sky.
It was a letter from Ruskin in the *Times* in our defence.[31]

*In 1851 Ruskin, at thirty-two, was the unchallenged dictator
of English art.* Modern Painters, The Seven Lamps of Architecture,
and recently the first volume of The Stones of Venice *had raised him
to dizzy heights of celebrity and authority. The intellectual world
applauded the genius whose superb literary style made his thoroughly subjective and inconsistent critical principles virtually irresistible; while a large middle class, utterly incompetent in matters
of taste, welcomed his pronouncements with relief and gratitude. To
Ruskin, Patmore now appealed on behalf of the shattered Pre-
Raphaelites. Though the great man had little personal liking for the
works of the Brotherhood, he welcomed an opportunity to destroy
the ignorant hosts of hack journalists who had presumed to judge
the Pre-Raphaelites so cruelly. The letter that came like thunder to
Hunt was published in* The Times *on May 13, 1851*.

Sir,—Your usual liberality will, I trust, give a place in your columns to this expression of my regret that the tone of the critique which appeared in *The Times* of Wednesday last on the works of Mr. Millais and Mr. Hunt, now in the Royal Academy, should have been scornful as well as severe.

I regret it, first, because the mere labour bestowed on these works, and their fidelity to a certain order of truth (labour and fidelity which are altogether indisputable) ought at once to have placed them above the level of mere contempt; and, secondly, because I believe these young artists to be at a most critical period of their career—at a turning point, from which they may either sink into nothingness or rise to very real greatness; and I believe also, that whether they choose the upward or downward path may in no small degree depend upon the character of the criticism which their works have to sustain. I do not wish in any way to dispute or invalidate the general truth of your critique on the Royal Academy; nor am I surprised at the estimate which the writer formed of the pictures in question when rapidly compared with works of totally different style and aim; nay, when I first saw the chief picture by Millais in the Exhibition last year I had nearly come to the same conclusion myself. But I ask your permission, in justice to artists who have at least given much time and toil to their pictures, to institute some more serious inquiry into their merits and faults than your general notice of the Academy could possibly have admitted.

Let me state, in the first place, that I have no acquaintance with any of these artists, and very imperfect sympathy with them. No one who has met with any of my writings will suspect me of desiring to encourage them in their Romanist and Tractarian tendencies. I am glad to see that Mr. Millais's lady in blue is heartily tired of her painted window and idolatrous toilet-table, and I have no particular respect for Mr. Collins' lady in white, because her sympathies are limited by a dead wall, or divided between some gold fish and a tadpole (the latter Mr. Collins may, perhaps, permit me to suggest *en passant*, as he is already half a frog, is rather too small for his age). But I happen to have a special acquaintance with the water plant, *Alisma Plantago*, among which the said gold fish are swimming, and, as I never saw it so thoroughly or so well drawn, I must take leave to remonstrate with you when you say sweepingly, that these men 'sacrifice *truth* as well as feeling to eccentricity.' For as a mere

botanical study of the water lily and *Alisma*, as well as of the common
lily and several other garden flowers, this picture would be invalu-
able to me, and I heartily wish it were mine.

But, before entering into such particulars, let me correct an impression which your article is likely to induce in most minds, and
which is altogether false. These pre-Raphaelites (I cannot compliment them on common sense in choice of a *nom de guerre*) do *not*
desire nor pretend in any way to imitate antique painting, as such.
They know little of ancient paintings who suppose the works of these
young artists to resemble them. As far as I can judge of their aim
—for, as I said, I do not know the men themselves—the pre-Raphaelites intend to surrender no advantage which the knowledge or in-
ventions of the present time can afford to their art. They intend to
return to early days in this one point only—that, as far as in them
lies, they will draw either what they see, or what they suppose might
have been the actual facts of the scene they desire to represent, ir-
respective of any conventional rules of picture-making; and they
have chosen their unfortunate though not inaccurate name because
all artists did this before Raphael's time, and after Raphael's time
did *not* this, but sought to paint fair pictures rather than represent
stern facts, of which the consequence has been that from Raphael's
time to this day historical art has been in acknowledged decadence.

Now, Sir, presupposing that the intention of these men was to
return to archaic *art* instead of to archaic *honesty*, your critic bor-
rows Fuseli's expression respecting ancient draperies—'snapped instead of folded,' and asserts that in these pictures there is a *'servile
imitation of false* perspective.' To which I have just this to answer:—

That there is not one single error in perspective in four out of
the five pictures in question, and that in Millais' 'Marianna' there is
but this one—that the top of the green curtain in the distant window
has too low a vanishing point; and that I will undertake, if need be,
to point out and prove a dozen worse errors in perspective in any 12
pictures containing architecture, taken at random from among the
works of the most popular painters of the day.

Secondly: that, putting aside the small Mulready and the works
of Thorburn and Sir W. Ross, and perhaps some others of those in
the miniature room which I have not examined, there is not a single
study of drapery in the whole Academy, be it in large works or small,
which for perfect truth, power, and finish, could be compared for an

instant with the black sleeve of the Julia, or with the velvet on the breast and the chain mail of the Valentine of Mr. Hunt's picture; or with the white draperies on the table in Mr. Millais' 'Marianna,' and of the right hand figure in the same painter's 'Dove returning to the Ark.'

And further: that as studies both of drapery and of every minor detail, there has been nothing in art so earnest or so complete as these pictures since the days of Albert Durer. This I assert generally and fearlessly. On the other hand, I am perfectly ready to admit that Mr. Hunt's 'Silvia' is not a person whom Proteus or anyone else would have been likely to have fallen in love with at first sight; and that one cannot feel any very sincere delight that Mr. Millais' 'Wives of the Sons of Noah' should have escaped the Deluge; with many other faults besides on which I will not enlarge at present, because I have already occupied too much of your valuable space, and I hope to be permitted to enter into more special criticism in a future letter.

I have the honour to be, Sir, your obedient servant,

THE AUTHOR OF 'MODERN PAINTERS.'[32]

Ruskin's letter at once reversed the tide of opinion. His cautiously qualified appreciation of the Pre-Raphaelites, mixed though it was with sharp criticism—criticism repeated and enlarged in a second letter published on May 30—was enough to persuade the British public that the Pre-Raphaelites were to be taken seriously. The fortunes of the Brotherhood soon improved. In October, Hunt's "Two Gentlemen from Verona" was awarded a prize by the Liverpool Academy. The next spring his "Hireling Shepherd" and Millais' "Ophelia" and "Huguenot" were hung "on the line" at the Royal Academy. In 1853 Millais became the youngest painter ever elected an associate of the august Academy.

Even before Ruskin had spoken, Madox Brown had foreseen the Pre-Raphaelites' eventual success. As to the pure white ground, *he wrote to a fellow painter in May, 1851,* you had better adopt that at once, as I can assure you you will be forced to do so ultimately, for Hunt and Millais, whose works already kill everything in the exhibition for brilliancy, will in a few years force everyone who will not drop behind them to use their methods. *Apropos* of these young men, you must be strangely puzzled to know what to

think of them if you see many of the English papers on the present
exhibition. For the amount of abuse that has been lavished on them
has been such as to impart dignity to a name which used to be looked
on more as a subject of mirth than anything else. You will remember
that with all of us, whatever used to be thought of Rossetti's, Hunt's,
and Millais' talents, the words Pre-Raphaelite Brotherhood, or the
letters P.R.B., used to be looked upon as the childish or ridiculous
part of the business. But now, I can assure you, that I pronounce
the words without hesitation as an ordinary term in the every day of
art. The term will now remain with them, and, in the course of time,
gain a dignity which cannot fail to attach to whatever is connected
with what they do.[33]

VI

*The last entries in William Rossetti's desultory journal con-
clude the history of the Pre-Raphaelite Brotherhood*.

1853, 23rd January.—I at last resume the P.R.B. Journal, not
too sanguine of continuing it for long.

Our position is greatly altered. We have emerged from reckless
abuse to a position of general and high recognition, just so much
qualified by adverse criticism as suffices to keep our once would-be
annihilators in countenance. I limit myself to the briefest recapitulation of last year's public doings and our present state.

Hunt, Millais, Stephens, and Woolner, exhibited at the R.A.—
Hunt sent *The Hireling Shepherd;* Millais, *Ophelia*, and *A Huguenot
on the Eve of St. Bartholomew;* Stephens, a small portrait of his
Mother; Woolner, his cast for the competition monument to Words-
worth, and medallion heads of Carlyle, Wordsworth, and Miss Orme.
Gabriel exhibited three designs (water-colour) in the Exhibition of
Sketches opened in December—*Giotto painting Dante's Portrait*,
Beatrice denying her Salutation, and a *Lady in Venetian Costume.*

At present Hunt is preparing for next exhibition. He purposes
exhibiting his old pictures from *Measure for Measure, Christ at the
Door*, a picture of Sheep commissioned by Maude, a portrait, and
probably two others of which I shall be able to speak more certainly
hereafter. Soon after sending in, he intends to go to Syria. Millais is
painting two subjects of invention—one of the Stuart period, the

other named *The Ransom*. Gabriel has in hand a picture in two compartments, symbolizing, in life-sized half-figures, Dante's resolve to write the *Divina Commedia* in memory of Beatrice. Woolner is absent from England since July last, having gone to the diggings in Australia, where he hopes to make money sufficient to enable him to return in a few years, and pursue sculpture with endurable prospects. Stephens is doing a portrait of his Father. I am still on *The Spectator*.

Monday 17th to Saturday 22nd.—Better than art-news signalizes this week—that, namely, of the arrival of Woolner's vessel, the Windsor, at Melbourne on the 22nd October last. It is the first we have heard about him since he reached Plymouth on his passage out. Another item of information is rather sad. Poor Collinson, our once P.R.B., is said to be on the eve of relinquishing art and entering a Jesuit college as a "working brother," I am told, whatever that may mean. Gabriel has been giving the finishing touches to some alterations he has made in his old *Annunciation* picture, consequent on an offer from McCracken of Belfast to buy it, on Hunt's recommendation, for the original price, £52. 10s. I have been sitting to him to assist his repainting of the Angel's head. Friday was to have been a P.R.B. meeting at Stephens's, but no one attended except myself. Hunt had to take advantage of the moonlight night for his picture *Christ at the Door*. The only change in domicile that has taken place since I dropped this journal is that Gabriel and I now have Chambers overlooking the river at Blackfriars Bridge, 14 Chatham Place. I should not have forgotten to premise that, though both Præraphaelism and Brotherhood are as real as ever, and purpose to continue so, the P.R.B. is not and cannot be so much a matter of social intercourse as it used to be. The P.R.B. meeting is no longer a sacred institution—indeed is, as such, well-nigh disused; which may explain the quasi-non-attendance at Stephens's. And the solemn code of rules which I find attached to these sheets reads now as almost comic. In fact it has been a proof of what Carlyle says in one of his *Latter-day Pamphlets*, that the formulation of a purpose into speech is destructive to that purpose—for not one of the new rules has been acted on, and the falling off of that aspect of P.R.Bism dates from just about the time when those regulations were passed in conclave.

Sunday 23rd to Saturday 29th.—Gabriel finished and sent off the *Annunciation* picture. It has now lost its familiar name of "The

Ancilla," the mottoes having been altered from Latin to English, to guard against the imputation of "popery." He is now possessed with the idea of bringing out his translation of the *Vita Nuova*, revised and illustrated. He had intended photographed designs a short time ago, but now again purposes etchings. . . .[34]

CHAPTER 5

Charles Darwin

———— ❀ ————

*"I have been engaged in a very presumptuous work,
and I know no one individual who would not say a
very foolish one."*

I

❧The House at Down was sixteen miles from London, a two-hour trip by carriage and train. In November, 1842, it stood, plain and graceless, among fallow fields surrounded by the bleak Kentish hills. It was not ideal, the young couple agreed, but they were weary of house-hunting, and the house was inexpensive and it did have possibilities. Most important, though it was not far from London, it was far enough, and sufficiently difficult of access, to assure the quiet and solitude they wanted. Balancing the good points against the bad, Charles Darwin was, on the whole, satisfied❧.

The country is extravagantly rural and quiet with narrow lanes and high hedges and hardly any ruts, ❧Darwin wrote to his sister❧. It is really surprising to think London is only 16 miles off.

255

The house stands very badly, close to a tiny lane and near another man's field. Our field is 15 acres and flat, looking into flat-bottomed valleys on both sides, but no view from the drawing-room, which faces due south, except on our flat field and bits of rather ugly distant horizon. Close in front there are some old (very productive) cherry trees, walnut trees, yew, Spanish chestnut, pear, old larch, Scotch fir and silver fir and old mulberry trees, [which] make rather a pretty group. They give the ground an old look, but from not flourishing much they also give it rather a desolate look. There are quinces and medlars and plums with plenty of fruit, and Morello cherries; but few apples. The purple magnolia flowers against the house. House ugly, looks neither old nor new—walls two feet thick—windows rather small—lower story rather low. Capital study 18 x 18. Dining-room 21 x 18. Drawing-room can easily be added to: is 21 x 15. Three stories, plenty of bedrooms. We could hold the Hensleighs and you and Susan and Erasmus all together.[1]

Charles Darwin was thirty-three when, in 1842, he brought his wife Emma and two infant children to live at Down. He was already a naturalist with an established reputation, fellow of the Geological and Zoological societies, propounder of a new theory of coral-reef formation, and author of the popular Journal of his five-year voyage aboard H.M.S. Beagle. *Already, too, he was plagued by that mysterious ill-health which, dating from his return to England in 1836, had made life in London increasingly unendurable. Regretfully, he doubted if he would ever be able to do substantial scientific work. At Down he expected to lead the retired life of a sickly, prematurely aging country gentleman.*

The Darwins' first reservations about the house at Down were short-lived. Physical alterations and the subtle chemistry of living soon transformed the unattractive house into a lovely and cherished family home. During their first year the grounds were landscaped, the lane lowered. A large bay extending the entire three floors was added to the house; fresh stucco was applied; in time a mass of creepers softened the plain lines. Within, the house was alive with frequent visitors and a growing family. There were ten children in all. One died in infancy, two in childhood; seven grew up at Down, knowing their father as a gentle, friendly, but rather august semi-invalid.

He was about six feet in height, but scarcely looked so tall, as he stooped a good deal, *Francis Darwin recalled of his father*; in later days he yielded to the stoop; but I can remember seeing him long ago swinging his arms back to open out his chest, and holding himself upright with a jerk. He gave one the idea that he had been active rather than strong; his shoulders were not broad for his height, though certainly not narrow. He walked with a swinging action, using a stick heavily shod with iron, which he struck loudly against the ground, producing as he went round the "Sand-walk" at Down, a rhythmical click which is with all of us a very distinct remembrance. As he returned from the midday walk, often carrying the waterproof or cloak which had proved too hot, one could see that the swinging step was kept up by something of an effort. Indoors his step was often slow and laboured, and as he went upstairs in the afternoon he might be heard mounting the stairs with a heavy footfall, as if each step were an effort.[2]

Darwin preserved his feeble resources by adhering to a daily schedule from which he departed ever more rarely as he grew older.

Francis Darwin again: He rose early, chiefly because he could not lie in bed, and I think he would have liked to get up earlier than he did. He took a short turn before breakfast, a habit which began when he went for the first time to a water-cure establishment. This habit he kept up till almost the end of his life. I used, as a little boy, to like going out with him, and I have a vague sense of the red of the winter sunrise, and a recollection of the pleasant companionship, and a certain honor and glory in it. He used to delight me as a boy by telling me how, in still earlier walks, on dark winter mornings, he had once or twice met foxes trotting home at the dawning.

After breakfasting alone about 7:45, he went to work at once, considering the 1½ hour between 8 and 9:30 one of his best working times. At 9:30 he came into the drawing room for his letters—rejoicing if the post was a light one and being sometimes much worried if it was not. He would then hear any family letters read aloud as he lay on the sofa.

The reading aloud, which also included part of a novel, lasted till about half-past ten, when he went back to work till twelve or a quarter past. By this time he considered his day's work over, and would often say, in a satisfied voice, "*I've* done a good day's work." He then went out of doors whether it was wet or fine; Polly, his white terrier, went with him in fair weather, but in the rain she refused or might be seen hesitating in the verandah, with a mixed expression of disgust and shame at her own want of courage; generally, however, her conscience carried the day, and as soon as he was evidently gone she could not bear to stay behind.

My father's midday walk generally began by a call at the greenhouse, where he looked over any germinating seeds or experimental plants which required a casual examination, but he hardly ever did any serious observing at this time. Then he went on for his constitutional—either round the "Sand-walk," or outside his own grounds in the immediate neighbourhood of the house. The "Sand-walk" was a narrow strip of land 1½ acres in extent, with a gravel-walk round it. On one side of it was a broad old shaw with fair-sized oaks in it, which made a sheltered shady walk; the other side was separated from a neighbouring grass field by a low quickset hedge, over which you could look at what view there was, a quiet little valley losing itself in the upland country towards the edge of the Westerham hill, with hazel coppice and larch wood, the remnants of what was once a large wood, stretching away to the Westerham road. I have heard my father say that the charm of this simple little valley helped to make him settle at Down.

Sometimes when alone he stood still or walked stealthily to observe birds or beasts. It was on one of these occasions that some young squirrels ran up his back and legs, while their mother barked at them in an agony from the tree. He always found birds' nests even up to the last years of his life, and we, as children, considered that he had a special genius in this direction. In his quiet prowls he came across the less common birds, but I fancy he used to conceal it from me, as a little boy, because he observed the agony of mind which I endured at not having seen the siskin or goldfinch, or whatever it might have been. He used to tell us how, when he was creeping noiselessly along in the "Big-Woods," he came upon a fox asleep in the day time, which was so much astonished that it took a good stare at him before it ran off.

Another favourite place was "Orchis Bank," above the quiet Cudham valley, where fly- and musk-orchis grew among the junipers, and Cephalanthera and Neottia under the beech boughs; the little wood "Hangrove," just above this, he was also fond of, and here I remember his collecting grasses, when he took a fancy to make out the

names of all the common kinds. He was fond of quoting the saying
of one of his little boys, who, having found a grass that his father
had not seen before, had it laid by his own plate during dinner, re-
marking, "I are an extraordinary grass-finder!"

Luncheon at Down came after his midday walk. After his lunch,
he read the newspaper, lying on the sofa in the drawing-room. I think
the paper was the only nonscientific matter which he read to himself.
Everything else, novels, travels, history, was read to him. After he
had read his paper, came his time for writing letters. These, as well
as the MS. of his books, were written by him as he sat in a huge
horse-hair chair by the fire, his paper supported on a board resting
on the arms of the chair. When he had many or long letters to write,
he would dictate them from a rough copy; these rough copies were
written on the backs of manuscript or of proof-sheets, and were almost illegible, sometimes even to himself. He made a rule of keeping
all letters that he received; this was a habit which he learnt from his
father, and which he said had been of great use to him.

When letters were finished, about three in the afternoon, he rested
in his bedroom, lying on the sofa and smoking a cigarette, and listening to a novel or other book not scientific. The reading aloud often
sent him to sleep, and he used to regret losing parts of a novel, for
my mother went steadily on lest the cessation of the sound might
wake him. He came down at four o'clock to dress for his walk, and he
was so regular that one might be quite certain it was within a few
minutes of four when his descending steps were heard.

From about half-past four to half-past five he worked; then he
came to the drawing-room, and was idle till it was time (about six)
to go up for another rest with novel-reading and a cigarette.

Latterly he gave up late dinner, and had a simple tea at half-past
seven (while we had dinner), with an egg or a small piece of meat.
After dinner he never stayed in the room, and used to apologise by
saying he was an old woman, who must be allowed to leave with the
ladies. This was one of the many signs and results of his constant
weakness and ill-health. Half an hour more or less of conversation
would make to him the difference of a sleepless night, and of the loss
perhaps of half the next day's work.

After dinner he played backgammon with my mother, two games
being played every night; for many years a score of the games which
each won was kept, and in this score he took the greatest interest.
After backgammon he read some scientific book to himself, either in

the drawing-room, or, if much talking was going on, in the study. In the evening, that is, after he had read as much as his strength would allow, and before the reading aloud began, he would often lie on the sofa and listen to my mother play the piano.

He became much tired in the evenings, especially of late years, when he left the drawing-room about ten, going to bed at half-past ten. His nights were generally bad, and he often lay awake or sat up in bed for hours, suffering much discomfort. He was troubled at night by the activity of his thoughts, and would become exhausted by his mind working at some problem which he would willingly have dismissed. At night, too, anything which had vexed or troubled him in the day would haunt him, and I think it was then that he suffered if he had not answered some troublesome person's letter.[3]

During the early years at Down, Darwin regularly visited London two or three times a month, and visitors were often entertained at home—numerous Wedgwoods (Emma's family, Charles' cousins), Charles' brother Erasmus, and scientific friends from London, especially the eminent geologist Charles Lyell, the rising botanist Joseph Dalton Hooker, and, after 1851, the brilliant young paleontologist Thomas Henry Huxley.

My first meeting with Mr. Darwin was in 1839, in Trafalgar square, *Hooker recalled*. I was walking with an officer who had been his shipmate for a short time in the *Beagle* seven years before, but who had not, I believe, since met him. I was introduced; the interview was of course brief, and the memory of him that I carried away and still retain was that of a rather tall and rather broad-shouldered man, with a slight stoop, an agreeable and animated expression when talking, beetle brows, and a hollow but mellow voice; and that his greeting of his old acquaintance was sailor-like—that is, delightfully frank and cordial. I observed him well, for I was already aware of his attainments and labours, derived from having read various proof-sheets of his then unpublished 'Journal.' These had been submitted to Mr. (afterwards Sir Charles) Lyell by Mr. Darwin, and by him sent to his father, Ch. Lyell, Esq., of Kinnordy, who (being a very old friend of my father, and taking a kind interest in my projected career as a naturalist) had allowed me to peruse them. At this time I was hurrying on my studies, so as to take my degree before volunteering to accompany Sir James Ross in the Antarctic

Expedition, which had just been determined on by the Admiralty; and so pressed for time was I, that I used to sleep with the sheets of the 'Journal' under my pillow, that I might read them between waking and rising. They impressed me profoundly, I might say despairingly, with the variety of acquirements, mental and physical, required in a naturalist who should follow in Darwin's footsteps, whilst they stimulated me to enthusiasm in the desire to travel and observe.

Very soon after the return of the Antarctic Expedition my correspondence with Mr. Darwin began (December, 1843) by his sending me a long letter, warmly congratulating me on my return to my family and friends, and expressing a wish to hear more of the results of the expedition, of which he had derived some knowledge from private letters of my own (written to or communicated through Mr. Lyell). Then, plunging at once into scientific matters, he directed my attention to the importance of correlating the Fuegian Flora with that of the Cordillera and of Europe, and invited me to study the botanical collections which he had made in the Galapagos Islands, as well as his Patagonian and Fuegian plants.

In the short intervals of good health that followed the long illnesses which oftentimes rendered life a burthen to him, between 1844 and 1847, I had many [invitations to Down], and delightful they were. A more hospitable and more attractive home under every point of view could not be imagined—of Society there were most often Dr. Falconer, Edward Forbes, Professor Bell, and Mr. Waterhouse—there were long walks, romps with the children on hands and knees, music that haunts me still. Darwin's own hearty manner, hollow laugh, and thorough enjoyment of home life with friends; strolls with him all together, and interviews with us one by one in his study, to discuss questions in any branch of biological or physical knowledge that we had followed; and which I at any rate always left with the feeling that I had imparted nothing and carried away more than I could stagger under. Latterly, as his health became more seriously affected, I was for days and weeks the only visitor, bringing my work with me and enjoying his society as opportunity offered. It was an established rule that he every day pumped me, as he called it, for half an hour or so after breakfast in his study, when he first brought out a heap of slips with questions botanical, geographical, &c., for me to answer, and concluded by telling me of the progress he had made in his own work, asking my opinion on various points. I saw no more of him till about noon, when I heard his mellow ringing voice calling my name under my window—this was to join him in his daily forenoon walk round the sand-walk. On joining him I found him in a rough grey shooting-coat in summer, and thick cape over his shoulders in winter, and a stout staff in his hand; away we trudged through the garden, where there was always some experiment to visit, and on to the sand-walk, round which a fixed number of turns were taken, during which our conversation usually ran on foreign lands and seas, old friends, old books, and things far off to both mind and eye.

In the afternoon there was another such walk, after which he again retired till dinner if well enough to join the family; if not, he generally managed to appear in the drawing-room, where seated in his high chair, with his feet in enormous carpet shoes, supported on a high stool—he enjoyed the music or conversation of his family.[4]

Francis Darwin testified to the burden of his father's ill-health. If the character of my father's working life is to be understood, the conditions of ill-health, under which he worked, must be constantly borne in mind. He bore his illness with such uncomplaining patience, that even his children can hardly, I believe, realise the extent of his habitual suffering. In their case the difficulty is heightened by the fact that, from the days of their earliest recollections, they saw him in constant ill-health,—and saw him, in spite of it, full of pleasure in what pleased them. Thus, in later life, their perception of what he endured had to be disentangled from the impression produced in childhood by constant genial kindness under conditions of unrecognised difficulty. No one indeed, except my mother, knows the full amount of suffering he endured, or the full amount of his wonderful patience. For all the latter years of his life she never left him for a night; and her days were so planned that all his resting hours might be shared with her. She shielded him from every avoidable annoyance, and omitted nothing that might save him trouble, or prevent him becoming overtired, or that might alleviate the many discomforts of his ill-health. I hesitate to speak thus freely of a thing so sacred as the life-long devotion which prompted all this constant and tender care. But it is, I repeat, a principal feature of his life, that for nearly forty years he never knew one day of the health of ordinary men, and that this his life was one long struggle against the weariness and strain of sickness. And this cannot be told without speaking of the one condition which enabled him to bear the strain and fight out the struggle to the end.[5]

In an autobiographical sketch composed for his family, Charles Darwin reflected on the retired life imposed upon him by his illness. Few persons can have lived a more retired life than we have done. Besides short visits to the houses of relations, and occasionally to the seaside or elsewhere, we have gone nowhere. During the first part of our residence we went a little into society, and received a few friends here; but my health almost always suffered from the excitement, violent shivering and vomitting attacks being thus brought on. I have therefore been compelled for many years to give up all dinner-parties; and this has been somewhat of a deprivation to me, as such parties always put me into high spirits. From the same cause I have been able to invite here very few scientific acquaintances.

My chief enjoyment and sole employment throughout life has been scientific work; and the excitement from such work makes me for the time forget, or quite drives away, my daily discomfort. I have therefore nothing to record during the rest of my life, except the publication of my several books.[6]

II

Two or three books published in the nineteenth century can truly be said to have changed the world. One was Darwin's The Origin of Species. *Darwin first grasped the species problem when, as a young man, he was attached without pay as naturalist to the survey ship* Beagle *on a celebrated circumnavigation of the globe between 1831 and 1836. The* Beagle *passed three years in South American waters, Darwin plunging enthusiastically into studies of the geology, botany, and zoology of an entire continent as yet almost unknown to European science. The experience transformed an uncertain and ill-equipped amateur into a devoted, disciplined man of science.*

Charles Darwin, from the autobiographical sketch: During the voyage of the *Beagle* I had been deeply impressed by discovering in the Pampean formation great fossil animals covered with armour like that on the existing armadillos; secondly, by the manner in which closely allied animals replace one another in proceeding southwards over the Continent; and thirdly, by the South American character of most of the productions of the Galapagos archipelago, and more especially by the manner in which they differ slightly on each island of the group; none of the islands appearing to be very ancient in a geological sense.

It was evident that such facts as these, as well as many others, could only be explained on the supposition that species gradually become modified; and the subject haunted me. But it was equally evident that neither the action of the surrounding conditions, nor the will of the organisms (especially in the case of plants) could account for the innumerable cases in which organisms of every kind are beautifully adapted to their habits of life—for instance, a woodpecker or a tree-frog to climb trees, or a seed for dispersal by hooks or plumes. I had always been much struck by such adaptations, and until these could be explained it seemed to me almost useless to endeavour to prove by indirect evidence that species have been modified.

After my return to England it appeared to me that by following the example of Lyell in Geology, and by collecting all facts which bore in any way on the variation of animals and plants under domestication and nature, some light might perhaps be thrown on the whole subject. My first note-book was opened in July 1837. I worked on true Baconian principles, and without any theory collected facts on a wholesale scale, more especially with respect to domesticated productions, by printed enquiries, by conversation with skilful breeders and gardeners, and by extensive reading. When I see the list of books of all kinds which I read and abstracted, including whole series of Journals and Transactions, I am surprised at my industry. I soon perceived that selection was the keystone of man's success in making useful races of animals and plants. But how selection could be applied to organisms living in a state of nature remained for some time a mystery to me.

In October 1838, that is, fifteen months after I had begun my systematic enquiry, I happened to read for amusement 'Malthus on Population,' and being well prepared to appreciate the struggle for existence which everywhere goes on from long-continued observation of the habits of animals and plants, it at once struck me that under these circumstances favourable variations would tend to be preserved, and unfavourable ones to be destroyed. The result of this would be the formation of new species. Here then I had at last got a theory by which to work; but I was so anxious to avoid prejudice, that I determined not for some time to write even the briefest sketch of it. In June 1842 I first allowed myself the satisfaction of writing a very brief abstract of my theory in pencil in 35 pages; and this was enlarged during the summer of 1844 into one of 230 pages, which I had fairly copied out and still possess.[7]

At the time of the Beagle's *epoch-making voyage, the immutability of species was a basic tenet of both scientific and religious orthodoxy. True, the fossil record revealed a progression of life forms, but each new species appeared abruptly, fully formed and in considerable numbers, in its stratum. For this fact the most plausible explanation, in that genuinely devout age, was that new species had been separately created. There was, certainly, no contrary evidence concerning their origin. Theories of evolution predicated on the transmutation of species, such as those advanced by the French naturalist Lamarck in 1809 or by the anonymous author of the notorious* Vestiges of Creation *in 1844—theories of the direct action of the environment upon the organism, of the inheritance of acquired characteristics, of some innate tendency of the organism to evolve in a particular direction, of the organism's willing its own modification—had no scientific standing. Darwin realized that his own hypothesis of evolution by means of natural selection would strike many of his contemporaries as no better than these fanciful speculations. For all his reverence for "true Baconian principles," his hypothesis was not founded on induction. He had no proof that living species, even under the most favorable conditions of domestic breeding, could be modified indefinitely and permanently. The geological record offered little evidence of those innumerable transitional forms between successive well-marked species that his theory required. The hypothesis was, in fact, a bold leap of the scientific imagination that justified itself, as every great scientific generalization does, by its success in relating and explaining large classes of facts. His theory, Darwin knew, would revolutionize all the biological sciences; very early he appreciated too its profound implications for philosophy, religion, ethics, and politics. The gentle invalid at Down, so careful to avoid the mildest excitement, was possessed of an idea that must inevitably challenge the entrenched orthodoxies in virtually every field of human thought.*

Provision had to be made to safeguard the theory in case of his death. Darwin put aside the sketch of 1844 with a letter to his wife⸗.

I have just finished my sketch of my species theory. If, as I believe, my theory in time be accepted by even one competent judge, it will be a considerable step in science.

I therefore write this in case of my sudden death, as my most solemn and last request, which I am sure you will consider the same as if legally entered in my will, that you will devote £400 to its publication, and further, will yourself, or through Hensleigh [her brother], take trouble in promoting it. I wish that my sketch be given to some competent person, with this sum to induce him to take trouble in its improvement and enlargement. I give to him all my books on Natural History, which are either scored or have references at the end of the pages, begging him carefully to look over and consider such passages as actually bearing, or by possibility bearing, on this subject. I wish you to make a list of all such books as some temptation to an editor. I also request that you will hand over [to] him all those scraps roughly divided in eight or ten brown paper portfolios. The scraps, with copied quotations from various works, are those which may aid my editor. I also request that you, or some amanuensis, will aid in deciphering any of the scraps which the editor may think possibly of use. As the looking over the references and scraps will be a long labour, and as the *correcting* and enlarging and altering my sketch will also take considerable time, I leave this sum of £400 as some remuneration, and any profits from the work. I consider that for this the editor is bound to get the sketch published at a publisher's or his own risk.

With respect to editors, Mr. Lyell would be the best if he would undertake it; I believe he would find the work pleasant, and he would learn some facts new to him. As the editor must be a geologist as well as a naturalist, the next best editor would be Professor Forbes of London. The next best (and quite best in many respects) would be Professor Henslow. Dr. Hooker would be *very* good. The next, Mr. Strickland. If none of these would undertake it, I would request you to consult with Mr. Lyell, or some other capable man for some editor, a geologist and naturalist. Should one other hundred pounds make the difference of procuring a good editor, request earnestly that you will raise £500.[8]

*Hooker was the first to whom he revealed, in 1844, the nature
of the work upon which he had embarked*. Besides a general interest about the southern lands, I have been now ever since my return
engaged in a very presumptuous work, and I know no one individual
who would not say a very foolish one. I was so struck with the distribution of the Galapagos organisms, &c., &c., and with the character of the American fossil mammifers, &c., &c., that I determined to
collect blindly every sort of fact, which could bear any way on what
are species. I have read heaps of agricultural and horticultural
books, and have never ceased collecting facts. At last gleams of light
have come, and I am almost convinced (quite contrary to the opinion
I started with) that species are not (it is like confessing a murder)
immutable. Heaven forfend me from Lamarck nonsense of a "tendency to progression," "adaptations from the slow willing of animals,"
&c! But the conclusions I am led to are not widely different from his;
though the means of change are wholly so. I think I have found out
(here's presumption!) the simple way by which species become exquisitely adapted to various ends. You will now groan, and think to
yourself, "on what a man have I been wasting my time and writing
to." I should, five years ago, have thought so.[9]

It took Darwin twenty years to write The Origin of Species;
*if circumstances had not compelled him to publish prematurely (as
he believed) he might have worked yet another twenty years, or indeed might never have finished the book at all. His poor health permitted him to work only a few hours each day, and sometimes required that all work be suspended for weeks at a time. Tenacious of
purpose though he was, he often procrastinated, perhaps intimidated
by the very importance of the work and certainly apprehensive about
the reception his book might receive and the scandal it would surely
cause. Above all, he was infinitely thorough, cautious, and patient,
firmly rejecting attractive speculations in his ceaseless pursuit of
fact. The range of his researches and experiments was considerable,
the mass and variety of materials slowly marshaled in support of
his theory enormous.*

*Scientific friends were systematically "pumped" for facts and
opinions on matters within their various specialties. From 1844 on,
his good friend Joseph Hooker, though not converted to Darwin's
views, was drawn closely into the work. Darwin's letters to Hooker,*

between his frequent visits to Down, were full of precise, insistent questionings.

Would you kindly observe one little fact for me, whether any species of plant, peculiar to any island, as Galapagos, St. Helena, or New Zealand, where there are no large quadrupeds, have hooked seed—such hooks as, if observed here, would be thought with justness to be adapted to catch into wool of animals.[10]

I am going to ask you some *more* questions. First for the Galapagos, you will see in my Journal, that the Birds, though peculiar species, have a most S. American aspect: I have just ascertained the same thing holds good with the sea-shells. It is so with those plants which are peculiar to this archipelago; you state that their numerical proportions are continental (is not this a very curious fact?) but are they related in forms to S. America. Do you know of any other case of an archipelago, with the separate islands possessing distinct representative species? How is it with the Azores?[11]

Have you any good evidence for the absence of insects in small islands? I found thirteen species in Keeling Atoll.[12]

I should like much to hear, if you make out, whether the N. or S. boundaries of a plant are the more restricted; I should have expected that the S. would be, in the temperate regions, from the number of antagonistic species being greater.[13]

Have you ever thought of G. St. Hilaire's "loi de balancement," as applied to plants? I am well aware that some zoologists quite reject it, but it certainly appears to me that it often holds good with animals. You are no doubt aware of the kind of facts I refer to, such as the great development of canines in the carnivera apparently causing a diminution—a compensation or balancement—in the small size of premolars, etc. I have incidentally noticed some analogous remarks on plants, but have never seen it discussed by botanists. Can you think of any cases in any one species in genus, or genus in family, with certain parts extra developed, and some adjoining parts reduced?[14]

The naturalist Leonard Jenyns was another of Darwin's correspondents. There is one subject, on which I am very curious, and which perhaps you may throw some light on, if you have ever thought of it; namely, what are the checks and what the periods of life,—by which the increase of any given species is limited. Just calculate the increase of any bird, if you assume that only half the young are reared, and these breed: within the *natural* (i.e., if free from accidents) life of the parents the number of individuals will become enormous, and I have been much surprised to think how great destruction *must* annually or occasionally be falling on every species, yet the means and period of such destruction is scarcely perceived by us.[15]

About 1845 the study of barnacles engaged Darwin's attention. Investigation of a single interesting problem opened new problems, and what was intended to be a brief digression from his species work extended to eight years and the publication of four monographs on fossil and living Cirripedes. The experience gave him essential training and authority in zoology, which now joined physical geography, geology, geographical distribution, and paleontology in his arsenal of sciences.

For the first time, too, he was able to verify his theory under the microscope and dissecting knife. To Hooker, in 1848: I have been getting on well with my beloved Cirripedia, and get more skilful in dissection. I have worked out the nervous system pretty well in several genera, and made out their ears and nostrils, which were quite unknown. I have lately got a bisexual cirripede, the male being microscopically small and parasitic within the sack of the female. I tell you this to boast of my species theory, for the nearest closely allied genus to it is, as usual, hermaphrodite, but I had observed some minute parasites adhering to it, and these parasites I now can show are supplemental males, the male organs in the hermaphrodite being unusually small, though perfect and containing zoosperms: so we have almost a polygamous animal, simple females alone being wanting. I never should have made this out, had not my species theory convinced me, that an hermaphrodite species must pass into a bisexual species by insensibly small stages; and here we have it, for the male organs in the hermaphrodite are beginning to fail, and independent males ready formed. But I can hardly explain what I mean, and you will perhaps wish my barnacles and species theory al Diavolo together. But I don't care what you say, my species theory is all gospel.[16]

By 1854 he could return to his major work. The stream of questions to friends and strangers resumed.

To Huxley : Is it not an extraordinary fact, the great difference in position of the heart in different species of *Cleodora?* I am a believer that when any part, usually constant, differs considerably in different allied species that it will be found in some degree variable within the limits of the same species. Thus, I should expect that if great numbers of specimens of some of the species of *Cleodora* had been examined with this object in view, the position of the heart in some of the species would have been found variable. Can you aid me with any analogous fact?[17]

To his cousin William Darwin Fox, a clergyman and naturalist : Now what I want to know is, at what age nestling pigeons have their tail feathers sufficiently developed to be counted. I do not think I ever saw a young pigeon.[18]

You will hate the very sight of my handwriting; but after this I promise I will ask nothing more, at least for a long time. As you live on sandy soil, have you lizards at all common? If you have, should you think it too ridiculous to offer a reward for me for lizard's eggs to the boys in your school; a shilling for every half-dozen, or more if rare, till you got two or three dozen and send them to me? If snake's eggs were brought in by mistake it would be very well, for I want such also; and we have neither lizards nor snakes about here. My object is to see whether such eggs will float on sea water, and whether they will keep alive thus floating for a month or two in my cellar. I am trying experiments on transportation of all organic beings that I can; and lizards are found on every island, and therefore I am very anxious to see whether their eggs stand sea water.[19]

I want you to observe one point for me, on which I am extremely much interested, and which will give you no trouble beyond keeping your eyes open, and that is a habit I know full well that you have. I find horses of various colours often have a spinal band or stripe of different and darker tint than the rest of the body; rarely transverse bars on the legs, generally on the under-side of the front legs, still more rarely a very faint transverse shoulder stripe like an ass. Mouse-coloured ponies, or rather small horses, often have spinal and leg bars. So have dun horses. So have sometimes chestnuts, but I have not yet got a case of spinal stripe in chestnut, race horse, or in quite heavy cart-horse. Any fact of this nature of such stripes in horses would be *most* useful to me.[20]

🖎*To Hooker*🖎 : Will you think of the largest genera with which you are well acquainted, and then suppose ⅘ of the species utterly destroyed and unknown in the sections (as it were) as much as possible in the centre of such great genera. Then would the remaining ⅕ of the species, forming a few sections, be, according to the general practice of average good Botanists, ranked as distinct genera? Of course they would in that case be clearly related genera. The question, in fact, is, are all the species in a gigantic genus kept together in that genus, because they are really so very closely similar as to be inseparable? or is it because no chasms or boundaries can be drawn separating the many species?[21]

🖎*In 1856 Darwin described his work to the American botanist Asa Gray, though at this time remaining silent (as he did with all but his most intimate colleagues) on his central doctrine of natural selection*🖎. It is not a little egotistical, but I should like to tell you (and I do not *think* I have) how I view my work. Nineteen years (!) ago it occurred to me that whilst otherwise employed on Nat. Hist., I might perhaps do good if I noted any sort of facts bearing on the question of the origin of species, and this I have since been doing. Either species have been independently created, or they have descended from other species, like varieties from one species. I think it can be shown to be probable that man gets his most distinct varieties by preserving such as arise best worth keeping and destroying the others, but I should fill a quire if I were to go on. To be brief, I *assume* that species arise like our domestic varieties with *much* extinction; and then test this hypothesis by comparison with as many general and pretty well-established propositions as I can find made out,—in geographical distribution, geological history, affinities, &c., &c. And it seems to me that, *supposing* that such hypothesis were to explain such general propositions, we ought, in accordance with the common way of following all sciences, to admit it till some better hypothesis be found out. For to my mind to say that species were created so and so is no scientific explanation, only a reverent way of saying it is so and so. But it is nonsensical trying to show how I try to proceed in the compass of a note. But as an honest man, I must tell you that I have come to the heterodox conclusion that there are no such things as independently created species—that species are only strongly defined varieties. I know that this will make you despise me. I do not underrate the many *huge* difficulties on this view, but yet it seems to me to explain too much, otherwise inexplicable, to be false.

I must say one word more in justification (for I feel sure that your tendency will be to despise me and my crotchets), that all my notions about *how* species change are derived from long continued study of the works of (and converse with) agriculturalists and horticulturists; and I believe I see my way pretty clearly on the means used by nature to change her species and *adapt* them to the wondrous and exquisitely beautiful contingencies to which every living being is exposed.[22]

✑§*A year later, too, he described his work to a young naturalist whom he had met briefly in London several years before and who had now written to him from the Malay Archipelago—Alfred Russel Wallace. Again, not a word about natural selection*§✑. This summer will make the 20th year (!) since I opened my first note-book, on the question how and in what way do species and varieties differ from each other. I am now preparing my work for publication, but I find the subject so very large, that though I have written many chapters, I do not suppose I shall go to press for two years. It is really *impossible* to explain my views (in the compass of a letter), on the causes and means of variation in a state of nature; but I have slowly adopted a distinct and tangible idea,—whether true or false others must judge; for the firmest conviction of the truth of a doctrine by its author, seems, alas, not to be the slightest guarantee of truth![23]

✑§*The species work was growing to monumental proportions. Lyell, concerned at the passage of years and fearing that someone else might publish first, advised him in 1856 to publish at least a sketch of his work as soon as possible*§✑.

With respect to your suggestion of a sketch of my views, ✑§*Darwin replied*§✑, I hardly know what to think, but will reflect on it, but it goes against my prejudices. To give a fair sketch would be absolutely impossible, for every proposition requires such an array of facts. If I were to do anything, it could only refer to the main agency of change—selection—and perhaps point out a very few of the leading features, which countenance such a view, and some few of the main difficulties. But I do not know what to think; I rather hate the idea of writing for priority, yet I certainly should be vexed if any one were to publish my doctrines before me.[24]

❧§*Hooker was consulted*§❧. I had a good talk with Lyell about my species work, and he urges me strongly to publish something. I am fixed against any periodical or Journal, as I positively will *not* expose myself to an Editor or a Council, allowing a publication for which they might be abused. If I publish anything it must be a *very thin* and little volume, giving a sketch of my views and difficulties; but it is really dreadfully unphilosophical to give a *resumé*, without exact references, of an unpublished work. But Lyell seemed to think I might do this, at the suggestion of friends, and on the ground, which I might state, that I had been at work for eighteen years, and yet could not publish for several years, and especially as I could point out difficulties which seemed to me to require special investigation. Now what think you? I believe I should sneer at any one else doing this, and my only comfort is, that I *truly* never dreamed of it, till Lyell suggested it, and seems deliberately to think it advisable.[25]

❧§*Hooker approved and work was started on a "Preliminary Essay." In a few months, however, Darwin changed his mind. In October, 1856, he reported to Fox*§❧: I remember you protested against Lyell's advice of writing a *sketch* of my species doctrines. Well, when I began I found it such unsatisfactory work that I have desisted, and am now drawing up my work as perfect as my materials of nineteen years' collecting suffice, but do not intend to stop to perfect any line of investigation beyond current work. Thus far and no farther I shall follow Lyell's urgent advice. Your remarks weighed with me considerably. I find to my sorrow it will run to quite a big book.[26]

❧§*To Lyell*§❧: I am working very steadily at my big book; I have found it quite impossible to publish any preliminary essay or sketch; but am doing my work as completely as my present materials allow without waiting to perfect them. And this much acceleration I owe to you.[27]

To Fox again, in February, 1858: I am working very hard at my book, perhaps too hard. It will be very big, and I am become most deeply interested in the way facts fall into groups. I am like Croesus overwhelmed with my riches in facts, and I mean to make my book as perfect as ever I can. I shall not go to press at soonest for a couple of years.[28]

III

On June 18, 1858, the postman deposited at Down a thin manuscript from Alfred Russel Wallace, written the previous February at Ternate in the Malay Archipelago. Its title was "On the Tendency of Varieties to Depart Indefinitely from the Original Type." Lyell was proved right.

At the time in question, *Wallace recalled*, I was suffering from a sharp attack of intermittent fever, and every day during the cold and succeeding hot fits had to lie down for several hours, during which time I had nothing to do but to think over any subjects then particularly interesting me. One day something brought to my recollection Malthus's "Principles of Population," which I had read about twelve years before. I thought of his clear exposition of "the positive checks to increase"—disease, accidents, war, and famine—which keep down the population of savage races to so much lower an average than that of more civilized peoples. It then occurred to me that these causes or their equivalents are continually acting in the case of animals also; and as animals usually breed much more rapidly than does mankind, the destruction every year from these causes must be enormous in order to keep down the numbers of each species, since they evidently do not increase regularly from year to year, as otherwise the world would long ago have been densely crowded with those that breed most quickly. Vaguely thinking over the enormous and constant destruction which this implied, it occurred to me to ask the question, Why do some die and some live? And the answer was clearly, that on the whole the best fitted live. From the effects of disease the most healthy escaped; from enemies, the strongest, the swiftest, or the most cunning; from famine, the best hunters or those with the best digestion; and so on. Then it suddenly flashed upon me that this self-acting process would necessarily *improve the race*, because in every generation the inferior would inevitably be killed off and the superior would remain—that is, *the fittest would survive.* Then at once I seemed to see the whole effect of this, that when sudden changes of land and sea, or of climate, or of food-supply, or of enemies occurred—and we know that such changes have always been taking place—and considering the amount of individual variation that my experience as a collector had shown me to exist, then it followed that all the changes necessary for the adaptation of the species to the changing conditions would be brought about; and as great changes in the environment are always slow, there would be ample time for the change to be effected by the survival of the best fitted in every generation. In this way every part of an animal's organization could be modified exactly as required, and in the very process of this modification the unmodified would die out, and thus the *definite* characters and the clear *isolation* of each new species would be explained. The more I thought over it the more I became convinced that I had at length found the long-sought-for law of nature that solved the problem of the origin of species. For the next hour I thought over the deficiencies in the theories of Lamarck and of the author of the "Vestiges," and I saw that my new theory supplemented these views and obviated every important difficulty. I waited anxiously for the termination of my fit so that I might at once make notes for a paper on the subject. The same evening I did this pretty fully, and on the two succeeding evenings wrote it out carefully in order to send it to Darwin by the next post, which would leave in a day or two.

I wrote a letter to him in which I said that I hoped the idea would be as new to him as it was to me, and that it would supply the missing factor to explain the origin of species. I asked him if he thought it sufficiently important to show to Sir Charles Lyell, who had thought so highly of my former paper.[29]

Darwin was crushed. In a state of stunned calm he immediately wrote to Lyell: Some year or so ago you recommended me to read a paper by Wallace in the 'Annals' [*Annals and Magazine of Natural History*, 1855], which had interested you, and, as I was writing to him, I knew this would please him much, so I told him. He has to-day sent me the enclosed, and asked me to forward it to you. It seems to me well worth reading. Your words have come true with a vengeance—that I should be forestalled. You said this, when I explained to you here very briefly my views of 'Natural Selection' depending on the struggle for existence. I never saw a more striking coincidence; if Wallace had my MS. sketch written out in 1842, he could not have made a better short abstract! Even his terms now stand as heads of my chapters. Please return me the MS., which he does not say he wishes me to publish, but I shall of course, at once write and offer to send to any journal. So all my originality, whatever it may amount to, will be smashed, though my book, if it will ever have any value, will not be deteriorated; as all the labour consists in the application of the theory.

I hope you will approve of Wallace's sketch, that I may tell him what you say.[30]

The calm soon passed. A week later, intensely agitated, he wrote to Lyell again: I am very sorry to trouble you, busy as you are, in so merely personal an affair; but if you will give me your deliberate opinion, you will do me as great a service as ever man did, for I have entire confidence in your judgment and honour.

There is nothing in Wallace's sketch which is not written out much fuller in my sketch, copied out in 1844, and read by Hooker some dozen years ago. About a year ago I sent a short sketch, of which I have a copy, of my views (owing to correspondence on several points) to Asa Gray, so that I could most truly say and prove that I take nothing from Wallace. I should be extremely glad now to publish a sketch of my general views in about a dozen pages or so; but I cannot persuade myself that I can do so honourably. Wallace says nothing about publication, and I enclose his letter. But as I had not intended to publish any sketch, can I do so honourably, because Wallace has sent me an outline of his doctrine? I would far rather burn my whole book, than that he or any other man should think that I had behaved in a paltry spirit. Do you not think his having sent me this sketch ties my hands? If I could honourably publish, I would state that I was induced now to publish a sketch (and I should be very glad to be permitted to say, to follow your advice long ago given) from Wallace having sent me an outline of my general conclusions. We differ only, [in] that I was led to my views from what artificial selection has done for domestic animals. I would send Wallace a copy of my letter to Asa Gray, to show him that I had not stolen his doctrine. But I cannot tell whether to publish now would not be base and paltry. This was my first impression, and I should have certainly acted on it had it not been for your letter.

This is a trumpery affair to trouble you with, but you cannot tell how much obliged I should be for your advice.

By the way, would you object to send this and your answer to Hooker to be forwarded to me, for then I shall have the opinion of my two best and kindest friends. This letter is miserably written, and I write it now, that I may for a time banish the whole subject; and I am worn out with musing.

My good dear friend forgive me. This is a trumpery letter, influenced by trumpery feelings.

I will never trouble you or Hooker on the subject again.[31]

But the next day: Forgive me for adding a P.S. to make the case as strong as possible against myself.

Wallace might say, "You did not intend publishing an abstract of your views till you received my communication. Is it fair to take advantage of my having freely, though unasked, communicated to you my ideas, and thus prevent me forestalling you?" The advantage which I should take being that I am induced to publish from privately knowing that Wallace is in the field. It seems hard on me that I should be thus compelled to lose my priority of many years' standing, but I cannot feel at all sure that this alters the justice of the case. First impressions are generally right, and I at first thought it would be dishonourable in me now to publish.

P.S.—I have always thought you would make a first-rate Lord Chancellor; and I now appeal to you as a Lord Chancellor.[32]

Hooker's response was prompt. He wanted Wallace's manuscript, along with Darwin's sketch of 1844 and a copy of the letter to Asa Gray. On July 1, 1858, Lyell and Hooker presented the three papers to the Linnean Society in London. Wallace's paper was read, and portions of Darwin's; the three were later published complete in the society's Journal.

Years after, Hooker recalled: I was present with Lyell at the meeting. We both I think said something impressing the necessity of profound attention (on the part of Naturalists) to the papers and their bearing on the future of Natural History, but there was no semblance of discussion.

The interest excited was intense, but the subject too novel and too ominous for the old School to enter the lists before armouring. It was talked over after the meeting, 'with bated breath.' Lyell's approval, and perhaps in a small way mine, as his Lieutenant in the affair, rather overawed those Fellows who would otherwise have flown out against the doctrine, and this because we had the vantage ground of being familiar with the authors and their themes.[33]

Now there was no question that Darwin must publish, and quickly. He started to work at once on an abstract of the large volume on which he had been engaged. Intended originally for publication in the Journal of the Linnean Society, the abstract soon assumed the proportions of a fair-sized volume.

There were regular progress reports to Hooker. In July: I pass my time by doing daily a couple of hours of my Abstract, and I find it amusing and improving work. I will be longer than I expected; it will take thirty-five of my MS. folio pages to give an abstract on variation under domestication alone; but I will try to put in nothing which does not seem to me of some interest, and which was once new to me. It seems a queer plan to give an abstract of an unpublished work.[34]

In October: I am working most steadily at my Abstract, but it grows to an inordinate length; yet fully to make my view clear (and never giving briefly more than a fact or two, and slurring over difficulties), I cannot make it shorter. It will yet take me three or four months; so slow do I work, though never idle.[35]

In December: I have now written 330 folio pages of my abstract, and it will require 150–200 [more]; so that it will make a printed volume of 400 pages, and must be printed separately, which I think will be better in many respects. The subject really seems too large for discussion at any Society, and I believe religion would be brought in by men whom I know.[36]

In the spring of 1859 a publisher was sought. Lyell persuaded John Murray, the publisher of his own great Principles of Geology, *to take Darwin's book. Though the* Principles *had been a revolutionary book in its time, Murray's own orthodoxy was well known, and Darwin was apprehensive about the publisher's attitude when he discovered the heretical thesis of the new book.*

Would you advise me, ⚜*Darwin worriedly asked Lyell*⚜, to tell Murray that my book is not more *un*-orthodox than the subject makes inevitable. That I do not discuss the origin of man. That I do not bring in any discussion about Genesis, &c., &c., and only give facts, and such conclusions from them as seem to me fair. Or had I better say *nothing* to Murray, and assume that he cannot object to this much unorthodoxy, which in fact is not more than any Geological Treatise which runs slap counter to Genesis.[37]

⚜*Murray accepted the book sight unseen. To Hooker, Darwin reported*⚜ : I wrote to him [Murray] and gave him the headings of the chapters, and told him he could not have the MS. for ten days or so; and this morning I received a letter, offering me handsome terms, and agreeing to publish without seeing the MS.! So he is eager enough; I think I should have been cautious, anyhow, but, owing to your letter, I told him *explicitly* that I accept his offer solely on condition that, after he has seen part or all the MS., he has full power of retracting. You will think me presumptuous, but I think my book will be popular to a certain extent (enough to ensure [against] heavy loss) amongst scientific and semi-scientific men; why I think so is, because I have found in conversation so great and surprising an interest amongst such men, and some o-scientific [non-scientific] men on this subject, and all my chapters are not *nearly* so dry and dull as that which you have read on geographical distribution. Anyhow, Murray ought to be the best judge, and if he chooses to publish it, I think I may wash my hands of all responsibility.[38]

⚜*The first chapters were ready for Murray's inspection a few days later*⚜. I send by this post, ⚜*Darwin announced to the publisher*⚜, the Title (with some remarks on a separate page), and the first three chapters. If you have patience to read all Chapter I., I honestly think you will have a fair notion of the interest of the whole book. It may be conceit, but I believe the subject will interest the public, and I am sure that the views are original. If you think otherwise, I must repeat my request that you will freely reject my work; and though I shall be a little disappointed, I shall be in no way injured.

If you choose to read Chapters II. and III., you will have a dull and rather abstruse chapter, and a plain and interesting one, in my opinion.[39]

A week later, to Hooker: I write one line to say that I heard from Murray yesterday, and he says he has read the first three chapters of one MS. (and this includes a very dull one), and he abides by his offer.[40]

During the spring, summer, and early fall of 1859 Darwin labored over his book. When the first proofs came from the printer he was alarmed to find the style incredibly bad, his meanings unclear. Endless, painstaking revisions were necessary on every page. He seemed to reach the limits of his strength.

To Asa Gray, in April: I work too hard for my much weakened health; yet I can do only three hours of work daily, and I cannot at all see when I shall have finished: I have done eleven long chapters, but I have got some other very difficult ones: as paleontology, classifications, and embryology, &c., and I have to correct and add largely to all those done. I find, alas! each chapter takes me on an average three months, so slow I am.[41]

To Hooker, in May: My health has quite failed. I am off to-morrow for a week of Hydropathy.[42] *In September*: I have corrected all but the last two chapters of my book, and hope to have done revises and all in about three weeks, and then I (or we all) shall start for some months' hydropathy; my health has been very bad, and I am becoming as weak as a child, and incapable of doing anything whatever, except my three hours daily work at proof-sheets. God knows whether I shall ever be good at anything again, perhaps a long rest and hydropathy may do something. I had a terrible long fit of sickness yesterday, which makes the world rather extra gloomy to-day, and I have an insanely strong wish to finish my accursed book, such corrections every page has required as I never saw before. It is so weariful, killing the whole afternoon, after 12 o'clock doing nothing whatever.[43]

To Fox, on September 23: My health has been as bad as it well could be all this summer; and I have kept on my legs, only by going at short intervals to Moor Park; but I have been better lately, and, thank Heaven, I have at least as good as done my book, having only the index and two or three revises to do. It will be published in the first week in November. Lyell has read about half of the volume in clean sheets, and gives me very great *kudos*. He is wavering so much about the immutability of species, that I expect he will come round. Hooker has come round, and will publish his belief soon. So much for my abominable volume, which has cost me so much labour that I almost hate it.[44]

On September 30, with enormous relief, he was able to write to Lyell : Well, good or bad, my work, thank God, is over; and hard work, I can assure you, I have had, and much work which has never borne fruit. Murray has printed 1250 copies, which seems to me rather too large an edition, but I hope he will not lose.[45]

IV

The book was published on November 24, 1859. It was a small volume of 490 pages, bound in green, and priced at 15 shillings. Its title was On the Origin of Species by Means of Natural Selection, of the Preservation of Favoured Races in the Struggle for Life. *Darwin's argument was measured and judicious, supported by an immense range of data marshaled with the utmost economy but with telling effect: first, the fact—the inexplicable fact—of variation, and the use made of it by skilled breeders in the production of domestic varieties that, by any classifier ignorant of their origins, would be considered separate species; second, variation under nature, and the effect of the unremitting struggle for existence in preserving and accumulating favorable modifications—natural selection; next, consideration of the difficulties of the theory, particularly the problem of the evolution of instinct, the sterility of hybrids, the imperfection of the geological record; finally, the successful application of the theory to account for the facts of geographical distribution, to justify the natural system of classification, to explain the data of morphology and embryology and the origins of rudimentary organs. In his last chapter, "Recapitulation and Conclusion," the author departed from his cautious tone to deliver a frank, confident challenge to the defenders of immutability and to predict the profound influence his doctrine would have* .

I have now recapitulated the chief facts and considerations which have thoroughly convinced me that species have changed, and are still changing by the preservation and accumulation of successive slight favorable variations. Why, it may be asked, have all the most eminent living naturalists and geologists rejected the view of the mutability of species? It cannot be asserted that organic beings in a state of nature are subject to no variation; it cannot be proved that the amount of variation in the course of long ages is a limited quantity; no clear distinction has been, or can be, drawn between species and well-marked varieties. It cannot be maintained that species when intercrossed are invariably sterile, and varieties invariably fertile; or that sterility is a special endowment and sign of creation. The belief that species were immutable productions was almost unavoidable as long as the history of the world was thought to be of short duration; and now that we have acquired some idea of the lapse of time, we are too apt to assume, without proof, that the geological record is so perfect that it would have afforded us plain evidence of the mutation of species, if they had undergone mutation.

But the chief cause of our natural unwillingness to admit that one species has given birth to clear and distinct species, is that we are always slow in admitting any great change of which we do not see the intermediate steps. The difficulty is the same as that felt by so many geologists, when Lyell first insisted that long lines of inland cliffs had been formed, and great valleys excavated, by the slow action of the coast-waves. The mind cannot possibly grasp the full meaning of the term of a hundred million years; it cannot add up and perceive the full effects of many slight variations, accumulated during an almost infinite number of generations.

Although I am fully convinced of the truth of the views given in this volume under the form of an abstract, I by no means expect to convince experienced naturalists whose minds are stocked with a multitude of facts all viewed, during a long course of years, from a point of view directly opposite to mine. It is so easy to hide our ignorance under such expressions as the "plan of creation," "unity of design," &c., and to think that we give an explanation when we only restate a fact. Any one whose disposition leads him to attach more weight to unexplained difficulties than to the explanation of a certain number of facts will certainly reject my theory. A few naturalists, endowed with much flexibility of mind, and who have already begun to doubt the immutability of species, may be influenced by this volume; but I look with confidence to the future, to young and rising naturalists, who will be able to view both sides of the question with impartiality. Whoever is led to believe that species are mutable will do good service by conscientiously expressing his conviction; for only thus can the load of prejudice by which this subject is overwhelmed be removed. . . .

When the views entertained in this volume on the origin of species, or when analogous views are generally admitted, we can dimly foresee that there will be a considerable revolution in natural history. Systematists will be able to pursue their labours as at present; but they will not be incessantly haunted by the shadowy doubt whether this or that form be in essence a species. This I feel sure, and I speak after experience, will be no slight relief. The endless disputes whether or not some fifty species of British brambles are true species will cease. Systematists will have only to decide (not that this will be easy) whether any form be sufficiently constant and distinct from other forms, to be capable of definition; and if definable, whether the differences will be sufficiently important to deserve a specific name. This latter point will become a far more essential consideration than it is at present; for differences, however slight, between any two forms, if not blended by intermediate gradations, are looked at by most naturalists as sufficient to raise both forms to the rank of species. Hereafter we shall be compelled to acknowledge that the only distinction between species and well-marked varieties is, that the latter are known, or believed, to be connected at the present day by intermediate gradations, whereas species were formerly thus connected. Hence, without quite rejecting the consideration of the present existence of intermediate gradations between any two forms, we shall be led to weigh more carefully and to value higher the actual amount of difference between them. It is quite possible that forms now generally acknowledged to be merely varieties may hereafter be thought worthy of specific names, as with the primrose and cowslip; and in this case scientific and common language will come into accordance. In short, we shall have to treat species in the same manner as those naturalists treat genera, who admit that genera are merely artificial combinations made for convenience. This may not be a cheering prospect; but we shall at least be freed from the vain search for the undiscovered and undiscoverable essence of the term species.

The other and more general departments of natural history will rise greatly in interest. The terms used by naturalists of affinity, relationship, community of type, paternity, morphology, adaptive characters, rudimentary and aborted organs, &c., will cease to be metaphorical, and will have a plain signification. When we no longer look at an organic being as a savage looks at a ship, as at something wholly beyond his comprehension; when we regard every production of nature as one which has had a history; when we contemplate every complex structure and instinct as the summing up of many contrivances, each useful to the possessor, nearly in the same way as when we look at any great mechanical invention as the summing up of the labour, the experience, the reason, and even the blunders of numerous workmen; when we thus view each organic being, how far more interesting, I speak from experience, does the study of natural history become!

A grand and almost untrodden field of inquiry will be opened, on the causes and laws of variation, on correlation of growth, on the effects of use and disuse, on the direct action of external conditions, and so forth. The study of domestic productions will rise immensely in value. A new variety raised by man will be a far more important and interesting subject for study than one more species added to the infinitude of already recorded species. Our classifications will come to be, as far as they can be so made, genealogies; and will then truly give what may be called the plan of creation. The rules for classifying will no doubt become simpler when we have a definite object in view. We possess no pedigrees or armorial bearings; and we have to discover and trace the many diverging lines of descent in our natural genealogies, by characters of any kind which have long been inherited. Rudimentary organs will speak infallibly with respect to the nature of long-lost structures. Species and groups of species, which are called aberrant, and which may fancifully be called living fossils, will aid us in forming a picture of the ancient forms of life. Embryology will reveal to us the structure, in some degree obscured, of the prototypes of each great class.

When we feel assured that all the individuals of the same species, and all the closely allied species of most genera, have within a not very remote period descended from one parent, and have migrated from some one birthplace; and when we better know the many means of migration, then, by the light which geology now throws, and will continue to throw, on former changes of climate and of the level of the land, we shall surely be enabled to trace in an admirable manner the former migrations of the inhabitants of the whole world. Even at present, by comparing the differences of the inhabitants of the sea on the opposite sides of a continent, and the nature of the various inhabitants on that continent in relation to their apparent means of immigration, some light can be thrown on ancient geography.

The noble science of Geology loses glory from the extreme imperfection of the record. The crust of the earth with its imbedded remains must not be looked at as a well-filled museum, but as a poor collection made at hazard and at rare intervals. The accumulation of each great fossiliferous formation will be recognised as having depended on an unusual concurrence of circumstances, and the blank intervals between the successive stages as having been of vast duration. But we shall be able to gauge with some security the duration of these intervals by a comparison of the preceding and succeeding organic forms. We must be cautious in attempting to correlate as strictly contemporaneous two formations, which include a few identical species, by the general succession of their forms of life. As species are produced and exterminated by slowly acting and still existing causes, and not by miraculous acts of creation and by catastrophes; and as the most important of all causes of organic change is one which is almost independent of altered and perhaps suddenly altered physical conditions, namely, the mutual relation of organism to organism,—the improvement of one being entailing the improvement or the extermination of others; it follows, that the amount of organic change in the fossils of consecutive formations probably serves as a fair measure of the lapse of actual time. A number of species, however, keeping in a body might remain for a long period unchanged, whilst within this same period, several of these species, by migrating into new countries and coming into competition with foreign associates, might become modified; so that we must not overrate the accuracy of organic change as a measure of time. During early periods of the earth's history, when the forms of life were probably fewer and simpler, the rate of change was probably slower; and at the first dawn of life, when very few forms of the simplest structure existed, the rate of change may have been slow in an extreme degree. The whole history of the world, as at present known, although of a length quite incomprehensible by us, will hereafter be recognised as a mere fragment of time, compared with the ages which have elapsed since the first creature, the progenitor of innumerable extinct and living descendants, was created.

In the distant future I see open fields for far more important researches. Psychology will be based on a new foundation, that of the

necessary acquirement of each mental power and capacity by grada-
tion. Light will be thrown on the origin of man and his history.

Authors of the highest eminence seem to be fully satisfied with the
view that each species has been independently created. To my mind it
accords better with what we know of the laws impressed on matter by
the Creator, that the production and extinction of the past and present inhabitants of the world should have been due to secondary
causes, like those determining the birth and death of the individual.
When I view all beings not as special creations, but as the lineal
descendants of some few beings which lived long before the first bed
of the Silurian system was deposited, they seem to me to become ennobled. Judging from the past, we may safely infer that not one living species will transmit its unaltered likeness to a distant futurity.
And of the species now living very few will transmit progeny of any
kind to a far distant futurity; for the manner in which all organic
beings are grouped, shows that the greatest number of species of
each genus, and all the species of many genera, have left no descendants, but have become utterly extinct. We can so far take a prophetic
glance into futurity as to foretel that it will be the common and
widely-spread species, belonging to the larger and dominant groups,
which will ultimately prevail and procreate new and dominant species.
As all the living forms of life are the lineal descendants of those
which lived long before the Silurian epoch, we may feel certain that
the ordinary succession by generation has never once been broken,
and that no cataclysm has desolated the whole world. Hence we may
look with some confidence to a secure future of equally inappreciable
length. And as natural selection works solely by and for the good of
each being, all corporeal and mental endowments will tend to progress
towards perfection.

It is interesting to contemplate an entangled bank, clothed with
many plants of many kinds, with birds singing on the bushes, with
various insects flitting about, and with worms crawling through the
damp earth, and to reflect that these elaborately constructed forms,
so different from each other, and dependent upon each other in so
complex a manner, have all been produced by laws acting around us.
These laws, taken in the largest sense, being Growth and Reproduction; Inheritance which is almost implied by reproduction; Variability from the indirect and direct action of the external conditions
of life, and from use and disuse; a Ratio of Increase so high as to
lead to a Struggle for Life, and as a consequence to Natural Selec-

tion, entailing Divergence of Character and the Extinction of less-improved forms. Thus, from the war of nature, from famine and death, the most exalted object which we are capable of conceiving, namely, the production of the higher animals, directly follows. There is grandeur in this view of life, with its several powers, having been originally breathed into a few forms or into one; and that, whilst this planet has gone cycling on according to the fixed law of gravity, from so simple a beginning endless forms most beautiful and most wonderful have been, and are being, evolved.[46]

V

What did Lyell, Hooker, and Huxley think? The opinion of the public at large, or even of the general scientific community, was less important to Darwin than the verdict of his friends, whose scientific competence he valued most highly. At the end of October, in those weeks of anxiety when his work was done but the book not yet published, he had written to Hooker: I remember thinking, above a year ago, that if ever I lived to see Lyell, yourself, and Huxley come round, partly by my book, and partly by their own reflections, I should feel that the subject is safe, and all the world might rail, but that ultimately the theory of Natural Selection (though, no doubt, imperfect in its present condition, and embracing many errors) would prevail. Nothing will ever convince me that three such men, with so much diversified knowledge, and so well accustomed to search for truth, could err greatly.[47]

Hooker, who had co-operated in Darwin's work for years and had seen much of the Origin *in manuscript, was at last converted*. I am a sinner, *he wrote to Darwin*, not to have written you ere this, if only to thank you for your glorious book—what a mass of close reasoning on curious facts and fresh phenomena—it is capitally written, and will be very successful. I say this on the strength of two or three plunges into as many chapters, for I have not yet attempted to read it. Lyell, with whom we are staying, is perfectly enchanted, and is absolutely gloating over it. I must accept your compliment to me, and acknowledgment of supposed assistance from me, as the warm tribute of affection from an honest (though deluded) man, and furthermore accept it as very pleasing to my vanity; but, my dear fellow, neither my name nor my judgment nor

my assistance deserved any such compliments, and if I am dishonest
enough to be pleased with what I don't deserve, it must just pass.
How different the *book* reads from the MS. I see I shall have much
to talk over with you.[48]

*Huxley's enthusiasm quickly expressed itself in the charac-
teristic belligerence that would soon earn him the sobriquet "Darwin's bulldog"*. Since I read Von Bär's essays, nine years ago, no
work on Natural History Science I have met with has made so great
an impression upon me, and I do most heartily thank you for the
great store of new views you have given me. Nothing, I think, can be
better than the tone of the book, it impresses those who know nothing
about the subject. As for your doctrine, I am prepared to go to the
stake, if requisite, in support of Chapter IX., and most parts of
Chapters X., XI., XII., and Chapter XIII. contains much that is
most admirable. As to the first four chapters, I agree thoroughly and
fully with all the principles laid down in them. I think you have
demonstrated a true cause for the production of species, and have
thrown the *onus probandi* that species did not arise in the way you
suppose, on your adversaries.

I trust you will not allow yourself to be in any way disgusted or
annoyed by the considerable abuse and misrepresentation which, unless I greatly mistake, is in store for you. Depend upon it you have
earned the lasting gratitude of all thoughtful men. And as to the
curs which will bark and yelp, you must recollect that some of your
friends, at any rate, are endowed with an amount of combativeness
which (though you have often and justly rebuked it) may stand you
in good stead.

I am sharpening up my claws and beak in readiness.[49]

For Lyell the publication of The Origin of Species *had a peculiarly personal, a poignant significance. For nearly thirty years, in
successive editions of his masterly* Principles of Geology, *the great
geologist had been a staunch proponent of the immutability of species. The doctrine of special creation, particularly of man, had a
profound emotional appeal to him that Darwin's argument, though
it convince his reason, could not overcome*. I have just finished
your volume, *he wrote to Darwin*, and right glad I am that I
did my best with Hooker to persuade you to publish it without wait-

ing for a time which probably could never have arrived, though you lived till the age of a hundred, when you had prepared all your facts on which you ground so many grand generalizations. It is a splendid case of close reasoning, and long substantial argument throughout so many pages; the condensation immense, too great perhaps for the uninitiated, but an effective and important preliminary statement. I have long seen most clearly that if any concession is made, all that you claim in your concluding pages will follow. It is this which has made me so long hesitate, always feeling that the case of Man and his races, and of other animals, and that of plants is one and the same, and that if a "vera causa" can be admitted for one, instead of a purely unknown and imaginary one, such as the word "Creation," all the consequences must follow.[50] *That those consequences remained painful to him he admitted at a later time to Hooker*. I plead guilty to going farther in my reasoning towards transmutation than in my sentiments and imagination, and perhaps for that very reason I shall lead more people to Darwin and you, than one who, being born later, has comparatively little to abandon of old and long cherished ideas, which constituted the charm to me of the theoretical part of the science in my earlier days, when I believed with Pascal in the theory, as Hallam terms it, of 'the archangel ruined.'[51]

With Hooker, Huxley, and Lyell converted, Darwin was confident that the subject was safe. Other friends, not numerous but all respected scientists, declared their adherence also; still others struggled conscientiously, and often painfully, with their doubts.

From the botanist H. C. Watson: Once commenced to read the 'Origin,' I could not rest till I had galloped through the whole. I shall now begin to re-read it more deliberately. Your leading idea will assuredly become recognised as an established truth in science, i.e., "Natural Selection." It has the characteristics of all great natural truths, clarifying what was obscure, simplifying what was intricate, adding greatly to previous knowledge. You are the greatest revolutionist in natural history of this century, if not of all centuries. Now [that] these novel ideas are brought fairly before the scientific public, it seems truly remarkable how so many of them could have failed to see their right road sooner. How could Sir C. Lyell, for instance, for thirty years read, write, and think, on the subject of species *and their succession,* and yet constantly look down the wrong road![52]

From his brother Erasmus: [Dr. Henry Holland] has not read much above half, so he says he can give no definite conclusion, and it is my private belief he wishes to remain in that state. He is evidently in a dreadful state of indecision, and keeps stating that he is not tied down to either view, and that he has always left an escape by the way he has spoken of varieties. I happened to speak of the eye before he had read that part, and it took away his breath—utterly impossible—structure—function, &c., &c., &c., but when he had read it he hummed and hawed, and perhaps it was partly conceivable, and then he fell back on the bones of the ear, which were beyond all probability or conceivability.

For myself I really think it is the most interesting book I ever read.[53]

From Hooker: I have had another talk with [George] Bentham, who is greatly agitated by your book: evidently the stern, keen intellect is aroused, and he finds that it is too late to halt between two opinions. How it will go we shall see. I am intensely interested in what we shall come to, and never broach the subject to him.[54]

Darwin to William B. Carpenter: I am perfectly delighted at your letter. It is a great thing to have got a great physiologist on our side. I say "our" for we are now a good and compact body of really good men, and mostly not old men. In the long run we shall conquer. I do not like being abused, but I feel that I can now bear it; and, as I told Lyell, I am well convinced that it is the first offender who reaps the rich harvest of abuse.[55]

Very early, however, there were intimations of the coming storm. I have heard, by roundabout channel, *Darwin reported to Lyell*, that [Sir John] Herschel says my book "is the law of higgledy-piggledy." What this exactly means I do not know, but it is evidently very contemptuous. If true this is a great blow and discouragement.[56]

⊷§A moving and prophetic letter came from Darwin's old teacher, Adam Sedgwick, professor of geology at Cambridge§⊷. I have read your book with more pain than pleasure. Parts of it I admired greatly, parts I laughed at till my sides were almost sore; other parts I read with absolute sorrow, because I think them utterly false and grievously mischievous. You have *deserted*—after a start in that tram-road of all solid physical truth—the true method of induction, and started us in machinery as wild, I think, as Bishop Wilkins's locomotive that was to sail with us to the moon. Many of your wide conclusions are based upon assumptions which can neither be proved nor disproved, why then express them in the language and arrangement of philosophical induction? As to your grand principle—*natural selection*—what is it but a secondary consequence of supposed, or known, primary facts! We all admit development as a fact of history: but how came it about? Here, in language, and still more in logic, we are point-blank at issue. There is a moral or metaphysical part of nature as well a physical. A man who denies this is deep in the mire of folly. 'Tis the crown and glory of organic science that it *does* through *final cause*, link material and moral; and yet *does not* allow us to mingle them in our first conception of laws, and our classification of such laws, whether we consider one side of nature or the other. You have ignored this link; and, if I do not mistake your meaning, you have done your best in one or two pregnant cases to break it. Were it possible (which, thank God, it is not) to break it, humanity, in my mind, would suffer a damage that might brutalize it, and sink the human race into a lower grade of degradation than any into which it has fallen since its written records tell us of its history.[57]

VI

⊷§In the ensuing campaign to capture the public mind Darwin took little direct part. It was rather the small band of Darwinians, led by Huxley, who carried the fight to the entrenched enemy. Lyell, at the Linnean Society in 1858 and at the annual meeting of the British Association for the Advancement of Science in 1859, had already ranged his considerable prestige on the Darwinian side, urging the scientific community to give the forthcoming Origin fair and unprejudiced consideration. Carpenter reviewed the Origin in the National Review, and earlier had occasion to mention it respectfully,

though noncommittally, in the columns of the Edinburgh Review; *that the* Edinburgh Review *should print even a neutral notice of the book could be considered a success of sorts, and Darwin was grateful.* Hooker *defended him in the* Gardeners' Chronicle. *For* Huxley, *the publication of* The Origin of Species *was the opening shot of a war into which he plunged with fierce joy. He expounded Darwin's doctrine in public lectures and reviewed the* Origin *effectively in* The Times, Macmillan's Magazine, *and the* Westminster Review. *Though influential, the Darwinians were, however, few in numbers, and the scientific opponents of the new theory, in alliance with the forces of outraged religious orthodoxy, had access to the largest and most respected periodicals and exploited their advantage to the full᷉.*

᷉The first blow fell even before publication when, on November 19, an unfriendly critic in The Athenaeum *belittled the* Origin *and resented its author's self-confident tone᷉.* We cannot pretend to follow our author in his wanderings through the whole series of phenomena associated with his subject. He omits nothing and he fears nothing. He does not shun objections, nor does he materially understate them; but he disposes of them all more or less confidently. Geographical distribution supplies strong arguments against him, but he considers them, and with evident self-satisfaction assures us that "if we make due allowance for our ignorance of all the changes of climate and of the level of the land, which have certainly occurred within the recent period, and for other similar changes which may have occurred within the same period,—if we remember how profoundly ignorant we are with respect to the many and curious means of occasional transport; if we bear in mind how often a species may have ranged continuously over a wide area, and then have become extinct in the intermediate tracts, the difficulties in believing that all the individuals of the same species, wherever located, have descended from the same parents are not insuperable." But might not the same style of reasoning, or rather of accommodating, be made use of with equal effect to support opposite views? Still onward, through other departments of research, the argument proceeds, and out of classification and embryology the author contrives to extract plain proofs that "the innumerable species, genera and families of organic beings, with which this world is peopled, have all been modified in the course of descent." Such is the object of every chapter, such the purport of the entire argument. The simple outline is sometimes lost sight of, in the crowd of manifold illustrations and considerations, but it is merely this throughout.[58]

It seems to me well done, ⒮*Darwin observed to Hooker*⒭, but the reviewer gives no new objections, and being hostile, passes over every single argument in favor of the doctrine. I fear from the tone of the review, that I have written in a conceited and cocksure style, which shames me a little.[59]

⒮*In March, 1860, Adam Sedgwick, bitterly hostile, attacked* The Origin of Species *in the* Spectator⒭. I need hardly go on any further with these objections. But I cannot conclude without expressing my detestation of the theory, because of its unflinching materialism;—because it has deserted the inductive track, the only track that leads to physical truth;—because it utterly repudiates final causes, and thereby indicates a demoralised understanding on the part of its advocates. Not that I believe that Darwin is an atheist; though I cannot but regard his materialism as atheistical. I think it untrue, because opposed to the obvious course of nature, and the very opposite of inductive truth. And I think it intensely mischievous.[60]

⒮*Darwin wrote to Asa Gray*⒭ : Sedgwick—as I and Lyell feel *certain* from internal evidence—has reviewed me savagely and unfairly in the *Spectator*. The notice includes much abuse, and is hardly fair in several respects. He would actually lead any one, who was ignorant of geology, to suppose that I had invented the great gaps between successive geological formations, instead of its being an almost universally admitted dogma. But my dear friend Sedgwick, with his noble heart, is old, and is rabid with indignation.[61]

⒮*The next month Richard Owen, the foremost comparative anatomist of the time, brought the* Edinburgh Review *firmly back into the orthodox fold with a poisonous review*⒭. The scientific world has looked forward with great interest to the facts which Mr. Darwin might finally deem adequate to the support of his theory on this supreme question in biology, and to the course of inductive original research which might issue in throwing light on 'that mystery of mysteries.' But having now stated the chief, if not the whole, of the original observations adduced by its author in the volume now before us, our disappointment may be conceived. Failing the adequacy of such observations, not merely to carry conviction, but to give a colour to the hypothesis, we were then left to confide in the superior grasp of mind, strength of intellect, clearness and precision of thought and expression, which might raise one man so far above his contemporaries, as to enable him to discern in the common stock of facts, of coincidences, correlations and analogies in Natural History, deeper and truer conclusions than his fellow-labourers had been able to reach.[62]

To Lyell, Darwin protested: I have just read the 'Edinburgh,' which without doubt is by Owen. It is extremely malignant, clever, and I fear will be very damaging. He is atrociously severe on Huxley's lecture, and very bitter against Hooker. It requires much study to appreciate all the bitter spite of many of the remarks against me; indeed I did not discover all myself. It scandalously misrepresents many parts. He misquotes some passages, altering words within inverted commas. It is painful to be hated in the intense degree with which Owen hates me.[63]

The North British Review, in May, anathematized the new heresy with horror and contempt. Mr Darwin's work is in direct antagonism to all the findings of a natural theology, formed on legitimate inductions in the study of the works of God; and it does open violence to everything which the Creator Himself has told us in the Scriptures of truth, of the method and results of His working. While in the foregoing remarks we have been careful to deal with the scientific claims of Mr Darwin's book, we have not scrupled to show that we have looked at it also from the point of view of revelation. In both aspects its publication is a mistake. Its author would have done well to science, and to his own fame, had he, being determined to write it, put it away among his papers, marked "A Contribution to Scientific Speculation in 1720." It would have thus preceded Linnaeus and Cuvier, with whom the dawn began to break into the brightness of noon, and might have been found interesting in 1860, as a prophecy of coming Vireys, Bory de St Vincents, and Lamarcks. But thrust upon us at this time of day, when science has walked in calm majesty out from the mists of prejudice, and been accepted as a sister by a sound theology, it has reminded us of a word in the oldest and best of books, which we commend to Mr Darwin and his followers: "Shadows as the night in the midst of the noonday."[64]

In the July Quarterly Review, *Samuel Wilberforce, Bishop of Oxford, indulged a well-known talent for ridicule before condemning the* Origin *ex cathedra*. This is the theory which really pervades the whole volume. Man, beast, creeping thing, and plant of the earth, are all the lineal and direct descendants of some one individual *ens*, whose various progeny have been simply modified by the action of natural and ascertainable conditions into the multiform aspect of life which we see around us. This is undoubtedly at first sight a somewhat startling conclusion to arrive at. To find that mosses, grasses, turnips, oaks, worms, and flies, mites and elephants, infusoria and whales, tadpoles of to-day and venerable saurians, truffles and men, are all equally the lineal descendants of the same aboriginal common ancestor, perhaps of the nucleated cell of some primeval fungus, which alone possessed the distinguishing honour of being the 'one primordial form into which life was first breathed by the Creator'— this, to say the least of it, is no common discovery—no very expected conclusion. But we are too loyal pupils of inductive philosophy to start back from any conclusion by reason of its strangeness. Newton's patient philosophy taught him to find in the falling apple the law which governs the silent movements of the stars in their courses; and if Mr. Darwin can with the same correctness of reasoning demonstrate to us our fungular descent, we shall dismiss our pride, and avow, with the characteristic humility of philosophy, our unsuspected cousinship with the mushrooms.[65]

It is uncommonly clever, *Darwin complained to Hooker*, it picks out with skill all the most conjectural parts, and brings forward well all the difficulties. I can plainly see, here and there, Owen's hand. The concluding pages will make Lyell shake in his shoes. By Jove, if he sticks to us, he will be a real hero.[66]

In Fraser's Magazine *the mathematician William Hopkins earnestly pondered the value of evolutionary progress*. Our author asserts that nature is always ready to render any variation permanent when it is for the good of the individual and its race. We quite believe that this is one way in which the beneficence of the Creator may be displayed. But what *is good* for an animal? Is it necessarily good that a sponge or a polyp should be promoted to the rank of an oyster, that the ambition of the oyster should aspire to the position of a cephalopod, or a cephalopod to that of a fish, and so on? We should have thought it far more likely that the advantage which may thus be accorded to any organic being was intended for its good in the sphere in which it was born, but not to raise it above that sphere.[67]

A writer for All the Year Round, *in a philosophical vein, predicted that the Darwinian theory must soon succumb in the very struggle for existence that it so picturesquely described*. For theories, as for organised beings, there is also a Natural Selection and a Struggle for Life. The world has seen all sorts of theories arise, have their day, and fall into neglect. Those theories only survive which are based on truth, as far as our intellectual faculties can at present ascertain; such as the Newtonian theory of universal gravitation. If Mr. Darwin's theory be true, nothing can prevent its ultimate and general reception, however much it may pain and shock those to whom it is propounded for the first time. If it be merely a clever hypothesis, an ingenious hallucination, to which a very industrious and able man has devoted the greater and the best part of his life, its failure will be nothing new in the history of science. It will be a Penelope's web, which, though woven with great skill and art, will be ruthlessly unwoven, leaving to some more competent artist the task of putting together a more solid and enduring fabric.[68]

Though he suffered under the critical buffeting, Darwin remained confident of the essential correctness of his theory. The very incapacity or unfairness of the reviewers nullified for him the force of their attacks. Of one reviewer he wrote to Hooker: Have you seen ——'s abusive article on me? It outdoes even the 'North British' and 'Edinburgh' in misapprehension and misrepresentation. I never knew anything so unfair as in discussing cells of bees, his ignoring the case of Melipona, which builds combs almost exactly intermediate between hive and humble bees. What has —— done that he feel so immeasurably superior to all us wretched naturalists, and to all political economists, including that great philosopher Malthus? This reviewer, however, and Harvey's letter have convinced me that I must be a very bad explainer. Neither really understand what I mean by Natural Selection. I am inclined to give up the attempt as hopeless. Those who do not understand, it seems, cannot be made to understand.[69]

Grimly, he wrote to Lyell: All these reiterated attacks will tell heavily; there will be no more converts, and probably some will go back. I hope you do not grow disheartened, I am determined to fight to the last.[70]

VII

While the apparent current of opinion continued overwhelmingly opposed, Darwin's argument made steady progress among numbers of competent scientists—startling, staggering, suggesting, clarifying, convincing. What was needed to bring that progress into the open and to give it added impetus was a direct public confrontation between representatives of the opposing camps. Darwin himself shrank from controversy, but his friends—most especially Huxley —only awaited a favorable opportunity. The opportunity was provided at the meeting of the British Association for the Advancement of Science, at Oxford, in 1860. Section D, which embraced zoology and botany, had scheduled for Saturday, June 30, a paper by Professor Draper of New York on "The Intellectual Development of Europe, Considered with Reference to the Views of Mr. Darwin." Darwin's opponents resolved to use the occasion to crush the new theory. They had the great advantage of an audience, largely clerical, that would be strongly prejudiced in their favor. They had, too, a formidable champion in the Bishop of Oxford, who, though profoundly ignorant of science, was a facile and clever speaker, adroit at ridicule and sure to mobilize all the forces of religious passion for a public condemnation of the Origin. *The little band of Darwin's defenders was disheartened and disgusted*.

The excitement was tremendous, *Hooker recalled many years later*. The lecture-room, in which it had been arranged that the discussion be held, proved far too small for the audience, and the meeting adjourned to the Library of the Museum, which was crammed to suffocation long before the champions entered the lists. The numbers were estimated at from 700 to 1000. Had it been term-time, or had the general public been admitted, it would have been impossible to have accommodated the rush to hear the oratory of the bold Bishop. Professor Henslow, the President of Section D, occupied the chair and wisely announced *in limine* that none who had not valid arguments to bring forward on one side or the other, would be allowed to address the meeting: a caution that proved necessary, for no fewer than four combatants had their utterances burked by him, because of their indulgence in vague declamation.

The Bishop was up to time, and spoke for full half-an-hour with inimitable spirit, emptiness and unfairness. It was evident from his handling of the subject that he had been 'crammed' up to the throat, and that he knew nothing at first hand; in fact, he used no argument not to be found in his 'Quarterly' article. He ridiculed Darwin badly, and Huxley savagely, but all in such dulcet tones, so persuasive a manner, and in such well-turned periods, that I who had been inclined to blame the President for allowing a discussion that could serve no scientific purpose now forgave him from the bottom of my heart. Unfortunately the Bishop, hurried along on the current of his own eloquence, so far forgot himself as to push his attempted advantage to the verge of personality in a telling passage in which he turned round and addressed Huxley: I forget the precise words, and quote from Lyell. 'The Bishop asked whether Huxley was related by his grandfather's or grandmother's side to an ape.' Huxley replied to the scientific argument of his opponent with force and eloquence, and to the personal allusion with a self-restraint, that gave dignity to his crushing rejoinder.

The excitement was now at its height; a lady fainted and had to be carried out, and it was some time before the discussion was resumed. Some voices called for [me,] and [my] name having been handed up, the President invited [me] to give [my] view of the theory from the Botanical side. This [I] did, demonstrating that the Bishop, by his own showing, had never grasped the principles of the 'Origin,' and that he was absolutely ignorant of the elements of botanical science. The Bishop made no reply, and the meeting broke up.[71]

◄§*Huxley described the event thirty years after*§►. The odd part of the business is, that I should not have been present except for

Robert Chambers. I had heard of the Bishop's intention to utilise the occasion. I knew he had the reputation of being a first-class controversialist, and I was quite aware that if he played his cards properly, we should have little chance, with such an audience, of making an efficient defence. Moreover, I was very tired, and wanted to join my wife at her brother-in-law's country house near Reading, on the Saturday. On the Friday I met Chambers in the street, and in reply to some remark of his, about his going to the meeting, I said that I did not mean to attend it—did not see the good of giving up peace and quietness to be episcopally pounded. Chambers broke out into vehement remonstrances, and talked about my deserting them. So I said, "Oh! if you are going to take it that way, I'll come and have my share of what is going on."

So I came, and chanced to sit near old Sir Benjamin Brodie. The Bishop began his speech, and to my astonishment very soon showed that he was so ignorant that he did not know how to manage his own case. My spirits rose proportionately, and when he turned to me with his insolent question, I said to Sir Benjamin, in an undertone, "The Lord hath delivered him into mine hands."

That sagacious old gentleman stared at me as if I had lost my senses. But, in fact, the Bishop had justified the severest retort I could devise, and I made up my mind to let him have it. I was careful, however, not to rise to reply, until the meeting called for me—then I let myself go.[72]

Lyell, who was present at Oxford but missed the memorable Saturday meeting of Section D, recounted: The Bishop of Oxford asked whether Huxley was related by his grandfather's or grandmother's side to an Ape. Huxley replied (I heard several varying versions of this shindy), 'that if he had his choice of an ancestor, whether it should be an ape, or one who having received a scholastic education, should use his logic to mislead an untutored public, and should treat not with argument but with ridicule the facts and reasoning adduced in support of a grave and serious philosophical question, he would not hesitate for a moment to prefer the ape.' Many blamed Huxley for his irreverent freedom; but still more of those I heard talk of it, and among them Falconer, assures me the Vice-Chancellor Jeune (a liberal) declared that the Bishop got no more than he deserved. The Bishop had been much applauded in the section, but before it was over the crowded section (numbers could not get in) were quite turned the other way, especially by Hooker.[73]

A battle—perhaps a decisive battle—had been won. Two days later Hooker, the faithful lieutenant, flushed with victory, reported to Darwin: I have just come from my last moonlight saunter at Oxford and been soliloquizing over the Radcliffe and our old rooms at the corner, and cannot go to bed without inditing a few lines to you, my dear old Darwin. I came here on Thursday afternoon and immediately fell into a lengthened reverie:—without you and my wife I am as dull as ditchwater, and crept about the once familiar streets feeling like a fish out of water. I swore I would not go near a Section and did not for two days, but amused myself with the College buildings and attempted sleeps in the sleepy gardens and rejoiced in my indolence. Huxley and Owen had had a furious battle over Darwin's absent body, at Section D, before my arrival, of which more anon. H. was triumphant; you and your book forthwith became the topics of the day, and I d—d the days and double d—d the topics too, and like a craven felt bored out of my life by being woke out of my reveries to become referee on Natural Selection, &c., &c., &c. On Saturday I walked with my old friend of the *Erebus*, Capt. Dayman, to the Sections and swore as usual I would not go in; but getting equally bored of doing nothing I did. A paper of a Yankee donkey called Draper on 'Civilisation according to the Darwinian Hypothesis,' or some such title, was being read, and it did not mend my temper, for of all the flatulent stuff and all the self-sufficient stuffers, these were the greatest; it was all a pie of Herbert Spencer and Buckle without the seasoning of either; however, hearing that Soapy Sam was to answer I waited to hear the end. The meeting was so large that they had adjourned to the Library, which was crammed with between 700 and 1000 people, for all the world was there to hear Sam Oxon.

Well, Sam Oxon got up and spouted for half an hour with inimitable spirit, ugliness and emptiness and unfairness. I saw he was coached up by Owen and knew nothing, and he said not a syllable but what was in the Reviews; he ridiculed you badly and Huxley savagely. Huxley answered admirably and turned the tables, but he could not throw his voice over so large an assembly, nor command the audience; and he did not allude to *Sam's* weak points nor put the matter in a form or way that carried the audience. The battle waxed hot. Lady Brewster fainted, the excitement increased as others spoke; my blood boiled, I felt myself a dastard; now I saw my advantage; I swore to myself that I would smite that Amalekite, Sam, hip and thigh if my heart jumped out of my mouth, and I handed my name up to the President (Henslow) as ready to throw down the gauntlet.

I must tell you that Henslow as President would have none speak but those who had arguments to use, and four persons had been burked by the audience and President for mere declamation: it moreover became necessary for each speaker to mount the platform, and so there I was cocked up with Sam at my right elbow, and there and then I smashed him amid rounds of applause. I hit him in the wind at the first shot in ten words taken from his own ugly mouth; and then proceeded to demonstrate in as few more: (1) that he could never have read your book, and (2) that he was absolutely ignorant of the rudiments of Bot. Science. I said a few more on the subject of my own experience and conversion, and wound up with a very few observations on the relative positions of the old and new hypotheses, and with some words of caution to the audience. Sam was shut up —had not one word to say in reply, and the meeting *was dissolved forthwith*, leaving you master of the field after 4 hours' battle. Huxley, who had borne all the previous brunt of the battle, and who never before (thank God) praised me to my face, told me it was splendid, and that he did not know before what stuff I was made of. I have been congratulated and thanked by the blackest coats and the whitest stocks in Oxford.[74]

At Down, far removed from the scene of combat, Darwin read the reports of the Oxford meeting with delight. I am indeed most thoroughly contented with the progress of opinion, *he wrote to Huxley*. From all that I hear from several quarters, it seems that Oxford did the subject great good. It is of enormous importance the showing the world that a few first-rate men are not afraid of expressing their opinion. I see daily more and more plainly that my unaided book would have done absolutely nothing.[75]

Now the tide began to turn, slowly at first but then with ever greater momentum with the publication of Hooker's Tasmanian

Flora (*1860*), *Huxley's* Man's Place in Nature (*1863*), *Lyell's* Antiquity of Man (*1863*), *and Darwin's* Descent of Man (*1871*).
*Within two decades the Darwinian hypothesis of evolution by means
of natural selection had captured the citadel of scientific orthodoxy.
Darwin lived to see the victory, to find himself transformed from an
object of obloquy and ridicule to one of veneration. Through it all
he found consolation in a simple philosophy* :—

Whenever I have found out that I have blundered, or that my work
has been imperfect, and when I have been contemptuously criticised,
and even when I have been overpraised, so that I have felt mortified,
it has been my greatest comfort to say hundreds of times to myself
that "I have worked as hard and as well as I could, and no man can
do more than that."[76]

VIII

*A generation that has lived through one of the great revolu-
tions of human thought, that in a short time has had its view of the
world radically transformed, bears the recollection of that experience
as it would of some major crisis of history it had survived. Some
twenty-five years after the publication of* The Origin of Species,
*Thomas Henry Huxley, a white-haired veteran of many memorable
battles waged in the name of science against ignorance, prejudice,
presumption, stupidity—indeed, against the eternally perverse in
human nature—recalled for a younger generation those momentous
days when Darwin's little green volume first confronted a hostile and
scorning public*.

To the present generation, that is to say, the people a few years
on the hither and thither side of thirty, the name of Charles Darwin
stands alongside of those of Isaac Newton and Michael Faraday;
and, like them, calls up the grand ideal of a searcher after truth and
interpreter of Nature. They think of him who bore it as a rare combination of genius, industry, and unswerving veracity, who earned
his place among the most famous men of the age by sheer native
power, in the teeth of a gale of popular prejudice, and uncheered by
a sign of favour or appreciation from the official fountains of hon-

our; as one who in spite of an acute sensitiveness to praise and blame, and notwithstanding provocations which might have excused any outbreak, kept himself clear of all envy, hatred, and malice, nor dealt otherwise than fairly and justly with the unfairness and injustice which was showered upon him; while, to the end of his days, he was ready to listen with patience and respect to the most insignificant of reasonable objectors.

And with respect to that theory of the origin of the forms of life peopling our globe, with which Darwin's name is bound up as closely as that of Newton with the theory of gravitation, nothing seems to be further from the mind of the present generation than any attempt to smother it with ridicule or to crush it by vehemence of denunciation. "The struggle for existence," and "Natural selection," have become household words and every-day conceptions. The reality and the importance of the natural processes on which Darwin founds his deductions are no more doubted than those of growth and multiplication; and, whether the full potency attributed to them is admitted or not, no one doubts their vast and far-reaching significance. Wherever the biological sciences are studied, the 'Origin of Species' lights the paths of the investigator; wherever they are taught it permeates the course of instruction. Nor has the influence of Darwinian ideas been less profound, beyond the realms of Biology. The oldest of all philosophies, that of Evolution, was bound hand and foot and cast into utter darkness during the millenium of theological scholasticism. But Darwin poured new life-blood into the ancient frame; the bonds burst, and the revivified thought of ancient Greece has proved itself to be a more adequate expression of the universal order of things than any of the schemes which have been accepted by the credulity and welcomed by the superstition of seventy later generations of men.

The contrast between the present condition of public opinion upon the Darwinian question; between the estimation in which Darwin's views are now held in the scientific world; between the acquiescence, or at least quiescence, of the theologians of the self-respecting order at the present day and the outburst of antagonism on all sides in 1858–59, when the new theory respecting the origin of species first became known to the older generation to which I belong, is so startling that, except for documentary evidence, I should be sometimes inclined to think my memories dreams.

On the whole, the supporters of Mr. Darwin's views in 1860 were numerically extremely insignificant. There is not the slightest doubt that, if a general council of the Church scientific had been held at that time, we should have been condemned by an overwhelming majority. And there is little doubt that, if such a council gathered now, the decree would be of an exactly contrary nature. It would indicate a lack of sense, as well as of modesty, to ascribe to the men of that generation less capacity or less honesty than their successors possess. What, then, are the causes which led instructed and fair-judging men of that day to arrive at a judgment so different from that which seems just and fair to those who follow them? That is really one of the most interesting of all questions connected with the history of science, and I shall try to answer it. I am afraid that in order to do so I must run the risk of appearing egotistical. However, if I tell my own story it is only because I know it better than that of other people.

I think I must have read the 'Vestiges' before I left England in 1846; but, if I did, the book made very little impression upon me, and I was not brought into serious contact with the 'Species' question until after 1850. At that time, I had long done with the Pentateuchal cosmogony, which had been impressed upon my childish understanding as Divine truth, with all the authority of parents and instructors, and from which it had cost me many a struggle to get free. But my mind was unbiassed in respect of any doctrine which presented itself, if it professed to be based on purely philosophical and scientific reasoning. It seemed to me then (as it does now) that "creation," in the ordinary sense of the word, is perfectly conceivable. I find no difficulty in imagining that, at some former period, this universe was not in existence; and that it made its appearance in six days (or instantaneously, if that is preferred), in consequence of the volition of some pre-existent Being. Then, as now, the so-called *a priori* arguments against Theism; and, given a Deity, against the possibility of creative acts, appeared to me to be devoid of reasonable foundation. I had not then, and I have not now, the smallest *a priori* objection to raise to the account of the creation of animals and plants given in 'Paradise Lost,' in which Milton so vividly embodies the natural sense of Genesis. Far be it from me to say that it is untrue because it is impossible. I confine myself to what must be regarded as a modest and reasonable request for some particle of evidence that the existing species of animals and plants did originate in that way, as a condition of my belief in a statement which appears to me to be highly improbable.

And, by way of being perfectly fair, I had exactly the same answer to give to the evolutionists in 1851–8. Within the ranks of the biologists, at that time, I met with nobody, except Dr. Grant, of University College, who had a word to say for Evolution—and his advocacy was not calculated to advance the cause. Outside these ranks, the only person known to me whose knowledge and capacity compelled respect, and who was, at the same time, a thorough-going evolutionist, was Mr. Herbert Spencer, whose acquaintance I made, I think, in 1852, and then entered into the bonds of a friendship which, I am happy to think, has known no interruption. Many and prolonged were the battles we fought on this topic. But even my friend's rare dialectic skill and copiousness of apt illustration could not drive me from my agnostic position. I took my stand upon two grounds: firstly, that up to that time, the evidence in favor of transmutation was wholly insufficient; and secondly, that no suggestion respecting the causes of transmutation assumed, which had been made, was in any way adequate to explain the phenomena. Looking back at the state of knowledge at that time, I really do not see that any other conclusion was justifiable.

By a curious irony of fate, the same influence which led me to put as little faith in modern speculations on this subject, as in the venerable traditions recorded in the first two chapters of Genesis, was perhaps more potent than any other in keeping alive a sort of pious conviction that Evolution, after all, would turn out true. I have recently read afresh the first edition of the 'Principles of Geology'; and when I consider that this remarkable book had been nearly thirty years in everybody's hands, and that it brings home to any reader of ordinary intelligence a great principle and a great fact —the principle, that the past must be explained by the present, unless good cause be shown to the contrary; and the fact, that, so far as our knowledge of the past history of life on our globe goes, no such cause can be shown—I cannot but believe that Lyell, for others, as for myself, was the chief agent in smoothing the road for Darwin. For consistent uniformitarianism postulates evolution as much in the organic as in the inorganic world. The origin of a new species by other than ordinary agencies would be a vastly greater "catastrophe" than any of those which Lyell successfully eliminated from sober geological speculation.

Thus, looking back into the past, it seems to me that my own position of critical expectancy was just and reasonable, and must have been taken up, on the same grounds, by many other persons. If Agassiz told me that the forms of life which have successively tenanted the globe were the incarnations of successive thoughts of the Deity; and that He had wiped out one set of these embodiments by an appalling geological catastrophe as soon as His ideas took a more advanced shape, I found myself not only unable to admit the accuracy of the deductions from the facts of paleontology, upon which this astounding hypothesis was founded, but I had to confess my want of any means of testing the correctness of his explanation of them. And besides that, I could by no means see what the explanation explained. Neither did it help me to be told by an eminent anatomist that species had succeeded one another in time, in virtue of "a continuously operative creational law." That seemed to me to be no more than saying that species had succeeded one another, in the form of a vote-catching resolution, with "law" to please the man of science, and "creational" to draw the orthodox. So I took refuge in that *"thätige Skepsis"* which Goethe has so well defined; and, reversing the apostolic precept to be all things to all men, I usually defended the tenability of the received doctrines, when I had to do with the transmutationist; and stood up for the possibility of transmutation among the orthodox—thereby, no doubt, increasing an already current, but quite undeserved, reputation for needless combativeness.

I remember, in the course of my first interview with Mr. Darwin, expressing my belief in the sharpness of the lines of demarcation between natural groups and in the absence of transitional forms, with all the confidence of youth and imperfect knowledge. I was not aware, at that time, that he had then been many years brooding over the species-question; and the humorous smile which accompanied his gentle answer, that such was not altogether his view, long haunted and puzzled me.

I imagine that most of those of my contemporaries who thought seriously about the matter, were very much in my own state of mind —inclined to say to both Mosaists and Evolutionists, "a plague on both your houses!" and disposed to turn aside from an interminable and apparently fruitless discussion, to labour in the fertile fields of ascertainable fact. And I may, therefore, further suppose that the publication of the Darwin and Wallace papers in 1858, and still more that of the 'Origin' in 1859, had the effect upon them of the flash of light, which to a man who has lost himself on a dark night,

suddenly reveals a road which, whether it takes him straight home
or not, certainly goes his way. That which we were looking for, and
could not find, was a hypothesis respecting the origin of known
organic forms, which assumed the operation of no causes but such
as could be proved to be actually at work. We wanted, not to pin our
faith to that or any other speculation, but to get hold of clear and
definite conceptions which could be brought face to face with facts
and have their validity tested. The 'Origin' provided us with the
working hypothesis we sought. Moreover, it did the immense service
of freeing us for ever from the dilemma—refuse to accept the creation hypothesis, and what have you to propose that can be accepted
by any cautious reasoner? In 1857 I had no answer ready, and I do
not think that anyone else had. A year later we reproached ourselves
with dulness for being perplexed by such an inquiry. My reflection,
when I first made myself master of the central idea of the 'Origin,'
was, "How extremely stupid not to have thought of that!" I suppose
that Columbus' companions said much the same when he made the
egg stand on end. The facts of variability, of the struggle for existence, of adaptation to conditions, were notorious enough; but none
of us had suspected that the road to the heart of the species problem lay through them, until Darwin and Wallace dispelled the darkness, and the beacon-fire of the 'Origin' guided the benighted.

Whether the particular shape which the doctrine of Evolution, as
applied to the organic world, took in Darwin's hands, would prove
to be final or not, was, to me, a matter of indifference. In my earliest
criticisms of the 'Origin' I ventured to point out that its logical
foundations were insecure so long as experiments in selective breeding had not produced varieties which were more or less infertile; and
that insecurity remains up to the present time. But, with any and
every critical doubt which my sceptical ingenuity could suggest, the
Darwinian hypothesis remained incomparably more probable than
the creation hypothesis. And if we had none of us been able to discern the paramount significance of some of the most patent and notorious of natural facts, until they were, so to speak, thrust under
our noses, what force remained in the dilemma—creation or nothing?
It was obvious that, hereafter, the probability would be immensely
greater, that the links of natural causation were hidden from our
purblind eyes, than that natural causation should be incompetent
to produce all the phenomena of nature. The only rational course
for those who had no other object than the attainment of truth was

to accept "Darwinism" as a working hypothesis and see what could
be made of it. Either it would prove its capacity to elucidate the facts
of organic life, or it would break down under the strain. This was
surely the dictate of common sense; and, for once, common sense
carried the day. The result has been that complete *volte-face* of the
present scientific world, which must seem so surprising to the present
generation. I do not mean to say that all the leaders of biological
science have avowed themselves Darwinians; but I do not think that
there is a single zoologist, or botanist, or paleontologist, among the
multitude of active workers of this generation, who is other than an
evolutionist, profoundly influenced by Darwin's view. Whatever may
be the ultimate fate of the particular theory put forth by Darwin, I
venture to affirm that, so far as my knowledge goes, all the ingenuity
and learning of hostile critics have not enabled them to adduce a
solitary fact, of which it can be said, this is irreconcilable with the
Darwinian theory. In the prodigious variety and complexity of organic nature, there are multitudes of phenomena which are not de-
ducible from any generalisations we have yet reached. But the same
may be said of every other class of natural objects. I believe that
astronomers cannot yet get the moon's motions into perfect accordance with the theory of gravitation.

The known is finite, the unknown infinite; intellectually we stand
on an islet in the midst of an illimitable ocean of inexplicability. Our
business in every generation is to reclaim a little more land, to add
something to the extent and the solidity of our possessions. And
even a cursory glance at the history of the biological sciences during
the last quarter of a century is sufficient to justify the assertion,
that the most potent instrument for the extension of the realm of
natural knowledge which has come into man's hands, since the publication of Newton's 'Principia,' is Darwin's 'Origin of Species.'

It was badly received by the generation to which it was first addressed, and the outpouring of angry nonsense to which it gave rise
is sad to think upon. But the present generation will probably behave
just as badly if another Darwin should arise, and inflict upon them
that which the generality of mankind most hate—the necessity of
revising their convictions. Let them, then, be charitable to us an-
cients; and if they behave no better than the men of my day to some
new benefactor, let them recollect that, after all, our wrath did not
come to much, and vented itself chiefly in the bad language of sanc-

timonious scolds. Let them as speedily perform a strategic right-about-face, and follow the truth wherever it leads. The opponents of the new truth will discover, as those of Darwin are doing, that, after all, theories do not alter facts, and that the universe remains unaffected even though texts crumble.[77]

CHAPTER 6

Charles George Gordon

---❖---

"I have done my best for the honour
of our country."

I

So you would abandon the Soudan?

⚬§Major-General Charles George Gordon, a slight, intense figure, spoke rapidly, with vigorous animation. Opposite him, on the leopard-skin couch, sat William T. Stead, editor of the Pall Mall Gazette. *Stead had sought out Gordon this January afternoon in 1884 to obtain his views on a report that the government had decided to evacuate the Sudan. At first reluctant to speak, Gordon had been persuaded that his views might yet affect the government's deliberations. It was the first time his opinion had been sought on the now crucial subject about which he, a former Governor-General of the Sudan in the employ of the Egyptian Khedive Ismail, knew more than any other Englishman.*

An enormous country of uncertain limits, the Egyptian Sudan

311

stretched from Egypt 1,200 miles south to the equator, and from the Red Sea 1,000 miles west into central Africa. For fifty years Egypt had extended her rule in the Sudan, elevating the town of Khartoum at the junction of the White and Blue Niles into the administrative center of the country. But now Egypt, nominally a part of the Turkish empire, had itself become virtually a British protectorate. Totally bankrupt, Egypt had been forced in 1876 to submit to an international control exercised jointly by England and France. The two powers had deposed the extravagant Ismail, placed his son Tewfik on the throne, and assumed the management of Egyptian revenues and expenditures. When a nationalist revolt of Egyptian army officers led by Arabi Pasha erupted in 1882, England had suppressed it alone. Now the English minister at Cairo, Sir Evelyn Baring, supported by an English army of occupation, dictated policy to a thoroughly subservient Egyptian government.

This state of affairs was a considerable embarrassment to the Liberal prime minister, William E. Gladstone, apostle of peace and retrenchment, who would have liked to divest himself of the imperial obligations incurred by doughtier Englishmen. He was determined that the English occupation of Egypt should be a brief one; as soon as Egyptian affairs were placed into businesslike order, the English would withdraw. Meanwhile he cherished the fiction that the Egyptian government was in fact sovereign, and scrupulously avoided interference in affairs that he was pleased to call purely Egyptian.

Gladstone's hopes for an early withdrawal from Egypt were threatened, however, by a serious revolt in the Sudan. In 1881, one Mohammed Ahmed, a fanatic Dongolese, had proclaimed himself the long-awaited Mahdi, successor to the prophet Mohammed, and had declared his intention of restoring Islam to its original purity by purging it of Turkish corruptions. From the start, his religious movement manifested itself as a revolt against the corrupt and incompetent Egyptian administration in the Sudan. In November, 1883, an Egyptian army of 10,000 men, led by a retired British officer, Colonel William Hicks (to whom Gladstone's government gave neither advice nor assistance), was annihilated by the Mahdi's dervishes. Egypt had no resources to finance a pacification of the Sudan, and Gladstone was determined that English money and men should not be used for that purpose. He had, therefore, decreed that Egypt must abandon the Sudan to the Mahdi; his decision had been duly transmitted to the Khedive by Baring. For those Englishmen who regarded Gladstone's policy as a parsimonious and shortsighted retreat from imperial responsibility, there was now no appeal but to public opinion. It was this consideration that had brought Stead to Gordon's door.

So you would abandon the Soudan? But the Eastern Soudan is indispensable to Egypt, *Gordon continued*. It will cost you far more to retain your hold upon Egypt proper if you abandon your hold of the Eastern Soudan to the Mahdi or to the Turk than what it would to retain your hold upon Eastern Soudan by the aid of such material as exists in the provinces. Darfour and Kordofan must be abandoned. That I admit; but the provinces lying to the east of the White Nile should be retained, and north of Sennaar. The danger to be feared is not that the Mahdi will march northward through Wady Halfa; on the contrary, it is very improbable that he will ever go so far north. The danger is altogether of a different nature. It arises from the influence which the spectacle of a conquering Mahometan Power established close to your frontiers will exercise upon the population which you govern. In all the cities in Egypt it will be felt that what the Mahdi has done they may do; and, as he has driven out the intruder and the infidel, they may do the same. Nor is it only England that has to face this danger. The success of the Mahdi has already excited dangerous fermentation in Arabia and Syria. Placards have been posted in Damascus calling upon the population to rise and drive out the Turks. If the whole of the Eastern Soudan is surrendered to the Mahdi, the Arab tribes on both sides of the Red Sea will take fire. In self-defence the Turks are bound to do something to cope with so formidable a danger, for it is quite possible that if nothing is done the whole of the Eastern Question may be reopened by the triumph of the Mahdi. I see it is proposed to fortify Wady Halfa, and prepare there to resist the Mahdi's attack. You might as well fortify against a fever. Contagion of that kind cannot be kept out by fortifications and garrisons. But that it is real, and that it does exist, will be denied by no one cognizant with Egypt and the East. In self-defence the policy of evacuation cannot possibly be justified.

There is another aspect to the question. You have 6000 men in Kartoum [the Egyptian garrison]. What are you going to do with them? You have garrisons in Darfour, in Bahr el Gazelle, and

Gondokoro. Are they to be sacrificed? Their only offence is their loyalty to their Sovereign. For their fidelity you are going to abandon them to their fate. You say they are to retire upon Wady Halfa. But Gondokoro is 1500 miles from Kartoum, and Kartoum is 350 only from Wady Halfa. How will you move your 6000 men from Kartoum—to say nothing of other places—and all the Europeans in that city through the desert to Wady Halfa? Where are you going to get the camels to take them away? Will the Mahdi supply them? If they are to escape with their lives, the garrison will not be allowed to leave with a coat on their backs. They will be plundered to the skin, and even then their lives may not be spared. Whatever you may decide about evacuation, you cannot evacuate, because your army cannot be moved. You must either surrender absolutely to the Mahdi or defend Kartoum at all hazards. The latter is the only course which ought to be entertained. There is no serious difficulty about it. The Mahdi's forces will fall to pieces of themselves; but if in a moment of panic orders are issued for the abandonment of the whole of the Eastern Soudan, a blow will be struck against the security of Egypt and the peace of the East, which may have fatal consequences.[1]

Stead's interview with Gordon appeared in the Pall Mall Gazette on January 9, together with an editorial calling upon the government to send Gordon, with full powers, to salvage what could yet be saved of the Sudan. The next day leading newspapers throughout England copied the interview and echoed the call for Gordon— victor over the Taiping rebels in China, destroyer of the slave trade in the Sudan, Gordon the soldier-saint and national hero.

For the government, the crisis in the Sudan was an unwelcome intrusion upon pressing domestic business. Evacuation had seemed a simple and expedient solution, but now Gordon had dramatized the plight of the Egyptian garrisons that would be sacrificed by a hasty withdrawal. The situation was daily becoming more urgent as the still loyal provinces wavered; in a few days or weeks the Sudan might completely disintegrate and the Egyptian garrisons and Europeans be lost. Clearly, an unpopular policy threatened quickly to become a disastrous one. The government, however, was inclined to temporize. The possibility of employing Gordon had already been considered and rejected; he was too eccentric, too unpredictable. Yet the popular clamor for Gordon was becoming irresistible. Could not the government employ Gordon in an advisory capacity, thereby identifying *the hero with the government's policy without actually committing itself to accept his recommendations—or to act at all? On January 16, however, Baring telegraphed urgently from Cairo for "a qualified British officer to go to Khartoum with full powers civil and military to conduct the retreat." The government stirred uncomfortably on the horns of its dilemma.*

On January 18, Gordon was summoned to a meeting at the War Office with Lord Wolseley, the Adjutant-General of the army, and four cabinet ministers—Lords Granville, Hartington, and North-brook, and Sir Charles Dilke. Accounts of that meeting written immediately afterward by several of the participants already revealed a fatal confusion as to whether Gordon's assignment was purely advisory or executive as well. Certainly the instructions drafted for him that afternoon spelled out advisory duties; but the ministers, who knew that Baring wanted an officer with full executive powers and would consider the sending of anyone else as useless, concluded their instructions by placing Gordon finally at the disposal of Baring and the Egyptian government.

Gordon's assignment, in Granville's verbose officialese, was:
To proceed to Suakim [on the Red Sea coast] to report on the military situation in the Sudan and on the measures to be taken for the security of the Egyptian garrisons still holding positions in that country and of the European population at Khartoum. He will consider the best mode of evacuating the interior of the Sudan and of securing the safety and good administration by the Egyptian Government of the ports on the Red Sea coast. He will pay special consideration to what steps should be taken to counteract the possible stimulus to the Slave Trade which may be given by the revolution which has taken place.

Colonel [sic] Gordon will be under the orders of Her Majesty's Minister at Cairo and will report through him to H. M. Government and perform such other duties as may be entrusted to him by the Egyptian Government through Sir Evelyn Baring.[2]

Thus the cabinet still refused to take responsibility for what was technically an Egyptian problem, even though Baring, to all practical purposes, was the Egyptian government.

In Gordon's mind there was never any doubt that his assignment was executive. Wolseley came for me and took me to the

Ministers, ❦*he wrote en route to a friend*❧. He went in and talked to the Ministers and came back and said "H.M.G. want you to understand this Government are determined to evacuate the Sudan, for they will not guarantee future government. Will you go and do it?" I said "Yes." He said "Go in." I went in and saw them. They said "Did Wolseley tell you our ideas?" I said "Yes; he said you will not guarantee future government of Sudan and you wish me to go and evacuate it?" They said "Yes," and it was over and I left at 8 P.M. for Calais.[3]

❦*Gordon carried a handbag and a metal case containing his general's uniform. With him went Colonel J. D. H. Stewart, a cavalry officer who had served in the Sudan and who was to be Gordon's chief assistant. On January 24 they were in Cairo. There were conferences the next day with Baring, the Khedive, and the Egyptian prime minister, from which Gordon emerged Governor-General of the Sudan once more, with orders to go to Khartoum and conduct the evacuation of the Egyptian garrisons without the use of force. On January 26 he and Stewart left Cairo by train for Assuit accompanied by a small party that included a friend of Crimean War days, General Gerald Graham. At Assuit the party boarded a steamer for the five-day journey up the Nile to Korosko, from which point Gordon and Stewart would cut directly across the desert to Abu Hamed*❧.

We reached Korosko on the evening of the 1st of February, ❦*Graham related*❧, and the next morning was that for saying good-bye, as here Gordon entered the great Nubian Desert. That morning we had a long talk together on deck after breakfast, when he told me what he meant to do, and how he felt for the misery of the natives. About eight o'clock he mounted his camel and said good-bye, but I walked beside him, and he shortly afterwards got down and walked with me. At last I left him, saying "good-bye" again, and "God bless you." Then he mounted again. A handsome young Arab, Ahmed, son of the Sheikh of Berber, rode beside him on a beautiful white camel. At the head of the caravan rode Ahmed's brother, both being armed with the great cross-hilted swords, and shields of rhinoceros hide, which Soudan warfare has now made familiar. These swords, together with a couple of very old double-barrelled pistols with flint locks, made up the Arab armament. Gordon carried no arms, but Stewart had a revolver. Before Gordon left he gave me a long heavy silver-mounted kourbash, or Soudan riding whip, of rhinoceros hide, and told me to say "that was a token that the reign of the kourbash in the Soudan was over." In exchange he took my white umbrella, having lost his own.

The place where I last saw Gordon is wild and desolate. The desert there is covered with a series of volcanic hills, looking, S. [Graham's aide-de-camp] said, like a miniature Switzerland. But here were no fertile valleys, no bright snow-clad peaks, no thriving population— nothing between the hills but black basins or ravines, dry, dark, and destitute of all vegetation, looking like separate entrances to the pit where those who entered, might leave all hope behind. I thought of Hicks with his doomed army coming into such a ravine after forty days in the wilderness, utterly spent and worn out, then finding the dark crests of the surrounding heights lined with a fierce exultant enemy, and of the sickening feeling he must have had, that all was lost for him and those he had led there. I climbed up the highest of these hills with S., and through a glass watched Gordon and the small caravan as his camels threaded their way along a sandy valley, hoping he would turn round that I might give him one more sign, but he rode on until he turned the dark side of one of the hills, and I saw him no more. Sadly we returned to our steamer, and I felt a gloomy foreboding that I should never see Gordon again.[4]

II

From Cairo, Gordon had telegraphed to the demoralized officials at Khartoum: "Do not be panic-stricken. You are men not women. I am coming." Now his arrival in the beleaguered city was awaited with rising excitement. On February 8 he was at Abu Hamed, on February 11 at Berber, on February 15 at Shendi. From Shendi a proclamation preceded him to Khartoum and was posted on the houses of the town. It announced that the Mahdi was appointed Sultan of Kordofan, that one-half the taxes was remitted, and that the slave trade could be resumed. On February 18, Gordon was in Khartoum.

General Gordon's arrival here this morning, *The Times corresIpondent and British consul in Khartoum, Frank Power, telegraphed to his newspaper on February 18*, led to a wonderful demonstration of welcome by the people, thousands of them crowding to kiss his hands and feet, and calling him the "Sultan of the Soudan."

His speech to the people was received with enthusiasm. He said:—

"I come without soldiers, but with God on my side, to redress the evils of the Soudan. I will not fight with any weapons but justice. There shall be no more Bashi-Bazouks [Turkish irregular troops]."

Since they heard that he was coming the aspect of the people has so changed that there are no longer any fears of disturbances in the town. They say that he is giving them more than even the Mahdi could give.

He is sending out proclamations in all directions.

Such is the influence of one man that there are no longer any fears for the garrison or people of Khartoum.[5]

A second dispatch followed the next day. Yesterday was one series of acceptable surprises for the people of Khartoum.

General Gordon's proclamation preceded him, and immediately on his arrival he summoned the officials, thus preparing the people for some salutary changes. He next held a levée at the Mudirieh, the entire population, even the poorest Arab, being admitted. On his way between the Mudirieh and the Palace about 1,000 persons pressed forward kissing his hands and feet, and called him "Sultan," "Father," and "Saviour of Kordofan."

General Gordon and Colonel Stewart at once opened offices in the Palace, giving to every one with a grievance admittance and a careful hearing. The Government books, recording from time immemorial the outstanding debts of the overtaxed people, were publicly burnt in front of the Palace. The kourbashes, whips, and implements for administering the bastinado from Government-house were all placed on the blazing pile. The evidence of debts and the emblems of oppression perished together.

In the afternoon General Gordon created a Council of the local notables, all Arabs. Then he visited the hospital and arsenal. With Colonel Stewart, Coetlogon Pasha, and the English Consul he visited the prison, and found it to be a dreadful den of misery. Two hundred wretches loaded with chains lay there. They were of all ages, boys and old men, some having never been tried, some having been proved innocent, but forgotten for over six months, some arrested on suspicion and detained there more than three years, many merely prisoners of war, and one a woman, who had spent 15 years in the prison for a crime committed when she was a girl.

General Gordon at once commenced to demolish this bastille. All the prisoners will be briefly examined, and if it be advisable set at liberty. Before it was dark scores of wretches had had their chains struck off, and to-day Colonel Stewart is continuing this work.

Last night the town was in a blaze of illumination, the bazaar being hung with cloth and coloured lamps and the private houses beautifully decorated. There was a fine display of fireworks by the negro population, who indulged in great rejoicings till midnight.[6]

As the only other Englishman in Khartoum, Power was admitted to the companionship of Gordon and Stewart. He was twenty-six years old, and it was only natural that he should succumb at once to Gordon's charm.

Gordon, Colonel Stewart, and I now mess and live together, *Power wrote to his mother on February 22*. Gordon is a most lovable character—quiet, mild, gentle, and strong; he is so humble too. The way he pats you on the shoulder when he says, "Look here, dear fellow, now what would you advise?" would make you love him. When he goes out of doors there are always crowds of Arab men and women at the gate to kiss his feet, and twice to-day the furious women, wishing to lift his feet to kiss them, threw him over. He appears to like me, and already calls me Frank. He likes my going so much amongst the natives, for not to do so is a mortal sin in his eyes. He is Dictator here; the Mahdi has gone down before him, and to-day sent him a "salam," or message of welcome. It is wonderful that one man could have such an influence on 200,000 people. Numbers of women flock here every day to ask him to touch their children to cure them; they call him the "Father and the Saviour of the Soudan." He has found me badly up in "Thomas à Kempis," which he reads every day, and has given me an "Imitation of Christ." He is indeed, I believe, the greatest and best man of this century. He asks me who I am writing to, and when I say "to you," he says he hopes you will some day give him a cup of tea, and like him. No one could help it. I stay on here to the end. I'll stop while he stays.[7]

A few days later, again to his mother: I like Gordon more and more every day; he has a most lovable manner and disposition, and is so kind to me. He is glad if you show the smallest desire to help him in his great trouble. How one man could have dared to attempt his task, I wonder. One day of his work and bother would kill another man, yet he is so cheerful at breakfast, lunch, and dinner; but I know he suffers fearfully from low spirits. I hear him walking up and down his room all night (it is next to mine). It is only his great piety carries him through.[8]

As soon as he arrived in Khartoum, Gordon began to organize the evacuation of the Egyptian troops and civilian employees and the European residents. It was obvious that a peaceful evacuation would require the co-operation of the tribes through whose territory the refugees must move. From Berber, while en route to Khartoum, Gordon had written to the Mahdi, offering him peace and the title of Sultan of Kordofan and accompanying the letter with a ceremonial gift of robes of honor. But the tribes in the eastern Sudan, between Berber and Suakim, had already revolted under a lieutenant of the Mahdi, Osman Digna, and other Mahdist agents were at work among the tribes on the northern escape route. Now that Egypt's intention of abandoning the Sudan was known, even those tribes hostile to the Mahdi would soon have to submit to him. The loyal tribes waited only to see what Gordon would do. It was therefore imperative, Gordon knew, to establish a strong native government to which the loyal tribes could adhere in preference to the Mahdi. At Cairo, and again from Khartoum, Gordon had urged the British government to approve the creation of an independent but subsidized Sudanese government under Zebehr Pasha, a notorious slave-trader and rebel then in confinement in Cairo. Zebehr, Gordon believed, was the only man capable of governing the Sudan. English public opinion, however, would not tolerate Zebehr, and on February 26 Gordon had Granville's telegram of refusal.

This was a crucial blow. In Cairo, Baring continued to press for Zebehr's appointment, but Gordon accepted the decision fatalistically and turned to an alternative plan. He had always been confident that, ultimately, behind his solitary person, was ranged the armed might of the British empire. A manifestation of that power, however small, he hoped, might be enough to check the deteriorating situation in the Sudan until the evacuation could be completed. Early in February General Graham had been sent to Suakim with 4,000 troops to relieve the Egyptian garrisons on the Red Sea coast.

Within a month he had defeated Osman Digna three times and awaited orders to advance across the 250 miles of desert to Berber on the Nile. Confident that Graham would come to Berber, Gordon promised the people of Khartoum that a British army was at hand. But again London refused. Though Graham had attacked the tribes of the eastern Sudan, the cabinet would not permit him to carry hostilities into the central Sudan. Graham returned to Cairo, leaving Osman Digna still blocking Gordon's eastern escape route to the Red Sea.

From London a telegram repeating the government's refusal of Zebehr and announcing its decision not to send troops to Berber was dispatched to Gordon on March 11. It was never received. The tribes north of Khartoum had by then gone over to the Mahdi, and on March 12 had cut the telegraph line to Cairo and begun the siege of Khartoum. Not until April 7 did a spy bring to Gordon Baring's terse report: "So far as I know, there is no intention on the part of the Government to send an English force to Berber."

On March 22 three dervishes arrived in Khartoum from the Mahdi. They returned to Gordon the robes of honor he had sent the Mahdi and offered him instead a gift of the patched and filthy jibbah that the Mahdi's followers wore as a uniform. They brought, too, a letter from the Mahdi in reply to Gordon's peace overtures.

Your letter has been received and its contents have been read and understood, *the Mahdi wrote*. You say you wish the progress of the Moslems, and that you are desirous of opening up the road to enable them to visit the tomb of the Prophet. You also express your desire to establish friendship between us and you, and ask us to set free the Christians and Moslems, promising also to declare me ruler of Kordofan.

How is it possible for one who is not a follower of the Prophet of God to wish to open the road to his tomb for pilgrims? The Prophet has no desire to be visited by dogs, for it is said, this world is a carcass, and those who seek after it are dogs. The Prophet cares not for those to visit him who worship other gods and who forget that God is over all, and knows every word he says, and is one who seeks the vanity of this world. If you pity the Moslems you should pity your own soul first, and save it from the anger of its Creator, and make it a follower of the true religion, by following our lord the Prophet Mohammed. God will not accept any religion except that of the Prophet. Come, therefore, and join his religion, and then you can pity his people, and guide them in the fulfilment of his laws; then only can you be considered a man of pity. Unless you do so, no true believer can be your companion.

Be it known to you that I am without pride, the promised Mahdi and the successor to the prophet. There is no need for me to be sultan or king of Kordofan, or any other country, nor have I any desire for the benefits or adornments of this world. I am a servant, and my duty is to show the way to God and to His kingdom. He who wishes to be happy should hear and follow me, but he who wishes to be miserable should turn away from my guidance; him shall God remove from his position, destroy, and torment perpetually.[9]

The Mahdi misjudged Gordon, but not more seriously than Gordon had misjudged him. Gordon had believed the Mahdi's religious pretensions were only a mask to cover an essentially political revolt that concessions by a vigorous and just administration could end. Gordon was now disabused. His reply to the Mahdi was abrupt and final :—

I have received the letters sent by your three messengers, and I understand all their contents; but I cannot have any more communication with you.[10]

The investment of Khartoum was not yet complete, and Gordon's messengers could still occasionally slip through the Arab lines to Berber and the telegraph. On April 17 The Times *printed the last dispatch it would have from its Khartoum correspondent for six months*.

Khartoum is at present the centre of an enormous rebel camp, *Power had written on April 7*. The rebels' tents are within sight, and their bullets often strike or go over the palace, in which a man was thus killed last week. We have killed several of the rebels, but our store of Krupp ammunition is rather short. The situation is now very critical.

We are trying to run a steamer through the rebel lines to Berber. Yesterday, owing to the severity of the rebel fire, she had to return. The day before yesterday an attack of the rebels on Omdurman was repulsed. We have mined the plain in front of the fortifications.

I have had only two sources of hope in this crisis—first, the ex-

pectation of an English relieving column; secondly, the plan of a retreat across the Equator. Because I am confident that General Gordon is abandoned by the Government, and that without Zebehr Pasha
he can never beat the rebels, I fear that he will be driven to retreat
by Central Africa. For to-day arrived an unciphered telegram sent
from Sir Evelyn Baring to Berber, saying that no English troops
would be sent to that place—in a word, clearly indicating that General Gordon and the others who have been faithful to the Government are thrown over.

To retreat on Berber is impossible. Sir Evelyn Baring's unciphered
telegram to that place will quickly be spread abroad, and the Arabs
will learn that the members of the English Government have turned
down their thumbs while General Gordon is struggling here.

A retreat on the Congo will entail great hardships.

General Gordon, Colonel Stewart, and your correspondent are in
good health.[11]

*Gordon was not planning a retreat to the equator. For the
honor of England he had been sent to the Sudan to evacuate the
Egyptian garrisons and he had failed. The honor of England must
eventually require the dispatch of an adequate military expedition to
effect that purpose. Until then he would defend Khartoum, and the
people who had entrusted their lives to him, at all hazards.*

III

*While his lieutenants were isolating and laying siege to Khar-
toum, the Mahdi himself remained in his camp at El Obeid, some 300
miles south of the capital. Amid the tumultuous horde that gathered
about him there was a small group of Europeans—missionaries, merchants, former officials of the Egyptian administration who had been
caught in the eruption of the Mahdist revolt. Some accepted Islam
and entered the service of the Mahdi in various capacities. Others
who refused to renounce their faith were, if for the present spared
torture and death, kept in degrading circumstances as prisoners of
war. One of these latter was an Austrian priest, Father Joseph Ohrwalder, who had been brought to El Obeid in September, 1882.*

From the sandhill Gianzara, *Ohrwalder recalled years later*,
almost up to the base of the Om Herezeh mountain, was one mass of

small huts; these were merely enclosures made of branches of euphorbia and (sorghum) dhurra stalks, just sufficient to keep off the burning rays of the sun. Here and there a white tent indicated the headquarters of some important emir. Fiki Minneh's camp adjoined that of Gianzara, and extended from Fulla (a small pond which runs dry in the summer months), up to the base of Om Herezeh. The huts were built so close to each other that constant fires took place, which spread rapidly, and caused great destruction.

This enormous camp presented a wonderful spectacle, more especially at night, when almost every one had his own cooking fire, and the whole plain resembled a sea of fires which were lost in the distant horizon. The din and noise created by hundreds of thousands of men, women, and children, can be better imagined than described. Every emir's dwelling was known by two flags which were always planted near the entrance, and beside them lay the war-drums, which were beaten day and night, almost without intermission. Besides all this, the neighing of thousands of horses rendered the din still more unbearable. The whole air was infected with the most sickening stench; but to these wretched people, pure or impure air makes no difference; they do not mind. All the filth was piled behind the huts, dead donkeys lay about unburied; no attempt was made to keep the place clean, and all this huge mass of people lived in the midst of an ever-increasing heap of rotting impurities. A daily market was held, and the people laid their goods on the ground, sheltering themselves under a strip of cloth, known as "Farda," stretched on the points of lances, the bases of which were stuck in the ground. There was a busy scene day and night at the Oshra well; here thousands of male and female slaves drew water, and frequent quarrels and fights took place.[12]

In April, 1884, the Mahdi moved to Rahad, where another European encountered him. Rudolf Slatin, a young Austrian officer, had entered Gordon's service in the Sudan in 1878; in 1881 he had become governor of Darfur. With the rise of the Mahdi his authority had steadily deteriorated, even though he had embraced Islam in an effort to retain the loyalty of his native officers. After the defeat of Hicks in November, 1883, Slatin had surrendered to the rebels, entering the Mahdi's service as a bodyguard to the Khalifa, the Mahdi's chief lieutenant and eventual successor. At Rahad, the Khalifa pre-

sented this prominent addition to his entourage to the Mahdi. Slatin
recalled the scene many years later⟨~⟩ :

At about two o'clock in the afternoon [the Khalifa] sent us a message to perform our ablutions and prepare to go to the Mesjed
(place of worship) ; a few minutes later he arrived himself, and told
us to follow him. He was on foot, as the mosque, which was close to
the Mahdi's hut, was only about three hundred yards off. On arrival,
we found the place crowded with devotees, ranged in closely packed
lines; and when the Khalifa entered, they made way for him with
great respect. A sheepskin was spread on the ground for us, and he
directed us to take our places beside him. The Mahdi's quarters, con-
sisting of several large straw huts fenced off by a thorn zariba, were
situated at the south-west end of the mosque. A gigantic tree afforded shade to a number of the worshippers, but those beyond had
no protection from the burning sun. A few paces from the front line,
and to the right, lay a small hut which was reserved for those with
whom the Mahdi wished to converse in private. The Khalifa now rose
and entered this hut, probably to inform his master of our arrival;
for in a few minutes he returned, again seated himself beside me, and
almost immediately the Mahdi himself came out. The Khalifa at once
arose, and with him Said Bey, Dimitri, and I, who were just behind
him, whilst the others quietly remained in their places. The Mahdi
being the Imam, or leader of prayers, his sheepskin was spread out in
front, and he then stepped towards us. I had advanced slightly, and
he greeted me with 'Salam aleikum,' which we at once returned by
'Aleikum es salam.' He then presented his hand for me to kiss, which
I did several times, and Said Bey and Dimitri followed my example.
Motioning us to be seated, he welcomed us, and turning to me said,
'Are you satisfied?' 'Indeed I am,' I replied readily; 'on coming so
near to you I am most happy.' 'God bless you and your brethren!'
(meaning Said Bey and Dimitri) said he; 'when news reached us of
your battles against my followers, I used to pray to God for your
conversion. God and His Prophet have heard my prayers, and as you
have faithfully served your former master for perishable money, so
now you should serve me; for he who serves me, and hears my words,
serves God and His religion, and shall have happiness in this world
and joy in the world to come.' We of course all made professions of
fidelity, and as I had been previously warned to ask him to give me

the 'beia,' or oath of allegiance, I now besought this honour. Calling us up beside him, he bade us kneel on the edge of his sheepskin, and placing our hands in his, he told us to repeat after him as follows:

'In the name of God the most compassionate and merciful, in the name of the unity of God, we pay God, His Prophet, and you our allegiance; (we swear) that we shall not associate anything else with God, that we shall not steal, nor commit adultery, nor lead anyone into deception, nor disobey you in your goodness; we swear to renounce this world and (look only) to the world to come, and that we shall not flee from the religious war.'

This over, we kissed his hand, and were now enrolled amongst his most devoted adherents. The muazzen (prayer caller) now gave the first signal to begin prayers, and we repeated the usual formulae after the Mahdi. When they were over, all those present raised their hands to heaven and besought God to grant victory to the faithful. The Mahdi now began his sermon. An immense circle was formed around him, and he spoke of the vanity and nothingness of this life, urging all to renounce the world, and to think only of their religious duties, and of the Jehad [religious war]; he painted, in most glowing terms, the delights of Paradise, and the heavenly joys which awaited those who paid heed to his doctrine. Every now and then he was interrupted by shouts of some fanatic in an ecstasy; and, indeed, I am convinced everyone present, except ourselves, really believed in him.

I had now a good opportunity of making a careful survey of Mohammed Ahmed; he was a tall, broad-shouldered man of light-brown colour, and powerfully built; he had a large head and sparkling black eyes; he wore a black beard, and had the usual three slits on each cheek; his nose and mouth were well shaped, and he had the habit of always smiling, showing his white teeth and exposing the V-shaped aperture between the two front ones, which is always considered a sign of good luck in the Sudan, and is known as 'falja.' This was one of the principal causes which made the Mahdi so popular with the fair sex, by whom he was dubbed 'Abu falja' (the man with the separated teeth). He wore a short quilted jibba, beautifully washed, and perfumed with sandalwood, musk, and attar of roses; this perfume was celebrated amongst his disciples as 'Rihet el Mahdi' (the odour of the Mahdi), and was supposed to equal, if not surpass, that of the dwellers in Paradise.[13]

The Mahdi remained at Rahad for several months, thinking always of the siege of Khartoum. Finally, at the end of Ramadan, he deemed the time propitious to move his people to Khartoum and bring the siege to a successful conclusion.

When the fast of Ramadan was over, *Slatin related*, Abu Anga and his entire fighting force were recalled from Jebel Dair; and the Mahdi then publicly announced that the Prophet had directed him to proceed to Khartoum and lay siege to it. Every Emir was enjoined to collect his men, and order them to prepare for the march; whilst any who remained behind were declared lawful prey, and liable to total confiscation of all they possessed. However, there was no hanging back on the part of the people, whose fanaticism knew no bounds, and who were well aware that treasure and plunder generally fell to the share of the faithful followers. The consequence was that the Mahdi's summons brought about a wholesale immigration of the entire population, such as had never before been seen in the Sudan.

We left Rahad on August 22, the Mahdist forces marching by three separate roads: the northern one, *viâ* Khursi, Helba, and Tura el Hadra, was selected by the camel-owning tribes; the central road, *viâ* Tayara, Sherkela, Shatt, and Duem, was taken by the Mahdi, Khalifas, and the majority of the Emirs; whilst the Baggaras and cattle-owning tribes adopted the southern route, which was well supplied with water, owing to the frequent rain pools which served as drinking places for the cattle. I, of course, in my capacity as mulazem of the Khalifa, followed my master.

[Every morning] the Khalifa's great war-drum, called 'El Mansura' (the victorious), was beaten; this was the signal for the march to begin again, and off we started. We generally marched from early morning till noon only, and thus our progress was not rapid.

After five days' march, we reached Shatt, where most of the wells were filled up, and had to be reopened, and several straw huts erected, for the Mahdi had decided to halt here for some days.

From Shatt we advanced to Duem [on the White Nile 120 miles above Khartoum], where the Mahdi held an enormous review; and, pointing to the Nile, he said, 'God has created this river; He will give you its waters to drink, and you shall become the possessors of all the lands along the banks.' This speech was greeted with shouts of joy by these wild fanatics, who at once believed that the wonderful land of Egypt was to be their prey.

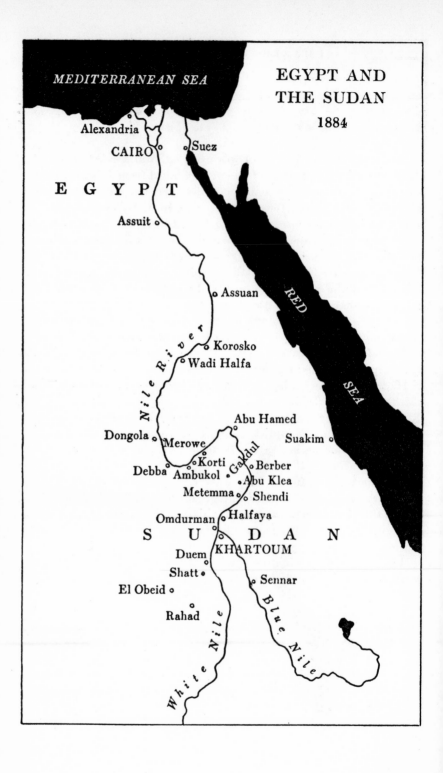

EGYPT AND
THE SUDAN
1884

MEDITERRANEAN SEA

Alexandria
CAIRO   Suez

E G Y P T

Assuit

Assuan

RED

Nile River

Korosko
Wadi Halfa

SEA

Abu Hamed

Dongola   Merowe   Suakim

Korti   Gakdul   Berber
Debba   Ambukol   Abu Klea

Metemma   Shendi

Omdurman   Halfaya

S U   D A N

Duem   KHARTOUM

Shatt   Sennar

El Obeid

Rahad

White Nile

Blue Nile

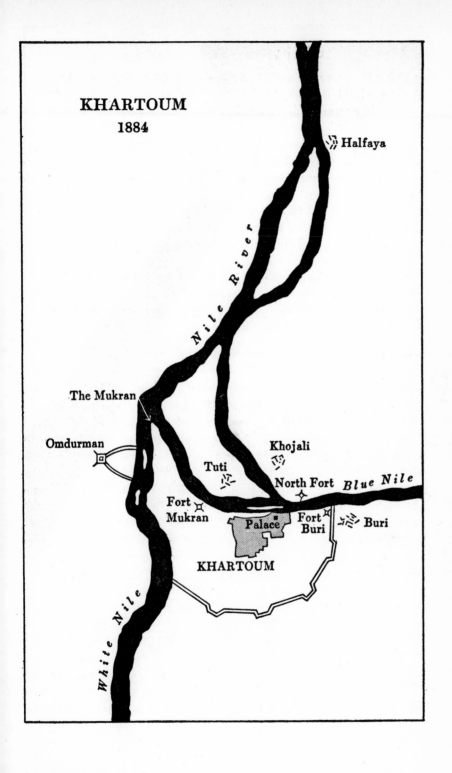

KHARTOUM
1884

Halfaya

Nile River

The Mukran

Omdurman

Khojali

Tuti

North Fort   Blue Nile

Fort
Mukran

Palace   Fort   Buri
                 Buri

KHARTOUM

White Nile

From Duem we proceeded to Tura del Hadra, where we spent the Feast of Great Bairam. At the Feast of Bairam the Mahdi repeated prayers in an unusually loud voice, and when he read the 'Khutba' he wept long and bitterly. We unbelievers well knew that this weeping was hypocrisy, and boded no good; but it had the desired effect on the fanatical crowds who had flocked to his banners from the river tribes, and who were roused by this touching sermon to the highest pitch of enthusiasm.

After a halt of two days, we again moved on, creeping forward like a great tortoise, so swelled were we by the thousands upon thousands who were now joining daily from every part of the Sudan.[14]

This enormous horde, which Ohrwalder estimated to comprise 200,000 people, moved slowly northward along the left bank of the Nile. On October 23 the Mahdi pitched his camp at Omdurman, across the river from Khartoum.

IV

Through the spring and summer of 1884, the cabinet ministers, when they thought of Gordon at all, thought of him with intense exasperation. The conflicting motives that had surrounded Gordon's employment, the ambiguity of his commission, and—not least—the alarming and seemingly erratic quality of his early communications now produced their full harvest of misunderstanding. Clearly, the hero who was to have salvaged the ministers' Sudan policy now threatened to embarrass them even further. Having denied his urgent requests first for Zebehr Pasha and then for a military force at Berber, the ministers were chagrined to find that Gordon was now trapped in Khartoum. They had no difficulty persuading themselves that, by irresponsibly exceeding his instructions, Gordon had brought his troubles upon himself; let him then extricate himself as best he could. To every anxious query from Parliament, Gladstone would reply confidently that, so far as he or anyone else knew, Khartoum was not in danger; before the government could take any action it must have from Gordon an authoritative statement of his situation. Gladstone would then draft a new set of inquiries to be dispatched to Khartoum. That these communications might not have reached Gordon seems never to have occurred to the government. Gordon's failure to reply was taken simply as further evidence of his intolerable perversity.

Gordon's situation that summer was serious but not yet desperate. Until September, the high waters of the Nile would keep the Arab besiegers at a distance. Morale in Khartoum was high; the population had confidence in Gordon and accepted his promises of the eventual arrival of an English army. Gordon had at his disposal a flotilla of steamers that he employed effectively to carry attacks behind the Arab lines. On three successive days at the end of July, Gordon's ablest native commander, Mohammed Ali Bey, inflicted defeats on the Arabs along the Blue Nile, thereby opening the route to Sennar where the steamers could buy grain. In August there were more successes on the Blue Nile and another north of Khartoum at Halfaya. As a result the besiegers were driven away from the city on three sides. Elated, Gordon planned an attack on Berber, which the Mahdists had taken in May. On September 5, however, Mohammed Ali Bey was ambushed and killed with a thousand of Gordon's best troops. Gordon's capacity for offensive action was now largely destroyed. Furthermore, the Nile was falling, which meant that Khartoum would be closely invested again; the Arabs were being reinforced with artillery; and there was no word of a relief force. Instead of an attack on Berber, Gordon resolved to send the steamer Abbas with word of his now precarious situation through the Arab lines to Dongola, where Major Herbert Kitchener constituted the sole British outpost in the Sudan. Stewart, Power, and Herbin, the French consul, volunteered to go. The mission was of vital importance to Gordon. Every precaution was taken, every conceivable contingency prepared for, to insure the safe descent of the Abbas.

The steamer *Abbas* left Khartoum [on September 9], *a member of the native crew told British officers six months later*, with Colonel Stewart, two European Consuls, twelve Greeks, and several natives on board. Two other steamers accompanied her beyond Berber, and four nuggars sailed with us, which were towed as far as Berber by the two steamers. We shelled the forts at Berber, and our steamer having safely passed them, the others returned, we proceeding with the nuggars, which we also left behind before reaching Abu Hamad.

On September 18 the steamer struck on a rock near a small island in the Wad Gamr country. We had previously seen many of the people running away to the hills on both banks of the river. Everything was landed on the island by means of a small boat. Colonel Stewart drove a nail into the steamer's gun, filed off the projecting end, and then threw the gun and its ammunition overboard.

Meanwhile several people came down to the bank shouting, 'Give us peace and grain.' We told them we had brought peace. Suleiman Wad Gamr, living in a house on the bank of the river, being asked for camels to take the party to Merawi, said that he would provide them, and invited Colonel Stewart and the two Consuls to the house of a blind man, named Fakrietman, telling them to come unarmed, lest the people should be frightened. The camels were not given to us. We all went unarmed, except Colonel Stewart, who had a small revolver in his belt.

Presently I saw Suleiman come out and make a sign to the people standing about the village, armed with swords and spears. These immediately divided into two parties, one running to the house of the blind man, the other to where the rest of Colonel Stewart's party were assembled. I was with the latter. When the natives charged we threw ourselves into the river. The natives fired and killed many of us, and others were drowned.

I landed on a small island, and remained there until it was dark, when I swam over to the left bank. After some time I made my way to Hamdab, where I was seized, and taken to Sheikh Omar, Suleiman's uncle, at Birteh. I have been at Birteh ever since, and remained there when the dervishes ran away the day before yesterday.

I heard that when the natives entered Fakrietman's house they fell upon Colonel Stewart and the Consuls, and killed all three. Hassan Bey held the blind man in front of him, thus escaping with a knife-wound only, and he afterwards went to Berber. Two artillery soldiers, two boat captains, and three of the native crew of the steamer are alive in Berber. A few slaves are also alive near Birteh. The money found was divided among the natives who murdered the party, everything else being sent to Berber. The bodies were thrown into the river.[15]

V

◄§ With Stewart and Power gone, Gordon's personal isolation was virtually complete. He was the only Englishman in Khartoum. A handful of Europeans remained, but none in whom he could truly confide or *to whom he could delegate a share of his heavy responsibility. From the natives Gordon was cut off not only by his position of authority but even more by his very imperfect knowledge of Arabic.*

The day after Stewart's departure, Gordon began to keep a journal. Ostensibly addressed to the commander of the inevitable Sudan Expeditionary Force, the journal was in one sense an official document. Here every night, and often hourly during the day, he recorded the events of the siege, great and trivial, serious and comic; proffered military advice to the English commander; and discoursed on the politics and diplomacy of Her Majesty's Government. But the journal was also an intensely personal document that chronicled his moods of optimism and despair, confidence and agonizing doubt, savage bitterness and earnest introspection. Here he discharged his wrath against timid and obtuse officialdom, made his sardonic jokes, pondered questions of religion—and, always, struggled with those eternal problems of conduct that confront a man who must bear terrible responsibility absolutely alone.

September 10.—Colonel Stewart, MM. Power and Herbin, left during the night for Dongola, *viâ* Berber.

It is wonderful how the people of the town, who have every possible facility to leave the city, cling to it, and how, indeed, there are hundreds who flock in, though it is an open secret we have neither money nor food. Somehow this makes me feel confident in the future, for it is seldom that an impulse such as this acts on each member of a disintegrated mass without there being some reason for it, which those who act have no idea of, but which is a sort of instinct. Truly I do not think one could inflict a greater punishment on an inhabitant of Kartoum than to force him to go to the Arabs.

With respect to letters written to the Mahdi and to the Arab chiefs, commenting on the apostasy of Europeans, they may [be], and are, no doubt, hard, but it is not a small thing for a European, for fear of death, to deny our faith; it was not so in old times, and it should not be regarded as if it was taking off one coat, and putting on another. If the Christian faith is a myth, then let men throw it off, but it is mean and dishonourable to do so merely to save one's life if one believes it is the true faith. What can be more strong than these words, "He who denies me on earth I will deny in heaven." The old martyrs regarded men as their enemies, who tried to prevent them avowing their faith. In the time of Queens Mary and Elizabeth, what men we had; and then it was for less than here, for it was mainly the question of the Mass, while here it is the question of the denial of our Lord and of his passion. It is perhaps as well to omit this, if this journal is published, for no man has a right to judge another. Politically and morally, however, it is better for us not to have anything to do with the apostate Europeans in the Arab camp. Treachery never succeeds, and, however matters may end, it is better to fall with clean hands, than to be mixed up with dubious acts and dubious men. Maybe it is better for us to fall with honour, than to gain the victory with dishonour, and in this view the Ulemas [preachers] of the town are agreed; they will have nought to do with the proposals of treachery.

We have completed the census, and have 34,000 people in the town.[16]

September 11.—Stewart's steamers, which had been delayed at Halfeyeh owing to some machinery accident, left last night for Berber.

[The steamers] *Talataween* and *Bordeen* left for Sennaar this morning to bring down dhoora [a cereal resembling corn].

There was an old belief among old Christians that every event which happens on earth is caused by some action being taken in heaven; the action in heaven being the cause of the event on earth, *vide* Revelation, when at the opening of seals the trumpet sounds, &c., &c., all events exercised in heaven are followed by events on earth. This being the case, how futile are our efforts to turn things out of their course. Vials are poured out on earth whence events happen. To me, it seems little what those events may be, but that the great object of our lives is how we bear those events in our individuality. If we trust in the flesh, thus saith the Lord, we are cursed; if we trust in Him we are blessed. I cannot think that there are any promises for answers to prayer made for temporal things; the promises are to hear prayer, and to give strength to bear with quiet what may be the Will of God. A vial is poured on earth; events happen; one is furious with the British Government for these events; but if we were logical, we should be furious with the pourer out of the vial, and that we shrink from being, for He is the Almighty who pours out the vial.[17]

§September 12§.—It is most dispiriting to be in the position I am, if it was not good for me, when I think that, *when I left* [in 1879], I could say, "no man could lift his hand or foot in the land of Soudan" without me (Gen. xli. 44) and now we cannot calculate on our existence over twenty-four hours. The people are all against us, and what a power they have; they need not fight, but have merely to refuse to sell us their grain. The stomach governs the world, and it was the stomach (a despised organ) which caused our misery from the beginning. It is wonderful that the ventral tube of man governs the world, in small and great things.

It certainly is a curious exemplification of how very lightly religions sit on men, and to note the fearful apostasy of both Mussulmans and Christians, when their lives or property are menaced. There is scarcely one great family of the Soudan, families who can trace their pedigree for five hundred years, who have not accepted Mahomet Achmet as Mahdi, to save their property, though they laugh at the idea afterwards. I am using this argument with them, in saying, "You ask me to become a Mussulman to save my life, and you yourself acknowledge Mahomet Achmet as the Mahdi, to save your lives; why, if we go on this principle, we will be adopting every religion whose adherents threaten our existence, for you know and own, when you are safe, that Mahomet Achmet is *not* the Mahdi."

I was awakened this morning by a woman crying out, "My son has been murdered, and I demand justice." Her little *only* boy had, it appears, been in one of the Arab water-wheels, which are moved by oxen, and a man had pushed him off; his skull was partially fractured, but he had been in hospital for some days, and we hoped for his recovery, when inflammation set in, and he died. He was a nice little bright-eyed, chocolate-coloured child of eight years old—the mother is a widow. One is drawn towards the children of this country, both browns and blacks; the former are of a perfect bronze colour.

During our blockade, we have often discussed the question of being frightened, which, in the world's view, a man should never be. For my part I am always frightened, and very much so. I fear the future of all engagements. It is not the fear of death, that is past, thank God; but I fear defeat, and its consequences. I do not believe a bit in the calm, unmoved man. I think it is only that he does not show it outwardly. Thence I conclude no commander of forces ought to live closely in relation with his subordinates, who watch him like lynxes, for there is no contagion equal to that of fear. I have been rendered furious, when, from anxiety, I could not eat, I would find those at same table were in like manner affected.[18]

September 13.— [Stewart's] steamers are reported to have passed the Shoboloha defile safely; they ought to be at Berber to-day. Berber is 200 miles from Merowé, where the cataracts cease, thence there is open water to Dongola, 150 miles distant from Merowé; he ought there to find the telegraph open, and so on the 20th of September he ought to be in communication with Cairo and Europe.

I think if, instead of 'Minor Tactics,' or books on art of war, we were to make our young officers study 'Plutarch's Lives,' it would be better; there we see men (unsupported by any true belief, pure pagans), making, *as a matter of course*, their lives a sacrifice, but in our days it is the highest merit not to run away. I speak for myself when I say I have been in dire anxiety, not for my own skin, but because I hate to be beaten, and I hate to see my schemes fail; but that I have had to undergo a tithe of what any nurse has to undergo, who is attached to a querulous invalid, is absurd, and not to be weighed together. When I emerge all are complimentary; when the invalid dies the question is, what should be given to the nurse for her services. We profess to be followers of our Lord, who, from his birth, when He was hunted, till his death, may be said to have had no sympathy or kindness shown Him; yet we (and I say myself especially) cry out if we are placed in any position of suffering, whereas it is our *métier*, if we are Christians, to undergo such suffering.

I have led the officers and officials the lives of dogs while I have been up here; it is spurs in their flanks every day; nothing can obliterate this ill-treatment from my memory. I may say that I have not given them a moment's peace; they are conies, but I ought to have been more considerate. It is quite painful to see men tremble so when they come and see me, that they cannot hold the match to their cigarette. Yet I have cut off no heads. Happy, as far as we can see, are those men who swing in small arcs; unhappy are those who, seeking the fields of adventure, swing from the extremes of evil and good. The neutral tint is the best for wear.[19]

September 14.—The news of the near approach of the Mahdi has not troubled me, for if he fails he is lost, and there will be no necessity for an expedition to Kordofan; if he succeeds, he may, by his presence, prevent any massacre. I have always felt we were doomed to come face to face ere the matter was ended.

I toss up in my mind, whether, if the place is taken, to blow up the palace and all in it, or else to be taken, and, with God's help, to maintain the faith, and if necessary suffer for it (which is most probable). The blowing up of the palace is the simplest, while the other means long and weary suffering and humiliation of all sorts. I think I shall elect for the last, not from fear of death, but because the former has more or less the taint of suicide, as it can do no good to any one, and is, in a way, taking things out of God's hands.

The Greek who came in told the Greek Consul that the Mahdi puts pepper under his nails, and when he receives visitors then he touches his eyes and weeps copiously; that he eats a few grains of dhoora openly, but in the interior of the house he has fine feeding and drinks alcoholic drinks.

The Greek told the Greek Consul that the Mahdi was perplexed to know what on earth I was doing up here, as I had no part or lot in the Soudan. I expect this question is more perplexing for others than the Mahdi (myself included). I must confess that the pepper business has sickened me; I had hitherto hoped I had to do with a regular fanatic, who believed in his mission, but when one comes to pepper in the finger nails, it is rather humiliating to have to succumb to him, and somehow I have the belief that I shall not have to do so. One cannot help being amused at this pepper business. Those who come in, for pardon, come in on their knees, with a halter round their neck. The Mahdi rises, having scratched his eyes and obtained a copious flow of tears, and takes off the halter! As the production of tears is generally considered the proof of sincerity, I would recommend the Mahdi's recipe to Cabinet Ministers, justifying some job. The nails (so say the Greeks) must be long! to contain the pepper.[20]

September 15.—This afternoon one of Seyd Mahomet Osman's family came up from Shendy; he reports the Stewart expedition having passed Shendy [95 miles from Khartoum], that they captured a large boat with grain and twenty-four slaves, which was collecting taxes for the Arabs. He reports as true the arrival of troops at Dongola.

Haunting the palace are a lot of splendid hawks. I often wonder whether they are destined to pick out my eyes, for I fear I was not the best of sons [cf. Prov. xxx. 17].²¹

≈§Reports that English troops were advancing, and that they were already at Dongola, were frequent. In fact, a much-delayed expeditionary force was then assembling at Assuan, 300 miles north of Dongola. Its commander, Lord Wolseley, and his staff were still in Cairo§≈.

≈§September 17§≈.—I have the strongest suspicion that these tales of troops at Dongola and Merowé are all gas-works, and that if you wanted to find Her Majesty's forces you would have to go to Shepheard's Hotel at Cairo.

The reports of the advance which we get from Seyd Osman are never supported by any written evidence from Dongola, and I expect they are invented. Whether the resurrection of Stewart, Power, and Herbin will have any effect remains to be seen, but, ill-natured or not, it is my firm impression that Her Majesty's Government will be most disagreeably surprised by their emerging.

If Stewart gets down, he ought to be in communication with Europe on the 22nd of September, and Power's telegrams ought to be in the *Times* 23rd September. It makes me laugh to think of the flutter in the dovecot which will follow. *"That beastly Soudan again!"*

I must say I do not love Diplomatists as a rule (and I can fancy the turning up of noses at my venturing to express an opinion of them), I mean in their official attire, for, personally, the few I know are most agreeable (and I specially except Alston, the chief clerk, and Weller, the hall porter, who has, of late years, become quite amiable); but taking them on their rostrums, with their satellites, from their chiefs down to the smaller fry, no one can imagine a more unsatisfactory lot of men to have anything to do with. I have seen ——, ——, ——, ——, at different times, and when one left their august presences, one marvelled at the policy of Great Britain being in such hands.

One would not so much mind if they did not inoculate with their virus those who get employed by them, but I have found Stokes of the Suez Canal, Wilson of Anatolia, and many others (I may say Stewart), all impregnated with their ideas of sun worship and expediency.

A man has come in who says Stewart and his steamers have cap-

tured a large convoy of two hundred camel-loads of stuff belonging
to the Arabs. They had passed Shendy, and had not been fired upon.
The Mahdi will be furious.[22]

September 19.—I own to having been very insubordinate to
Her Majesty's Government and its officials, but it is my nature, and
I cannot help it. I fear I have not even tried to play battledore and
shuttlecock with them. I know if *I* was chief I would never employ
myself, for I am incorrigible. To men like Dilke, who weigh every
word, I must be *perfect poison*. I wonder what the telegrams about
Soudan have cost Her Majesty's Government? It has been a truly
horrid question. There is the Town El Obeyed and the SHEIKH El
Obeyed; there is the Haloman of Cairo and the Haloman of Kartoum. Sanderson must have a hard time of it. "The *city* moves
about!" "Why, if Haloman is attacked, Cairo must be in danger!
Send for Wolseley! Kartoum forces defeated by Sheikh el Obeyed!
Why, the town must have moved! Is not El Obeyed the place Hicks
went to take? Most extraordinary! Send for Wolseley!"

"Eureka, I have found it out; there is a *man* called *El Obeyed* and
a *town* called *El Obeyed*. When a movement occurs, it is the *man*,
not the *town*, which has moved!"

"Blessed is the man who does not sit in the seat of the *scornful*"
(Ps. i. 1). I own it is not right to scoff at one's superiors, but I do
not do it in malice, and I hope those who are remarked upon will not
be offended. Life is a very leaden business, and if any one can
lighten it, so much the better. Because I criticise Baring, Egerton,
and the Foreign Office, it is not that I think I am their superior, but
because I would like them to see how others, outside themselves, view
things. Because I may differ with them it is no reason why they may
not be right, and acting uprightly, and I may be utterly wrong.[23]

September 20.—Spy in Halfeyeh states Stewart's steamers
have recaptured the two steamers I had lost at Berber, and had no
fighting to speak of; that the English troops are advancing on Ambukol, half way between Debbeh and Merowé, and had defeated the
Arabs.

A man has come in from Shendy, who corroborates the advance of
the expeditionary force and the defeat of the Arabs. Another came
in, who says the *Abbas* passed down safely, and that the steamers

Mansowrah and *Saphia* are on their return, but says nothing of capture of the two steamers at Berber.[24]

On the 20th, three Arabs arrived from Dongola with a packet of letters, both personal and official. It included two cipher messages from E. H. Egerton (who was temporarily filling Baring's place in Cairo) that Gordon could not read. But of great importance was a note from Gordon's friend E. A. Floyer, newly appointed Inspector-General of the Sudan Telegraph, and, on the same piece of paper, a note to Stewart from Kitchener. These, containing the first trustworthy news of a relief expedition, were cause for rejoicing.

September 21.—The three messengers from Dongola came in with two cipher telegrams from Egerton of same import, not legible, for want of cipher, which Stewart carried off. Some photograph letters which I could only partially make out, and notes from Floyer and Kitchener, saying forces were coming up. I have ordered *three* [rounds] to be fired from all guns at 4 P.M. as a salute, and to warn the Arabs something is up. I shall send down spies to-morrow. I gave the *three* £50, and gave them each £10, with promise they will be paid £10 more when they get to Dongola. They say they had nothing given them on starting! which is curious if true.

We fired a salute of three rounds from each gun on lines, to let the Arabs know of the advance expeditionary force. The men who came in say the Arabs were fully expecting an attack, and were in a great way.[25]

On the 22nd there were two further letters from Kitchener. The more recent, dated August 31 at Debbeh, read: "Mr. Egerton has asked me to send you the following:—August 30th. Tell Gordon steamers are being passed over second Cataracts, and that we wish to be informed through Dongola exactly when he expects to be in difficulties as to provisions and ammunition." Then Kitchener added: "Lord Wolseley is coming out to command. The 35th Regiment is now being sent from Halfa to Dongola. Sir E. Wood is at Halfa. Generals Earle, Dormer, Buller, and Fremantle are coming up Nile with troops. I think an expedition will be sent across from here to Kartoum, while another goes with steamer to Berber. A few words about what you wish done would be very acceptable." In high spirits, Gordon could feel kindly even toward Egerton.

September 22d.—I am sure I should like that fellow Egerton. There is a light-hearted jocularity about his communications, and I should think the cares of life sat easily on him. He wishes to know *exactly* "day, hour, and minute" that he (Gordon) expects to be in "difficulties as to provisions and ammunition."

Now I really think if Egerton was to turn over the "archives" (a delicious word) of his office, he would see we had been in difficulties for provisions for some months. It is as if a man on the bank, having seen his friend in river already bobbed down two or three times, hails, "I say, old fellow, let us know when we are to throw you the life buoy; I know you have bobbed down two or three times, but it is a pity to throw you the life buoy until you really are *in extremis*, and I want to know *exactly*, for I am a man brought up in a school of exactitude."

Egerton's cipher telegram, which I cannot decipher through Stewart having taken the book, is short, but I feel sure is weighty, and I regret deeply I cannot get at its contents, which I think would afford matter for amusing comment.[26]

September 24th.—My view is this, as to the operations of British forces. I will put three steamers, each with two guns on them, and an armed force of infantry at disposal of any British authority; will send these steamers to either Metemma, opposite Shendy, or to the Cataract below Berber, to there meet any British Force which may come across country to the Nile. These steamers, with this force coming across country, will (*D.V.*) capture Berber and then communicate with Kartoum. I would not attempt to pass the *bulk* of British Force across country, only the fighting column, to co-operate with the three steamers. When Berber is taken I should keep the bulk of the forces there, and send up the fighting column to Kartoum.

I cannot too much impress on you that this expedition will not encounter any enemy worth the name in an European sense of the word; the struggle is with the climate and destitution of the country. It is one of time and patience, and of small parties of determined men, backed by native allies, which are got by policy and money. A heavy lumbering column, however strong, is nowhere in this land. Parties of forty or sixty men, swiftly moving about, will do more than any column. If you lose two or three, what of it—it is the chance of war. Native allies above all things, at whatever cost. It is the country of the irregular, not of the regular. If you move in mass you will find no end of difficulties; whereas, if you let detached parties dash out here and there, you will spread dismay in the Arab ranks. The time to attack is the dawn, or rather before it (this is stale news), but sixty men would put these Arabs to flight just before dawn, which one thousand could not accomplish in daylight. The reason is that the strength of the Arabs is their horsemen, who do not dare to act in the dark. I do hope you will not drag on that artillery: it can only produce delay and do little good.

Nevertheless, Gordon cautioned, the enemy should not be underestimated. The wretched peasant, with that filthy cloth, which you see, is a determined warrior, who can undergo thirst and privation, who no more cares for pain or death than if he were of stone. The young fellows even have a game by which they test who will bear the lash of the hippopotamus' whip best. They are in their own land; the pains of war are their ordinary life; and they are supported by religion of a fanatical kind, influenced by the memory of years of suffering at the hands of an effete set of Bashi Bazouks.

From addressing advice to the commander of the expeditionary force, Gordon now shifted abruptly to a soliloquy on a subject that troubled him considerably. It is the most extraordinary thing, quite incomprehensible, that with only one exception not one single messenger has entered this place on the proper initiative of outsiders. It has been invariably *my* messengers, who were sent out by me, from Kartoum, who did bring me any news. It would seem as if those outside seemed to think it was my duty to send out and bring in news for myself, and that they had nothing to do with it. Either these officers outside do not care to spend a sou in spies to give me information, or else they think it is a matter of supreme indifference whether I know what is going on or not; and I must say when my messengers do come back, they bring me scarcely any information of import. There is a lot of "I hope you are well," &c.; men like Kitchener and Chermside might be expected to have more brains than that. If I had not exerted myself in the spy business, we never would have had a word, I verily believe. I never saw such a poor lot as these outsiders. Even if they had had to pay £20 out of their own pockets, one might have expected them to do it, considering the circumstances. They might have been paid back. But neither Her Majesty's Ministers in Cairo, nor these men have seemed to care a jot to inform us. Silly foolish questions are all we ever have got from them, and it is not to be wondered at, that I am indignant with such unpatriotic conduct, and not inclined to be over civil beyond my duty. I never saw such a feeble lot in my life! One has only to compare the telegrams, &c., we sent down, with the *rubbish* sent in by *our own messengers I* paid for.

Read Floyer's telegram, with Kitchener's note to Stewart on same paper—it perfectly exasperates one. Kitchener asks Stewart "what he can do for him"—nothing of what has gone on with respect to the Soudan since Graham's expedition. Of course men are not *obliged* to write at all.

I altogether *decline* the imputation that the projected expedition has come to *relieve me*. It has *come to SAVE OUR NATIONAL HONOUR in extricating the garrisons, &c., from a position our action in Egypt has placed these garrisons. I was relief expedition No. 1.* They are *relief expedition No. 2.* As for myself I could make good my retreat at any moment if I wished. Now realise what would happen if this *first relief expedition* was to bolt and the steamers fell into the hands of the Mahdi: *this second relief expedition* (for the honour of England engaged in extricating garrisons) would be somewhat hampered. We the *first* and *second* expeditions are equally engaged for the honour of England. This is fair logic. *I came up to extricate the garrisons and failed. Earle comes up to extricate garrisons and (I hope) succeeds. Earle does not come to extricate me.* The extrication of the garrisons was supposed to effect our "national honour." If Earle succeeds the "national honour" thanks him and I hope rewards him, but it is altogether independent of me, who for failing incurs its blame. I am not the *rescued lamb*, and I will not be.

What is Kitchener doing at Debbeh? that he could not write a better letter than to tell me the names of the generals and regiments —a matter of the most supreme indifference to Kartoum.[27]

◆§*September 25*§◆.—You can scarcely imagine the state (well known to Stewart, Power, and Herbin) one gets in, when one is constantly hearing explosions; what with the guns, mines, and musketry, one's nerves get strained, and nothing can drop without one thinking it is an explosion. What the Russians underwent at Sevastopol must have been terrible. As Hansall, the Austrian Consul, says, it is *abrutissant*. It has slackened off now, but still any loud noise, in this clear air, makes me jump (*i.e.* be, for a moment, afraid) like any man who rides knows, when his horse, as it were, sinks completely beneath him, on a sudden start.[28]

September 26.—4 P.M. Steamers from Sennaar in sight. Now we shall be all together again, thank God!

The Arabs off the south front are all agog at sight of the steamers coming down. Those on the Blue Nile are firing on the steamers. I sent up *Mansowrah* to help them. The Arabs are in the houses. Expenditure of ammunition is enormous, I should think. The three steamers have passed the place where the Arabs are. They came down one by one, which was not wise.

From the top of the Serail one commands view all round for miles.

It will be a satisfaction to Her Majesty's Navy to know that it is our navy which has, humanly speaking, saved us. It really is a splendid fleet and naval arsenal. The steamers have come in; the Arabs were numerous and had five guns; seven of their shells struck the steamers (Arabs had also two rocket tubes). The steamers brought down 2000 ardebs, and report Sennaar well off, and no Arabs in arms in all their district. Our loss in passing the gauntlet was three killed and eight wounded.

I declare my people do, in a feeble way, what is wanted, and do not deserve the character of cowards; they bear defeat far better than other peoples, and they are good-tempered over it. *We* English are the cream, all acknowledge that, but we will not exist on two dates a day, as these people do, without a murmur.

The steamer *Bordeen* was struck by two shots, one near water-line. The *Ismailia* steamer received three, the *Talataween* steamer received two shots. Happily all got down safe. The Arabs fired from guns and rifles with fury—we could see that from the roof. All the steamers have got small-pox from bullet-marks! Our chief of arsenal, Hussein Bey, had been sharp enough to have bits of old tents ready to stop shot-holes. Had we not had these we might have lost the *Bordeen* steamer.[29]

September 27.—I have arranged to send down three steamers to Shendy to co-operate with Dongola forces. It is of no use sending up to Sennaar again for dhoora, for we have no money to pay for it, and it is a risk with these Arab guns. Our steamers are of about the same consistency as the Thames steamboats, so you may imagine the risk there is of putting them under artillery fire.

Great female squawking under the window of the serail, approaching to yells. On examination I find the noise comes from a black female fighting the cavass. On enquiry I find my lady had gone down to buy dhoora with two dollars in her hand, and had been pushed by some ungallant fellow, and the dollars fell into the river. Though I do not see that the responsibility was upon me, I gave her the two dollars, and comforted her black soul. It would be a comfort if all the troubles of life were got rid of so cheaply.

I made Nutzer Bey a Pasha for his Sennaar trip, and sent him down with Cassim el Mousse to Metemma to await advance of Her Majesty's forces. Ibraham Tongi and Mousse Beys refused, or rather declined to go unless also made Pashas, which I did not see, so these worthies stay here.

B. to A.—"Well you know I had to send on the telegram, and I added I hoped Stewart was well. That fellow G. takes exception to this, and says *va sans dire*, that I would not have wished that Stewart was ill. Most unjust. Had I added anything to this telegram, I might have got into a row, which would never do, but what was the use of pampering to inordinate curiosity?"

A. to B.—"Well he pitched into me for asking Stewart to tell me if I could do anything for him (the communications being so easy), and for telling *him* the names of the Generals (to my mind a most important matter, for it would strike terror among the Arabs), *he* says *he* does not care who the Generals are (which is sheer heresy and perfectly sickening). I shall write nothing more to *him* except the purest official documents. It is very clear his liver is out of order, to go and attack officers of his own corps like that. It is atrocious!"[30]

On October 1 the steamers Tell Hewein, Safia, *and* Mansura *left Khartoum to go down the Nile to Metemma, there to await the fighting column from Debbeh, only 150 miles away, whose arrival Gordon expected in a few weeks. Gordon would have been dismayed to know that the advance party of the expeditionary force, numbering but 250 troops, had reached Dongola only the day before, and that Lord Wolseley had left Cairo for the main English encampment at Assuan only three days before. For the present, the steamers* Tewfikieh, Bordein, *and* Ismailia *remained at Khartoum to resist the ever tightening circle of besiegers.*

October 2.—Arabi's clerk, Ahmet-Eff-Awaan (Stewart knows him well) was, on Stewart's departure, represented to me as in utter misery, so I gave him back £10 a month. *To-night* I heard my friend had been positively preaching for the Mahdi! so I have shut him up. An attempt was made the day before yesterday morning to set fire to one of the houses near the magazine at the Roman Catholic Mission. It was discovered; it was evidently the work of an incendiary. I have ordered all houses to be pulled down in the neighborhood. This is not comfortable, for it shows we have some evil-disposed people here.[31]

October 3.—An inquiry is going on about the fire near the magazine. Some little suspicion that Awaan is mixed up with it, for his house was near; indeed, it adjoins the place where the fire was. It burned four tents. It will go hard with him if he is found guilty: certainly his preaching in favour of the Mahdi is against him.

I visited the place of the fire, and also Awaan's house. My impression is against Awaan's being the culprit; but I have no doubt the Court of Inquiry will find him guilty. I am paying for the houses pulled down. There is no doubt the fire was the work of an incendiary.

Stewart will not believe it of Awaan; but it appears that in disputing about the Mahdi, Awaan took off his slipper and struck his opponent [an extreme insult]—he was so strong in his opinion. A more fawning, wretched fellow one never saw. I should send him to the Mahdi, but that he knows English, and is a born intriguer.[32]

October 4.—Awaan, Arabi's clerk, has been telling, in the town, that the letters I got saying, "Her Majesty's troops are advancing," were written by him and sent down, and then returned. There is an evident wish to take off his head; but I think he is more fool than knave, and shall try and resist the wish of town.[33]

October 6.—Owing to a discovered intrigue and the risk of having too much power in the hands of one man, I have sent Ibrahim Ruckdi to Malia as chief clerk, and Gugliz Bey of Malia is made my chief clerk. Nothing like change of air for these fellows.

I own I am suspicious, *i.e.* I judge by the eye, by little signs, &c., for I do not know the language; but I cannot help thinking I am more often right than wrong with my suspicions. One comes on a group of clerks, heads all together, in the chief clerk's room; one sees disturbed countenances at once. I cannot help thinking "You are concocting deviltry!" and I look out for some "*tricks*."[34]

October 7.—I will mention a secret in all Egyptian administrations, *i.e.* if you give an order, it is totally inefficient in three days' time if not repeated again and again at intervals; it seems as if its essence evaporated in the heat of these countries. The officers would laugh you to scorn if you said, "Why, I gave a *standing order* respecting this or that." It would be to them perfectly ridiculous and absurd to expect a "standing order" to be obeyed, unless *repeated* at intervals. In most services, standing orders are regarded, but certainly not in Egypt; this is the reason why all those beautiful proclamations and laws issued by the Control and their successors are *dead letters* after ten days; they are constructed for the European Press. What is needed, is continual hammering at seeing your orders obeyed.

Fearful row to-night because, after one and a half days' warning, the *Bordeen* was going to start for Halfeyeh, no soldiers were found on board, and this after repeated orders to Ferratch Pasha. Men may say what they like, but one is bound to lose one's temper in such cases.[35]

October 9.—A boy came in four days absent from the Mahdi's camp, which is at a place opposite Gitana. He says the Mahdi is moving along the left bank towards Omdurman, and that he has with him all the Europeans, Elias Pasha, and Slatin; that he will try and take the place before the advance of the English, who are said to be near Berber.[36]

October 12.—When you say to any escaped soldier, "Why do you come here?" he replies, "Why, the Arabs give us nothing. Why, with you I can get this or that." It is merely a question of what they can *get*. The belly governs the whole world.

I declare solemnly, that if it were not for the honour's sake of our nation, I would let these people slide; they are of the very feeblest nature, and the Arabs are ten times better; but because they are weak, there is so much more the reason to try and help them; for I think it was because we were such worthless creatures, that Our Lord came to deliver us. These Shaggyeh [a river tribe that remained loyal] know no shame. It is an unknown quantity with them. What a life one has to live. I wish I commanded the Arabs (speaking professionally). I think it is a great shame not giving me Zubair Pasha, for he would know how to deal with these people. They are the weariness of my life. From February until now they have been one continued worry to me.

The *Towfikia* was to have left this morning [to join the flotilla at Metemma]; but late last night, happening to go to the telegraph office, and asking whether she was ready? the captain replied he had no wood! so there was an end of her start to-day.

Another *plot?* In town a man was discovered taking out a note couched in mysterious language from one of the clerks in a Government office. With the note was £34, supposed to be a present to the Mahdi from Sheikh el Islam (the blind man) here. The efforts to square the circle are extraordinary. The people here, I expect, have all hedged. I am going to make a sort of general arrest to-night (similar to that made by Napoleon III. on the night of the 1st December [1851]) of all who are supposed to be in communication with the Mahdi. I shall not hurt them, but shall send them out to the Mahdi.

5 P.M.—The arrests are out. Sheikh el Islam, Cadi, and a host of swells are to be kept in their homes—sixteen in all! A good swoop; among them the Mudir Achmet Bey Jelaba. I have made Moussa Bey Mudir. There will be quite a scare about it. I have not sent any away to the Mahdi.

A mouse has taken Stewart's place at table; she (judging from her swelled-out appearance) comes up and eats out of my plate without fear.[37]

October 13.—We are a wonderful people; it was never our Government which made us a great nation; our Government has been ever the drag on our wheels. It is, of course, on the cards that Khartoum is taken under the nose of the expeditionary force, which will be *just too late.*

The expeditionary force will perhaps think it necessary to retake it; but that will be of no use, and will cause loss of life uselessly on both sides. It had far better quietly return, with its tail between its legs; for once Kartoum is taken, it matters little if the Opposition say "You gave up Kartoum," or "You gave up Kartoum, Sennaar," &c., &c.; the sun will have set, people will not care much for the satellites. England was made by adventurers, not by its Government, and I believe it will only hold its place by adventurers. If Kartoum falls, then go quietly back to Cairo, for you will only lose men and spend money uselessly in carrying on the campaign.[38]

October 14.—I have been obliged to make some more arrests.

This evening, some twelve of those arrested and allowed to stay in their houses are to be taken to the barracks; I hate those arrests, but one can scarcely doubt so many informants, who declare there was "trahison" meditated, not from any wish to join Mahdi, but for fear I was not strong enough to hold the city, and owing to Awaan's statement, *that he had written the letters* I had received from Debbeh announcing that the expeditionary force was coming.

I confess I am more perplexed about these arrests than I like; is it a good thing? or is it not? If I could be sure that the majority wished to go to the Mahdi, I could make up my mind at once what to do; it would be an immense relief to me, but does the mass wish it? If they do not, I ought to take all precautions against such an event. Then comes the query. Am I not, in these arrests, being made a tool of by the Turkish and Cairo elements? Are they not gratifying spites? Paul said, "*I have learned*" (as in a school) "*in whatsoever state I am to be content.*" I can only say, "*I am learning,*" but have "*not learned.*"[39]

October 15.—I had to make three more arrests—when once one begins this detestable practice, one never can stop. As far as I can judge the mass of people approve of the arrests. I am now going on the principle "in for a penny, in for a pound."

A lot of people were pressing for harder measures, but my new chief clerk said "we would wish to leave it to you to do or not to do," which is lively, as I am innocent of what goes on, or who is a traitor, or who is not; if ever there was a happy-go-lucky government, it is this in Kartoum. I declare that, sometimes, I give a decision, and have no more idea of what the decision is about than a cow; these, however, are exceptional cases. I have had about six bad slips in ten years, not more, and these I have managed to rectify, with loss of prestige.[40]

The Mahdi was now only a few days' march from Omdurman. In a last effort to move Gordon he instructed Slatin to write to his former chief advising him to surrender. Instead Slatin wrote to both Gordon and the Austrian consul, justifying his past conduct and asking to rejoin the government side. Gordon was unmoved. A remark in one of Slatin's letters, however, was the first suggestion Gordon had received that Stewart had failed to reach Dongola.

October 16.—The letters of Slatin have arrived. I have no remarks to make on them, and cannot make out why he wrote them.

Slatin's letter to Austrian Consul contains the remark that "if he comes over to me I must promise never to surrender the city, *as he would then suffer terrible tortures and death.*" He evidently is not a Spartan; he also says that "he changed his religion because he had not had much attention paid to his religious belief when young." If he gets away I shall take him to the Congo with me; he will want some *quarantine;* one feels sorry for him.

Slatin says there is a rumour that a boat of Stewart's expedition, down Nile, was captured by Arabs at the Cataract Dar Djumna, below Abou Hamed, but he doubts its truth.[41]

On October 19 the steamer Tell Hewein *returned to Khartoum from Shendi with late—and egregiously false—news. The Arabs, went the report, had captured two small boats of Stewart's expedition, but Stewart himself had got safely through to Debbeh; and English troops were now only two days from Berber. Apparently the Mahdi and the English were converging on Khartoum simultaneously; the outcome would be close. To assist the English, Gordon now sent the steamer* Bordein *to accompany the* Tell Hewein *down to Shendi. There remained at Khartoum only the* Ismailia *and the small* Husseinyeh, *newly constructed out of parts found stored in the Khartoum arsenal. But on October 22 Gordon was disturbed to receive a long letter from the Mahdi announcing the capture of the* Abbas; *as proof, the Mahdi itemized the papers Stewart had been carrying. Another letter from Slatin corroborated the Mahdi's story. Gordon was unconvinced but full of foreboding*.

October 22.—A man came in with a letter from Slatin, in which he says the *Abbas* was captured near Dar Djumna. Stewart killed, with nine men, and all the papers captured.

I am very anxious about the *Abbas;* it would be terrible, if it is true, that she is captured.

Slatin's letter mentions the 'Rapport Militaire'; it seems odd he should have known it was on board, unless the *Abbas* was captured; yet we have two men who declare she passed down. Perhaps the captured Greeks knew of the existence of this famous Journal, and told the Arabs of it, or Awaan may have written it; it is odd he (Slatin) says nothing of Power and Herbin.[42]

October 23.—The Arab horsemen cut the telegraph which goes out of the lines at Bourré to the North Fort. I declined to allow its repair, since I had lost a major and had six men wounded when last we went out of the lines, and besides which I had another cable to the north side. No sentries at the North Fort or Bourré, or on the Mudirat; these people are enough to break one's heart. Fortunately, from the roof of the Palace one watches all these things, and can bully them into obeying orders; but it is (as Hansall says) a *vie abrutissante*, to be always snarling and growling.

If these Arabs (one's servants) are not *eating*, they are *saying* their *prayers;* if not *saying their prayers*, they are *sleeping;* if not *sleeping*, they are *sick*. One snatches at them at intervals. Now figure to yourself the position; you cannot do anything with them while in these fortresses, *eating, saying prayers, sleeping*, or *sick*, and they know it. You would be a brute if you did (which I fear I often am). You want to send an immediate order, and there is your servant bobbing up and down, and you cannot disturb him. It is a beautiful country for trying experiments with your patience.

It is very curious, but if I am in a bad temper, which I fear is often the case, my servants will be always at their prayers, and thus religious practices follow the scale of my temper; they are pagans if all goes well.[43]

October 24.—I calculated that the advance force of troops arrived at Wady Halfa on 22nd September, that they took twenty days from there to Debbeh, so that on 12th October they were at Debbeh (Stewart (*D.V.*) arrived at Debbeh on 28th September), and I calculate they could not be at Metemma—Shendy—before 10th November, which will give them twenty-nine days for 150 miles, thence it is five days here for a steamer, so that 15th November ought to see them or their advance guard.

If they do not come before 30th November the game is up, and Rule Britannia. In this calculation I have given every latitude for difficulties of transport, making forts, &c., and on the 15th November I ought to see Her Majesty's uniform. I suppose a part of the force will go to attack Berber on the 10th November (when I calculate they will be at Metemma—Shendy), and that a small party will come on here; so we have now 7 days in October and 15 days in November to wait = 22 days—three weeks to add to the 226 days we have already passed.[44]

October 27.—Stewart's servant, Macktar, must needs go and marry another wife. How they can go on like this, marrying and giving in marriage, when one can never say, that to-morrow is our own, is wonderful. Tangi had taken two wives up here!

The sergeant-major, soldiers, and two men, Shaggyeh, who came in to-day, say that one of our soldiers escaped from Omdurman three days ago. On inquiry, I find that it is true, and the officer in command never reported it. The sergeant-major says the Arabs meditate an attack on Omdurman, in consequence of what the deserter told them. This is the *fourth* desertion since March that I know of, and it is the *first* desertion among the soldiers (with saving clause) that I know of.

Some time ago I gave Ferratch Pasha £100 a month, and I afterwards made him a Ferile, or General of Division, for political reasons. He had the cheek to ask me to give him £150 a month. He put in an application a few days ago for the £150, and forage for eight horses! Quite ignoring the state of the dhoora exchange, I said, "Wait." He was foolish enough to renew the application, which I tore up. He may go to the Arabs if he likes.

I must say I rather revel at the thought of the dismay which will attend the reduction of salaries to quarter their present rate, they have been so very selfish about these things. I believe if the Mahdi would only give them half the present rate, they would go to the Mahdi; but the Mahdi's service is *gratuitous*, so there is no fear of that. I go out, a black Bashi Bazouk addresses me on the inadequacy of his pay and rations. I whisper to him, *"Go to Sheikh el Obeyed,"* he grins and evaporates. I do not care a bit now.

It amuses me to find people here holding on to the delusion that the old state of affairs is likely to come back as to the Government, and saying, "You are going to stay with us as Governor-General, and things are to be as of old." I answer, "I would not take you again at any price after your meanness." They say, "Oh, yes, the people are not well behaved, &c., &c., but you will stay *for the glory of God"* (*i.e.* our interests). They are an amusing lot: Allah on lips, self interest at heart, and such self interest as is *positively naked,* and they even laugh at it.[45]

October 30.—This morning the Arabs came to Halfeyeh, capturing some of our heedless people. Not being able to sleep last night, I was late in getting up, and consequently every one also slept and no proper look-out was kept on the Arabs. I should think I had written twenty orders about their keeping a look-out, but it is of no use.

I believe we (*i.e.* those Shaggyeh) lost to-day twenty-three soldiers taken prisoners, one killed, one wounded; seventeen cows, five women, eight slaves, three donkeys, seven horses, twenty-four Remington rifles captured; and this after I had repeatedly warned them of an impending attack, and specially warned them last night after the capture of the three spies. They, these Shaggyeh, number 1200; on the other side, with 30 horses, the Arabs were not 200; they made no attempt to defend themselves; dreadful lot, how I look forward to their disbandment![46]

October 31.—It turns out that the Shaggyeh chief who commanded in the North Fort slept in town the day before yesterday night, and so was absent at yesterday morning's catastrophe; also the officer Osman Bey never reported this man's absence; I have turned them out, and cut them each a month's pay. (No sentry as usual, on North Fort. They are incorrigible. I ordered them thirty blows: *i.e.* the sentries.)

I have ever felt the greatest insecurity respecting the lines, for I believe one hundred determined men would carry them with ease, if they made their attack on the Shaggyeh or Bashi Bazouk part. These creatures used to shut themselves into the houses at about 7 P.M., and never go out till it was broad daylight; they were not eighty yards from the river. The Cairo Turkish Bashi Bazouks, the Shaggyeh, and the fellaheen soldiers, I will back against any troops in the world for *cowardice!* The worst of it is, that it is taken generally as a thing of "*matter of course*" by the Kartoum people, and, one may say, officers; no one is a bit put out or ashamed; it teaches no experience. *Vide* the absence of sentries on the fort to-day, who, I expect, cannot sit down over-comfortably to-night after their thirty blows.

One cannot help feeling amused at these Shaggyehs, for they are the most arrant braggadocios, as are the Cairo Turkish Bashi Bazouks. They have little kettledrums about a span in diameter; whenever I hear them I feel viciously inclined. The Shaggyeh are very quiet to-day; they are all boxed up in the houses; very few have ventured out more than 2000 yards. The report is that they are ashamed, which, if words could make them so, they ought to be; but I doubt it. They have not beaten their kettledrums to-night; yes, they have begun to beat them now.[47]

⋙*November 1*⋘.—These people are a fine lot. The merchants of the market have been refusing to give more than three and a half reals for a sovereign, five to six reals being the proper rate; so I captured nine of the chief of them, and have sent them to the lines with a pretended order to send them out to Waled a Goun [the Mahdist commander], but with orders to keep them on the lines. I hope this will cure them. I shall let them in again when they sign a paper agreeing to my terms. Of course it is tyranny, but there is no other course to be pursued. The nine culprits, three soldiers with fixed bayonets before, three soldiers with ditto behind, and a mounted cavass on each flank, are wending their way to the lines through the market. Quite a procession! My servants are my staff. I never hear these sort of things from the officials, who are bribed, I expect, to keep silence.[48]

⋙*On November 3 the* Bordein *fought its way into Khartoum with the post from Shendi. There were some personal letters, a cipher telegram from Lord Wolseley, and a letter from Kitchener. "Please inform me by this present messenger, who is paid to return," Kitchener had written from Debbeh on October 14, "who were on board the steamer that came down from Kartoum. I am sorry to say, whoever they were, they have fallen into the hands of Suleiman Wady Goun, Sheikh of the Minassir, and have, I am afraid, been killed." Stewart dead—it was certain now. "Lord Wolseley is now at Wady Halfa," Kitchener went on, "and it is expected this expedition will definitely start from Dongola on or about the 1st November. Special boats are coming out from England for the passage up the Nile. There are a considerable number of troops now at Dongola." English troops were then only ten days away. Gordon wrote to Wolseley a full report of his position; he could, he believed, hold out "with ease" another forty days—until the middle of December. Unfortunately, Gordon could not read Wolseley's cipher telegram; Kitchener too was ignorant of Wolseley's plan. The troops then at Dongola were, in fact, only a garrison. The main body of the expedition would not*

*be assembled there until December 15. The push across the desert
from Korti to Metemma and thence to Khartoum would not be possible before Christmas. Cautious and thorough, Wolseley was unaware how perilous Gordon's situation was. Stewart would have been
able to tell him*.

November 5.—Steamer *Bordeen* left this evening for Metemma.

I cannot get out of my head the *Abbas* catastrophe; that the
Abbas (with her 970 bullet marks on her, her gun, and her parapets,
which were bullet-proof), could be captured by force, seems impossible; that she ran upon a rock seems unlikely, for she had her sides
defended by buffers, sunk one foot in water. I also had warned them
against ever anchoring by the bank, also to take wood from isolated
spots; in fact, as far as human foresight goes, I did all possible.
Why did you let them go? The matter was thus. I determined to send
the *Abbas* down with an Arab captain. Herbin asked to be allowed
to go. I jumped at his offer. Then Stewart said he would go, if I
would exonerate him from deserting me. I said you do not desert me.
I: I cannot go; but if you go, you do great service. I then wrote him
an official; he wanted me to write him an order. I said "No, for
though I fear not responsibility, I will not put you in any danger in
which I am not myself." I wrote them a letter, couched thus: "*Abbas*
is going down; you say you are willing to go in her, if I think you can
do so in honour—you can go in honour, for you can do nothing here,
and if you go you do me great service in telegraphing my views."
You will notice the number of Greeks. They were a body-guard I
ordered and paid highly, to prevent any treachery on the part of
the crew. Thus the question of treachery was duly weighed by me
and guarded against, as far as I could—both on the part of the
crew and on the part of the inhabitants—and I told them to anchor
mid stream, and not to take wood except in isolated spots.

I escorted them by two steamers past every place where danger
could be apprehended, viz., Berber and Shendy. They appear to have
been captured in a comparatively thinly populated place, below Abou
Hamed. I feel somehow convinced they were captured by treachery—
the Arabs pretending to be friendly—and surprising them at night.
I will own that, without reason (apparently, for the chorus was,
that the *trip was safe*) I have never been comfortable since they left.
Stewart was a man who did not chew the cud, he never thought of

danger in prospective; he was not a bit suspicious (while I am made up of it). I can see in imagination the whole scene, the Sheikh inviting them to land, saying, "Thank God the Mahdi is a liar"— bringing in wood—men going on shore and dispersed. The *Abbas* with her steam down, then a rush of wild Arabs, and all is over!

A curious thing has happened; my friend Kitchener sent up the post; he wrapped the letters in some old newspapers (he gave me no news in his letter), the old newspapers were thrown out in the garden: there a clerk who knew some English found them blowing about, and gave them to the apothecary of the hospital, who knows English. The Doctor found him reading them, saw date *15th September*, and secured them for me; they are like gold, as you may imagine, since we have had no news since 24th February, 1884.

These papers gave us far more information than any of your letters. Did K. send them by accident or on purpose? Abyssinian ambassadors in London, Walmer Castle, &c.; my black troops beating back Ras Aloula at Keren, not recognizing the Hewitt Treaty, and killing 194 of the Abyssinians, at Keren, *vide Standard*, 1 and 15 September. Lord Wolseley seen off at Victoria Station, for the *Gordon relief expedition!! NO! for the relief of Soudan garrisons.* Khedive expressing delight at seeing Lord N., while during the audience the Khedive displayed great cordiality towards Lord N. Abdel Kader saying you would have four hard fights. I do not believe it.[49]

November 12 .—Last night three slaves came into Omdurman. At 11 P.M. they reported Arabs meant to attack to-day at dawn. It was reported to me, but the telegraph clerk did not choose to tell me till 7 A.M. to-day. We had been called up at 5.30 A.M. by a violent fusillade at Omdurman. The Arabs came out in considerable force, and, as I had not been warned, the steamers had not steam up. From 5.30 A.M. to 8.30 Arabs came on and went back continually. All the cavalry were out; the expenditure of ammunition was immense. The Arabs had a gun or guns on the bank. Details further on, as the firing is still going on.

10.20 A.M.—For half an hour firing lulled, but then recommenced, and is still going on. The *Ismailia* was struck with a shell, but I hear is not seriously damaged. The *Husseinyeh* is aground (I feel much the want of my other steamers at Metemma). 11.15 A.M.—Firing has lulled; it was very heavy for the last three quarters of an hour from the *Ismailia* and Arabs; it is now desultory, and is dying away.

Husseinyeh is still aground. The *Ismailia* is at anchor. What a six hours of anxiety for me, when I saw the shells strike the water near the steamers from the Arabs; imagine my feelings! Noon. The firing has ceased, I am glad to say. I have lived *years* in these last *hours!* Had I lost the *Ismailia*, I should have lost the *Husseinyeh* (aground), and then Omdurman, and the North Fort! And then the town! 1 P.M. —The Arabs are firing on the steamers with their two guns. The *Husseinyeh still aground;* that is the reason of it. Firing, 1.30 P.M., now has ceased. The *Ismailia*, struck by three shells, had one man killed, fifteen wounded on board of her; she did really very well. I boxed the telegraph clerk's ears for not giving me the telegraph last night (after repeated orders that no consideration was to prevent his coming to me); and then, as my conscience pricked me, I gave him $5. He said he did not mind if I killed him—I was his father (a chocolate-coloured youth of twenty). I know all this is brutal— *abrutissant*, as Hansall calls it—but what is one to do? If you cut their pay, you hurt their families. I am an advocate for summary and quick punishment, which hurts only the defaulter. Had this clerk warned me, of course, at daybreak, the steamers would have had their steam up, and been ready. We have a Krupp at Mogrim Fort. Ferratch Pasha reports he has dismounted one of the Arab guns. The Arabs had a show of four hundred horsemen, who kept far off. Telegraph was, and is, interrupted between this and the Omdurman Fort (whether by bullet or otherwise is not known as yet). Considering that the Arab mountain gun can (and has) made holes *two feet square* in the steamer, my anxiety is not to be wondered at. (I feel as if I had walked thirty miles.) We fired eighty-three rounds of Krupp at the Arabs from Mogrim, forty-three rockets. The Arabs fired three hundred and seventy rounds from their guns at the steamers. As for ammunition (Remington), we fired from *our steamers*, forts, &c., fifty thousand rounds; and I certainly think the Arabs fired as much. Omdurman certainly was "over-eager to fire on the enemy" in the early dawn, and consequently wasted ammunition. This ends the greatest battle (*as yet*) of our second blockade. Spies (of last night) say it was undertaken against the Mahdi's wish, by his Khalifa or Vizier, who persuaded him to allow it. During all through, the Arabs of the South and East never moved a peg. Like the Chinese, one may calculate they will never assist one another.

This is our *first* encounter with the Mahdi's personal troops. One tumbles at 3 A.M. into a troubled sleep; a drum beats—tup! tup! tup!

It comes into a dream, but after a few moments one becomes more awake, and it is revealed to the brain that *one is in Kartoum.* The next query is, where is this tup, tupping going on? A hope arises it will die away. No, it goes on, and increases in intensity. The thought strikes one, "Have they enough ammunition?" (the excuse of bad soldiers). One exerts oneself. At last, it is no use, up one must get, and go on to the roof of the Palace; then telegrams, orders, swearing, and cursing goes on till about 9 A.M. Men may say what they like about glorious war, but to me it is a horrid nuisance (if it is permitted to say anything is a nuisance which comes on us). I saw that poor little beast the *Husseinyeh* (a Thames launch) fall back, stern foremost, under a terrific fire of breech-loaders. I saw a shell strike the water at her bows; I saw her stop and puff off steam, and I gave the glass to my boy, *sickened unto death.* My boy (he is thirty) said, "*Husseinyeh is sick.*" I knew it, but said quietly, "Go down and telegraph to Mogrim, 'Is *Husseinyeh* sick?'" Answer, "No." I asked again; answer, "No." Then telegraph said, "She was aground."

2.45 P.M. The *Ismailia* tried to take the *Husseinyeh* off, and got struck twice, in addition to the three times before mentioned, with shells, so she desisted from the attempt. The Arabs are firing on the *Husseinyeh.* I have ordered the Krupp at Mogrim to play on the Arab guns, and shall wait till night to take off the *Husseinyeh.* She is nearer to the *left* bank than to the *right* bank; it is not clear if she is aground or half sunk (equally a trouble). 3.30 P.M. The Arabs are bringing their guns nearer to the aground or half-sunken *Husseinyeh.* The *Ismailia* reports that the two last shells have done her no material damage. 4.30 P.M. The Arabs have now three guns bearing on the *Husseinyeh.* 6 P.M. The firing has ceased. I hope to get the *Husseinyeh* off at night. 7 P.M. The Arabs keep up a dropping fire on the *Husseinyeh,* who, I hear, has two shell holes in her, and has six men, including the captain, wounded. I must say the Arabs to-day showed the greatest of pluck; over and over again they returned to the attack, though overwhelmed with the musketry fire of the castellated *Ismailia.* I think they must have lost heavily, for at times they were in dense groups. I believe that by the *Arabs* we may understand *our own regulars captured in Kordofan and Darfur, &c.* We are going to get the *Husseinyeh* off to-night *if we can.* No Royal Navy vessels would have behaved better than the *Ismailia* to-day; she passed and repassed the Arab guns upwards of twenty times, when any one well-placed shell would have sunk her. Whether the crew knew it or not does not matter. *I did, and felt comfortable accordingly.* The Arab guns were not 1200 yards distant from her, and even less at times. She was struck five times with shell. Remember that the *Ismailia* is only a superior penny boat, and that the Egyptian mountain gun is as superior to our wretched seven-pounders as a three-pounder is to a twelve-pounder howitzer, both for range and for effect. You want a gun to make a hole, not a gimlet-hole, which these seven-pounders do, and what wearisome work to carry them!

All this worry is (humanly speaking) due to that chocolate-coloured clerk of the telegraph not warning me. This evening there was an ominous sign that the Arabs on the Blue Nile knew of our troubles with the *Husseinyeh.* They came up against Bourré, but two gunshots drove them off. At 4 p.m. the Arabs on the right bank of the White Nile fired twelve shells against the lines, and opened a fire of musketry for a short time, but did no harm. I have given half a month's pay to the *Ismailia* and to the *Husseinyeh* crews, and $2 for the men who have gone to get the latter off; she is *not half sunk,* but *is aground.* There is (8 p.m.) a fire on the left bank of the White Nile, opposite to Halfeyeh. The Arabs got into the ditch of the entrenched camp at Omdurman, which is theirs. We only occupy the fort.

8.15 p.m. The Arabs have still their guns on the river bank, and are firing at the *Husseinyeh,* whom I am trying, by my men, to get off. Evidently they are not cowed, for generally they take their guns back at night to their camp. Report from the *Husseinyeh* steamer: 10.20 p.m. Wounded, 6; killed, 3; efforts as yet are ineffectual as to taking off the steamer *Husseinyeh.*[50]

The Arabs had penetrated the outer defences of Omdurman and cut the telegraph connecting the fort with Khartoum. Omdurman was isolated and must inevitably fall when its supplies were exhausted—a matter of a few weeks at best. When Omdurman fell, the end of Khartoum would be near. Outside, the activity of the besiegers increased. Within, Gordon counted the grim, final days and watched the Nile for a sign of the relief force.

November 15.—I think I have been rather unjust towards the fellaheen soldier, for though he is not brave enough to take the field, he has done good work on board the steamers, and a good many of their officers and men have been killed and wounded (thanks to the policy that has been followed elsewhere) in a quarrel which does not concern them. These remarks are produced by a visit I made to the hospital to-day, when I saw the mass of the wounded were fellaheen soldiers, whom I put in the steamers, because, when in action, they could not run away, while I kept the blacks for the defence of the lines. As I was leaving the hospital to-day, a dead man was carried out by four men in chains (convicts) on a stretcher, accompanied by two soldiers with fixed bayonets—to be buried as a dog! This is part of the glory of war![51]

✍§*On November 25 the* Bordein *again ran the gauntlet of Arab guns to Khartoum. It brought Gordon his final disappointment*§✍.

✍§*November 25*§✍.—1.15 P.M. Steamers in sight; the Doctor saw them first. The steamers are firing; only one steamer in sight.

The Arabs had three guns at Halfeyeh against the coming-in steamer. 2.30 P.M. I have sent down the *Ismailia* to cover the incoming steamer. The Arabs are grunting with their Nordenfeldt, and firing from their gun. Mogrim is playing on them with the Krupp, and Tuti with their mountain gun. 2.45 P.M. For the last half hour the firing on the part of Arabs on the advancing steamer has been most furious with guns and musketry; we replying. I am grateful to say that, after this hot reception, she has got in safe to Mogrim.

If any officer of the Expedition is on board, he will know what it is to be in a penny boat! under cannon fire. The *Bordeen* has come in; she has seven wounded. There are *no Arabs* at Shoboloha, or (consequently) *guns;* the wounded were from two shells fired by the Arabs from Halfeyeh. The Expeditionary Force is at Ambukol (which is LIVELY!); the Arabs had four guns at Halfeyeh; one woman was killed in the *Bordeen:* the letters received by the *Bordeen* are of no great import, for they do not tell me the route the Expedition will take, and I have received a later post—that of 14th October.[52]

✍§*The* Bordein *brought three official cipher telegrams from London, including the cabinet's last message, dated July 24, which ended: "Her Majesty's Government continue to be anxious to learn from himself his views and position, so that, if danger has arisen or is likely to arise in the manner they have described, they may be in a position to take measures accordingly." Gordon pasted the tele-grams, undeciphered, in his journal. There was also a telegram in Arabic from the Khedive, written at Gladstone's behest on Septem-ber 21, which in effect transferred most of Gordon's authority in the Sudan to the commanders of the relief expedition. Fortunately, Gor-don failed to grasp the significance of this message.*

November 26.—I am sure we are deprived of a treat in not being able to decipher the long telegram on the preceding page. It also is delicious to find not one civil word from any official personage except Kitchener; it relieves me immensely (also I must except Tow-fik, who in his despatch was civil and polite). Evidently I am in dis-grace! How fearful![53]

The Bordein remained at Khartoum nearly three weeks. When it left to return to Shendi it carried the final portion of Gor-don's journal. The last entry was dated December 14.

December 14.—Arabs fired two shells at the Palace this morning; 546 ardebs dhoora! in store; also 83,525 okes of biscuit! 10.30 A.M. The steamers are down at Omdurman, engaging the Arabs, consequently I am on *tenterhooks!* 11.30 A.M. Steamers returned; the *Bordeen* was struck by a shell in her battery; we had only one man wounded. We are going to send down the *Bordeen* to-morrow with this journal. If I was in command of the two hundred men of the Ex-peditionary Force, which are all that are necessary for the move-ment, I should stop just below Halfeyeh, and attack the Arabs at that place before I came on here to Kartoum. I should then com-municate with the North Fort, and act according to circumstances. Now MARK THIS, if the Expeditionary Force, and I ask no more than two hundred men, does not come in ten days, *the town may fall;* and I have done my best for the honour of our country. Good bye.

C. G. Gordon.

You send me no information, though you have lots of money.

C.G.G.[54]

VI

Impelled at last by a revolt within his cabinet, Gladstone, on August 5, 1884, asked the House of Commons to vote £300,000 for

*a Sudan expeditionary force. The sum was small, and Gladstone still
hoped an expedition would not be necessary. The War Office, however, was more zealous than the Prime Minister to rescue Gordon.
Immediately, long-prepared plans were put into effect. The short
but hazardous route from the Red Sea port of Suakim across 250
miles of desert to Berber had already been rejected in favor of a
river route—1,600 miles fom Cairo to Khartoum. Command of the
expedition was given to Lord Wolseley. At Assuan a camp was established for 7,000 picked troops; equipment and supplies for the
troops, and for 8,000 refugees who were expected to accompany the
expedition back from Khartoum, were shipped from England. To
transport the expedition up the Nile and over the cataracts, Wolseley, who had once campaigned on the Red River in Canada, ordered
the manufacture of 400 flat-bottomed boats on the Canadian model
and proceeded to import Canadian boatmen to man them.*

*English officers in Egypt were already despairing when Wolseley
reached Cairo on September 4. September was passed at Cairo, October at Assuan and Wadi Halfa assembling and organizing the
expedition. The first river boats did not leave England until September 10 and did not reach Wadi Halfa until the end of October. During November and half of December boats, steamers, troops, and
supplies were hauled 200 miles over the cataracts to Dongola. By
the end of December the expedition was finally assembled at Korti,
140 miles south of Dongola. Wolseley planned for the main body of
the expedition to continue up the Nile to Berber while a specially
constituted camel corps of 2,000 men cut directly across country 150
miles to Metemma where Gordon's steamers waited. There communications could be re-established with Gordon. If his situation was serious, the camel corps could advance to his aid at once. The main body
of the expedition, however, was not expected to reach Khartoum before March.*

*On December 30 a message was received from Gordon urging
speed. That same day a supply column left Korti for Gakdul, half-
way to Metemma, where it established a depot and returned—a pro-
cedure made necessary by a shortage of camels. Not until January 8
did the camel corps, commanded by General Herbert Stewart and
including units of the Royal Sussex Regiment and a naval brigade,
leave Korti for Metemma. Night marches in rough and unfamiliar
country, mishandling of the camels, untrustworthy native drivers,*

and a shortage of water delayed and harassed the force. Further-
more, the preliminary advance to Gakdul had alerted the Arabs. On
January 16 the camel corps found 10,000 Arabs barring its way
to the wells at Abu Klea.

The events of the next day were recorded in his journal by Colonel
Charles Wilson, the column's intelligence officer.

As it became evident that the enemy intended to keep up a harass-
ing fire on us, and not deliver an attack, Stewart determined to
march out and give battle, leaving a force behind to hold the zeribah.
The square was then formed up, and we marched down the valley
towards the row of flags which stretched across it, whilst Barrow
with the cavalry moved off to the left to keep the enemy on the hills
in check. The square was formed up thus: Guards and Mounted Infantry in front, the Heavies and Sussex Regiment in rear, and the
Naval Brigade with the Heavies. As we moved on, the firing continued. We halted several times and returned the fire with Martinis
and the screw guns: these had some effect, for we could see numbers
of men streaming off from the enemy's right in the valley. We kept
to the right until we got out of the grass and had clear ground round
us; and then moved on, with Campbell's company of Mounted Infantry out as skirmishers on our left front. When the skirmishers got
within about 200 yards of the flags, the square was halted for the
rear to close up, and at this moment the enemy rose from the ravine
in which they were hidden, in the most perfect order. It was a beautiful and striking sight, such a one as FitzJames must have seen when
Roderick Dhu's men rose out of the heather; nothing could be more
applicable than Scott's description. How they managed to conceal
their horses I know not, but they did so very effectually. The formation was curious, a sort of variety of the old phalanx. It was as if
there were portions of three phalanxes with rows of men behind. At
the head of each rode an emir or sheikh with a banner, accompanied
by personal attendants, and then came the fighting men. They advanced at a quick even pace as if on parade, and our skirmishers had
only just time to get into the square before they were upon us: one
poor fellow who lagged behind was caught and speared at once.
When the enemy commenced their advance, I remember experiencing
a feeling of pity mixed with admiration for them, as I thought they
would all be shot down in a few minutes. I could not have believed be-

forehand that men in close formation would have been able to advance for 200 or 400 yards over bare ground in the face of Martini-Henrys. As they advanced the feeling was changed to wonder that the tremendous fire we were keeping up had so little effect. When they got within 80 yards, the fire of the Guards and Mounted Infantry began to take good effect, and a huge pile of dead rose in front of them. Then to my astonishment the enemy took ground to their right as if on parade, so as to envelop the rear of the square. I remember thinking, "By Jove, they will be into the square!" and almost the next moment I saw a fine old sheikh on horseback plant his banner in the centre of the square, behind the camels. He was at once shot down, falling on his banner. He turned out to be Musa, Emir of the Duguaim Arabs, from Kordofan. I had noticed him in the advance, with his banner in one hand and a book of prayers in the other, and never saw anything finer. The old man never swerved to the right or left, and never ceased chanting his prayers until he had planted his banner in our square. If any man deserved a place in the Moslem Paradise, he did. When I saw the old sheikh in the square, and heard the wild uproar behind the camels, I drew my revolver; for directly the sheikh fell, the Arabs began running in under the camels to the front part of the square. Some of the rear rank now faced about and began firing. By this fire Herbert Stewart's horse was shot, and as he fell three Arabs ran at him. I was close to his horse's tail, and disposed of the one nearest to me, about three paces off; and the others were, I think, killed by the Mounted Infantry officers close by. Almost immediately afterwards the enemy retired, and loud and long cheering broke out from the square. Our men had by this time got somewhat out of hand, wild with excitement. It was for a few moments difficult to get them into their places; and if the enemy had charged again, few of us would have escaped. At one time this seemed likely, as they retired slowly, and for a short time hesitated in the valley before they made their final bolt.[55]

◄§The next day the camel corps pushed on toward Metemma. On January 19, almost within sight of the Nile, there was another fight with the Arabs in which Stewart was mortally wounded. The command then fell to Wilson. On the 21st, thoroughly exhausted and with heavy casualties, the column reached the Nile and found Gordon's steamers§►.

VII

⊷§The news of Abu Klea quickly reached the Mahdi's camp, where Slatin, whose correspondence with Gordon asking to rejoin his former chief had been discovered, was now a prisoner, loaded with chains and under constant guard. Slatin recorded⧂⦙ :

Six days after the fall of Omdurman [on January 15], loud weeping and wailing filled our camp; since I had left Darfur I had not heard anything like it. The Mahdi's doctrine forbade the display of sorrow and grief for those who died, or were killed, because they had entered into the joys of Paradise. Something very unusual must therefore have happened to make the people dare to transgress the Mahdi's regulations. My guards, who were old soldiers, were so curious to know the cause that they left me to make inquiries, and in a few minutes brought back the startling news that the English advanced guard had met the combined force of Barabra, Jaalin, Degheim, and Kenana, under Musa Wad Helu, at Abu Teleh (Abu Klea), and had utterly defeated them; thousands had fallen, and the few who had survived had returned, many of them wounded. The Degheim and Kenana had been almost annihilated; Musa Wad Helu, and most of the Emirs, had fallen.

What news!—my heart was literally thumping with joyous excitement. After all these long years a crowning victory at last! The Mahdi and Khalifa at once gave orders that all this noise should cease; but for hours the weeping and wailing of the women continued. Instructions were now given to Nur Angara to start off with troops towards Metemmeh. But what good would this do? Even if he had the will—which he had not—what could he do with a few troops when thousands and thousands of wild fanatics had failed? Within the next two or three days came the news of other defeats at Abu Kru and Kubba (Gubat), and of the erection of a fort on the Nile close to Metemmeh. The Mahdi and his principal Emirs now held a consultation. All the wonderful victories they had gained up to the present were at stake, for those besieging Khartum were terrified and had retired. It was now the question of a few days only, and the Mahdi was done. They must risk everything. Consequently, orders were sent out to the besiegers to collect and make all preparations. Why did the long-expected steamers with the English troops not come? Did their commanders not know Khartum, and the lives of all in it, were hanging by a thread? In vain did I, and thousands of others, wait for the shrill whistle of the steamer, and for the booming of the guns announcing that the English had arrived, and were passing the entrenchments made by the Dervishes to oppose them. Yes, in vain! The delay was inexplicable; what could it mean? Had new difficulties arisen?

It was now Sunday, the 25th of January [1885]—a day I shall never forget as long as I live. That evening, when it was dark, the Mahdi and his Khalifas crossed over in a boat to where their warriors were all collected ready for the fight. It was known during the day that Khartum would be attacked the next morning, and the Mahdi had now gone to brace up his followers for the fray by preaching to them the glories of Jehad, and urging them to fight till death. Pray Heaven Gordon may have got the news, and made his preparations to resist in time!

On this occasion the Mahdi and his Khalifas had most strictly enjoined their followers to restrain their feelings, and receive the last injunctions in silence, instead of with the usual shouts and acclamations, which might awaken the suspicions of the exhausted and hungry garrison. His solemn harangue over, the Mahdi recrossed, and returned to the camp at dawn, leaving with the storming party only Khalifa Sherif, who had begged to be allowed to join in the holy battle.

That night was for me the most excitingly anxious one in my life. If only the attack were repulsed Khartum would be saved, otherwise all would be lost. Utterly exhausted, I was just dropping off to sleep at early dawn when I was startled by the deafening discharge of thousands of rifles and guns; this lasted for a few minutes, then only occasional rifle-shots were heard, and now all was quiet again. It was scarcely light, and I could barely distinguish objects. Could this possibly be the great attack on Khartum? A wild discharge of firearms and cannon, and in a few minutes complete stillness?

The sun was now rising red over the horizon; what would this day bring forth? Excited and agitated, I awaited the result with intense impatience. Soon shouts of rejoicing and victory were heard in the distance, and my guards ran off to find out the news. In a few minutes they were back again, excitedly relating how Khartum had been taken by storm, and was now in the hands of the Mahdists. Was it possible the news was false? I crawled out of my tent and scanned the camp; a great crowd had collected before the quarters of the Mahdi and Khalifa, which were not far off; then there was a movement in the direction of my tent, and I could see plainly they were coming towards me. In front marched three Black soldiers; one named Shatta, formerly belonging to Ahmed Bey Dafalla's slave bodyguard, carried in his hands a bloody cloth in which something was wrapped up, and behind him followed a crowd of people weeping. The slaves had now approached my tent, and stood before me with insulting gestures; Shatta undid the cloth and showed me the head of General Gordon!

The blood rushed to my head, and my heart seemed to stop beating; but with a tremendous effort of self-control I gazed silently at this ghastly spectacle. His blue eyes were half-opened; the mouth was perfectly natural; the hair of his head and his short whiskers were almost quite white.

'Is not this the head of your uncle, the unbeliever?' said Shatta, holding the head up before me.

'What of it?' said I quietly. 'A brave soldier, who fell at his post. Happy is he to have fallen; his sufferings are over.'[56]

VIII

⮑§At Metemma, Col. Wilson's first concern was for his troops. They needed rest, and their position had to be safeguarded against attack. January 21 and 22 were spent in reconnaissance on the Nile above and below Metemma. Finally, on January 24, Wilson, with 20 red-coated soldiers of the Royal Sussex Regiment and 250 of Gordon's native troops, started upstream with the **Bordein** *and* **Tell Hewein** *to Khartoum, 100 miles away. Progress up the difficult channels was slow; nights were passed at anchor. On the morning of January 28, the steamers were approaching Khartoum§⮑.*

Started at 6 A.M. My orders were, the 'Bordein' to lead, the 'Talahawiyeh' to conform to her movements; the Sussex men to fire volleys at the embrasures of the batteries, which were also to be engaged by the guns of the steamers; the blacks to fire away as hard as they could; the 'Bordein' to go ahead full speed into Khartoum, followed by her consort. Wortley and his signaller, who had a heliostat, were to try and attract Gordon's attention. At 7.30 we passed Jebel Seg et Taib, a steep hill close to the bank of the river, where there had been at one time a battery with guns, to prevent the passage of the steamers up and down the river. It was a good position, and, luckily for us, unoccupied. We went on past Abu Alim, where one of the Mahdi's chief emirs lives, and soon after could see Khartum in the far distance above the trees of Tuti Island. About this time a Shagiyeh on the right bank shouted out to the 'Talahawiyeh' to stop, and told them that Khartum had been taken and Gordon killed two days before.

Occasional firing had been going on all the morning, but as we approached Fighiaiha the enemy opened a regular fusilade. The fight had now commenced, and I went with Khashm and Ibrahim to the midship turret, where I remained throughout the action. Gascoigne joined us shortly afterwards, and was there or with the Sussex on the deckhouse. In the turret I was close to the captain and *reis* [pilot], and also to the engineer, so that I could give orders at once. It made a capital conning tower, for by standing on a stool and looking over, one could see all round. The tower was also bulletproof, an advantage which old Khashm seemed to appreciate, for he doubled himself up in a corner, and only moved to get out of the way of the gun.

When we came full in sight of Halfiyeh I noticed that the palm-grove had been burned and the houses wrecked—a picture of the desolation of war—and also that there were several large boats lying by the bank. I called Khashm's attention to this, and he at once replied, "Gordon's troops must be there, as the Mahdi has no boats." Directly after, a heavy fire was opened upon us from four guns and many rifles at from 600 to 700 yards. The guns were well placed, one in a *sakieh* pit, two in a little battery above, and one in the village. The bullets began to fly pretty thickly, tapping like hail against the ship's sides, whilst the shells went screeching overhead or threw up jets of water in the stream round us. Our men replied cheerily, and the gun in the turret was capitally served by the black gunners under their captain Abdullah Effendi, who laid the gun each time and fired it himself. The gunners, who had nothing on but a cloth round their waists, looked more like demons than men in the thick smoke; and one huge giant was the very incarnation of savagery drunk with war. The shooting was fairly good, and we heard afterwards that we had dismounted one of the guns in the battery; but at the time we could not see the effect. After we had run the gauntlet and the fire was turned on our consort, the Sudanese sent up a wild cry of delight, raising their rifles in their hands and shaking them in the air.

It was a strange weird sight, these black savages with their blood up, quivering with excitement.

I now had leisure to watch the 'Talahawiyeh' coming through the thick of it, scathless as we had done, the red flag streaming bravely above the smoke, which hung in a dense cloud round her. The firing now ceased for a few minutes, and we could see the large Government House at Khartum plainly above the trees. Khashm was very anxious to know whether we could see the Egyptian flag, which he said Gordon always kept flying; but neither Gascoigne nor I could see a trace of one anywhere. Khashm now began to get anxious, and said he felt certain something must have happened at Khartum, and that the place must be in the Mahdi's hands, otherwise there would have been no boats at Halfiyeh, and the flag would be flying. I could not believe this; at any rate, we could not stop now until we were certain all was over.

We had only a short respite, for, directly after passing Shamba, two guns on the right bank opened upon us, with a heavy rifle-fire from both banks, and this was kept up until we came within range of the guns at Omdurman. When about half-way up Tuti I thought for a moment that the island was still in Gordon's hands. A sort of dike ran along the edge of the island, and behind this there was a long line of men firing away as hard as they could. I heard the bullets singing overhead, and saw them strike the sand amongst the enemy's sharpshooters on the opposite bank, and thought they were helping us. I then ordered the steamer to run close to the bank, stop, cease firing, and ask for news. This we did, getting within 60 or 70 yards. I felt so persuaded at first that they were Gordon's men that I got outside the turret, but the only reply to our shouts was a sharper and better directed fire, which soon drove me inside again.

It was clear that the enemy's riflemen were on Tuti; but Khartum might still be holding out—so after a delay of about a quarter of an hour we went on, old Khashm protesting it was all up, and predicting terrible disaster to ourselves. No sooner did we start upwards than we got into such a fire as I hope never to pass through again in a "penny steamer." Two or more guns opened upon us from Omdurman fort, and three or four from Khartum or the upper end of Tuti; the roll of musketry from each side was continuous; and high above that could be heard the grunting of a Nordenfeldt or a mitrailleuse, and the loud rushing noise of the Krupp shells, fired either from Khartum itself or from the upper end of Tuti Island.

We kept on to the junction of the two Niles, when it became plain to every one that Khartum had fallen into the Mahdi's hands; for not only were there hundreds of dervishes ranged under their banners, standing on the sandspit close to the town ready to resist our landing, but no flag was flying in Khartum and not a shot was fired in our assistance; here, too, if not before, we should have met the two steamers I knew Gordon still had at Khartum. I at once gave the order to turn and run full speed down the river.[57]

NOTES TO THE CHAPTERS

1. LORD ASHLEY

1. *Report from the Committee on the "Bill to regulate the Labour of Children in the Mills and Factories of the United Kingdom,"* p. 14.
2. *Ibid.,* pp. 18–19.
3. *Ibid.,* p. 96.
4. *Ibid.,* p. 192.
5. *Ibid.,* pp. 195–99.
6. Edwin Hodder, *The Life and Work of the Seventh Earl of Shaftesbury, K.G.* (London, 1888), I, 148–49.
7. *Ibid.,* I, 100–101.
8. *Ibid.,* I, 153.
9. *Ibid.,* I, 342–43.
10. *Ibid.,* I, 346.
11. *Ibid.,* I, 404–5.
12. *Ibid.,* I, 405–6.
13. *Ibid.,* I, 408–11.
14. *Ibid.,* I, 411, 418.
15. *Ibid.,* I, 418–20.
16. *Parliamentary Debates,* 3rd series, LXIII, 1321–52.
17. Hodder, *op. cit.,* I, 421–22.
18. *Parliamentary Debates,* 3rd series, LXIII, 1356.
19. *Ibid.,* LXIII, 1353.
20. *Ibid.,* LXIV, 424.
21. *Ibid.,* LXIV, 1001.
22. Hodder, *op. cit.,* I, 426, 428–29.
23. *Ibid.,* I, 428–30.
24. *Parliamentary Debates,* 3rd series, LXV, 118.
25. *Ibid.,* LXIV, 539.
26. *Ibid.,* LXIV, 539.
27. *Ibid.,* LXV, 120.
28. *Ibid.,* LXIV, 540.
29. *Ibid.,* LXV, 119.
30. *Ibid.,* LXV, 582.
31. Hodder, *op. cit.,* I, 430–31.
32. *Ibid.,* I, 431–32.
33. *Ibid.,* II, 29.
34. *Ibid.,* II, 29–30.
35. *Ibid.,* II, 33–34.
36. *Parliamentary Debates,* 3rd series, LXXIII, 1407–8.
37. *Ibid.,* LXXIII, 1392–93.
38. *Ibid.,* LXXIII, 1422–23.
39. *Ibid.,* LXIII, 1418–19.
40. *Ibid.,* LXXIII, 1434–36.
41. *Ibid.,* LXXIII, 1453–56.
42. Hodder, *op. cit.,* II, 35–36.
43. *Ibid.,* II, 36.
44. *Ibid.,* II, 43–44.
45. *Ibid.,* II, 44–45.
46. *Parliamentary Debates,* 3rd series, LXXIV, 914.
47. Hodder, *op. cit.,* II, 48.
48. *Parliamentary Debates,* 3rd series, LXXIV, 1093–94.
49. Hodder, *op. cit.,* II, 50.
50. *Ibid.,* II, 50–51.
51. *Ibid.,* II, 135.
52. *Ibid.,* II, 137.
53. *Ibid.,* II, 190.
54. *Ibid.,* II, 193.
55. *Ibid.,* II, 195–96.

2. JOHN HENRY NEWMAN

1. John Henry Cardinal Newman, *Apologia pro vita sua* (New York, 1950), pp. 207–8, 239–43.
2. *Ibid.,* pp. 58–59.
3. John Henry Newman, *Autobiographical Writings* (New York, 1957), pp. 124–27.
4. *Apologia,* pp. 62–63.
5. R. W. Church, *The Oxford Movement* (London, 1932), pp. 159–61.
6. John Keble, *National Apostasy* (London, 1931), pp. 10–12.
7. *Apologia,* pp. 70–71.
8. *Tracts for the Times* (London,

1838), Vol. I, No. 1.

9. John Henry Newman, *Letters and Correspondence* (London, 1891), I, 488.

10. James Anthony Froude, *Short Studies on Great Subjects* (New York, 1910), IV, 179–80.

11. J. C. Shairp, *Studies in Poetry and Philosophy* (Edinburgh, 1876), pp. 244–46.

12. *Apologia*, pp. 83–85.

13. Shairp, *op. cit.*, pp. 246–49.

14. John Henry Newman, *Parochial and Plain Sermons* (London, 1868), I, 309–24.

15. *Apologia*, p. 99.

16. *Letters and Correspondence*, II, 112.

17. *Ibid.*, II, 252.

18. *Ibid.*, II, 256–57.

19. *Ibid.*, II, 257–58.

20. *Apologia*, p. 114.

21. *Ibid.*, pp. 132–35.

22. *Letters and Correspondence*, II, 286.

23. *Dublin Review*, XII n.s. (April 1869), 327–28.

24. Isaac Williams, *Autobiography* (London, 1892), pp. 100–102, 103–4.

25. *Letters and Correspondence*, II, 292–93.

26. *Ibid.*, II, 299–300; Maisie Ward, *Young Mr. Newman* (London, 1948), p. 360.

27. *Letters and Correspondence*, II, 303.

28. *Apologia*, p. 146.

29. *Ibid.*, pp. 147–48.

30. *Tracts for the Times*, Vol. VI, No. 90, pp. 12–13.

31. Williams, *Autobiography*, pp. 108–9.

32. *Letters and Correspondence*, II, 326.

33. *Ibid.*, II, 334.

34. *Ibid.*, II 335–36.

35. *Ibid.*, II, 341.

36. *Ibid.*, II 341.

37. *Ibid.*, II, 342.

38. *Ibid.*, II, 345–46.

39. *Ibid.*, II, 356.

40. *Ibid.*, II, 386.

41. *Ibid.*, II, 386–87.

42. *Ibid.*, II, 388.

43. *Apologia*, pp. 183–84.

44. *Letters and Correspondence*, II, 417.

45. *Ibid.*, II, 417–18.

46. *Ibid.*, II, 421–22.

47. *Ibid.*, II, 423.

48. John Henry Newman, *Sermons Bearing on Subjects of the Day* (London, 1869), pp. 406–9.

49. *Apologia*, pp. 205–7.

50. *Letters and Correspondence*, II, 429.

51. *Ibid.*, II, 429–30.

52. *Ibid.*, II, 431.

53. *Ibid.*, II, 435.

54. *Ibid.*, II, 445–46.

55. *Ibid.*, II, 457–58.

56. *Ibid.*, II, 459.

57. *Ibid.*, II, 468.

58. *Apologia*, p. 236.

3. ELIZABETH BARRETT BROWNING

1. *The Letters of Robert Browning and Elizabeth Barrett Browning, 1845–1846* (New York and London, 1899), I, 43.

2. *Ibid.*, I, 1–2.

3. *Ibid.*, I, 2–4.

4. *Ibid.*, I, 4–6.

5. *Ibid.*, I, 6–9.

6. *Ibid.*, I, 9–11.

7. *Ibid.*, I, 11–12.

8. *Ibid.*, I, 26.

9. *Ibid.*, I, 29.

10. *Ibid.*, I, 33–34.

11. *Ibid.*, I, 35–37.

12. *Ibid.*, I, 42.

13. *Ibid.*, I, 62.

14. *Ibid.*, I, 65–66.

15. *Ibid.*, I, 66–68.

16. *Ibid.*, I, 72.

17. *Ibid.*, I, 73–74.

18. *Ibid.*, I, 74–75.

19. *Ibid.*, I, 76–78.

20. *Ibid.*, I, 80–82.

21. *Ibid.*, I, 173–77.

22. *Ibid.*, I, 181–82.

23. *Ibid.*, I, 184–85.

24. *Ibid.*, I, 197–200.

25. *Ibid.*, I, 201–4.

26. *Ibid.*, I, 204–6.
27. *Ibid.*, I, 210–11.
28. *Ibid.*, I, 213–14.
29. *Ibid.*, I, 209.
30. *Ibid.*, I, 212.
31. *Ibid.*, I, 218–19.
32. *Ibid.*, I, 219–22.
33. *Ibid.*, I, 223–24.
34. *Ibid.*, I, 241–42.
35. *Ibid.*, I, 405–6.
36. *Ibid.*, I, 440–41.
37. *Ibid.*, I, 517.
38. *Ibid.*, II, 274–75.
39. *Ibid.*, II, 484.
40. *Ibid.*, II, 486–88.
41. *Ibid.*, II, 491.
42. *Ibid.*, II, 492–95.

43. *Ibid.*, II, 499–500.
44. *Ibid.*, II, 503–4.
45. *Ibid.*, II, 531–32.
46. *Ibid.*, II, 534–35.
47. *Ibid.*, II, 535.
48. *Ibid.*, II, 536.
49. *Ibid.*, II, 537–38.
50. *Ibid.*, II, 538–40.
51. *Ibid.*, II, 546–49.
52. *Ibid.*, II, 556.
53. *Ibid.*, II, 557–58.
54. *Ibid.*, II, 559.
55. *Ibid.*, II, 559.
56. *Ibid.*, II, 559–60.
57. *Ibid.*, II, 560–61.
58. *Ibid.*, II, 561–62.

4. DANTE GABRIEL ROSSETTI

1. Hall Caine, *My Story* (New York, 1909), pp. 101–6, 113–15.
2. William Holman Hunt, *Preraphaelitism and the Preraphaelite Brotherhood* (New York, 1905), I, 105–10.
3. *Autobiographical Notes of William Bell Scott* (New York, 1892), I, 248–50.
4. Hunt, *Preraphaelitism*, I, 163–65.
5. *Ibid.*, I, 154–55.
6. *Ibid.*, I, 144–45.
7. *Autobiographical Notes of W. B. Scott*, I, 289–91.
8. John Guille Millais, *The Life and Letters of Sir John Everett Millais* (New York, 1899), I, 54–55.
9. *Dante Gabriel Rossetti, His Family Letters* (Boston, 1895), I, 404–5.
10. William Holman Hunt, "The Pre-Raphaelite Brotherhood," *Contemporary Review*, IL (April, 1886), 480–81.
11. Ford Madox Ford, *Ford Madox Brown* (London, 1896), p. 63.
12. *Dante Gabriel Rossetti, His Family Letters*, I, 133–34.
13. *Ibid.*, I, 136.
14. *Præraphaelite Diaries and Letters* (London, 1900), pp. 209–12.
15. Hunt, *Preraphaelitism*, I, 158–60.
16. *Præraphaelite Diaries and Letters*, pp. 214–22.
17. Basil Champneys, *Memoirs and Correspondence of Coventry Patmore* (London, 1900), I, 82–84.
18. *Præraphaelite Diaries and Letters*, pp. 223–35.
19. *Letters of Dante Gabriel Rossetti to William Allingham* (New York, 1897), pp. 65–67.
20. *Præraphaelite Diaries and Letters*, pp. 235–66.
21. *William Allingham, A Diary* (London, 1907), pp. 58–59.
22. Hunt, *Preraphaelitism*, I, 199–200.
23. *The Athenaeum*, April 20, 1850, p. 424.
24. Hunt, *Preraphaelitism*, I, 203.
25. *The Times*, May 9, 1850.
26. *Blackwood's Edinburgh Magazine*, LXVIII (July, 1850), 82.
27. *Household Words*, June 15, 1850, pp. 265–66.
28. Hunt, *Preraphaelitism*, I, 219–22.
29. *Præraphaelite Diaries and Letters*, pp. 275–76.
30. Hunt, *Preraphaelitism*, I, 206.
31. Hunt, "The Pre-Raphaelite Brotherhood," *Contemporary Review*, IL (May, 1886), 747.
32. *The Times*, May 13, 1851.
33. Ford Madox Ford, *Ford Madox Brown*, p. 77.
34. *Præraphaelite Diaries and Letters*, pp. 305–9.

5. CHARLES ROBERT DARWIN

1. Francis Darwin and A. C. Seward (eds.), *More Letters of Charles Darwin* (London, 1903), I, 32–33.
2. Francis Darwin (ed.), *The Life and Letters of Charles Darwin* (New York, 1887, I, 87–88.
3. *Ibid.,* I, 90–102.
4. *Ibid.,* I, 380–81, 387–88.
5. *Ibid.,* I, 135–36.
6. *Ibid.,* I, 64–65.
7. *Ibid.,* I, 67–68.
8. *Ibid.,* I, 377–79.
9. *Ibid.,* I, 384.
10. Darwin and Seward, *More Letters,* I, 40.
11. Darwin, *Life and Letters,* I, 385.
12. *Ibid.,* I, 391.
13. Darwin and Seward, *More Letters,* I, 42.
14. *Ibid.,* I, 57.
15. Darwin, *Life and Letters,* I, 392–93.
16. Darwin and Seward, *More Letters,* I, 64–65.
17. *Ibid.,* I, 74.
18. Darwin, *Life and Letters,* I, 406.
19. *Ibid.,* I, 413.
20. *Ibid.,* I, 468–69.
21. Darwin and Seward, *More Letters,* I, 107.
22. Darwin, *Life and Letters,* I, 437–38.
23. *Ibid.,* I, 453–54.
24. *Ibid.,* I, 426–27.
25. *Ibid.,* I, 427–28.
26. *Ibid.,* I, 442.
27. *Ibid.,* I, 443.
28. *Ibid.,* I, 467–68.
29. Alfred Russel Wallace, *My Life* (New York, 1905), I, 361–63.
30. Darwin, *Life and Letters,* I, 473.
31. *Ibid.,* I, 474–75.
32. *Ibid.,* I, 475.
33. Leonard Huxley, *Life and Letters of Sir Joseph Dalton Hooker* (New York, 1918), II, 300–301.
34. Darwin, *Life and Letters,* I, 488–89.
35. *Ibid.,* I, 493.
36. *Ibid.,* I, 499.
37. *Ibid.,* I, 507.
38. *Ibid.,* I, 508–9.
39. *Ibid.,* I, 510–11.
40. *Ibid.,* I, 511.
41. *Ibid.,* I, 510.
42. *Ibid.,* I, 513.
43. *Ibid.,* I, 518.
44. *Ibid.,* I, 522–23.
45. *Ibid.,* I, 525.
46. Charles Darwin, *On the Origin of Species* (London, 1859), pp. 480–490.
47. Darwin, *Life and Letters,* I, 529–30.
48. *Ibid.,* II, 23.
49. *Ibid.,* II, 26–27.
50. *Ibid.,* II, 2.
51. Lyell, Mrs. (ed.), *Life, Letters and Journals of Sir Charles Lyell, Bart.* (London, 1881), II, 361–62.
52. Darwin, *Life and Letters,* II, 21–22.
53. *Ibid.,* II, 28–29.
54. Darwin and Seward, *More Letters,* I, 134.
55. Darwin, *Life and Letters,* II, 34.
56. *Ibid.,* II, 37.
57. *Ibid.,* II, 43–44.
58. *The Athenaeum,* XXXIV (Nov. 19, 1859), 660.
59. Darwin, *Life and Letters,* II, 19.
60. *Spectator,* March 24, 1860, quoted in Darwin, *Life and Letters,* II, 91–92.
61. Darwin, *Life and Letters,* II, 90.
62. *Edinburgh Review,* CXI (April, 1860), 495–96.
63. Darwin, *Life and Letters,* II, 94.
64. *North British Review,* XXXII (May, 1860), 486.
65. *Quarterly Review,* CVIII (July, 1860), 231.
66. Darwin, *Life and Letters,* II, 117–18.
67. *Fraser's Magazine,* LXII (July, 1860), 75.
68. *All the Year Round,* III (July 7, 1860), 299.
69. Darwin, *Life and Letters,* II, 110.
70. *Ibid.,* II, 109.
71. *Ibid.,* II, 114–16.

72. Leonard Huxley, *Life and Letters of Thomas Henry Huxley* (New York, 1900), I, 202.

73. Lyell, *Life, Letters and Journals*, II, 335.

74. Huxley, *Life and Letters of Hooker*, I, 525–27.

75. Darwin and Seward, *More Letters*, I, 156–57.

76. Darwin, *Life and Letters*, I, 72–73.

77. *Ibid.*, I, 533–58.

6. CHARLES GEORGE GORDON

1. *Pall Mall Gazette*, January 9, 1884, quoted in Henry William Gordon, *Events in the Life of Charles George Gordon* (London, 1886), pp. 297–300, 303–35.

2. Bernard M. Allen, *Gordon and the Sudan* (London, 1931), pp. 231–32.

3. *Ibid.*, p. 229.

4. Gerald Graham, "Last Words with Gordon," *Fortnightly Review*, XLVII (Jan. 1, 1887), 41–42.

5. *The Times*, February 19, 1884.

6. *The Times*, February 20, 1884.

7. Frank Power, *Letters from Khartoum* (London, 1885), pp. 96–98.

8. *Ibid.*, pp. 98–99.

9. F. R. Wingate, *Mahdiism and the Egyptian Sudan* (London, 1891), pp. 111–15.

10. *Ibid.*, p. 115.

11. *The Times*, April 17, 1884.

12. Joseph Ohrwalder, *Ten Years' Captivity in the Mahdi's Camp, 1882–1892* (London, n.d.), pp. 54–55.

13. Rudolf C. Slatin, *Fire and Sword in the Sudan* (London, 1897), pp. 159–62.

14. *Ibid.*, pp. 174, 182, 183–84, 184–85.

15. *The Times*, February 5, 1885.

16. *The Journals of Major-Gen. C. G. Gordon, C.B. at Kartoum* (Boston, 1885), pp. 3, 3–4, 5–6, 7.

17. *Ibid.*, pp. 7, 9, 11.

18. *Ibid.*, pp. 12–13, 13–14, 14–15, 18–19.

19. *Ibid.*, pp. 20, 23, 23–25.

20. *Ibid.*, pp 28–29, 29–30.

21. *Ibid.*, pp. 31, 33.

22. *Ibid.*, pp. 35, 39–40.

23. *Ibid.*, pp. 54, 55.

24. *Ibid.*, pp. 60, 61.

25. *Ibid.*, pp. 63–65.

26. *Ibid.*, pp. 67–68.

27. *Ibid.*, pp. 77, 82–83, 84, 85–87.

28. *Ibid.*, p. 90.

29. *Ibid.*, pp. 97–98.

30. *Ibid.*, pp. 99, 100, 101.

31. *Ibid.*, pp. 122–23.

32. *Ibid.*, pp. 124–25.

33. *Ibid.*, p. 131.

34. *Ibid.*, pp. 143, 144.

35. *Ibid.*, p. 149.

36. *Ibid.*, p. 158.

37. *Ibid.*, pp. 172, 172–73, 175–76.

38. *Ibid.*, pp. 178–79.

39. *Ibid.*, pp. 179, 180, 181.

40. *Ibid.*, pp. 182, 184.

41. *Ibid.*, pp. 185, 187.

42. *Ibid.*, pp. 200, 202–3.

43. *Ibid.*, pp. 207–8.

44. *Ibid.*, pp. 209–10, 212.

45. *Ibid.*, pp. 227–29.

46. *Ibid.*, pp. 237, 238, 239.

47. *Ibid.*, pp. 244, 246–47.

48. *Ibid.*, p. 248.

49. *Ibid.*, pp. 257–59, 266–67.

50. *Ibid.*, pp. 289–95.

51. *Ibid.*, p. 306.

52. *Ibid.*, p. 330.

53. *Ibid.*, p. 332.

54. *Ibid.*, pp. 364–65.

55. Charles W. Wilson, *From Korti to Khartum* (Edinburgh and London, 1885), pp. 25–30.

56. Slatin, *Fire and Sword in the Sudan*, pp. 204–6.

57. Wilson, *op. cit.*, pp. 167–74.

INDEX

(Prepared by the author)

THE AUTHOR AND HIS BOOK

Robert A. Rosenbaum was born March 9, 1926, in Cincinnati, Ohio where—in 1948—he received his B.A. at the University of Cincinnati. In 1949 he took his Masters at Columbia University in New York. He was in the United States Army between 1944 and 1946, and, at present, is an editor with Grolier Inc., the encyclopedia publishers in New York. Mr. Rosenbaum has been an editor in several New York publishing houses but for several years has been doing doctoral research on the Victorian era. This extensive research is the source of EARNEST VICTORIANS, *his first book.*

EARNEST VICTORIANS (*Hawthorn, 1961*) *was designed by Sidney Feinberg, and completely manufactured by American Book–Stratford Press, New York. The body type was set in Scotch, originally designed and cut by Alexander Wilson and Son Foundry of Scotland in the early nineteenth century.*

A HAWTHORN BOOK